Change in Bengal Agrarian Society *c.* 1760-1850

RATNALEKHA RAY

Original Edition with a New Introduction by

ANANDA BHATTACHARYYA

MANOHAR
2026

First published 1979
Reprinted 2026

ISBN 978-93-90035-87-8

Published by
Ajay Kumar Jain *for*
Manohar Publishers & Distributors
4753/23 Ansari Road, Daryaganj
New Delhi 110 002

Printed at
Replika Press Pvt. Ltd.

To
My Parents
Dr. Golapchandra Ray Chaudhuri
&
Sarama Ray Chaudhuri

Preface

This work seeks to trace the course of change in the agrarian society of Bengal under the rule of the East India Company with special reference to the impact of the Permanent Settlement. Part One is an attempt to describe the nature of land tenures and the different categories of land rights, as they prevailed before the Permanent Settlement and as they were affected by the Regulations of 1793. It will emerge that in traditional agrarian society there was an incredible variety of land rights, which differed from district to district, and we shall observe that the attempt to simplify the situation by creating a single category of landlords by the Permanent Settlement only succeeded in creating fresh complications in each locality. On the premise that these local circumstances need to be thoroughly explored before reaching general conclusions, I shall undertake five area studies in Part Two of my book. The selected districts, chosen from West, North and East Bengal, will cover a broad spectrum of geographical and social conditions in the Bengali-speaking region of Eastern India. In each area study I shall note the lie of the land and the composition of the population, the local conditions of land tenure before the Permanent Settlement, the distinctive settlement of the district in 1793, the sale of 'estates' after the Permanent Settlement, the resulting rent-sharing structure, and the impact of changes in the upper levels of tribute collection on the land-holding structure in the village and on the position of dominant village groups in the lower rungs of the hierarechy of landlords. Although my period will be roughly 1760-1850, wherever possible I shall look forward in time and relate changes in local land tenure systems to broader social and political movements in the nineteenth and twentieth centuries.

Conversely, I shall go back repeatedly to the Ain-i-Akbari, Murshid Quli Khan and the decline of the Nizamat to get a better perspective on change under the rule of the East India Company. Having explored local detail over a broad span of time, I shall finally try to assess in Part Three change and continuity in the rural order as it emerged in the nineteenth century from the 1790s, when 'landlords' were chosen and declared, 'tenants' identified and their rights circumscribed by successive regulations, thousands of 'estates' sold for arrears of revenue, and the structures of rule in the countryside transformed by revolutionary innovations such as courts, collectorates, magistracies and police stations (thanas).

My deepest debt in writing this work is to Professor Eric Stokes who supervised my research on this subject in Cambridge. I am also very much indebted to Dr. Anil Seal and Professor Benoy Bhushan Chaudhuri, who looked after my research at various stages. I thank Mr. Christopher Emerie for working out the statistical tables. I benefited much from conversations with my friends and colleagues in Cambridge, Calcutta, and Bangladesh. I also wish to record the help that I received from the Directors, Librarians and Staff of the India Office Library, the libraries of Cambridge, the West Bengal State Archives and the Calcutta High Court, the District Record Offices and the various zamindari kacharies. I am grateful in particular to my father, Dr. Golapchandra Ray Chaudhuri and my father-in-law Shri K.K. Ray, for their substantial help in collecting materials.

RATNALEKHA RAY

Contents

PART II

Case Studies

PART III

Conclusion

Abbreviations

BR	Board of Revenue
BRC	Bengal Revenue Consultations
BRP	Board of Revenue Proceedings

Introduction

Ananda Bhattacharyya

Ratnalekha Ray's *Change in Bengal Agrarian Society c. 1760-1850*, (1979) may be considered the most vigorous attempts at situating them in the total structure of Bengal agrarian society during early British rule. Ray doubtlessly offered a very attractive and far-reaching frame of reference. Ray's important contribution to the understanding of Bengal's agrarian structure was the clear-cut distinction that she made between the revenue-receiving and the landholding structure. She contented that the so-called 'landed property' conferred upon the zamindar by the introduction of the Permanent Settlement of 1793. Ray also provided us with important clues to the regional characteristics of Bengal agrarian society. She implicitly showed that her conceptual frame was relevant to almost all the localities in Bengal with certain modifications. Ray defined the changes brought about in the position of the zamindars by the Permanent Settlement as one which destroyed the zamindari as a public to revenue collection. It goes to the credit of Ratnalekha Ray to pick up these threads, weave them together and extend their logic to a study of the impact of the Permanent Settlement on Bengal's agrarian society of 1760-1850. Her supporting data are apparently collated from a wide range of original source materials, her methodology is inter-disciplinary and her presentation is neat.

Land revenue and its collection was the most important issue in policy debates during this period. The structure of revenue rights which the East India Company inherited in Bengal had been largely shaped from early in the eighteenth century by a series of powerful Nawabs, the increasingly autonomous Mughal governors of the province.[1] Few subordinate chieftains with long-standing claims to

[1]P.J. Marshall, *The Making and Unmaking of Empires: Britain, India and America c. 1753-1783*, Oxford: Oxford University Press, 2005: 244; B.B.

exercise authority over land and people had survived their dominance. The Nawabs had also succeeded in greatly reducing the number of *jagirs*, imperial grants to noblemen in return for military and other service to the Mughal Empire[2] appointed for limited terms.[3] Historians of South Asia quite regularly apply the term 'Gentry Class' to the Bengali zamindars, who, under the Mughals[4] unquestionably performed

---

Chaudhuri, 'Rural Power Structure and Agricultural Productivity in Eastern India, 1757-1947', in Meghnad Desai, Susanne Hoeber Rudolph, and Ashok Rudra, eds., *Agrarian Power and Agricultural Productivity in South Asia*, New Delhi: Oxford University Press, 1984: 100-68.

[2]Pranab Ray, 'Rebel Zamindars Sobha Singh and Some Contemporary Records', *Proceedings of the Indian History Congress*, New Delhi: Indian History Congress, vol. 61, pt. 1, 2000-1: 345-51. Aniruddha Ray, *Towns and Cities of Medieval India: A Brief Survey*, New Delhi: Manohar, 2015: 518-52; idem, *Adventurers, Landowners and Rebels: Bengal c. 1575-c. 1715*, New Delhi: Munshiram Manoharlal, 1998). Chatterjee (Kumkum Chatterjee, *The Cultures of History in Early Modern India: Persianization and Mughal Persianization and Mughal Culture in Bengal*, New Delhi: Oxford University Press, 2009. The role of the Mughals in creating and destroying zamindars has been studied extensively by Ratnalekha Ray (*Change in Bengal Agrarian Society, c. 1760-1850* (heretofore refer to *Change*), New Delhi: Manohar, 1979), Shirin Akhtar (*The Role of Zamindars in Bengal, 1707-1772*, Dacca: Asiatic Society of Bangladesh, 1982), J.R. McLane (*Land and Local Kingship in Eighteenth Century Bengal*, Cambridge: Cambridge University Press, 1993) and others. Ludden (Ratnalekha Ray, *Change in Bengal Agrarian Society, c. 1760-1850*, New Delhi: Manohar, 1979, reviewed by David Ludden, *The Journal of Economic History*, The Economic History Association, Cambridge University Press, vol. 43, no. 2, June 1983: 518-19) has admitted the fact that the central question of Ratnalekha Ray is an 'old one' but 'its method and conclusions are quite new'. It establishes a base from which to build in future. Ray studied the economic organization of agrarian Bengal and demonstrated the sweeping changes in land law embodied in the 1793 Permanent Settlement. Ray made a clear distinction in Taniguchi's words between 'revenue-receiving and the landholding structure'. B.B. Chaudhury (*Peasant History of Late Pre-Colonial and Colonial India*, vol. VIII, pt. 2, New Delhi: Pearson Education India, 2008: 5-11) has stressed on the role of the Indian society, i.e. the indigenous institutions in this undertaking.

[3]Rajat Datta, *Society, Economy and the Market: Commercial in Rural Bengal, c. 1760-1800*, Delhi: Manohar, 2000; S. Taniguchi,'The Peasantry of Northern Bengal in the Late Eighteenth Century', in Peter Robb, K. Sughira and H. Yanagisawa, eds., *Local Agrarian Societies in Colonial India: Japanese Perspectives*, London: Curzon Press, 1996.

[4]C.A. Bayly, *Rulers, Townsmen, and Bazaars: North Indian Society in the Age of British Expansion, 1770-1870*, Cambridge/New York: Cambridge University Press, 1983: 36.

much of the grass-roots work of revenue collection.[5] Affected by the currency inflation of the late seventeenth century which rendered existing assignments less profitable, they found it almost impossible to extract enough money from the peasantry to keep up the cavalry contingents required by their rank; they, rather than the state *per se*, therefore turned 'to bankers and speculators from the cities'.[6] The dominance of a small number of large zamindars was the distinctive feature of eighteenth century Bengal's revenue system.[7] Eighteenth-century Indian states prospered and perished by their ability to enforce the collection of the land tax, by far the major contributor to state treasuries.[8] In this sense, the landlord effectively had property rights on the land. In some of these areas, the British declared the landlord's revenue commitments to the government to be fixed in perpetuity (the Permanent Settlement).[9] The old version in the context of Permanent Settlement stressed the growth of 'landlord powers' meaning the power of the zamindars. Ramkrishna Mukherjee,[10] like

---

[5]Howard Dick, Michael Sullivan and John Butcher, eds., *The Rise and Fall of Revenue Farming: Business Elites and the Emergence of the Modern State in Southeast Asia (Studies in the Economies of East and South-East Asia)*, 1st edn., Basingstoke: Palgrave Macmillan, 1993: 52.

[6]Irfan Habib, *The Agrarian System of Mughal India (1556-1707)*, New York: Asia Publishing House, 1963; M. Athar Ali, *The Mughal Nobility Under Aurangzeb,* New Delhi and New York: Oxford University Press, 1970; Dharma Kumar and Tapan Raychaudhuri, eds., *The Cambridge Economic History of India*, vol. I: *c. 1200-c. 1750*, Cambridge: Cambridge University Press, 1st pub. 1982: 178.

[7]John Wilson, *The Domination of Strangers: Modern Governance in Eastern India*, New York: Palgrave Macmillan; 2008; see also Ratnalekha Ray, *Change*: 29; David L. Curley, 'Voluntary Relations and Royal Gifts of Pan in Mughal Bengal', in Stewart Gordon, ed., *Robes of Honour*: *Khilat in Pre-colonial and Colonial Bengal*, New Delhi: Oxford University Press, 2003: 50-79; Tilottama Mukherjee, 'The Co-ordinating State and the Economy: The Nizamat in the Eighteenth Century Bengal', *Modern Asian Studies* (heretofore refer to *MAS*) 42, 1, Cambridge: Cambridge University Press, 2008: 1-48.

[8]S. Arasaratnam, 'Trade and Political Domination in South India, 1750-1790: Changing British-India Relations', in Patrick Tuck, ed., With an Introduction, *The East India Company 1600-1858: Trade, Finance and Power*, vol. IV, London and New York: Routledge, 1998: 145-90.

[9]The definition of the term 'peasant' has been defined by Islam and Chaudhuri (Sirajul Islam, *Bengal Land Tenure*, Calcutta: K.P. Bagchi, 1988 and B.B. Chaudhuri, *Peasant History of Late Pre-Colonial and Colonial India*).

[10] Ramkrishna Mukherjee, *The Dynamics of a Rural Society,* Berlin: Akademie-Verlag, 1957:110.

others, strongly argues that the land belonged to the village community, and that allotment of land in any form required the consent of the village *panchayat*.[11] The rights of the state were largely theoretical.

According to Taniguchi 'such was the broad historical background that eventually necessitated the creation of the Patni system'.[12] The typical arrangement under which zamindars granted away permanent leases (*patnis*) of portions of their estates was first tried by the Burdwan Raj with two ends in view: getting rid of the difficulties in collecting rent from all parts of a far-flung estate. Amit Bhaduri analysed the implications of the system for the rural economy. As a result the normal exchange between agricultural and manufactured products went into process for which 'agricultural output in Bengal did not rise enough to absorb these increasing claims by the expanding class of rent-receiving intermediaries'.[13] Both of them paved the way for the proliferation of subinfeudation on an unprecedented scale by laying down rules for arranging in order various conflicting landed interests and for protecting the interests of each rung in the tenurial structure. The zamindari system of our period thus took the form of a network of diverse landed interests from zamindari estates down to *se-patni* or *osat-taluk* lower kinds of tenures. The traditional view or an ideological debate raised by a social anthropologist.[14]

The *jotedars* had a crucial role, too, in the 'mechanics of rural control'. 'Any breakdown in the system of rural control was . . . local and partial, and a consequence of breakdown of collaboration of owners of estates and village leaders in particular estates'. It implies that the domination of *jotedars* determined the rural agrarian structure: 'Over two centuries of British rule the dominant character of the production relations within Bengal villages was semi-feudal,

---

[11] Biplab Dasgupta, *European Trade and Colonial Conquest,* London: Anthem Press, 2005: 143; Ramkrishna Mukherjee, op. cit.: 18-22; Niharanjan Ray, *History of the Bengali People: Ancient Period*, New Delhi: Orient Longmans, 1994: 153.

[12] S. Taniguchi, 'The Patni System: A Modern Origin of the "Sub-Infeudation" of Bengal', *Hitotsubashi Journal of Economics*, Hitotsubashi University, vol. 22, no. 1 (June 1981): 32-60.

[13] Amit Bhaduri, 'The Evolution of Land Relations in Eastern India under British Rule', *IESHR,* Sage, January-March 1976: 45-53.

[14] E.R., Leach, ed., *Aspects of Caste in South India, Ceylon and North-West Pakistan*, Cambridge: Cambridge University Press, 1960. Ratnalekha Ray questions the entire premise on which this argument rests and came to the conclusion that 'such an assumption is factually incorrect'.

marked by the small size of plots, labour-intensive farming, and the master-serf type of relationship between *jotedars* and *bargadars* (sharecroppers), reinforced by usury'.[15] Examining the fact Chaudhuri said that 'zamindari was admittedly not a unit of production. This partly followed from its composition, often a considerable number of scattered villages'.[16]

There is no evidence that *jotedars* as a separate class before the battle of Plassey. Those who take this view cite references that are four to five decades into British rule, such as Colebrooke and Buchanan-Hamilton, two great scholars of the period. To infer from these references that this class of *jotedar* existed even before Plassey is hazardous in the extreme. The two authorities also refrained in their writings from making such inferences. The important question is whether it was possible for the differentiation to reach a stage where not only would there be peasants who were considerably richer than others, but that they would constitute a separate class altogether, when the land and labour markets were developed, and money played a minor role in the transactions in which the peasantry took part. It is also questionable whether such a class of *jotedars* could emerge without a section of the peasantry being entirely or nearly pushed out of the ownership of land and reduced to sharecroppers and landless labourers. It is true that landlessness was not a feature of village life in pre-Plassey Bengal. There are conflicting views as regards the emergence of *jotedars*. The first view coined by Kalyan Kumar Sengupta,[17] Ratnalekha Ray, Rajat Kanta Ray[18] who assert that 'there was a spectrum of rich peasants who dominated village society almost all over the Bengal province'.[19] The second view is supported by

---

[15] Rajat Ray and Ratna, 'The Dynamism of Continuity in Rural Bengal under the British Imperium', *IESHR*, Sage, June 1973: 103-28.

[16] Chaudhury 'Rural Power Structure and Agricultural Productivity in Eastern India, 1757-1947', in Meghnad Desai, Susane Hoeber Ruddolph and Ashok Rudra, eds., *Agrarian Power and Agricultural Productivity in South Asia*, op. cit.: 100-70.

[17] Kalyan Kumar Sengupta, *Pabna Disturbances and the Politics of Rent 1873-1885*, New Delhi: People's Publishing House, 1974.

[18] 'The Retreat of the Jotedars?', *IESHR*, Sage, vol. XXV, no. 2. 1988: 237-47.

[19] Shinkichi Taniguchi, 'Rethinking the Bengal Peasantry in History', in Shubhra Chakrabarti and Utsa Patnaik, eds., *Agrarian and Other Histories: Essays for Binay Bhushan Chaudhuri*, New Delhi: Tulika: 41-63. Taniguchi also admits the first view which has also been explained in elsewhere (S. Taniguchi, 'The Peasantry of Northern Bengal in the Late Eighteenth Century', in Peter Robb, K. Sughira

Partha Chatterjee,[20] Sugata Bose,[21] Rajat Datta[22] and others. Binay Bhushan Chaudhuri, is of the opinion that while the former went a bit too far in asserting that Bengal's village society was totally dominated by rich peasants or *jotedars*. The traditional landlords or zamindars had scarcely any presence in it, the latter also went too far in claiming that Bengal's village society was almost exclusively composed of small peasants and that there was scarcely any differentiation among them.[23] Chaudhury admits 'that there were rich peasants almost all across Bengal'.[24] The rural power primarily derived from 'control over land' and a close connection with the organization of agricultural production, would deny that zamindars had ever constituted a significant component of the rural power structure.[25] Rajat Datta's argument was that the so-called *jotedars* or rich peasants existed only in the frontier districts, Dinajpur and Rangpur and Datta argued that 'it is difficult to show the domination of rich peasants with large landholdings' and came to the conclusion that 'it is not justifiable to characterise eighteenth-century Bengal as *jotedar*-dominated'. Taniguchi has summarized Datta's point wise arguments but thinks that 'Ray's conceptual frame is still useful for our research'. It is Taniguchi's firm conviction that contrary to Datta's assertion 'the jotedars extended their holdings at the cost of both the zamindar and the poorer peasants', and 'jotedar class was present over almost all of Bengal'. But whether her view regarding *jotedar* domination remained unchanged or not B.B. Chaudhuri's comment should be kept in mind. There was a remarkable rise of 'new' *jotedars* in the late nineteenth century as a consequence of the further involvement in the peasant economy in commercial agriculture and the market

and H. Yanagisawa, eds., *Local Agrarian Societies in Colonial India: Japanese Perspectives*, London: Curzon Press, 1996).

[20] 'Agrarian Structure in Pre-partition Bengal', in *Perspectives in Social Sciences 2: Three Studies on the Agrarian Structure in Bengal, 1850-1947*, ed. Asok Sen, Partha Chatterjee and Saugata Mukherji, Calcutta: Oxford University Press, 1982: 113-224.

[21] *Agrarian Bengal: Economy, Social Structure and Politics, 1919-1947*, Cambridge: Cambridge University Press, 1986.

[22] *Society, Economy and the Market: Commercialization in Rural Bengal, c. 1760-1800*, New Delhi: Manohar, 2000.

[23] S. Taniguchi, in Shubhra Chakrabarty and Utsa Patnaik, op. cit.

[24] B.B. Chaudhuri, *Peasant History of Late Pre-Colonial and Colonial India.*

[25] Rajat K. Ray and Ratnalekha Ray', 'Zamindars and Jotedars: A Study of Rural Politics of Bengal', *MAS*, 9, 1975: 81-102; Ray, *Change*: chs. 2, 3, 10.

economy at a time of increasing pressure of population'.[26] Taniguchi and Chaudhuri have come to the conclusion that these 'new' *jotedars* acquired their *jotes*, through land markets of various types, while the 'old' *jotedars* extended their holdings mainly through political pressure within the village and against the zamindars.

If the timing of the emergence of the *jotedar* as a separate class is in dispute, more controversial is the notion of 'power'. Was the local feudal lord, who directly controlled the destiny of his subjects, more powerful than the emperor whose influence was indirect? Was the *daroga* of the local thana, having a greater capacity to inflict damage on people residing in the area under his jurisdiction, more powerful than the district-level superintendent of police, operating from his faraway headquarters? As Dasguta commented 'In all these cases, the questions are wrongly posed – the local loss, though he matters more to people living within his jurisdiction, nevertheless operates within a framework defined by his superior'.[27] A great deal of the confusion, created by this controversy as to who was more powerful, zamindars or *jotedars*, can be avoided if the notion of 'power' is carefully defined. In this respective domains, both were powerful, but in case of a conflict between the two, the person at the higher hierarchical level always enjoyed a comparative advantage.

Coming to sharecroppers, one can make a distinction between sharecropping as a practice, and sharecropping as a separate class. Even at the time of Buchanan-Hamilton, in early-nineteenth century, Dinajpur sharecroppers usually owned two or three bighas (1-1.15 acres) of land[28] and 'employ their leisure time in cultivating land for their neighbours'.[29] In addition, half the farming population, having one or two ploughs, would go in for sharecropping if their ploughs could not be fully used on their own land.[30] If they produced only one crop, and hence had time on their hands for the rest of the year, 'they hire themselves out as day labourers, to those who cultivate soils, or act as porters or labourers to merchants and manufacturers

[26] Chaudhuri, 'Rural Power', in Robb: 100-70.

[27] Biplab Dasgupta, *European Trade and Colonial Conquest*, London: Anthem Press, 2005: 160.

[28] Francis Buchanan-Hamilton, *A Geographical, Statistical and Historical Description of the District . . . of Dinagepore*, Calcutta: Baptist Mission Press, 1833: 234-5.

[29] Ibid.: 235.

[30] Ibid.: 235.

of sugar and indigo'.[31] Sinha contends that the process of depeasantization was not in evidence even in 1786 and that the figure of 150,000 sharecroppers mentioned by Buchanan-Hamilton in the case of Dinajpur in 1808, is 'no indication of the number of *adhiyars* [sharecroppers] in other districts'.[32] Buchanan-Hamilton's figure of 34 per cent of sharecroppers, in Dinajpur, in 1808, contrasts sharply with the estimate of Floud Commission, at 13.8 per cent for that district, in 1938. For Rangpur, the figures were 39.4 per cent in Buchanan-Hamilton and 19.1 per cent in the Floud Commission.[33]

But the theory of the emergence of this priviledged tenantry (*jotedar* as viewed by Ray) in a big way under the unsettled conditions of 1760-93, particularly of the post-famine generation, cannot be dismissed so lightly as the author does. The situation was no less than revolutionary in so far as it created a great body of pauperized, footless peasants who could look forward to rehabilitation only under the patronage of men who could spare livestock, grain and other forms of capital. It is likely that the former entered into patron-client relationships with the latter by way of commendations with a view to reclaiming their lands turned waste as well as jungle lands in other districts.

Ray sees the priviledged tenantry (of both peasant and non-peasant castes) of her period, 1760-1850, as a class of village landlords in whose hands *ryoti* land rights and control over the labour of the village poor, engaged as sharecroppers and labourers, were concentrated. The *gantidars* of Jessore and Twenty-four Parganas, the *chaukidars* of the Sundarbans; the *jotedars* of Rangpur, Dinajpur and eastern Jessore; the *hoaladars* of Jessore, Bakarganj and Noakhali; the *talukdars* of Chittagong and the *mandals* of the Midnapore jungle mahals – such people are said to have constituted this class. However, these were but different names for the large-scale reclaimers of wastelands. We come across such substantial tenant farmers both before and after the Permanent Settlement, wherever there was scope for large-scale land reclamation. But can we generalize this observation for the whole of Bengal? Ray's answer is largely in the affirmative,

---

[31] Ibid.

[32] Sinha, vol. 2, 1968: 43.

[33] Francis Floud, *Report of the Land Revenue Commission Bengal,* vol. II: *Appendices (I to IX) and Indian Land System Ancient, Medieval and . . .*, Bengal Land Revenue Commission, Government of Bengal, vol. 2, Calcutta: Bengal Secretariat Press, 1940: Table VIII(d).

though with some qualifications. Her data, however, remain inadequate for convincing us that during her period, such a class flourished not only at the fringe, but also in the heartland the relatively more densely populated and long-settled central rice plains of Bengal. She shows further that many of the new men amongst the auction purchasers were not able to take possession of their new purchases, while others with rural roots could. Some zamindars therefore came back through *benami* purchases and re-purchases. On the whole, it was the 'smaller class of *talukdars* and zamindars who succeeded in buying up the greatest number of the titles brought into circulation by the sale of the zamindaris' upto 1819. Did this pattern of land transfers continue to be the same even after the business crisis of 1829-33 and 1847-8? Ray did not have resources to give us 'to come to a conclusion in this respect'. In any case, the break-up of the Raj and the need for adjustment to the rigidities of the British collection system led to the growth of smaller properties, 'both vertically down a chain of sub-infeudation as well as, laterally by way of subdivision and fragmentation. Thus the Permanent Settlement effected 'a broader distribution of tribute from the land among a large number literate gentry' and, however small, rent incomes provided an incentive to these mobile elements. Holding of lands increasingly defined an economic and political as well as a social and cultural relationship.[34]

Besides the traditional structure the rajas of Bishnupur had the tenures known as *be-panchak* (rent-free) and *panchak* (nominal quit-rent). There were two types of service tenures in the district one paying their *panchaki* directly to the government and another to the zamindars. In Mahiara *be-panchak* or entirely rent-free tenures existed, and in Gangajalghati police circle the *ghatwals* paid their *panchaks* to the zamindars or *talukdars. Ghatwals* and *chaukidars* usually derived their income from the service rendered to the authority. With the behaviour of raja of Bishnupur the hierarchical relation became strained. The prominence of the large landed estates, such as, Burdwan Natore and Nadia, is to be seen in the context of the seventeenth century Mughal need for loyal and non-threatening allies in Bengal, who could help bring the newly conquered territory under imperial government control. In 1576, Akbar defeated Daud Khan, the last

[34]Anand A. Yang, *Bazaar India: Markets, Society, and the Colonial State in Bihar,* Berkeley, Los Angeles, Oxford: University of California Press, 1999: 67-8.

ruler of the short-lived Karrani dynasty and added Bengal to the Mughal Empire.[35] It was at this juncture when the raja of Burdwan Tejchand tried to dismantle the existing realm by imposing a new section of puppet landlords in Bankura. What the raja failed to understand that the imposition of a superstructure cannot ensure the development of the economy, what followed afterwards was the series of clashes between the *patnidars* with the existing older communities who tried to protect their rights at cost of their life. Eighteenth century Bengal witnessed substantial political and economic transformations.

The ambigious laws and the substantial privatization of rent recovery inevitably implied conflict between landlord and tenant. Tirthankar Ray has pointed out the power struggle that cropped up on the promulgation of Permanent Settlement. At one level, the role of Jay Krishna Mukherjee, zamindar of Uttarpara, near Calcutta, may be mentioned. Even his biographer admitted the fact that 'his methods of dealings with his tenants were of a rather summary nature' and mentions his use of enforcers who used clubs (*lathiyals*). It was a common practice of the zamindars who also filed a large number of suits against his tenants and resumed a large number of rent-free estates. In Part One of the book, Ray sets the problem and defines her conceptual frame and related terminology. She traces the evolution of the zamindars and *jotedars* as two distinctly separate social categories with pre-colonial roots; shows that the working of the Permanent Settlement owed for its origins more to the immediate realities of the East India Company's need to maximize the tribute on a secure and long-term basis, than to the radical Western ideology of the times. She argues that the polity in course of the changes was affected more – and this fundamentally – than its underlying socio-economic structures. Five area studies, covering the zamindars of Burdwan, Bishnupur, Midnapur, Dinajpur-Rangpur and Dacca-Jalalpur containing a wealth of micro-data, are presented in Part Two in support of her arguments. Her supporting data is apparently collated from a wide range of original source materials, her methodology is inter-disciplinary and her presentation crystal clear. As Guha has rightly observed that 'that the resultant work therefore reflects a perspective as well as an awareness of the regional and caste-oriented

[35]Rachel Fell Mcdermott, *Mother of My Heart, Daughter of My Dreams: Kali and Uma in the Devotional Poetry of Bengal*, New York: Oxford University Press, 2001: 17.

variations in the emerging revenue-managing/landholding patterns. But her interpretation and major conclusions somewhat suffer from overtones and her data on the social background of certain peasant castes like the Rajbangsis far from adequate'.[36] In Midnapore the powerful agricultural caste (Kaivarta) provided the rent-receiving class, the village oligarchy, and the landholding body. Taniguchi has agreed with Ray's assertion and comes to the decision to say that 'her conceptual frame was relevant to almost all the localities in Bengal with certain modifications'. Rich peasants were very much found in Bengal and the position and function of this important groups remained unchanged during the colonial rule. Ratnalekha Ray has also shown these types of zamindars and argued by saying that many zamindars had to come to terms with tenants who were in fact powerful landlords at the village level (*jotedars*). Post-permanent Settlement changes, according to her, had taken place at two distinct levels; (i) at the level of territorial control and land revenue management, i.e. the sphere of zamindari rights; and (ii) at the level of land holding proper with cultivation rights, i.e. the sphere of *ryot* rights. In both the spheres, the respective bundles of proprietary rights were organized hierarchically. All revenue-payers with proprietary rights in the revenue-management are categorized by Ray as zamindars, irrespective of their gradations (as *talukdars*, etc.). All landholders with proprietary rights in the soil, along with command over poor villagers' labour for its cultivation, are categorized by the convenient term *jotedar*. *Jotedars*, also called village landlords, carried on some trading/moneylending activities as well, through which ties their control over the dependent peasantry was reinforced. The revenue management through hereditary zamindars was not a British innovation. Such an institutional arrangement, says Ray, was very much an established feature of the early eighteenth century Bengal polity and could even be traced back to an earlier period. *Jotedars* were in physical control of the land. They might cultivate some, lease out the rest to sharecroppers, and also operate as moneylenders. Ray's view of the status of the *jotedar* is reflected in an unusual description 'peasant landlord'. The two categories of zamindars and *jotedars* were quite distinct. The zamindar occupied the upper level within a system of graded hierarchies. He was the territorial lord while the

[36]Ratnalekha Ray, *Change in the Bengal Agrarian Society*, reviewed by Amalendu Guha, *Book Review Literary Trust*, no. 2, 1981: 13-14.

jotedar was the lord of the soil. In other words the zamindar operated at a higher level of the agrarian structure, while the *jotedar* operated at the level of the village. The two sometimes overlapped, but the roles were distinct. The zamindars who had proprietory rights in the collection of revenue often belonged to higher castes, with a distinctive style of life, whereas the *jotedars* usually belonged to agricultural castes who were dominant in the region, but ritually low in all-India scheme. Their style of life was closer to that of others around them. Ray merely mentions this but does not discuss the theoretical implications of the two different systems – that of revenue collection and that of landownership – which existed simultaneously. Ray also emphasizes the extreme complexity of the facts on the ground and mentions the fact there was considerable variation within the categories of zamindars and *jotedars*, both socially and economically. She does not, however, lay sufficient stress on yet another dimension of complexity. Even major conceptual categories like the *jotedar* did not have uniform application, everywhere in Bengal. For instance, Beteille mentions that the term was also used to denote sharecroppers in Burdwan.[37] The zamindars could not increase the *jotedars*' rents at will and had to share the surplus they exacted from the sharecroppers with them. Ray's identification of the *jotedars* depends to a large extent on surveys by Francis Buchanan, one of which was in Dinajpur district. This illustrates the potential gap between the structure of incentives the Permanent Settlement intended to create and what actually came into being. The British tried to apply concepts and categories alien to the reality of the Indian agrarian society. In looking for a 'landlord' of the kind that existed in England, the British made a clear case for mistaken identity. The imposition of zamindars as landlords brought in a new set of changes which created fresh complications. To understand the kind of agrarian change Ray tries to analyse the anthropological concepts of 'organizational change' and 'structural change' might have been useful as analytical tools. Organizational change is change in the superstructure of a society whereas structural change is change in the basic structure of a society. While the earlier generation of scholars claimed that rural Bengal had undergone a structural change as a result of the Permanent

[37] A. Beteille, *Studies in Agrarian Social Structure*, New Delhi: Oxford University Press, 1974.

Settlement, Ray points out admirably, with the help of area studies that the change was in fact organizational.

Late eighteenth century Bengal also witnessed the emergence of a new class of political and financial notables. These were moneylenders, merchants, and traders who collaborated first with the Nawabs of Bengal and later with the British. These new class of elites, however, underwent further transformations under the effects of the permanent settlement of Bengal. Big and small landlords who were unable to meet the fixed revenue demands were forced to sell off their lands, which now passed into the hands of a more recent class of wealthy elites – artists and merchants who made their fortunes as a result of participating in the new economic order under the English East India Company, and from moneylending and trading with the British, Dutch, and Portuguese. Many of them hailed from middle to low castes such as the Subarnabanik, Sadgop, and Tanti. The patriarch of the Sadgop family that came to own the Midnapore zamindari had worked as the *diwan* of the Khaira [*sic*] raja whom Ratnalekha Ray calls a tribal chief.[38] Distribution of Sadgops more or less overlapped with that of the Bagdi. Though Midnapur district as a whole was not ranked among the top fifteen tribal-majority districts, certain tracts of the district showed a very strong tribal presence. Fiercely enforced ties of kinship and ethnicity allowed jungle zamindars to successfully resist the transfer of their estates to outsiders. While these ties facilitated a strong loyalty, they did not interfere with a loosely structured administration. Even the Midnapore zamindari under Sadgop ownership, the only one with a strong and extensive control over substantial areas in both the jungle and riverine areas, followed the practice of leaving jungle, parganas on small quit rents with Paik sardars. When these Paiks were displaced they often paralysed the revenue collection. If the Paiks and Chuars were characterized derogatory as savage and prone to violence, the jungle

[38]Ray, *Change*: 137. This reference is probably to the Khaira hill tribes of Manbhum, a branch of the Lodhas of Midnapore, and confirms that the currently impoverished Lodhas and Kharias were the original kings of the forest. He was an exception. Most Jungle zamindaris remained with the families that owned them and fought to regain them when temporarily dispossessed, like Durjan Singh of Raipur and the Raja of Pachet (K. Sivaramkrishnan, *Modern Forests: Statemaking and Environmental Change in Colonial Eastern India*, Stanford: Stanford University Press, 1999: 50.

landlords dared no better.[39] They were described as rude and illiterate, thereby incapable of comprehending anything but the simplest and easiest regulations, while possessed of a character that made them 'ignorant, savage, vicious, selfish and corrupt'. The jungle zamindars were also deeply averse to attending court proceedings as it involved travelling larger distances and they hesitated to move far from their Jungle strongholds. To one commentator, this was at least partly due to the fact that every zamindar having been at sometime a criminal in the eye of the law.[40] Ratnalekha Ray argues against this picture by pointing out that the transferring that occurred were more to zamindari servants, employees of the collectorate and local businessmen. The point remains that they were Bengali and not related to the original jungle zamindars.[41]

Ratnalekha Ray, in her study on agrarian Bengal, advanced the hypothesis that some members of the dominant cultivators who had in possession of superior tenancy rights, called *jotedars* and occasionally by other names, were locally powerful enough to resist zamindars' attempts to collect more rent and therein eviction. Indeed, early administrative writings on the permanent settlement hint that these groups needed often to be pacified and co-opted. The argument held

---

[39]John R. McLane like Basudev Chattopadhyay (*Crime and Control in Early Colonial Bengal 1770-1860*, Calcutta: K.P. Bagchi) commences his discussion with the Permanent Settlement. His account explains the emergence of banditry in terms of the impact of this settlement on rural social relations, and the centralizing tendencies of colonial state making that he traces from this 1793 watershed. Ratnalekha Ray seeks to explain Chuar disturbances as an anarchic consequence of this breakdown (Ray, *Change*: 70). Ray in her discussion point to the leadership of chaukidars and other displaced service tenure holders who lost rent-free lands to the combined onslaught of resumption by the state and landlords (Ray, *Change*: 70). A recent research on Chuar rebellion is found in the work of Bhattacharyya (*Adivasi Resistance in Early Colonial India Comprising the Chuar Rebellion of 1799 by J.C. Price* and *Relevant Midnapore District Collectorate Records from the Eighteenth Century*, edited with an Introduction by Ananda Bhattacharyya, Manohar, 2017).

[40]Letter from Magistrate Midnapore to Secy. Rev., extract Bengal Consultation 1 May 1800, IOLR; H. Ricketts, *Papers Relating to the South West Frontier, Comprising Reports on Purulia or Manbhum, Chotanagpur, Hazaribagh, Sambalpore and South West Frontier Agency, Selections from the Records of Government, Bengal XX*, Calcutta: Thomas Jones, Calcutta Gazette Office, 1855: 7; Extract Bengal Judicial Consultations, 31 July 1800, D. Campbell, Magistrate Birbhum to Secy. GOB, JUD and Rev: 84-5.

[41]Ray, *Change*: 153.

by Ray to conclude that the new property rights in land long regarded as the propelling force behind a revolution in Bengali rural society, would appear to have effected a less fundamental change than is usually supposed. Often referred to as the *jotedar* thesis, the idea of a dominant group capable of providing collective resistance to eviction and exploitation by superior right-holders leaves the pre-history and the post-history of the dominant groups open to question, even speculation.[42] Ray even examined the course of change from the pre-modern agrarian societies of Bengal to that at the time of the Permanent Settlement, and noted that the upper level of the agrarian society was always shifting from the time of Murshid Quli Khan to that of Cornwallis.

Ratnalekha Ray's book had grown out of a Cambridge thesis done under Eric Stokes, with an aim to examine the nature of the impact of the Permanent settlement (1793) on the agrarian society of Bengal. She had also attempted with detailed case studies to show that any idea that the agrarian social fabric in the pre-British period was simple and comparatively more egalitarian than the post-Permanent Settlement. There is an opinion that as a result of the Permanent Settlement, a new idea of absolute property was vested on the zamindars, and that created a market for zamindari titles. Manoshi Mitra rightly argued that the 'new rigour of government demand soon caused a massive transfer of landed property rights from the ancient zamindars with time honoured rights to the surplus, to a band of profit hungry 'businessmen' who systematically began to turn the screw on an otherwise egalitarian peasantry.'[43]

Ratnalekha Ray had a small analysis of the landholding pattern in the pre-British period in chapters 2 and 3. She has pointed out that while it is difficult to date the emergence of this class of village oligarchs, the famine of 1770 and the developments of the succeeding years helped this class which could take over abandoned holdings and bring them back to cultivation, due to their control over capital, and could also take advantage of the increased monetization of the economy and commercial agricultural production. This situation in

---

[42] For an excellent overview, see P.J. Marshall, *Bengal: The British Bridgehead – Eastern India 1740-1828*, Cambridge: Cambridge University Press, 1988.

[43] Ratnalekha Ray, *Change in Bengal Agrarian Society, c. 1760-1850*, New Delhi: Manohar, 1979, reviewed by Manoshi Mitra in *Indian Journal of Agricultural Economics,* vol. XXXVII, nos. 1-2, January-March 1982, Indian Society of Agricultural Economics, Bombay, 1982: 105-8.

Bengal can be compared to that which prevailed over parts of Bihar specially Purnea where this phenomenon of a powerful village based landholding class known variously as *gutchdars, kumdurrah* ryots, etc., holding large areas which were cultivated by sharecroppers *adhiyars* functioning as rural creditors, traders, and posing a challenge both to the zamindars and the government in their favour. This phenomenon of a village – based dominant peasantry which could hardly be dislodged even with changes in the upper echelons of the zamindari hierarchy was to be found in other areas of Bihar in greater or lesser degree.

Case studies of select zamindaries by Ratnalekha Ray show different outcomes in different cases but even with the zamindar who adapted most successfully to the changed situation created by the Permanent Settlement by sub-infeudation, the Burdwan Raj, changes at the top hardly went down to the village level. The Sadgop caste of dominant peasantry continued and improved their positions specifically under the *patni*[44] system. The high caste Hindu groups were typically found in the districts of Burdwan, Bishnupur and Dacca and formed the core of the local gentry. The districts of Dinajpur and Rangpur did not witness the existence of high-caste Hindus and local gentry.

The term *patni* system is most ambiguous one and probably had its origin from the Bengali word *pattani* system which means constituency or settlement. Unlike most of the other tenures of its time *pattani* had no pedigree. It had originated from the estate of Burdwan within a few years after Permanent Settlement and consecutively after availing its legal recognition through Regulation VIII of 1819 it spread rapidly like wildfire throughout in the district of

[44]By 1802 unofficially this system had become the practice and the *patni* leaseholders leased out their land in similar manner resulting into the growth of similar form of intermediate tenures in the 2nd and 3rd strata known as *dar-patni, se-patni, chahram-patni*. The exact number of *dar-patni* and *se-patni* in the district at the beginning of the late century is unknown. The Bankura estates belonging to the maharaja of Burdwan continued 241 *patni* taluk alone (W.W. Hunter, *A Statistical Account of Bengal*, vol. IV: *Bardwan, Bankura and Birbhum*, London: Trubner & Co., 1875: 251). Regarding the other estates that were within the realm of Bankura many of them had fallen under the newly built political unit known as jungle mahals, the number of the *patnidars* were comparatively to those which was under the supervision of Tejchand. The same situation was prevalent even in the year 1825 when the entire estate of Bankura except that of west Burdwan was let out as *patni* tenures.

Bengal. The creation of the *patni* tenure saved the nascent family of Burdwan Raj and his newly built estate from the verge of starvation. The idea of *patni* had its origin within the pros and cons of the Permanent Settlement. As Sirajul Islam observes, 'one of the major drawback of the permanent settlement was its failure to take to account the enormous changes that had been occurring in the agrarian relation from the beginning of the eighteenth century'.[45] The *patni* tenure rapidly spread over the extensive estate of Burdwan, and by 1818 it covered almost the whole of it. It appears from the official records that there were near about 1,495 tenures which comprised near about 8,737 villages and the total government revenue was 3,225,494. The *patnidars* possessed 5.8 villages with the government revenue of Rs. 2,158 and paid Rs. 658 as the price of the tenure.[46]

Thus a process of subinfeudation began which further increased the burden on the peasants who had to take recourse to moneylenders. Commercialization of agriculture contributed to the spread of rural indebtedness and a class of landless labourers and sharecroppers emerged at the lower end of the scale. Ratnalekha Ray has convincingly argued on the basis of detailed case studies that such a view of things tends to ignore the reality. In actual terms agrarian society in pre-British Bengal was much more complex with the rights to the surplus being shared between a wide range of claimants from ancient principalities to territorial magnates to co-sharers of parganas, to a class of village based land holders, the *jotedars* on whose acquiescence the system of rent collection either by the zamindari *amlah* or the revenue farmers depended. Ray had shown how the *jotedars* managed to have large holdings at extremely low rates of rent on the basis of their links with the zamindari *amlah* and the revenue farmers, as well as their position of almost complete domination over the mass of the peasantry through their control over land, capital and labour. Their position as rural moneylenders and financiers of cultivation and participation in trade further helped reinforce their position of control. Their lands were cultivated by a mixture of sharecroppers, as well as tied labourers, who were bound to them for sheer survival. Their caste composition might vary with area to area, but their relationship with the zamindar was full of contradictions. If the zamindar was

[45] Sirajul Islam, *Bengal Land Tenure: The Origin and Growth of Intermediate Interest in 19th Century*, Calcutta: K.P. Bagchi & Co, 1988: 10.

[46] Judicial Proceedings 8 October 1819, no. 28.

strong he might wrest some more of the surplus. But on the other hand, 'when the zamindar happened to be a female or a minor, or when there was a dispute over succession to the zamindar dominant village groups were encouraged by this struggle for power above them to withhold revenues'. Ratnalekha Ray defines the change brought about in the position of the zamindars by the Permanent Settlement as one which destroyed the zamindari as a public to revenue collection. Bankura or Baancorah, an integral part of Rarh Bengal, and simultaneous introduction of new land revenue system, the socio-economic structure changed slowly which led to the breakdown of the Bishnupur Raj and converted Bankura into semi-feudal tract affecting the landed relations of the region.[47] The *patni* system was a new trend of sub-infeudation system which was implanted by the Burdwan Raj in soil of Bankura. The *patni* tenure was first 'constituted (*pattan*)' by the raja of Burdwan around the turn of the century, and two decades elapsed before it was legally sanctioned by the regulation 8 of 1819 known as the *patni* sale law.[48] Scholarly British administrators of the late nineteenth century saw the peculiarity of the land system of Bengal in this excessive subinfeudation and wrote detailed accounts of it.[49] The famous chart prepared by C.D. Field makes a good example of their efforts in this direction. They tended to emphasize that the zamindars were separated from the actual tillers of the soil by innumerable rungs of intermediate tenure-holders.In the Patni tenure system a sale-deed, usually known as *byanamah* was signed in between raja and the purchaser who was known as *kabuliyat*. The *patni* tenure of Kaitoonath Ghose consisted of 22 villages and an annual rent of Rs. 12,541 was accrued from it. Thus by this contract he obtained complete possession of the lot and according to Taniguchi 'it relates to the profits arising from rents,

[47]Arundhuti Sen, 'Patni System and Sub-infeudation Rights in Bankura', *Journal of Bengali Studies*, vol. 4, no. 2, December 2015: 26-37.

[48]Shinkichi Taniguchi, 'The Patni System: A Modern Origin of the "Sub-Infeudation" of Bengal', *Hitotsubashi Journal of Economics*, vol. 22, no. 1, June 1981: 32-60.

[49]B.H. Baden-Powell, *The Land-Systems of British India,* 3 vols., London: 1892, Clarendon Press, vol. 1: 501-53; C.D. Field, *Land-holding and the Relation of Landlord and Tenant in Various Countries*, Calcutta: Thacker Spink, 1883: 705-42; W.W. Hunter, *A Statistical Account of Bengal*, vol. V: *Districts of Dacca, Bakarganj, Faridpur and Maimansinh,* London: Trubner & Co., 1875, vol. 5: 96-100, 324-5, 365-79, 448-53.

produce of lands not leased out, *chackeran* lands, cultivated and waste lands, jungle, *julker* [fee on fishery], *bunker* [fee on gatherer of forest products], gardens, tanks, lakes, *jheels* and all zamindary rights and privileges'. Three different years were given as the year of its initiation: *Bengal District Gazetteer, Burdwan* gives AD 1799, while documents recorded in the proceedings of the Judicial Department (8 October 1819) give AD 1801 and 1803 at different places. This short period of about two decades witnessed considerable agrarian tensions between the raja and the *patnidars* of several gradations, which eventually ended up with the enactment of the above regulation.

The raja of Burdwan used to sell and re-sell the tenure of the defaulting *patnidar*. The *patnidars* and the *dar-patnidars* would claim their *patni* lands as a taluk as it was defined in the proceedings of the Board of Revenue. There is a detailed analysis of the *patni* tenure system in the work of Taniguchi. The archival documents of West Bengal State Archives, particularly, the Board of Revenue Proceedings and Judicial Proceedings frequently refer the confrontation which occurred between the *patni* and *dar-patni talukdars* and the raja of Burdwan himself failed to pay near about Rs. 1,900,000. There were near about 460 applicants who were involved in litigation for sale of the defaulting *patnis*.

With the legalization of *patni* tenure in 1819, the system gradually spread it tentacles throughout in Bankura affecting the patterns and the trends of the land revenue administration in Bankura.[50] There were three factors behind the creation of *patni* tenure, as viewed by Taniguchi.[51] The raja himself wrote in his petition to the government that he expected the *patnidar*, by giving out a tenure at fixed rent in perpetuity, to encourage the improvement of the cultivation.[52] There was an urgent need for money on the part of the raja and the latter demanded a considerable sum of purchase money for the grant of

[50]Bankura during medieval period was been part of ancient Bishnupur with the exception of thanas Raipur and Khatra and of the western portions of the Bankura. When Bankura was seized, the raja of Bishnupur was more or less reduced to the status of feudatory chief.

[51]There is a detailed study in his ph.d dissertation (S. Taniguchi, 'Structure of Agrarian Society in Northern Bengal, 1765 to 1800', unpublished Ph.D. dissertation submitted to the University of Calcutta, 1977), cited in Shubhra Chakrabarti and Utsa Patnaik, eds., *Agrarian and Other Histories: Essays For Binay Bhushan Chaudhuri*, New Delhi: Tulika, 2017.

[52]Proceedings of the Judicial Department, 8 October 1819, no. 30.

the *patni* tenure. With the British accession of Bishnupur the settlement was made with Raja Chaitnya Singh, the *hustabood* being fixed at Rs. 3,86,708 payable to the government. The Great Famine of 1769-70 drastically affected the vertical structure of Bishnupur Raj which was so long based upon the allegiance of the local community who either perished or were apparently eliminated from the scene within the few years after the introduction of Permanent Settlement. Immediately before the creation of the *patni* tenures, the Burdwan estate incurred heavy arrears of revenue due to the government and portion of it was actually sold at public auction in 1797.[53] The crisis of the Bishnupur Raj was accelerated by the mismanagement of the estate and the fratricidal struggle of the Bishnupur Raj. By the year 1806 the whole of the ancient Bishnupur Raj had been sold at public auction in lots from which originated the ten revenue paying estates of Bishnupur subdivision of Bankura in the late-nineteenth century out of which eight deserves mention: Bishnupur, Karigunda, Jungle Mahals, Kuchaikol, Panchal, Jamatra, Shahjora, Maliara.[54]

Ratnalekha Ray presents an interesting study of Burdwan Raj in the context of the disarmament process.[55] The Raj had almost 33,000 paik and barkandaz (guards) and a lot of *nagadin* troupes (household troupers) which cost almost Rs. 33,000[56] in 1761 and was cut down to Rs. 8,660 in 1767 and the grant to maintain the force was totally abolished in 1768. The huge militia of Raj were mostly disbanded and were replaced by regular police force.[57]

---

[53] *Bengal District Gazetteer, Burdwan,* 1910: 149; K.A.L. Hill, *Final Report on the Survey and Settlement Operations in the District of Burdwan, 1927-1934*, vol. 1, Culcutta: Bengal Government Press, 1940; Ray, *Change*: 89-109. Ratnalekha Ray made it clear that most of the lots sold at the auction were purchased by the raja himself in fictitious names (Ray, *Change*: 102). It would be argued that he was subject to heavy private debts in order to purchase these lots, and that he was urgently in need of ready money to repay them (I am indebted to Professor Shinkichi Taniguchi for providing his published documents in establishing this argument).

[54] Ray, *Change*: 119.

[55] Jati Sankar Mondal, 'The Spark of Rebellion: Dacoits and Bushrangers', in Paul Brown, Deb Narayan Bandyopadhyay and Christopher Conti, eds., *Landscape, Peace and Culture: Linkages between Australia and India*, Newcastle: Cambridge Scholars Publishing: 138-48.

[56] Ray, *Change*: 97.

[57] Ibid.: 180.

Against this background the first major work in the theme of continuity and change in Bengal appeared in the late 1970s by Ratnalekha Ray. She arguing against the contemporary wisdom which emphasized dramatic change pointed out the continuities in the Bengal countryside. At one level she established that the sale of zamindaris did not result in any qualitative change in the ownership of the auctioned estates. The buyers being the *amlas* or the scions of the old estates ensued a continuity in the nature of ownership. She argued that the real power had continued unabated in the post-permanent settlement era. Most of the points made in the book were more cogently and forcefully laid down in an earlier research which was co-authored by Rajat Kanta Ray.

As opposed to the numerous works on nineteenth century agrarian history, the eighteenth century remained relatively untouched by scholars for some time and with it the issues of continuity and change. Recently, the arguments of the Rays have been subjected to critical assessment by Rajat Datta. The main tenet of Datta's argument is that in the late eighteenth century it was the zamindars and the merchants and not the *jotedars* who dominated the countryside through their control over production. Datta explicitly denied the domination, or even the existence, of this class of rural gentry in the late eighteenth century, but appears to have implicitly accepted that this class may have emerged in the nineteenth century.

As contributions to the debate on the nature of continuity and change between the pre-colonial and colonial eras (in terms underlying social and economic structures) both the arguments seem rather narrowly conceived. The first important problem with them is the period from which the sources are drawn. The earliest sources referred to are the Company documents of the last quarter of the eighteenth century and most of the other sources belong to the last decades of the eighteenth century. One of the most important sources used by all of them, Buchanan-Hamilton's surveys, actually belong to the early nineteenth century. Datta's account, in tracing the ascendancy of the merchants and the zamindars, underplays the importance of the changes following the battle of Plassey. In the light of the fact that after Plassey the Company ceased to import bullion into Bengal and insisted 'used the proceeds of political power-cash revenues to finance its trade' leading to a 'severe credit crisis in eastern India', it appears that the increased activity of the zamindars and the merchants at the village level was more recent and had its origin in the operation of the Company rather than in the pre-colonial era as has been implied.[58]

Two recent studies by Kumkum Chatterjee and John Mclane apparently contradict the argument raised by Subhajyoti Ray. Their assertion that big business as well as large landed magnates continued to thrive in certain areas of eastern India even after the decline of the Mughal empire is generally accepted and seems to confirm Bayly's findings from north India. Their assertion about the deep inroads that the zamindars and the merchants had made in the countryside is also well known. But it appears to Subhajyoti Ray that their models are tenable in areas which had a long history of settled and ranked peasantry. Thus while Chatterjee focuses on a band of territory in Bihar on either side of the river Ganges. Mclane's sources are drawn from south-west Bengal, both of which are among the oldest continuously settled tracts of the subcontinent. These were the core areas of the post-Mughal 'state' systems in Bihar and Bengal. It is not surprising that a 'regionally oriented group', to quote Philip Calkins,[59] emerged in these areas following the weakening of Mughal authority. In addition, McLane's model presupposes the penetration of certain indefinite but what Washbrook[60] has criticized as 'irreducible'. The argument regarding the continuity of the power of the *jotedars* put forward by the Ray's is also based on similar sources as Datta's. In addition, it is seen that it is a logical argument rather than a substantive one. Irrespective of their different names in different parts of Bengal the *jotedar* of the nineteenth century obviously evolved from a position of power he had in the eighteenth century. In this sense there was continuity. After the mid-nineteenth century he may have been a *chaukidar* or even a *dar chaukidar*. But more importantly, the nature of *jotedar's* power in the nineteenth century was of a different type, its basis was different, as (it can be argued) was its function.

The Company gave the zamindar considerable powers to recover

[58]Subhajyoti Ray, *Transformations on the Bengal Frontier: Jalpaiguri 1765-1948,* London: Routledge Curzon, 2002: 2-3.

[59]Philip B. Calkins, 'The Formation of a Regionally Oriented Group in Bengal, 1700-1740', *Journal of Asian Studie*s, vol. 29(4) (Aug. 1970), Cambridge: Cambridge University Press: 799-806.

[60]A. David, 'Law, State and Agrarian Society in Colonial India', *Modern Asian Studies*, Cambridge: Cambridge University Press, vol. 15, no. 3: 649-721.

rent. The *Haptam* (Seventh) Regulation of 1799 was notorious in this respect. It allowed the zamindar to seize and sell the defaulting tenant's property while waiting for a judicial decision. If a zamindar filed a legal complaint against the tenant, he could be arrested even before any investigation. But, perhaps most important, 'no part of the existing regulations was meant to deprive the zamindars and other landholders of the power of summoning, and if necessary of compelling the attendance of their tenants, for the adjustment of their rents, or for any other just purpose'. This gave the zamindar license to personally coerce the tenant. The 1812 regulation subsequently placed some restrictions on the zamindar's rights to sell the tenant's property, but the provision permitting coercion remained in place until 1859.

But the original scheme was overtaken by the unintended effect of a rapidly emerging market in sub-tenurial rights in land. It is in this light one should see the *patni* system, particularly Patni Regulation VIII of 1819, which legally recognized the sub-letting right of the superior tenure-holder. This dichotomy between the intended and the actual outcome of the Permanent Settlement, that it influenced the later stages in the evolution of land-relations in Bengal. It triggered off a rapid process of differentiation among the landholders from above. It was a process generated by the zamindars themselves in their attempt to hedge risk. Thus a significant market in the sub-tenurial and sub-letting rights of land developed, which made such rights an easily marketable commodity. The *patni* system gave legal recognition to this providing a distinct landmark in the first phase in the commercialization of sub-tenurial rights in land on an unprecedented scale. Perhaps, the most serious implication of this commercialization of sub-tenurial rights in land was the tendency for rapid growth in the number of intermediate rent-receivers (between the zamindar and the direct cultivator) which accompanied the process. As a consequence, it paid no invest individually in the improvement of land. Profit from increased productivity of land had usually to be shared by the various layers of intermediaries, while there was no viable mechanism of sharing the cost of land improvement collectively. This seems to have been a crucial economic factor in vitiating the original intention of the Permanent Settlement, which had expected that high land revenue would compel the zamindars to raise the productivity of land to make the holding of estates an attractive economic proposition over time.

The Permanent Settlement did cause a diversion of part of the mercantile or urban capital to purchase of land, but it is doubtful whether this was a big part. The land market was scarcely dominated by the so-called 'Calcutta *banians*'. It is true that the scope for participation in trade on the part of indigenous merchants and traders tended to be restricted, but it scarcely disappeared. Their role as independent traders became sharply limited, but in various forms as junior partners to the Europeans was still profitable, particularly because of the expansion of both internal and external trade.

In Dinajpur, the situation was different as viewed by Buchanan-Hamilton during his visit. He says 'no zamindar cleared less than 10 per cent and none of the larger zamindar more than 25 per cent of the gross rental'. It appears from the evidence furnished by Buchanan that the raja of Dinajpur cleared only 15.5 per cent. The estate of a famous merchant Odwait Chaudhuri yielded only 18 per cent.[61] Chaudhury has shown that 'this small profit was liable to be reduced by crop failures or other hazards'. This heaviness of the land revenue demand partly accounted for the phenomenon called 'trading in land'. The collector of Midnapore put it, i.e. to collect as much as possible from peasants and then to wilfully default.

The sale law of 1793 combined coercion with economic coercion. Revenue had then to be paid monthly, and where zamindars failed to pay one-third of a monthly instalment by the 15th of the following month they were imprisoned and their estates were attached by the government. Rents were collected by the government as long as the arrears remained unpaid, and monthly sales were insisted upon. The system of imprisonment was abolished in 1794, except where the sale of estates was not enough for the realization of arrears. At the same time a new penalty was imposed – interest at 12 per cent charged on the arrears. Regulation VII of 1799 did away with imprisonment altogether but the utmost punctuality was insisted upon in the payment of revenue. In the district of Bengal proper the conflict of the new purchasers with the rent-free holders was particularly acute in the big estates held by Hindu zamindars who made many of these grants, such as Bishnupur, Nadia, Dinajpur, Rajshahi, and Midnapore. In Bishnupur purchasers 'found it impossible to secure full possession of the purchased mahals . . . their purchase money with interest was returned to them'. Even the zamindar of Burdwan 'into whose hands the bulk of the zamindari fell found it difficult to secure possession'.

[61] *Dinajpore Report, 1951 Census edn.*, Calcutta: 247-9.

His suggestion to the government to cancel the sales and give him back the purchase money was not accepted, and 'it is probably only because he was himself a wealthy and powerful nobleman that he was eventually able to secure peaceful possession of the property'.[62]

Two other changes effected by Regulation VII of 1799 had also a role in the rising value of landed property. The sub institution of year-end sales for monthly ones greatly reduced the strain on the zamindar's resources. Secondly, the Regulation strengthened the hands of zamindars against various groups from which they collected rents.

Ratnalekha Ray's analysis of landholders and peasantry in Midnapore at the beginning of British rule reveals that in the jungle parganas the zamindari of Midnapore alone passed out of the hands of a tribal raja into Sadgop hands, before the permanent settlement of 1793; and after 1793, only three other parganas were brought by Bengali speculators, and retained, out of at least seventeen district estates.[63] She notes that in the Jungle mahals 'the zamindars were aboriginal bhuiya or Bhumij chiefs who had assumed the status of Rajput or khandait'.[64]

Ratnalekha Ray in *Change in Bengal Agrarian Society* has shown that even during the mighty rule Moyna as well as Tamluk was practically a self government 'almost an autonomous state'. Moynaraj also used to take the responsibility of playing the role of a 'samajpati' (leader of society) through generations. Thus, these 'rajas had the rare quality of combing two important factors – controlling of government as well as keeping a close contact with the common people. This was extremely rare in the background of the middle ages. Bayly has mentioned that from the days of the Nawabs till the first seven years of Hastings there was a custom, the *foujdars* used to send horses and gold annually to the zamindars of Kashijora, Moynachoura, Medinipur, and Narayangarh. In a separate context while naming several zamindars he has referred to *taluk*, Narayangarh and Moynachura as the real rajas. Before the ten year settlement James Grant has mentioned eight families evaluating their revenue-collection and hereditary prestige, and Moynachura is one of them. Edward Becher wrote a letter to Warren Hastings dated 6 February

[62]F.W. Robertson, *Final Report on the Survey and Settlement Operations in the District of Bankura, 1917-24*, Calcutta: Bengal Secretariat Book Depot, 1926: 35-6.

[63]Ray, *Change*: 131-73.

[64]Ibid., 147.

1773 where it is mentioned that 'the fort in which the Raja lives is surrounded by two moats both of which are wide and deep; he used to shut himself up in his fort in order to put off unwanted persons and then it is impossible to reach him'.

In spite of these efforts by many eminent historians, Tanguchi feels 'that there still remains not only lots of gaps to be filled in our knowledge on regional variations, but also contradicting views, which need to be reconciled, regarding some basic aspects of the Bengal agrarian societies'.[65]

To sum up, the author has no doubts left to her that the formation of the Bengali *jotedar* class predates colonial period, even though supporting historical evidence is still awaited. She further holds that the Permanent Settlement had hardly any impact on the consolidation of 'the pre-existing *jotedar* class' and its domination over the peasantry. In her opinion, the domination of the *ryots* by *jotedars* in Bengal in her period was a general phenomenon, and rural Bengal had, by and large, long ceased to have a small peasant subsistence economy as its dominant feature. In some areas, she concedes, powerful zamindars were able to reduce the village elite almost to the uniform dead level of ordinary *ryots*. In other areas, the latter were able not only to retain their position, but also to appropriate a larger share of the economic rent than the zamindars. Availability of waste lands nearby, potentiality of cash crop cultivation and the locus of the zamindar within or outside the pargana – these were the crucial factors that determined the *jotedar's* position vis-à-vis his, zamindar. The author believes that, except in old settled parganas 'surrounded by intensively cultivated rice producing plains', everywhere else, *jotedars* continued to retain a substantial share of the rent all over Bengal. For, according to the author, in most parganas there was considerable scope for extension of cultivation after the Permanent Settlement. As has already been said, many will not agree with this generalization, particularly with the statement that there was already a powerful Muslim *jotedar* class in larger parts of East Bengal during the author's period. We do not think that this was possible until jute

[65] Shinkichi Taniguchi, 'Regional Structure of Bengal Agrarian Societies in the Late Nineteenth Century', in *Development and Culture in Asia: Comparative Study on Grassroots Solidarity among Peoples in Asian Countries,* A project report sponsored by the Ministry of Education, Japan, Hitosubashi University, Tokyo, 2000.

came in, in a big way after 1850, in the railway age. Even then, Teli/ Tili and Saha/Sunri traders and moneylenders started not only buying up zamindari rights but also *ryoti* rights.

ACKNOWLEDGEMENTS

In order to bring out the reprint edition of Ratnalekha Ray's *Change in Bengal Agrarian Society* I am highly indebted to Professor Deba Prosad Choudhury, Professor B.B. Chaudhuri, Professor Rajat Kanta Ray, Professor Sirajul Islam, Professor Shinkichi Taniguchi, Professor David Ludden and Professor John R. McLane for providing me with new insights in studying the agrarian history of Bengal. I am also indebted to Professor Chandak Sengupta, Professor S. Taniguchi, Miss Sonia Wigh, PhD fellow and Miss Fatima Hamid for providing me so many published papers for writing my introduction. I am also indebted to the employees of The National Library, Calcutta and the staff and Archivists of The National Archives, New Delhi and the India Office Library, London. Special acknowledgement is due to Sri Aryama Ghosh, PhD fellow, Department of History, Jadavpur University for providing valuable feedback in preparing my introduction. The original work has been reproduced verbatim without any editorial intervention. Finally, I am duly indebted to Shri Ramesh Jain of Manohar Publishers & Distributors, who kindly agreed to bring out a reprint edition of this classic volume.

BIBLIOGRAPHY

PRIMARY SOURCES

(A) *India Office Library and Records, London*

Bengal Consultation F/4/1770.

Letter from Magistrate Midnapore to Secy. Rev., Extract Bengal Consultation, 1 May 1800, IOLR.

Extract Bengal Judicial Consultations, 31 July 1800, D. Campbell, Magistrate Birbhum to Secy. GOB, Jud. and Rev: 84-5.

(b) *West Bengal State Archives, Kolkata*

Judicial Proceedings, 8 October 1819, no. 28.

Proceedings of the Judicial Department, 8 October 1819, nos. 80.

Secondary Sources

Akhtar, Shirin, *The Role of Zamindars in Bengal, 1707-1772*, Dacca: Asiatic Society of Bangladesh, 1982.

Arasaratnam, S., 'Trade and Political Domination in South India, 1750-1790: Changing British – India Relations', in Patrick Tuck, ed., with an Introduction, *The East India Company 1600-1858: Trade, Finance and Power*, vol. IV, London and New York: Routledge, 1998.

Baden-Powell, B.H., *The Land Systems of British India,* 3 vols (rpt.), New Delhi: Oriental Publishers, 1974.

Bayly, C.A. *Rulers, Townsmen, and Bazaars: North Indian Society in the Age of British Expansion, 1770-1870*, Cambridge / New York: Cambridge University Press, 1983.

Beteille, Andre, *Studies in the Agrarian Social Structure*, New Delhi: Oxford University Press, 1974.

Bhattacharyya, Ananda, *Adivasi Resistance in Early Colonial India Comprising the Chuar Rebellion of 1799 by J.C. Price and Relevant Midnapore District Collectorate Records from the Eighteenth Century*, edited with an Introduction by Ananda Bhattacharyya, New Delhi: Manohar, 2017.

Bose, Sugata, *Agrarian Bengal: Economy, Social Structure and Politics*, Cambridge: Cambridge University Press, 1986.

Calkins, Philip B. 'The Formation of a Regionally Oriented Group in Bengal, 1700-1740', *Journal of Asian Studies*, vol. 29(4) (Aug. 1970), Cambridge: Cambridge University Press.

Chatterjee, Kumkum, *The Cultures of History in Early Modern India: Persianization and Mughal Culture in Bengal*, New Delhi: Oxford University Press, 2009.

Chattopadhyay, Basudev, *Crime and Control in Early Colonial Bengal, 1770-1860*, Kolkata: K.P. Bagchi, 2002.

———, 'Agricultural Growth in Bengal and Bihar, 1770-1860: Growth of Cultivation since the Famine of 1770', *Bengal Past and Present*, January-June, Calcutta: Calcutta Historical Society, 1976.

———, 'Rural Power Structure and Agricultural Productivity in Eastern India, 1757-1947', in Meghnad Desai, Susane Hoeber Ruddolph and Ashok Rudra, eds., *Agrarian Power and Agricultural Productivity in South Asia*, New Delhi: Oxford University Press, 1984.

———, *Peasant History of Late Pre-Colonial and Colonial India*, vol. VIII, pt. 2, New Delhi: Pearson Education India, 2008.

Cohn, Bernard S., 'Political Systems in Eighteenth Century India: The Banaras Region', *Journal of the American Oriental Society*, Ann Arbor: American Oriental Society, University of Michigan, 82(3), 1962.

Curley, David L., 'Voluntary Relations and Royal Gifts of Pan in Mughal Bengal', in Stewart Gordon, ed. *Robes of Honour*: *Khilat in Pre-colonial and Colonial Bengal*, New Delhi: Oxford University Press, 2003.

Dasgupta, Biplab, *European Trade and Colonial Conquest,* London: Anthem Press, 2005.

Datta, Rajat, *Society, Economy and the Market: Commercial in Rural Bengal, c. 1760-1800*, New Delhi: Manohar, 2000.

Dick, Howard, Michael Sullivan and John Butcher, eds., *The Rise and Fall of Revenue Farming: Business Elites and the Emergence of the Modern State in Southeast Asia (Studies in the Economies of East and South-East Asia,* 1st edn., London: Palgrave Macmillan, 1993.

Dinajpore Report, 1951 Census edn., Calcutta, 1952.

Field, C.D., *Land-holding and the Relation of Landlord and Tenant in Various Countries*, Calcutta: Thacker Spink, 1883.

Firminger, Walter Kelly, ed., *Fifth Report on East India Affairs*, vol. II, Calcutta: R. Cambray, 1918.

Floud, Francis, *Report of the Land Revenue Commission Bengal*, vol. II: *Appendices (I to IX) and Indian Land System Ancient, Medieval and . . . Bengal Land Revenue Commission*, Government of Bengal, vol. 2, Calcutta: Bengal Secretariat Press, 1940.

Habib, Irfan, 'Studying a Colonial Economy – Without Perceiving Colonialism', *Modern Asian Studies* (heretofore refer to *MAS*), Cambridge: Cambridge University Press, 19, 3, 1985.

———, 'Theories of Social Change', Riazul Islam Memorial Lecture, Dhaka, May 1986.

Hill, K.A.L., *Final Report on the Survey and Settlement Operations in the District of Burdwan, 1927-1934*, vol. 1., Calcutta: Bengal Government Press, 1940.

Hunter, W.W., *A Statistical Account of Bengal,* vol. IV: *Bardwan, Bankura and Birbhum*, London: Trubner & Co., 1875.

———, *A Statistical Account of Bengal,* vol. V: *Districts of Dacca, Bakarganj, Faridpur and Maimansinh,* London: Trubner & Co, 1875.

Islam, Sirajul, *Bengal Land Tenure: The Origin and Growth of Intermediate Interest in 19th Century*, Calcutta: K.P. Bagchi & Co., 1988.

Leach, E.R., ed., *Aspects of Caste in South India, Ceylon and North-West Pakistan*, Cambridge: Cambridge University Press, 1960.

Marshall, P.J., *Bengal: The British Bridgehead – Eastern India 1740-1828*, Cambridge: Cambridge University Press, 1988.

Mcdermott, Rachel Fell, *Mother of My Heart, Daughter of My Dreams: Kali and Uma in the Devotional Poetry of Bengal*, New York: Oxford University Press, 2001.

McLane, J.R., *Land and Local Kingship in Eighteenth Century Bengal*, Cambridge: Cambridge University Press, 1993.

Mondal, Jati Sankar, 'The Spark of Rebellion: Dacoits and Bushrangers', in Paul Brown, Deb Narayan Bandyopadhyay and Christopher Conti, eds., *Landscape, Peace and Culture: Linkages between Australia and India*, New Castle Upon Tyne: Cambridge Scholars Publishing, 2010.

Mukherjee, Tilottama, 'The Co-ordinating State and the Economy: The Nizamat in the Eighteenth Century Bengal', *MAS*, 42, 1, Cambridge: Cambridge University Press, 2008

Ray, Aniruddha, *Towns and Cities of Medieval India*: *A Brief Survey*, New Delhi: Manohar, 2015.

———, *Adventurers, Landowners and Rebels: Bengal c. 1575-c. 1715*, New Delhi: Munshiram Manoharlal, 1998.

Ray, Niharanjan, *History of the Bengali People: Ancient Period*, New Delhi: Orient Longmans, 1994.

Ray, Pranab, 'Rebel Zamindars Sobha Singh and Some Contemporary Records', *Proceedings of the Indian History Congress*, vol. 61, pt. 1, New Delhi: Indian History Congress, 2000-1.

Ray, Rajat and Ratnalekha Ray, 'The Dynamism of Continuity in Rural Bengal Under the British Imperium', *IESHR*, June 1973.

———, 'Zamindars and Jotedars: A Study of Rural Politics of Bengal', *MAS*, Cambridge: Cambridge University Press, 9, 1, 1975.

———, 'The Retreat of the Jotedars? *IESHR*, vol. XXV, no. 2. 1988.

Ray, Ratnalekha, *Change in Bengal Agrarian Society, c. 1760-1850*, New Delhi: Manohar, 1979, reviewed by Manoshi Mitra in *Indian Journal of Agricultural Economics*, vol. XXXVII, nos. 1-2, January-March, *Indian Society of Agricultural Economics*, Bombay, 1982.

———, *Change in Bengal Agrarian Society, c. 1760-1850*, New Delhi: Manohar, 1979, reviewed by David Ludden, *The Journal of Economic History*, The Economic History Association, Cambridge University Press, vol. 43, no. 2, June 1983.

———, *Change in the Bengal Agrarian Society*, reviewed by Amalendu Guha, *Book Review Literary Trust*, no. 2, 1981.

Ray, Subhajyoti, *Transformations on the Bengal Frontier: Jalpaiguri 1765-1948,* London: Routledge Curzon, 2002.

Raychaudhuri, Tapan, Irfan Habib, Dharma Kumar and Meghnad Desai, eds., *The Cambridge Economic History of India*, vol. I: *c. 1200-c. 1750*, Cambridge: Cambridge University Press, 1982.

Ricketts, H., *Papers Relating to the South West Frontier, Comprising Reports on Purulia or Manbhum, Chotonagpur, Hazaribagh, Sambalpore and South West Frontier Agency, Selections from the Records of Government,* Bengal XX, Calcutta: Thomas Jones, Calcutta Gazette Office, 1855.

Robertson, F.W., *Final Report on the Survey and Settlement Operations in the District of Bankura, 1917-24*, Calcutta: The Govt. of India Press, 1926.

Sen, Arundhuti, 'Patni System and Sub-infeudation Rights in Bankura' *Journal of Bengali Studies*, vol. 4, no. 2, December 2015.

Sen, Asok, Partha Chatterjee and Saugata Mukherji, *Perspectives in Social Sciences 2: Three Studies on the Agrarian Structure in Bengal 1850-1947*, published for the Centre for Studies in Social Sciences, Calcutta: Oxford University Press, 1982.

Sengupta, Kalyan Kumar, *Pabna Disturbances and the Politics of Rent 1873-1885*, New Delhi: People's Publishing House, 1974.

Sinha, N.K., *Economic History of Bengal: From Plassey to the Permanent Settlement*, vol. 2, Calcutta: Firma K.L. Mukhopadhyay, 1968.

Sivaramkrishnan, K., *Modern Forests: State Making and Environmental Change in Colonial Eastern India,* Stanford: Stanford University Press, 1999.

Taniguchi, Shinkichi, 'Structure of Agrarian Society in Northern Bengal, 1765 to 1800', unpublished Ph.D. Dissertation submitted to the University of Calcutta, 1977.

———, 'Rethinking the Bengal Peasantry in History', in Shubhra Chakrabarti and Utsa Patnaik, eds., *Agrarian and Other Histories: Essays For Binay Bhushan Chaudhuri*, New Delhi: Tulika Books, 2017.

———, 'The Peasantry of Northern Bengal in the Late Eighteenth Century', in Peter Robb, K. Sughira and H. Yanagisawa, eds., *Local Agrarian Societies in Colonial India: Japanese Perspectives*, London, Curzon Press, 1996.

———, 'The Patni System: A Modern Origin of the "Sub-Infeudation" of Bengal', *Hitotsubashi Journal of Economics*, Hitotsubashi University, vol. 22, no. 1 (June 1981).

———, 'Regional Structure of Bengal Agrarian Societies in the Late Nineteenth Century', in *Development and Culture in Asia-Comparative Study on Grassroots Solidarity among Peoples in Asian Countries,* A Project Report Sponsored by the Ministry of Education, Japan, Tokyo: Hitosubashi University, 2000.

Thorner, Daniel & Alice Thorner, *Land and Labour in India*, Bombay: Asia Publishing House, 1962.

Washbrook, David A., 'Law, State and Agrarian Society in Colonial India', *MAS,* vol. 15, no. 3, Cambridge: Cambridge University Press.

Wilson, John, *The Domination of Strangers: Modern Governance in Eastern India*, London: Palgrave Macmillan, 2008.

Yang, Anand A., *Bazaar India: Markets, Society, & the Colonial State in Bihar,* Berkeley, Los Angeles and Oxford: University of California Press, 1998.

1

The Problem

The Permanent Settlement of 1793 provided the legal and administrative framework within which agrarian relations were determined in Bengal until the zamindari abolition acts of the 1950s. It is the purpose of this study to examine the idea, reiterated time and again since its first authoritative formulation in the Fifth Report of the Select Committee of 1812,[1] that the Permanent Settlement fundamentally altered the structure of rural society. The tendency to associate the rise of the East India Company with the disappearance of an old order and the emergence of a new set of relations in the land arises from the assumption that colonial rule transformed the basis of Bengal's society from status to contract. But recent detailed local studies based on contemporary records have tended to dispel many romantic notions about the traditional village community which found uncritical acceptance among generations of administrators and scholars earlier.[2] Once it is appreciated that rural society on the eve of the British occupation was a complex society in a comparatively advanced stage of evolution, the problem of agrarian change under British rule no longer remains a simple matter of contrasting a changing scheme of things with a static order regulated by age-old custom.

---

[1]Fifth Report of the Select Committee on the Affairs of the East India Company, *Parliamentary Papers*, Vol. 7, sess. 1812.

[2]For the growing challenge to hitherto accepted notions of traditional rural society, see Dharma Kumar, *Land and Caste in South India: Agricultural Labour in the Madras Presidency during the Nineteenth Century*; (Cambridge 1965) and Tapan Ray Chaudhuri, 'The Agrarian System of Mughal India', *Enquiry*, Spring 1965.

The stratified rural community of the twentieth century, with its landlords and rich farmers on the one hand and landless peasants and agricultural labourers on the other, is often contrasted with an egalitarian and self-sufficient village society before British rule. According to this view, a superior stratum of Muslim officers of state and local Hindu magnates (zamindars) existed in the villages, but within village society there was supposed to be no stratification of the kind based on class differences between different agricultural households. There were, supposedly, no landless villagers and no class of rich agriculturists monopolizing land and employing hired labour. In a self-sufficient subsistence economy, where each peasant family produced for its own consumption by means of family labour, there was said to be no scope for such class differences. Commercial agriculture, it was assumed, had not yet developed, cash transactions were supposed to be limited, and there was said to be no usurious system of rural debt which would enrich a class of money-lenders at the expense of the peasants.[3]

In Bengal, it has been claimed, the Permanent Settlement changed all this. Under the operations of this settlement, in the course of the nineteenth century, a three-tier class system emerged: landlords (zamindars) and rich farmers (jotedars), self-sufficient peasants with tenancy rights in land (raiyats), and sharecroppers (bargadars) and agricultural labourers (krishaks). All this was said to have resulted from a process of concentration of land-holding and expropriation of peasants initiated by the Permanent Settlement. It was held that this settlement introduced a rule of property for Bengal derived from French physiocratic notions,[4] which led to the creation of landed estates. By creating absolute property in the soil the Permanent Settlement brought into existence, according to prevailing notions, a market for land. Within two decades, it was said, from one-third to one-half of the whole landed property in

[3]For a statement of these assumptions, see Ramkrishna Mukherjee, *The Dynamics of a Rural Society* (Berlin 1957); Daniel and Alice Thorner, *Land and Labour in India* (London 1962); Narendra Krishna Sinha, *The Economic History of Bengal*, Vol. II (Calcutta, 1962), admits the existence of class differences in village society, but tends to minimize their importance; see pp. 131-144, 196-198.

[4]Ranajit Guha, *A Rule of Property for Bengal* (Paris 1963).

Bengal was sold on account of arrears of revenue.[5] The older aristocracy of zamindars, who had ancient rights in the land (but not the exclusive property of it), were said to have been destroyed during these convulsions in the land market. On the ruins of the ancient zamindaris there arose, according to this view, a new class of 'sharks and rapacious businessmen', 'a shrewd, opportunist and self-seeking commercialized group of interests who invested their capital in the purchase of land'.[6] This urban capitalist landlord class raised rents to an unprecedented degree, and since the demand of the government was permanently limited by statute, the increase in rents created a powerful incentive towards subinfeudation. Soon after the Permanent Settlement there emerged a complex rent-collecting structure with many grades of intermediary tenure-holders between the landlords and the tenants.[7] There was thus an increasing burden on the peasantry, and since taxes of a fixed and inflexible amount had now to be paid in cash (which substituted payments in kind), the peasants were forced to have recourse increasingly to money-lenders.[8] Meanwhile, commercial agriculture had spread in Bengal under the encouragement of the colonial regime, and land had acquired value as a means of producing commercial crops. A system of rural credit on the security of the land thus quickly developed and, inevitably, land began to pass from debtors to creditors. A class of landless sharecroppers and agricultural labourers emerged in this process of concentration of landholding, and on the other end of the scale there emerged a new class of rich farmers giving loans, who themselves held large farms which were cultivated by hired labour.[9]

Such, in brief, have been the conceptions of agrarian change in Bengal among generations of critics of the Permanent Settlement: the creation of a land market, the emergence of profit-oriented landlordism and the disintegration and increasing land

---

[5]William Wilson Hunter, *Bengal Ms. Records*, Vol. 1 (London 1894), p. 101.

[6]R. Palme Dutt, *India Today*, (Bombay 1949), p. 216; B.B. Misra, *The Central Administration of the East India Company*, 1773-1834 (Manchester 1959), p. 195. See also Narendra Krishna Sinha, op. cit., pp. 177-178.

[7]B.B. Misra, *The Indian Middle Classes* (London 1961), p. 133.

[8]Daniel and Alice Thorner, op cit., pp. 54.

[9]Ramkrishna Mukherjee, op. cit., pp. 27-40.

differentiation of the peasantry under the growing burden of rent and usury. If, however, it can be shown that landless labour, rural indebtedness and a village land-holding class among the peasantry were already significant features of rural society before 1793, then the whole question of agrarian change in Bengal under the Permanent Settlement will deserve reconsideration from a fresh angle. What was the nature of zamindari and how exactly was it changed by the Permanent Settlement? How did this change, if any, at the upper stratum of rural society transform its agrarian base and alter the land-holding pattern at the village level?

Quite recently there have been attempts to quantify the extent and direction of change resulting from the Permanent Settlement. Bernard Cohn for the Benaras region (which was then under the Bengal Presidency) and Sirajul Islam for the Bengal region (Bengal proper excluding Midnapur) have produced figures for land transfers giving very interesting results.[10] Both conclude that people traditionally connected with the land (though possibly, as Cohn points out, strangers to the locality and in that sense 'new men') and not commercial magnates alien to the countryside, were the predominant group among the auction purchasers of properties brought to the hammer by the sale regulations of the Permanent Settlement for covering revenue deficits.[11] Islam has calculated that during 1793-1819, about 68.2 per cent of the land (in terms of the assessment fixed on lands and not in terms of area) underwent transfer,[12] at any rate, on paper (real transfers were less on

[10]M.S. Islam, 'Permanent Settlement and the Landed Interest in Bengal 1793-1819', Ph. D. thesis, SOAS 1972; Bernard S. Cohn, 'Structural Change in Indian Rural Society', in Robert Eric Frykenberg, *Land Control and Social Structure in Indian History* (Madison, Wisconsin 1969).

[11]M.S. Islam, op. cit., p. 239; Bernard S. Cohn, op. cit. The earlier writings by Cohn on the Benaras region suggest a more fundamental change in local society than he seems to admit in his later essay in *Land Control and Social Structure*. See Bernard E. Cohn, 'The Initial British Impact on India', *Journal of Asian Studies*, August 1960. Nevertheless he still made provision for a structural shift in local land control rights due to the intrusion of strangers, even though they mostly came from traditional land-holdings castes like Rajputs and Brahmans.

[12]Op cit., Appendix B, Jama of lands advertised for sale and actually sold.

account of fictitious transfers made by zamindars to their servants and dependents while retaining actual possession of the properties). The effect was most devastating for the so-called 'capital' zamindars who paid 51 per cent of the land revenue of Bengal; together they lost 61 per cent of their properties, while the lesser zamindars lost no more than 26 per cent.[13] On account of these convulsions in the land market, the market value of land (by this term Islam refers to the purchase prices offered for zamindaris at auction) declined between 1779-1800, but after 1800 the zamindars who emerged from the turmoil benefited from the increased value of land due to growth of population, extension of cultivation, liquidation of all rights of the tenants by the dreaded Regulation of 1799, and greater confidence in the permanence of the Permanent Settlement.[14] Both Islam and Cohn have tended to equate the figures of transfer of zamindaris available to them with the transfer of the actual control of the land and Islam, in particular, equates the market price of zamindaris with the market price of land. For want of relevant statistics, Islam leaves out of account the under-tenure holders below the zamindars who might have continued in occupation of the land while above them the zamindari changed hands. This possibility Cohn explores in much greater detail for the Benaras region and concludes that many transfers of land remained merely paper transactions as the new purchasers were often obliged to accommodate the former zamindars within the local land control system by some form of subleasing of the management and collection of revenue. The purchase of a title at auction could not by itself mean much if the purchaser—as happened so often in the Benaras region—failed to impose full raiyati rates on the ex-proprietors' private lands (sic) and could not manage to collect directly from the non-proprietary cultivators.

The tacit assumption that zamindars under the Permanent Settlement were landlords and that the auction sale of their zamindaris established a market for land arises almost unconsciously from the application of English terms and concepts to Indian realities for which they were not quite suitable. In order

---

[13]Ibid., pp. 213=214, 236.

[14]Ibid., p.248 ff.

to avoid this snare and to reach a deeper understanding of the process of agrarian change we have to be quite clear, at the outset, of the meaning of such basic terms as 'land' and 'landlord' in the particular context of eighteenth and nineteenth century Bengal.

A Fundamental Distinction: Zamindar and Jotedar

The term zamindar (zamin=land, dar=holder) literally meant a land-holder. But the land-holders' rights over land, that solid and comforting entity from which men derive their sustenance, had quite different meanings. They might mean the physical occupation of a visible piece of ground producing crops; or they might mean the superior control of a defined stretch of territory administered by an authority who collected dues (known as jama or assessment) from the villages within it. For different kinds of land-control rights, depending on whether these meant direct occupation of the soil or control over territory, there would be different kinds of holders or owners. Above the villages would stand the superior tribute-collecting landlords ruling over their territorial jurisdictions, while within the villages would exist subordinate village landholders possessing crop-bearing lands. Within each basic category, there might be many layers of proprietary rights, existing in a graded hierarchy. Land ownership was, therefore, a complex phenomenon that did not lend itself to a straightforward definition in terms of Roman law. As a later Bengal Civilian expressed it: 'there is no ownership of land, but simply a system of possessory interests. These interests are piled one on top of another, and none can be got rid of unless the interest holder fails to pay his dues to his superior "landlord."'[15]

In order to subject this complex situation to proper analysis, it is necessary to comprehend the fundamental distinction between (a) the various grades of hereditary revenue payers with proprietary rights in revenue management and (b) the dominant landed village groups in effective possession of land and commanding the labour of poor villagers. For the sake of convenience, the first group of revenue-collecting proprietors

[15]Bell Papers, file no. 2, 1940-1946, 'Agriculture in India', University of Cambridge, Centre of South Asian Studies.

might be referred to by the shorthand term zamindar, though many grades of revenue payers below the zamindar known under innumerable terms all fell within this group. For the second group, we might employ the convenient term jotedar, though there were other terms too.

The distinction between the revenue-collecting structure through which an agricultural surplus was extracted from the villages and the land-holding structure through which the economic resources of the villages were differentially distributed among the villagers needs to be emphasised. The distinction was not, of course, absolute: zamindars might hold small amounts of private lands (called nankar or khamar) which they cultivated personally through hired or tied labour, and jotedars might collect the tribute assessed (jama) on their villages on behalf of the receiver of the tribute immediately above them. In other words, persons in the revenue-collecting hierarchy might have a niche in the land-holding structure and vice versa. But the duality of roles played by a single person must not obscure the difference between the roles as such.

The zamindar had a proprietary right in collecting the jama of a fiscal and administrative unit of territory called the pargana and paying this assessed revenue to the government after retaining for himself a certain percentage of the assessment (theoretically 10 per cent, but in practice more) as his malikana (proprietor's allowance). The basic fiscal units called mauzas (corresponding in theory to villages), which constituted the pargana, might be made over by the zamindar to the charge of taluqdars and revenue farmers who would collect the jama from the villages within the portions of the pargana assigned to them and pay the sum to the zamindar after retaining an allowance for themselves. The zamindars and taluqdars were the lords of the territory, with heritable proprietary rights, not in the land itself, but in the office of collecting (hasil) the assessment.

The holders of the land, as distinct from the lords of the territory, were the raiyats recorded on the assessment register (jamabandi) of the mauzas kept by the village registrars of lands (patwaris). At one end of this land-holding structure there would be the landless people of the village who were denied by social custom the status of raiyats in spite of being the actual tillers of the land; at the other end, the superior raiyats with excess lands, who would lease out the lands which they could not cultivate themselves to under-tenants, share croppers and hired labourers; in between were the self-sufficient peasant proprietors who enjoyed a right of occupancy so long as they paid the sum assessed on them. The superior raiyats who dominated this village land-holding structure, though recorded by the Mughals and the British as 'tenants', formed in economic reality a landlord class closely approximating to the village zamindar group in North India.

The early British administrators in Bengal, who carried out a painstaking search for 'landlords' in order to conclude a settlement, were not unaware of the complexities of land ownership in the province which they had but recently conquered. But after voluminous researches recorded in the lengthy proceedings of the Governor-General-in-Council and the Board of Revenue, the framers of the Permanent Settlement concluded that the zamindars and taluqdars were the owners of the land, or at any rate, the nearest approximations to the British concept of landlords. It was expected that they would, given the right kind of incentive, carry out the improvements in agriculture necessary for securing a growing volume of exports (the so-called 'Investment' of the East India Company) from Bengal. With this idea proprietary rights were conferred by Lord Cornwallis on the zamindars and taluqdars in 1793 and their territorial jurisdictions were declared to be 'estates'. When the zamindars failed to live up to the model of an improving landlord class—they did not after all hold land on a significant scale—a reaction among administrators led to the spread of the belief, earlier recorded by James Grant in his 'Analysis of the Bengal Finances', that there were no landlords in India in a real sense and that proprietary rights, in so far as they existed, were vested either in the state or in the body of resident tenants (khudkast raiyats).

As a matter of fact, both the framers and the critics of the Permanent Settlement failed to make the important distinction between the lords of the territory—the zamindars and the lords of the soil—the jotedars. Strange as it might appear, the Permanent Settlement constituted what could almost be described as a case of mistaken identity. In order to understand the true implications of the Permanent Settlement for the structure of land ownership in Bengal, it is necessary to go into the position of the different kinds of landlords before the Settlement with some degree of detail, as well as to examine the exact character of the rights conferred on them by the Permanent Settlement.

PART I

BENGALI AGRARIAN SOCIETY AND THE PERMANENT SETTLEMENT

2

The Evolution of Pre-Modern Agrarian Society in Bengal: Zamindars

The Mughal System 1575-1707

Much of the controversy regarding the revenue settlement of Bengal among rival factions of the Company's government tended to centre round the question—Who were the zamindars? Not only senior Company servants like Boughton Rouse and James Grant but high-ranking native revenue officers expressed diametrically opposite opinions on the subject. Shitab Rai, the naib diwan (deputy finance minister) for Bihar, expressed the view that 'the revenue belongs to the king, but the land to the Zemindar'. Rai Raiyan Rajvallabh put forward the opposite view: 'The Proprietor or the lord of the soil is the Emperor. Zemindars and Chaudhuris are written as officers, and depend, conditionally on the carrying on of the improvement of cultivation, and discharging the revenue of the government, together with the duties of protecting the highways, and of their respective limits and boundaries, and the chastisement of evil-doers'.[1] These differences of opinion, even

[1]Qanungo Ramram Chaudhuri combined both views in his statement: 'A zemindari and Chowdhry is, according to the Raje-ul-Mulk, an object of inheritance; and the zemindars and Chowdhries are there in hereditary themselves; but inasmuch as the payment of the revenue of Government, the maintenance of the peace, and the protection of the country, and the carrying on of its cultivation and improvement, are committed to them on the part of his Majesty: it is therefore an office; neither are they independent of the approbation of Government.' Boughton Rouse, *A Dissertation on the Landed Property of Bengal,* India Office Library Tract No. V. 3325, Appendices containing the opinions of the native reference officers, pp. 272-299.

among experienced native revenue officers who were not guided by the European misconceptions of Indian practices, arose from the complexity of zamindari rights due to developments over time and differences between localities.

For the province of Bengal at any rate, the term zamindar was a Mughal revenue innovation introduced for the first time by Akbar[2] to denote all categories of existing landholders (the most prominent being the so-called 'twelve bhuiyas'[3] who were crushed by the Mughal armies) and was in this sense as much a blanket term invented for administrative convenience as the British shorthand category of 'landlord'. The Mughal system, with its insistence on standardization of revenue arrangements through uniform appointment or confirmation of zamindars to the charge of regularly defined parganas, substantially modified the fluid structure of land rights headed by the practically independent bhuiyas who had mushroomed during the anarchy of the transition from Afghan to Mughal rule. The most substantial change was the destruction of resisting bhuiyas by

[2]Zamindar is a Persian compound-word, but was not in use in Persia. In India it was used in the fourteenth century by the Persian historians, Barani and Afif, to denote Hindu chieftains, but the term was not then a revenue-administrative category and the official terms for landholders of various types within the Delhi Sultanate were khuts, muqaddams and chaudhuris. Irfan Habib, *The Agrarian System of Mughal India, (1556-1707)* (Bombay 1963), p. 10; Ziauddin Barani, *Tarikh-i-Firozshahi*, translated in H.M. Elliot, *The History of India as Told by Its Own Historians*, Vol. III, (London 1871), pp. 182-183. A Hindu local chieftain called Raja Kans (identified with Raja Ganesh) who temporarily seized the independent Muslim state of Bengal after the breakup of the Delhi sultanate was described by the author of the *Riyazu-s-Salatin* as the zamindar of Bhaturia, but it must be remembered that this work was composed as late as 1786 when the term zamindar had supplanted older contemporary terms by which Kans had been known. Ghulam Hussain Salim, *Riyaz-us-Salatin*, translated by Maulavi Abdus Salam, (Calcutta 1902), pp. 112-113. The term used most commonly by Bengalis to denote landholders before the invention of the administrative category 'zamindar' was bhuiya.

[3]Many of the chiefs subjugated by the Mughals, some of the 'Bara Bhuiyas' in particular, were Hindu or Pathan upstarts who grabbed territories during the transition from Afghan to Mughal rule, but a few—such as the Rajas of Bishnupur, Susang and Chandradvip—were older Hindu princes who had ruled independently from time immemorial. Tapankumar Raychaudhuri, *Bengal under Akbar and Jahangir. An Introductory Study in Social History*, (Calcutta 1953), pp. 17-18.

large armies, such as Pratapaditya of Jessore and the Afghan chiefs of Bhati (Sundarbans including tracts along the Meghna in Dacca and contiguous districts), and their replacement by more amenable zamindars and taluqdars who were regarded by theoreticians of Mughal statecraft as officials appointed for collecting the revenue and administering the territory of the parganas and sarkars recorded in the manuals of administration. In the East Bengal tracts formerly held by the bara bhuiyas, numerous petty zamindaris and taluqs sprang up after the fall of the bhuiyas and their position came to be regulated, in theory at any rate, by official rules.[4] The administrative regulations of Akbar introduced a device called the diwani sanad (title-deed given by the finance ministry), which was uniformly given to all kinds of landholders grouped under the category of zamindar.[5] In the sanad, their position was explicitly stated to be the khidmat or service of collecting the land revenue. The sanad was granted without an explicit mention of the right of transference and inheritance which was allowed by custom. The supreme owner of the land, the state, gave a sanad to whom it appointed to the office of zamindar.[6] The zamindar did not have the right to alienate one bigha of revenue-paying land without the sanction of the government,[7] nor to sell it, though by custom he could inherit, alienate or sell his revenue management rights, which contained unmistakable features of property.

According to the high Mughal theory of government, then, the zamindar held his office upon the pleasure of the government

[4]Ibid, pp. 20-21.

[5]S. Nurul Hasan, 'Three Studies of Zamindari System', *Medieval India: A Miscellany*, Vol. I (Aligarh 1969), p. 234.

[6]In the course of time the zamindars themselves came to accept this theory, though in practice their position might be different. In a petition relating to the Decennial Settlement the zamindars of Rangpur stated: 'The country belongs to the Company and we, the zamindars, are only appointed for the purpose of transacting the business of it.' Quoted in *A Statistical Account of Bengal*, W.W. Hunger, Vol. VII, p. 319.

[7]But in Bengal zamindars were able, because of their entrenched local position, to alienate large quantities of malguzari (revenue-paying) land as devottar (temple), brahmottar (priestly) and other types of revenue-free property. The Nadia Raj Papers contain a list of devottar lands appropriated by the Raj family (see Table 1.1).

TABLE 2.1

Devottar Lands of Nadia Raj Family

	Name of deity	*Name of donor*	*Name of property*	*Area in bighas*	*Date of gift*
1.	Britti Srimati Maharajni	Raja Krishnachandra	Isvarnagar	3553	1768
2.	Devottar Sri Sri Chandi Thakurani	Do	Sahebnagar	2427	1742
3.	Devottar Sri Sri Thakurani	Do	Do	2427	1742
4.	Sri Sri Devottar Krishnachandra Thakur	Do	Do	1578	1755
5.	Sri Sri Gopal Thakur	Do	Dudhsar	2150	1752
6.	Devottar Sri Sri Lakshminarayan	Raja Rudra Ray	Dakatia Pata	1000	1700
7.	Devottar Sri Sri Thakur	Raja Raghuram Ray	Sandah	2111	1728
8.	Sri Sri Rajesvar Thakur	Krishnachandra	Hummia Pata	1854	1752
9.	Devottar Sri Sri Gopinath Thakur	Raghuram	Gopinath Ray	1900	1728
10.	Devottar Sidhveswari Thakurani	Krishnachandra	Bishnupur	708	1742
11.	Devottar Govindadei Thakur	Raghuram	Jatrapur	1589	1701
12.	Do	Ramjivan Ray	Baikuntha Sarak	225	1714
13.	Do	Do	Natun Sarak	—	—
14.	Do	Raghuram	Mrigipota	502	1702
15.	Do	Do	Adapota	580	1701
16.	Devottar Krishnader Thakur	Krishnachandra	Ghugragachi	1230	1748
17.	Devottar Jalesvar Thakur	Do	Teghari Kalinagar	2296	1768
18.	Anandadeb Thakur	Do	Haradham	509	1754
19.	Do	Do	Do	67	1751
20.	Devottar Krishna Ray Thakur	Raghav Ray	Jagannathpur	3467	1671

Source : List of Devottars entered in the 1202 B.S. Taidad in the possession of Maharaja Girishchandra Ray, Nadia Raj Papers.

that is to say, upon the due performance of the duties of revenue collection and rural administration assigned to him by the sanad.[8] How far was this theory translated into practice? The division of the suba (province) of Bengal into 19 sarkars and 688 parganas enumerated in the *Ain-i-Akbari*, implied the extension of a regular imperial administrative machinery over the whole territory of Bengal.[9] But these territorial divisions were largely theoretical (since much of the territory was not under the political control of the Mughal government) and the revenue demand of 472,726,681 dams on Bengal mentioned by Abul Fazl was merely an estimation of the land tax which could be realized from the province when brought under proper sarkar administration.[10] Throughout the reigns of Akbar and Jahangir, the zamindars were local chiefs—both Hindu and Afghan—who paid tribute as vassals.[11] In other areas of Hindustan, the Mughal government insisted

---

[8]Board of Revenue Proceedings, 13 March 1789, No. 14, answer of the Roy Royan to the questions put to him by the Board of Revenue, dated 27 February 1789.

[9]Abul Fazl-i-Allami, *Ain-i-Akbari*, Vol. 11, translated by H.S. Jarrett (Calcutta 1949), p. 141.

[10]It was not until the administration of the governor Islam Khan (1575-1627) that the Afghan chiefs of Bhati were subjugated and regular political control imposed over the whole province. Long after Abul Fazl had drawn up the ideal scheme for the administrative divisions of the province of Bengal, local military officers of the imperial government were pushing on the administrative boundaries of the empire by pacifying the areas assigned to them, and by collecting tribute from the local chiefs who had offered submission. At this stage there was little sign of the usual activities of a regular civil administration by local officers at sarkar or pargana level. *Riayazu-s-Salatin*, pp. 165-179. Tapan Raychaudhuri remarks, 'In the literature of the period, even the small zamindars appear as Rajas, omnipotent within their territories, while the representatives of the imperial power seem to be a distant reality hardly intruding into the zamindar's sphere of influence.' Tapan Raychaudhuri, op. cit., p. 22. These conditions persisted throughout the reigns of Akbar and Jahangir. As pacification progressed, faujdars and shiqdars took charge of sarkars and parganas, but they did not press hard on the local tribute-collecting political systems. By the time of the Viceroy Shah Shuja, who made a new revenue settlement of Bengal, 15 more sarkars and 688 more parganas had been added to the older divisions. Atul Chandra Roy, *History of Bengal, Mughal Period (1526-1765)* (Calcutta 1965), p. 339.

[11]Tapan Raychaudhuri, op. cit., pp. 17, 31-32.

on fixing revenue rates on the peasants through its own local revenue machinery and the zamindars were allowed a separate case as their malikana in addition to their private revenue-free lands. But in Bengal the zamindars paid a fixed sum of tribute over long periods instead of a varying land tax from year to year,[12] and made collections from peasants at rates fixed by custom or by themselves. Even as late as the reign of Aurangzeb, only about 1.5 per cent of the villages had been measured in Bengal, though in the Mughal Empire as a whole (excluding Bijapur and Hyderabad), 49 per cent of the villages had been measured and settled by the government. In Agra, only 9 per cent of the villages were left unmeasured, in Allahabad 5 per cent, in Lahore 9 per cent.[13]

In Bengal, unlike Hindustan, the government had no direct contact with the villages.[14] Those rulers who offered submission

[12]Irfan Habib, op. cit., pp. 145, 177-179. An asal jama or original revenue was estimated by Akbar's finance minister, Todar Mal, for Bengal in 1586 which remained virtually unchanged until the next revenue settlement by Shah Shuja in 1658 at an increment of revenues of 15½ per cent over the sum estimated by Todar Mal. The increase was derived mainly from territories annexed in the interval. The next settlement was made in the time of Murshid Quli Khan. James Grant, 'Historical and Comparative Analysis of the Finances of Bengal', Appendix No. 4 to the Fifth Report of the Select Committee on the Affairs of the East India Company, *Parliamentary Papers*, sess. 1812, Vol. VII.

[13]The following was the area measured in the different subas in bighas: Bengal—3 lakh 34 thousand; Bihar—1 crore 27 lakh; Allahabad—1 crore 97 lakh; Awadh—1 crore 90 lakh; Agra—4 crore 1 lakh; Delhi—6 crore 1 lakh; Lahore—2 crore 43 lakh; Multan—44 lakh. If we compare these figures with the number of villages in each suba, the extent to which Bengal was under-administered stands out clearly; Bengal—112 thousand, Bihar—55 thousand, Allahabad—47 thousand, Awadh - 52 thousand. Agra—30 thousand, Delhi—45 thousand, Lahore—27 thousand, Multan—9 thousand. Irfan Habib, op. cit., p. 4.

[14]The only exception was the sarkar of Purnia, a faujdari area (as distinct from diwani areas where revenue was collected by the diwani department) where the faujdar (a military officer of the nizamat department) collected revenue almost wholly from raiyats and not from taluqdars, revenue-farmers and zamindars as was general in Bengal. The only advantage enjoyed by the zamindars in Purnia was an allowance called nankar, and not village and mufassal charges for tax collection (saranjami) as in other parts of Bengal, *Proceedings of the Controlling Council of Revenue at Murshidabad*, Walter K. Firminger ed., Vol. II, proceedings on 13 December 1970, to Richard Becher from Ducarel dated 3 December 1770.

to the Mughal Emperor as the sovereign continued to form the de facto government of their territories, which bore the political characteristic of 'principalities' (Rajs) within the Mughal state. Because of the weakness of the Mughal state in Bengal, not only did many old principalities survive,[15] but new principalities were built up within Mughal territory by mushroom zamindars through regular warfare against neighbouring magnates.[16] The Mughal state, which enjoyed no monopoly of the instruments of coercion and administration, permitted these violent activities of its more prominent subjects and remained content with a distant overall control exerted by a relatively small number of town-based officials.[17] Since it was the weakness of the supreme government in the countryside which permitted the existence of the system of intermediary government known as the zamindari system, the exact nature of the presence of the Mughal government in rural Bengal deserves closer study.

---

[15]Most notably, the Bishnupur, Susang and Chandradvip Rajs, which were already quite old. The more recent principalities built up by mushroom bhuiyas like Pratapaditya of Jessore and Isa Khan of the Bhati tract were crushed out of existence.

[16]A striking example was the buildup of the Jessore Raj, created under Mughal rule by a Kayastha soldier of Man Singh's army which crushed Pratapaditya of Jessore. Bhabeswar Ray, the soldier of fortune, got hold of a part of the territory of the fallen bhuiya and his descendants expanded the zamindari by conquest. See p. 28.

[17]Bengal was so under-administered even at the end of Aurangzeb's reign that the foundation of Mughal rule remained shaky in Bengal and the province was periodically disturbed by revolts of powerful barons. In 1691 Nurulla Khan was the joint faujdar of Jessore, Hugli, Burdwan, Midnapur and Hijli, though there should have been a faujdar for each of these important sarkars according to the manual of administration drawn up by Abul Fazl a century before. This laxity of control encouraged the zamindar of Chitwa, Sobha Singh, to raise the banner of revolt against Mughal rule in association with Rahim Khan, the leader of the Afghans in Orissa. When the revolt broke out in Midnapur and Burdwan, Nurulla Khan marched out from his distant headquarters in Jessore, but the enemy had already secured the strategic points, so that he was compelled to fall back on the fort of Hugli and subsequently to retreat precipitately from it. Half the province of Bengal, west of the Ganges from Burdwan to Rajmahal was occupied by the rebels. The revolt was suppressed only after pitched battles fought by an experienced general appointed by Aurangzeb. *Riyazu-s-Salatin*, p. 231-237.

According to the manual of administration drawn up by Abul Fazl, the government was represented in the mauza by the patwari and in the pargana by the amin (surveyor) and shiqdar (police officer and revenue collector).[18] But in practice, the patwaris, shiqdars and amins were officers manning the zamindari establishments in the interior (mufassal) and were under the control of zamindari officials at the headquarters (sadr).[19] The basic fiscal jurisdictions, mauzas and parganas, were thus virtually out of reach of the supreme government and were controlled by the subordinate government of the zamindars. The parganas were grouped together in a number of sarkars (districts) which constituted the Bengal suba (province). Theoretically each sarkar should have had a faujdar, a military officer representing the Nizamat who was responsible for law and order, and an amil who was the revenue collector representing the diwani or the revenue department. In practice faujdars, where they existed at all (there were none for Bishnupur and Birbhum), held a large number of sarkars under their jurisdictions,[20] and for the whole of Bengal Salimulla mentions only nine faujdars, stationed in Chittagong (Islamabad), Midnapur, Purnia (Jalalgarh), Rajshahi, Sylhet, Rangpur, Rangamati, Burdwan and Hugli.[21]

As for amils who were supposed to collect the revenue from each sarkar, it seems that these revenue officials did not usually reside as permanent officers stationed at the district

[18] *Ain-i-Akbari*, pp. 46-60.

[19] Home Miscellaneous Series, Vol. 206, Amini Commission Report.

[20] The task of the faujdar was to prevent rebellion against the government rather than to perform police and judicial functions at the village or pargana level, which were exercised by village and pargana officers under the zamindar. The faujdar had under him a daroga, a qazi and a naib qazi who constituted the criminal court of the sarkar, but the jurisdiction of these criminal courts (nizamat adalats) seldom reached out of the headquarters into the localities, where disputes were settled locally as far as possible (see B.B. Misra, *Central Administration of the East India Company, 1773-1834* (Manchester 1959), pp. 224-225. The local police establishments—paikan establishments at village level and thanadari establishments at county level—were under the authority of zamindars, who were answerable to the government for law and order. India Office Library Mss. Eur. 231, 'Regulations for Criminal Courts in Bengal, 1790'.

[21] W.K. Firminger, *Historical Introduction to the Bengal Portion of the Fifth Report* (Reprint, Calcutta 1962), p. 43.

headquarters,[22] but were sent annually from Murshidabad to different zamindaris to take charge of collection. With the purpose of checking fraud on the part of the zamindars and the amils, the Mughal government maintained an establishment of qanungos down to the pargana level. The qanungos kept all pargana accounts relating to land and had the authority to summon village papers from the patwaris. Nevertheless, the efficiency of the qanungo establishment as a check on fraud was much impaired by the fact that local families acquired the office of qanungo on a hereditary basis (just like the office of zamindar and chaudhuri) and utilized their position to augment their own rent-free properties.[23] Whatever the theory of government set forth by Abul Fazl in the *Ain-i-Akbari*, in Bengal throughout the Mughal and Nawabi periods the government at Murshidabad did not have a regular system of district administration approaching the collectorate network built up by the East India Company for concluding the Decennial (subsequently Permanent) Settlement. The Mughal government in Bengal had no systematic control of the business of the interior; the real units of local, and even district, administration were the zamindaris.

The sphere of zamindari thus lay in the polity rather than in the economy.[24] A zamindari was not, like an English estate of the eighteenth century, a unit of production. The basic unit of production was the village and the raiyati holdings appertaining to it. Zamindari was a pyramidal revenue-

---

[22] *Proceedings of the Controlling Council of Revenue at Murshidabad*, Vol. 2, proceedings on 3 December 1770, Naib Diwan's representation, p. 8.

[23] See the case study of Midnapur below. The head Qanungo of Bengal himself built up the extremely under-assessed zamindari of Rokunpur by acquiring choice mahals in all parts of Bengal. Dispersed in minute divisions of territory, taken from different zamindaris as reward for suitably doctoring the accounts, this zamindari naturally escaped regular assessment as it could not be subjected as a whole to the local surveys which took place from time to time. James Grant considered this zamindari to be the richest of its size in Bengal. James Grant, 'Analysis of the Finances of Bengal', *Parliamentary Papers*, sess. 1812, Vol. VII, p. 269.

[24] Except in so far as the polity affected the economy, particularly through the levy and apportionment of the jama and abwabs (irregular cesses).

collecting and tribute-sharing structure through which revenue (mal) and customs duties (sayer) were collected for distribution between the Mughal state and the rural classes of high caste origin above the peasantry who manned the subordinate government of the country. This subordinate local government, at the head of which stood the zamindar of the area, extracted as tribute (jama with abwabs) a sizeable portion of the social surplus of the villages, leaving a margin of the surplus for the village landholders and a bare subsistence for the majority of cultivators and labourers. The zamindars were able to do this because they represented authority and government to the raiyats, controlled within their territory superior force, and provided the minimum administrative conditions for the maintenance and extension of cultivation by giving official loans to agriculturists (taqavi) and maintaining embankments (pulbandi).[25] The traditional social authority of the zamindars, their hereditary local influence and their paternal image among the raiyats helped materially in the maintenance of the subordinate government of the country over the villages, each of which had its own oligarchy seeking collaboration with the zamindari government for bolstering their own position within the village. In addition to land revenue the zamindars also collected sayer which was imposed on hats, ganjs and bazars, the rural markets, commercial centres and urban marts, where merchandise like grain, tabacco, sugar and silk were bought and sold. Zamindars claimed an equal right in the revenue arising from marts and entrepots as in the revenue from lands (a fact further illustrating the point that they were territorial rather than landed magnates). In times of agricultural scarcity, the subordinate government of the zamindars could thus make up the deficiency in the tribute from land with the duties from trade which continued

[25]Cultivators looked up to their zamindars for the provision of these essential needs of cultivation. There was a rather touching instance of this in 1790 when the Collector of Birbhum conveyed a petition of the raiyats for the immediate repair of the embankments, pleading that as the Raja of Birbhum was in confinement (for arrears of revenue), there was nobody to take care of them. BRP, 20 August 1790, No. 1, Collector of Birbhum to BR, 2 August 1790.

throughout the year and gave them a certain extra authority within their territories.[26]

The process of social conflict in rural areas was channelled through the zamindari establishment in the form of rival factions of zamindari officials, for the zamindari was the unit of government within which, by the operation of its own administrative establishment, the distribution of power, social prestige (caste and family precedence) and economic resources (rent-free grants, service lands, revenue farm and mokarari, i.e., permanent leases was determined. The zamindari establishment operated as a machinery of distribution through the exercise of the customary and de facto power (though not recognized in the diwani sanad) of the zamindars to make sales, conveyances and donations of land.[27] The numerous dependent landed rights which were created in this way within a zamindari contained the characteristics of property for there was a brisk selling market for these rights which freely

---

[26]BRP, 15 April 1790, No. 41, Questions relative to gunges, hats and bazars with answer from Collector of Burdwan; *Bengal District Records, Dinajpur,* Vol. II, No. 226, p. 145, Collector of Dinajpur to Shore, 30 October 1787. The territorial magnates maintained armies, dispensed criminal justice, enforced law and order and decided disputes of boundaries within their territory. When a raiyat delayed or withheld his revenue, when any inhabitant of the zamindari infringed the laws of the state and the customs of the country, or when any officer employed in the mufassal abused his trust, the zamindar had the right and privilege of punishing, fining, or banishing the offender from the district. He had the power of hearing and enquiring into complaints, summoning people before him when necessary, and of inflicting punishment (not capital) according to the magnitude of the offence. BRP, 13 March 1789, No. 15. Answers of the Qanungos 27 February 1789.

[27]BRP, 13 March 1789, No. 14. Answer of the Roy Royan. The right confirmed by the Roy Royan did not imply any power to alienate malguzari land from the revenue-roll without the sanction of the government. Nevertheless, zamindars had vastly extended their power of distributing malguzari lands. The accounts of the baze-zamin or alienated lands of the zamindars of Mahishadal settlement show great quantities of lands in these zamindaris alienated to various classes of people: priests (devottar), Brahman (brahmottar), mandals (mahattran), barbers, washermen, leather workers, blacksmiths, milkmen, book binders (mindaran) and the zamindars and their relatives themselves (nij jote.)

circulated within the zamindari.[28] The local gentry of grihastha[29] status who sought to secure these titles to the land, necessarily had to develop connections with one or other of the factions in the zamindari to ensure their own share in the resources of the local society.

The Nawabi System 1707-1760

From an analysis of the functional content of the zamindari system during the Mughal period it becomes clear that zamindari was essentially a function of the governance of the country and was an integral part of the political and administrative structure of Bengali society. Since the political and administrative framework changed considerably with the emergence of a practically independent nawabi in Bengal under Murshid Quli Khan, the zamindari system in turn underwent substantial modification. Three important measures of policy adopted by Murshid Quli Khan permanently changed the political system in Bengal. In the first place, the continuous inflow of Muslim nobles and mansabdars (high officers) who were paid in jagirs (assignments of revenue made by the state to its officers in lieu of salaries) ceased, and by transferring the jagirs (which had so long intervened between the provincial government and the local barons) to Orissa,[30] Murshid Quli Khan established direct political alliances with selected local barons, on whom the Nizamat henceforth became more and more dependent for managing the countryside. Secondly, the area measured in Bengal and fixed with new revenue rates on the basis of measurement

---

[28]Midnapur Collectorate Records, Permanent Settlement Records including resumed estates Kabuliyats, Serial No. 2, which contains old Bengali and Persian sanads. Two instances may be given. Raja Naranarayan of Kasijora gave 3 bighas of household land in lease to Sheikh Marhum of Pargana Kasijora, in 1154 B.S. (1747-48). His son Sheikh Sanaullah sold the household and landed property to Sheikh Muhammad Shah at Rs. 21. In Pargana Kurulchour of Chakle Jaleswar, Nabanikar Chaudhuri sold 111½ bighas of rent free land in village Keot Khalsa at Rs. 90 to Rahman Khan in 1178 B.S.

[29]Grihasthas were respectable householders (griha=house, stha=resident) of good caste enjoying bhadrasan or ancestral household and cultivable lands.

[30]*Riyazu-s-Salatin*, p. 249.

was extended to some new areas by Murshid Quli Khan who put recalcitrant and defaulting zamindars into prison at Murshidabad and made over their zamindaris to the charge of Bengali amils for survey and measurement. Certain areas—especially faujdars' areas like Rangpur and areas of small zamindaris and taluqs like Dacca—were brought under a regular system of amils who exercised supervisory control over the zamindaris under their charge even if they did not directly collect revenue from the raiyats.[31] Thirdly, in the much larger

[31]Salim-alla in *Tarikh-i-Bangla* and Ghulam Husain Salim in *Riyaz-us-Salatin* stated that the Bengali amils sent shiqdars (collectors) and amins (measurers) to all the villages of the parganas for measuring the cultivated and waste lands in order to conclude a settlement village by village, plot by plot, and raiyat by raiyat. After the completion of the settlement, the amils continued to collect directly from the raiyats according to rates fixed by the survey (hast-o-bud) and the zamindars, deprived of their management of the revenues, were pensioned off with nankar (private lands) for subsistence. Salim-alla seems to imply that this process of measurement, direct raiyatwari management through amils and abolition of the revenue management rights of the zamindars occurred throughout Bengal, but Ghulam Husain Salim is careful to mention only defaulting zamindars and to imply by inference that the process of measurement occurred only in the areas where the zamindars were put into prison for default. Both Salim-alla and Ghulam Husain Salim make frequent references to zamindars engaged in collecting revenues even after the new revenue reforms had been carried out. Francis Gladwin, *A Narrative of Transactions in Bengal*, being a translation of Salim-alla's *Tarikh-i-Bangla* (London 1788), pp. 42-57; *Riyazu-s-Salatin*, pp. 254-259. Salim-alla himself mentions that the zamindaris of Birbhum and Bishnupur remained free from these new regulations and continued to pay a fixed tribute in cash (peshkash); he also mentions that trustworthy and faithful zamindars were allowed to realize the revenues for the state from their respective zamindaris. It is probable that in their case no measurement took place at all. It is known for a fact that the zamindari of the English East India Company, consisting of the three towns of Calcutta, was not measured. After carefully considering the evidence, a modern biographer of Murshid Quli Khan concludes that Salim-alla's evidence must be accepted with some reservation and that the survey was by no means as thorough as he implied. Abdul Karim, *Murshid Quli Khan and His Times* (Dacca 1963), pp. 82-89. The question as to how extensive was the area in which the survey and appointment of amils for revenue collection was put into effect can be answered only by inference and by reading history back from the conditions prevailing at the time of the British takeover of the revenue administration. It seems that in the larger zamindaris with powerful barons, who came to control in course of time more than half the territory in Bengal, no survey took place. The

areas not affected by these regulations for regular revenue management, Murshid Quli Khan encouraged the concentration of zamindari rights by placing a large number of parganas under a few trusted revenue-farmers and officials like Raghunandan (his peshkar) of Natore, who imposed a new zamindari jurisdiction over former proprietors throughout the huge Raj of Rajshahi.[32] Murshid Quli Khan and his successors found it

---

amils were appointed in these zamindaris merely to receive the revenues and they exercised no supervision over the large zamindaris unless the zamindar was aminor. These big zamindaris were formed in the diwani areas, where temporary amils sent from Murshidabad by the diwani department collected the revenues on tour. In the faujdari areas, where a resident faujdar collected the revenue and appointed amils for receiving the dues from the parganas, a more regular revenue administration prevailed. Dacca, which was not a faujdari but was regularly administered by a niabat, also fell in this category. The zamindars of the niabat of Dacca were numerous and held only small parganas and necessarily there were amils who collected revenues from groups of parganas, exercising supervision over the zamindar of each parganas. At the time of the British takeover of the revenue administration, a number of smaller zamindars and taluqdars were under the regular district-based supervision of faujdars and amils in the following areas: the faujdaris of Purnia, Rangpur, Sylhet, Chittagong and Midnapur, and the niabat of Dacca. It is possible that Murshid Quli Khan's revenue measures affected these districts more closely than the rest of Bengal. For the comparative study of conditions of revenue administration and control of zamindaris during the administration of the naib diwan Reza Khan (1765-1772), see *The Letter Copy Books of the Resident at Durbar at Murshidabad 1769-1770*, Walter K. Firminger, ed., (Calcutta 1919); and *Proceedings of the Controlling Council of Revenue at Murshidabad 1770-1772*, Vols I-XI, Walter K. Firminger, ed, (Calcutta 1919); see also Abdul Majed Khan *The Transition in Bengal 1756-1775: A Study of Saiyid Muhammad Reza Khan* (Cambridge 1969).

[32]The Raj of Rajshahi was a result of the weeding out of disaffected and refractory zamindars by Murshid Quli Khan and the conferment of their zamindaris on Ramjivan, his peshkar (assistant) Raghunandan's brother. A powerful baronage was created in this case by the deliberate action of the Nizamat. There were three revolts by zamindars during the administration of Murshid Quli Khan: first, by Udaynarayan, zamindar of Chakla Rajshahi; second, by Sitaram, zamindar of Bhusna; third, by the Afghan zamindars of Mahmudshahi. After the suppression of each revolt Murshid Quli Khan conferred the confiscated zamindaris on Ramjivan of Natore, a small zamindar who had been punctual in payment of revenue and whose brother was a trusted official of the Nawab. The pursuit of the policy of political alliances with loyal and powerful barons permanently changed the political map of Bengal, *Riyazu-s-Salatin*, pp. 259, 265-267, 278.

profitable to assist the expansion of a few favoured zamindaris for such a policy resulted in substantial reduction of the costs of peace-keeping and revenue-collection. Only a small force of 2,000 cavalry and 4,000 infantry represented the military power of the Nizamat under Murshid Quli Khan.[33] But he and the succeeding Nawabs managed to control the countryside and collect the revenue at little cost by working through a dozen big zamindars who enormously expanded their dominions by the independent use of force against neighbouring zamindars and taluqdars. As a result of this process of agglomeration by private warfare and public favouritism, at the time of the British occupation nearly 60 per cent of the land revenue of Bengal was paid by 15 large zamindaris, comprising 615 parganas out of 1,256 in the province. This can be seen in Table 2.1, and it appears that the only really ancient zamindaris were Bishnupur, Birbhum, Lashkarpur, Tippera and Pachet, each of which were former kingdoms which submitted to Mughal sovereignty. The large zamindaris of Burdwan, Rajshahi, Dinajpur, Rokunpur, Mahmudshahi and Idrakpur were mushroom growths which underwent their real expansion in the first half of the eighteenth century. Nadia and Jessore, which also attained their huge size during this period, were of somewhat older status. Many of these zamindaris, such as Burdwan, Rajshahi, Nadia, Rokunpur and Mahmudshahi, were built up through official patronage or misuse of office. The close correlation between office-holding and zamindari was striking. Except for a few Rajput, Pathan and Khatri adventurers of non-Bengali extraction, all the magnates sprang from the Rarh (West Bengal), Varendra (North Bengal) or Vanga (East Bengal) samajs (regional subsection of caste) of the Brahman and Kayastha gentry, and were thus related by kinship to the high caste gentry of smaller fortunes who constituted the literati of the countryside.

Below the Rajas (magnates), but related to many of them by blood and marriage, stood the various local samajs or clans of ritually pure groups collectively known as the grihasthas (gentry). The traditional rural community of Bengal was stratified, in terms of social esteem, into the two socially distinct estates of grihastha and chasi (cultivator). The status

---

[33] Ibid., p. 257.

TABLE 2.2

Names of Zamindaris 1	*No. of Parganas* 2	*Assessment* 3	*Caste* 4	*Remarks* 5
Burdwan	57	20,47,506	Khatri	Founded by Abu Khetri, a revenue collector appointed in 1680. Described by Grant as an 'enlarged compact and fertile Zamindary in grain, cotton, silk and sugarcane'. This Raj was put together by the conquests of Maharaja Kirtichund between 1701-1739.
Rajshahi	139	16,96,087	Brahman	Founded by Raghunandan, peshkar of Murshid Quli Khan. The largest zamindari in Bengal, the Nator Raj was built up between 1710-1740 through active favour by the Nizamat.
Dinajpur	89	4,62,964	Kayastha	Founded by Sukdeb Ray, an officer of the zamindari of Khetlal who obtained a zamindari sanad in 1650. The Dinajpur Raj was built up by the conquests of his successors Prannath and Ramnath between 1682-1760.
Nadia	73	5,94,846	Brahman	Founded by Bhabananda, recorder of the Hugli qanungo daftar (office of land registrar) in the reign of Jahangir.
Birbhum	22	3,66,509	Pathan	Formerly an ancient Hindu Kingdom, seized by a Pathan adventurer and held as a border march from 1697.
Calcutta	27	2,22,958	British	Granted to the British in 1760.
Jessore	23	1,87,754	Kayastha	Founded by Bhabeswar Ray, a soldier of the Mughal army under Man Singh, who reduced the Bengal chieftains during the reign of Akbar.

1	2	3	4	5
Bishnupur	2	1,29,803	Rajput	A kingdom founded in the legendary past, the independent Bishnupur Raj was reduced to a zamindari by Murshid Quli Khan in 1715.
Laskarpur	15	1,25,516	Brahman	Enclosed on all sides by the Nator Raj, the Putia Raj (Lashkarpur) was the only older zamindari, founded probably in the seventeenth century, which survived the rapid expansions of the Rajshahi zamindari in this area under official favour.
Rokunpur	62	2,42,943	Kayastha	Conferred on Shaw Narayan, qanungo of the suba in the first half of the eighteenth century.
Mahmudshahi	29	1,10,633	Brahman	Conferred on Ramdeb in 1722; this zamindari was dependent on the Nator Raj.
Fatehsing	11	1,86,421	Brahman	Conferred on Hari Prasad, a zamindari south of Murshidabad city.
Idrakpur	60	81,975	Kayastha	Founded at the same time as the Dinajpur Raj by another officer of the Khetlal zamindari in the middle of the seventeenth ceutury.
Tipperah	—	47,993	Rajput	The independent Rajas of Tripura held Hill Tipperah as their independent state and plains Tipperah as a zamindari under the Mughal Government.
Pachet	2	18,203	Rajput	Old and imperfectly reduced jungle zamindari.
Other zamindaris	1,140	43,95,973		
Total	1,256	1,09,18,084		

Source & Notes: James Grant, 'Analysis of the Finances of Bengal', *Parliamentary Papers*, Sess. 1812, Vol. VII, pp. 267–269. Series of articles entitled 'The Territorial Aristocracy of Bengal', *Calcutta Review*, 1872.

group of grihasthas consisted of Brahmans, Vaidyas Kayasthas, Qazis, Maulvis, Khondkars, etc., who, however humble in their circumstances, considered it derogatory to their honour to hold the plough. The chasis in all cases were agriculturists, though in each village there would be families of rich peasants (sampanna chasis) whose heads might imitate neighbouring agriculturist grihasthas by confining their role in agriculture to supervision and direction. The chasis proper (excluding Brahman or Kayastha agriculturists) were either Muslims of agricultural stock or Hindus of semi-clean or unclean caste, such as Kaivartas, Namasudras, Sadgops, Rajbangshis and Pods.[34] From region to region the social composition of the grihastha and chasi strata varied, and the revenue-collecting and land-holding structures of each region bore unmistakable signs of these local variations.[35] In East Bengal the classical social model of pargana Bikrampur was characterized by a relatively neat equation of Brahman, Vaidya, and Kayastha castes with grihastha status and of Muslim and Namasudra castes with chasi status. In the socially peculiar region of Hijli (Tamluk and Contai sub-divisions of the present Midnapur district), on the other hand, Brahmans and Kayasthas were few in number, and the respectable agriculturist Kaivartas of the area formed the grihastha class, though in other regions their caste fellows were treated with contempt as chasis. In Bishnupur the number of Brahmans was so large that many of them performed all agricultural operations, short of holding the plough; the existence of a considerable number of poor cultivators among the Brahmans and Kayasthas of Bishnupur, Burdwan and other parts of West Bengal marked the high caste Rarhis sharply off from their Varendra or Vangaja caste fellows.[36]

But whatever the local caste composition of the grihasthas (Brahman and Kayastha was the norm), all over Bengal there existed a local gentry, very numerous in some places (as in

---

[34]'The Zamindar and the Ryot', *Calcutta Review*, Vol. VI, 1846, Part II, p. 325.

[35]Compare, for instance, the case study of Dacca with Midnapur, and of Bishnupur and Dinajpur and Rangpur.

[36]See Jogendranath Bhattacharya, *Hindu Castes and Sects* (Reprint, Calcutta 1968), p 33.

Bikrampur) but quite thin in ranks in others (as in Patiladaha and many other parganas of North Bengal). Their local influence varied from region to region in relation to their number; but the bigger zamindars could seldom bypass the local gentry in the collection of tribute from the villages. By virtue of their literacy, the Brahmans, Kayasthas and Vaidyas manned indispensable services and professions. They staffed the Nizamat and zamindari administration as officials, clerks and writers (mainly Kayasthas), and filled the various professions as priests (Brahmans), teachers (Brahmans and Kayasthas) and physicians (Vaidyas). Naturally they claimed a share in the tribute from land and without making terms with them neither the Mughal state nor the territorial magnates could collect it. They obtained their share in the tribute of the land in three forms: (a) taluqs which contained the property features of zamindari but were smaller in size and which paid the revenue to the state through a big zamindar (except in the case of huzuri or independent taluqs); (b) farms (ijaras) and sub-farms (dar-ijaras) of revenue given by the zamindars to their own dependents and officials and influential local people; and (c) small rent-free or quit-rent holdings (devottar, brahmottar, aima etc.) and large jotes with under-rated assessments which were granted by the state or the territorial magnates. Inevitably the revenue-collecting structure was complicated by these different forms of land tenure. The pyramidal shape of revenue-collecting structure was deeply rooted in the social and economic gradations in Bengal and enabled the literate rural stratum of local gentry to exist.

The contours of the revenue-collecting structure, and the extent of formalization of the rights of the local gentry within it, changed from district to district according to various factors like the number of gentry, the size of zamindaris and the amount of waste land. The rights of the smaller gentry were most solid in the Niabat of Dacca, where there were thousands of small taluqs with distinct features of property. The zamindaris in this area were not very large and the zamindars were appointed and changed at pleasure by the deputy governors of Dacca (called naibs of Dacca, hence niabat) for the task of collecting revenues from innumerable petty taluqdars. The taluqdars continued in possession while zamindars came and went. The taluqs were created mostly by grants of jungle lands, (of which there were plenty in the delta near the sea, covered by the Sunderbans) which were eagerly taken up by the dense ranks of the Bikrampur gentry in the neighbourhood of Dacca. In the zamindari of Dinajpur in the north, where the number of rural high caste gentry was very small, the Raj (which had been built up by conquest and reduction of existing proprietary rights) collected revenue directly from the jotedars in most villages and the number of intermediary taluqdars was not great. The high caste literate Hindus who had influence were accommodated as sadr and mufassal officers within the zamindari establishment which went down in several tiers from Dinajpur sadr to the individual mauzas. In the zamindari of Burdwan, an even bigger Raj built up by equally sanguinary methods of conquest, the much larger number of local gentry were accommodated by a long chain of farms and sub-farms going down from the sadr mustajirs in Burdwan town to the qutqinadars in the villages; these farms were temporary both in theory and practice. In Bishnupur the very numerous Brahman gentry held considerable rent-free brahmottar and devottar properties which gave them better security of livelihood. But, in general, wherever big Rajs had come into existence by conquest, the revenue-collecting rights of the smaller gentry were rather inchoate compared with the extremely secure tenures of the taluqdar class in districts of small zamindaris like Dacca and Midnapur.

Until the breakup of the big Rajs under the Permanent Settlement, therefore, the local gentry in Bengal were a dependent vassal class, subject to the caprice of powerful Rajas. Even in areas where they enjoyed secure taluqs, as in Dacca (where, moreover, there were no aggressive Rajas of the size of Burdwan or Dinajpur) the policy of the Mughal government to deal with small revenue-payers only through zamindars of one or more parganas subjected them to vexatious exactions by superior proprietors. The zamindars of Buzrugumedpur, who got themselves appointed to the zamindari through official influence (Maharaja Rajvallabh, the founder of the family, was the deputy-governor of Dacca), liquidated the rights of a considerable number of taluqdars, whose properties they annexed as nij (own) taluqs of the zamindar. On the other hand, many among these dependent gentry showed a considerable aptitude for seizing opportunities and rising to the more exalted walks of life. Maharaja Rajvallabh was himself originally a petty taluqdar who rose in the service of the Nizamat and acquired three lucrative parganas. The Raj families of Nadia, Dinajpur and Rajshahi were all at one time insignificant grihasthas (however high in caste rank) who built up their fortunes by exploiting the opportunities of office under the Mughal government. The majority of grihasthas, who probably never left their rural homes, contented themselves with the dues from their small properties; but there was always to be found among them a number of enterprising men who supplemented their income from properties by service, either in the revenue (diwani) and records (qanungo) branches of the government or in the sadr and mufassal establishments of the big zamindars. In these offices or land administration, there were splendid openings for unscrupulous and quick-witted men to acquire zamindaris for themselves by defrauding their masters—whether the government or private persons. The composition of the zamindar class was thus quite fluid and it was estimated by Shore that at least half of the properties in Bengal changed hands from the beginning of the eighteenth century to the establishment of British rule.[37] The local gentry of Bengal under the Nawabs of Murshidabad were a dependent but mobile social element who stood poised to seize the new opportunities of the British revenue arrangements.

The British revenue arrangements thus intruded on a highly fluid and differentiated state of land rights for which the abstract and all inclusive concept of zamindari was no adequate guide to understanding. From the Nawabi period the British inherited two main categories of hereditary revenue-managing rights that had emerged from the revenue policies implemented by Murshid Quli Khan: the smaller zamindaris and taluqs that had survived the process of agglomeration and the extensive Rajs of proven loyalty to the Nizamat that had suddenly mushroomed after 1700. The smaller zamindaris and taluqs characterized the areas around active centres of Mughal government, such as the faujdari of Midnapur and the niabat

[37]But there were also a few surviving ancient kingdoms, such as Bishnupur and Birbhum, which must be included in the category of extensive baronages.

of Dacca. The smaller zamindaris and huzuri taluqs (independent taluqs paying revenue directly to the government) were grouped together under faujdars and amils who supervised their management from sarkar headquarters; the mazkuri (dependent) taluqs were made over to the supervising authority of government-appointed zamindars and chaudhuris,[38] who exercised their authority over the taluqdars from pargana headquarters. These petty landlords were subject to exactions by the superior authorities appointed over them.[39] Their revenue-managing rights could be either traditional ritualized local rights or mushroom products of connections with government establishments. In Midnapur many Brahman and Kayastha qanungos and other officers in the employ of the faujdar's government had acquired portions of the parganas under their charge and entered them as their hereditary taluqs. But there were also very old families of Kaivarta agriculturists, long-settled in the country, who acquired revenue management rights over the villages in which they held agricultural lands in the form of dependent taluqs held under the Kaivarta Rajas who had led the original settlements and migrations.[40] In Dacca, similarly there were jangalbari (forest-clearance) taluqdars under zamindars who had acquired their rights by clearing forests and settling the country. But many among these Brahman, Kayastha, and Vaidya taluqdars were also officials employed at the niabat of Dacca who acquired taluqs by fraud or purchase whenever they got an opportunity.[41]

---

[38]Hereditary collectors of revenue appointed by sanad to parganas whose position in this period was practically identical with that of the zamindars.

[39]*Riyazu-s-Salatin*, pp. 305-306, 299-300, gives instances of the oppressive conduct of the assistant to the Deputy-Governor of Dacca and the faujdar of Rangpur towards the zamindars in their districts.

[40]See case study of Midnapur.

[41]In a detailed recent study of the Natore Raj, which was a typical example of the mushrooming baronages patronized by the Nizamat, it has been remarked that throughout the vast area of the zamindari of Rajshahi, the well remembered Rani Bhavani and her officials constituted the government in the eyes of the mass of the people. From the palace of Natore, there spread out across the zamindari an intricate network of zamindari officials representing authority in the mufassal. The Rani's paiks maintained the peace of the country, her revenue officials kept embankments in repair, her agents constructed numerous tanks, temples

Leaving aside the niabat of Dacca and the border faujdari areas which were controlled by local revenue authorities, the revenue administration of the interior of Bengal was under the direct charge of the distant diwani department in Murshidabad which managed the collection of the revenue through peripatetic amils. In the first half of the eighteenth century, large principalities had sprung up in this area, owing allegiance to the Mughal state and collecting tribute from the village oligarchies. By the time of Alivardi Khan the Nizamat had become dependent to an extraordinary degree on the loyal and influential baronages which governed the countryside through a complex zamindari bureaucracy and supplied the feudal levies which the state needed in times of external threat.[42] A moderate revenue demand enabled the zamindars during the time of Alivardi Khan to accumulate riches and to maintain large armies, both of which proved crucial contributions to the defence against the Maratha invaders. By the time the Marathas

and serais (inns), her munificence supported the priests, teachers, and medical practitioners. A.B.M. Mahmood, The Land Revenue History of the Rajshahi Zamindari (1765-1793), SOAS thesis 1966, pp. 298-299. Before the organization of the collectorate system in Bengal by the British government, the territories of the big magnates formed in effect states within the State, from which emanated the administrative authority and action which affected the villages and their ruling cliques.

[42]The army of Nawab Sarfaraz Khan which marched out from Murshidabad against the invader Alivardi Khan was composed of high Muslim officers of state, faujdars mansabdars and zamindars of Bengal. *Riyazu-s-Salatin*, pp. 311-312. After Alivardi Khan conquered Bengal and turned against Orissa, it was the arrival of an auxiliary force of the Raja of Burdwan under the command of Manikchand at a crucial moment that turned defeat into victory against the Orissa army. Ibid., pp. 329-330. When the Marathas invaded Bengal, the Rajas of Burdwan and Bishnupur sunk their hereditary enmity and combined with Alivardi Khan in the common defence of their territories. After the capture of the tract from Rajmahal to Midnapur, the Marathas themselves started diplomatic negotiation with the zamindars for consolidating their hold on the captured territory. Ibid., pp. 343-344. The revenue demanded by Alivardi Khan from the zamindars was very moderate but as a result of his policy of allowing the zamindars to flourish financially he was able during the Maratha invasion to raise the enormous contribution of one crore rupees at one time and fifty lakhs on another occasion. *The Letter Copy Books of the Resident at the Durbar*, op. cit., pp. xi-xiv, extract of a letter from Mr. Becher to the Honourable the President, 24 May 1769.

erupted on the Bengal scene in the 1740s, a mutually advantageous relationship had been worked out between the Rajas and the Nawab, which enabled the former to live 'in a State of power, Parade and Independence in their Zemindarries'[43] and the latter to collect a regular revenue at little cost and to call on extraordinary financial and military resources in emergency. It should, however, be noted that the effectiveness of the Raj as a centre of power vis-a-vis its own territories depended very much on whether or not an adult male of at least moderate ability with an undisputed claim to the succession presided over the zamindari. There was a tendency for the large zamindaris to be torn by faction from the sadr kachari (head office) downwards to the village establishments which only adult male zamindars with undisputed authority among the officers of the zamindari establishments could keep in check effectively. When the zamindar happened to be a female or a minor, or when there was a dispute over succession to the zamindari, rival factions among the zamindari servants contended with each other for misappropriating the resources of the zamindari and the dominant village groups were encouraged by this struggle for power above them to withhold revenues.[44] Even where an undisputed adult male zamindar presided over a large zamindari, the system of farming out revenues which seems to have been a widespread practice in many of the major Rajs of Bengal before 1760 implied certain limits to his power with regard to the farmed out villages and parganas of his zamindari.[45]

To sum up, there were in Bengal under the Nawabs independent chiefs, whose kingdoms lay outside Mughal territory, such as the Rajas of Kuch Bihar, Assam and Tripura; autonomous chiefs who tendered submission to Mughal sovereignty but retained their kingdoms by paying a tribute, such as the

[43]*Proceedings of the Controlling Council of Revenue at Murshidabad*, Vol. II, 3-31 December 1770, (Calcutta 1920), pp. 5-7, proceedings of 3 December 1770, minute by Richard Becher.

[44]See the case studies of Burdwan, Dinajpur and Bishnupur.

[45]See case study of Burdwan where revenue-farming had been carried to a further extent than in any other zamindari before 1760 and many of the revenue-farmers were hereditary farmers who held their farms almost as ancestral properties.

frontier Rajas of Birbhum and Bishnupur; office-holding families who staked out in the course of a few generations a hereditary claim to jurisdictions over large areas, such as the Rajas of Burdwan and Nadia. Also more recent revenue-farming or record-keeping families who under official favour acquired the status of territorial magnates, such as the Rajas of Natore and the Qanungo Mahashayas of Rokunpur; smaller zamindars who held single parganas or shares in parganas as co-sharing proprietors, such as the Ponabalia Raychaudhuris who held a six-anna share of the small parganas of Haveli Selimabad in Bakarganj; and in some areas, a numerous body of taluqdars, some of whom might have enjoyed influential local positions of long standing (antedating the zamindars over them, as in the case of the Bikrampur taluqdars) while others had merely acquired by exploiting official connections scattered revenue-collecting rights over certain mahals under different zamindaris (such as the notorious Muslim dacoit of Dacca, Ainuddin Shiqdar, who or whose ancestor apparently held the post of shiqdar under the niabat).[46] The complexities of these historical developments were compounded by the regional differences in the structure of zamindars at any point in time. There was a strong contrast between the border Rajs of Birbhum and Bishnupur in West Bengal with the numerous petty Bikrampur taluqs in the closely administered niabat of Dacca during the time of Murshid Quli Khan.

The rise of the East India Company 1760-1790

The political system of Bengal, of which the large baronages in the diwani areas under Murshidabad, the petty vassalages in the niabat of Dacca, and the faujdari areas under the sadr towns of the sarkars formed so integral a part in the days of Alivardi Khan, began to break down gradually after the battle of Plassey. The localized subordinate governments designated as zamindaris and taluqs by the Mughals came under great pressure as a result of the politieal changes in the structure of the supreme government. The pressure at the intermediate levels of the political system (i.e., the levels between the state and the villages) became evident from 1760, when the British took

[46]See the case studies of Dacca.

over the revenue administration and farmed out the revenue of the districts of Midnapur, Chittagong and Burdwan (and earlier in 1757 the 24 Parganas). In the rest of Bengal, which was made over to Mir Qasim, the Nizamat badly mauled its time-honoured revenue arrangements in a last desperate bid to save itself from further British expansion. When this final bid for survival lay in ruins on the battle-field of Buxar, the zamindari system had started cracking both in the baronages and in the faujdaris as a result of tremendous exactions by the Nizamat in its efforts to mobilize financial resources for defence against the East India Company. In its attempt to save itself, the uppermost level of the political system, the Nizamat, tried to crush the intermediate level of the zamindaris, with which it had co-existed ever since the Mughal conquest of Bengal.

The revenue settlement of Murshid Quli Khan in 1722 had fixed the land revenue of Bengal at Rs 1 crore and 42 lakhs.[47] Mir Qasim, in his settlement of 1763, fixed an additional sum of Rs 1 crore and 26 lakhs on the territory remaining under his revenue administration, so that in the shrunken territory under the Nizamat (excluding Burdwan, Midnapur, Chittagong and 24 Parganas) the revenue stood at Rs 2 crore and 56 lakhs. By imposing abwabs, resuming profits of jagirs and carrying out hast-o-buds (surveys), Mir Qasim nearly doubled the revenue of his territory in course of three years—from 1760 to 1763.[48] This impossible additional demand was never collected in full, but the strenuous efforts to realize it began to produce structural distortions in the zamindari system. Dispossessing the zamindars, Mir Qasim let loose a horde of faujdars, amils and revenue-farmers on both the diwani and faujdari areas, who quickly exhausted the resources of the territories made over to them. In this process the distinction between the diwani and faujdari areas was effectively swept aside.[49] The

[47]By the time of Alivardi Khan subadari abwabs (cesses collected by the Nizamat) had raised this sum to Rs 1 crore and 56 lakhs.

[48]Shore minute of 18 June 1789, *Parliamentary Papers*, sess. 1812, Vol. VIII.

[49]The baronages in the diwani areas which came under the greatest pressure were Dinajpur, Nadia and Rajshahi. Leaving aside irregular contributions, the increase of revenue by hast-o-bud on a permanent basis was for Dinajpur Rs 11½ lakhs, for Nadia 7½ lakhs, for Rajshahi 4½ lakhs. Ibid.

Dinajpur Raj was placed practically on the same footing as the neighbouring faujdar of Rangpur. In Rangpur the faujdar, Abid Ali Khan, took a farm of the district at an enormously increased revenue; in Dinajpur the Raja was replaced by the revenue-farmer Ramnath Bhaduri who engaged to pay more than double the existing revenue. Mir Qasim threw into prison the zamindars of Dinajpur, Nadia, Rajshahi, Birbhum and Fatesingh, along with Jagat Seth and Rajvallabh (zamindar of Rajnagar and deputy-governor of Dacca). He subsequently killed Jagat Seth, Rajvallabh and some of the other zamindars[50] because he suspected them of conspiring with the British.

Two years after the overthrow of Mir Qasim in 1765, Clive obtained the diwani of Bengal which was made over to the naib diwan, Reza Khan, for administering according to established Mughal forms under the supervision of a British Resident at Murshidabad. But although Reza Khan prided himself on having restored the Mughal system, important changes crept into it on account of the continuous pressure of the British demand for increased collections of land revenue. Under the Mughal system, as we have seen, malguzari agreements with zamindars and taluqdars had been the common form of revenue management. Tahuds (temporary revenue engagements) with amils and faujdars had been extremely rare in diwani areas (though not in faujdari areas like Rangpur and Purnia) until Mir Qasim entered into revenue engagements with amils, faujdars, and ijaradars at a massive increase of revenues. The British were equally insistent on increased collections and to satisfy the demand Reza Khan employed 'numerous tribes of fougedars, Aumils and Sikdars'[51] for realizing greater amounts of tribute. Richard Becher, the Resident at Murshidabad, noted that in Alivardi Khan's times the amount of revenue put into the treasury was much smaller

[50]*Riyazu-s-Salatin*, pp. 393-396. The author does not mention the names of the murdered zamindars. It is known that the Raja of Dinajpur survived and got back his zamindari; so did Krishnachandra, Maharaja of Nadia, after Mir Qasim's overthrow. Their escape was narrow in view of the murder of Rajvallabh.

[51]*Fort William-India House Correspondence* (*Public Series*), N.K. Sinha ed., Vol. 5, 1767-1769 (Delhi 1949), letter from Court of Directors to President and Council at Fort William, 30 June 1769, p. 212.

than the large sums brought in at Murshidabad under Reza Khan's management and wrote to his government in Calcutta:

> When the English first received the grant of the Dewannee their first consideration seems to have been the raising of as large sums from the country as could be collected. . . . The zamindars not being willing or able to pay the sums required, aumils have been sent into most of the Districts. These aumils on their appointment agree with the Ministers to pay a fixed sum for the districts they are to go to and the man that has offered most has generally been preferr'd. What a destructive system is this for the poor inhabitants! The aumils have no connection or natural interest in the welfare of the country where they make the collections, nor have they any certainty of holding their places beyond the year. . . .[52]

Spelling out the consequences of this altered form of revenue management for the zamindari system, Becher observed in a minute:

> Be it remember'd also the situation these Zemindars & ca found themselves in when under the Government of the Soubahs, Who tho' arbitrary and despotic to the highest degree, left the Zemindar to live in a State of power, Parade and Independence in their Zemindarries (demanding from them) except on emergent Occasions only the punctual payment of the Malguzzary settled annually to be paid to the Government. . . . As certain it is that since the English have been in possession of the Dewannee, the Zemindars have been reduced to a much inferior Situation to that enjoyed under the Soubahs, & that in general they are now poor, when it

[52]*Letters Copy Books of the Resident at Durbar*, extract of letter from Becher to the Honourable the President dt. 24 May 1769, pp. xi-xiv. The amildari system under Reza Khan, which practically amounted to annual revenue-farming, was fundamentally different from that used by Murshid Quli Khan, under which amils were employed with the regeular administrative purpose of measuring the lands and fixing the revenue rates.

is considered what numerous Families and dependants they have to provide for . . . .[53]

The famine of 1770, which engulfed the majority of the large zamindars of West and North Bengal in financial ruin, put an end to the dual government at the centre and the administration by amils in the districts. Assuming direct administration of the diwani in 1772, Warren Hastings introduced for the whole of Bengal a five-year experiment of farming out revenues at outcry that had already been tried in 24 Parganas and Burdwan.[54] Some big zamindars were temporarily dispossessed by revenue-farmers of the Calcutta banian (merchant) type, though others managed to retain possession as farmers of their own zamindaris, or as under-farmers below the Calcutta banians. The intrusion of the native commercial and official classes of Calcutta into the revenue system of the interior started from 1772 though the penetration was probably not very deep as the majority of the zamindars managed to retain possession of their properties.[55] Nevertheless, their financial and political position suffered a decline from which many had no hope of recovery. Hastings' revenue policy, as Francis put it in rather violent terms, was to raise from the land the enormous sum required for financing the Company's 'Investment' (purchased goods for export) and commercial charges (formerly met by import of specie) and 'to effect this, together with some other purposes, perhaps equally interesting to himself, by reducing every Native of every Rank to what he calls a *competent subsistence*'.[56] The quinquiennial farming

[53]*Proceedings of the Controlling Council of Revenue at Murshidabad*, Vol. II, proceedings of 3 December 1770, minute by Becher, pp. 6-7. An example of the pressure on the zamindari system caused by the sending of amils was the zamindari of Idrakpur, where the diwan of the Raja combined with the amil to ruin the Raja and his country. The zamindar could scarcely get sufficient allowance to maintain his family, far less to support the rank which his position implied. So great was his financial distress that he was willing to give up his zamindari to the British in return for a sufficient allowance for himself and his family.

[54]The farming system of the 1772-1777 has been treated at length by N.K. Sinha, op. cit., and need not be analyzed here.

[55]*Ibid.*, p. 83.

[56]Francis Mss. Eur. E. 13 C. Letter from Francis to Mr. Ellis dt. 20 November 1776.

experiment, specially, was simply a great loot in which not only the East India Company, but also its seniormost European officers and their native assistants participated for purposes of private gain in addition to the public objective of financing from the Bengal revenues the Investment, the territorial expansion and the China trade of the Company. It was estimated by Maharaja Nabakrishna Deb, the former diwan of Clive, that Hastings, Barwell, Middleton, Vansittart and other senior officers who concluded the settlement received from the zamindars, taluqdars, and farmers cash presents to the amount of Rs 42 lakhs.[57]

The high ruling prices of grain immediately after the famine induced many revenue-farmers to bid beyond the real value of their farms, and due to the spreading depopulation across the countryside large balances accumulated. When the quinquiennial farming settlement was thus thoroughly discredited, Hastings restored the zamindari system in 1777 in practically the older forms, though the system had by now been badly mauled.[58] Police, embankments, customs duties on markets

---

[57]The following are the particulars supplied by Nabakrishna to Henry Strachey, though he could not produce any evidence to back his somewhat extravagent accusations: 'An account of the Money received by Governor Hastings and other Gentlemen from the Zemindars, Talookdars and Farmers of the soubah of Bengal from his accession to the Government till the arrival of the General and other Gentlemen; exclusive of Nuzzers (presents), Pearls, Jewels, cloths and complementary present. . .' Appendix to letter from Raja Nobkishen to Henry Strachey, 23 March 1776, Francis Mss. Eur. F.7.

[58]A typical example of the deterioration of the system was to be found in the Dinajpur Raj. The extremely able and warlike Raja Ramnath had ruled this zamindari autonomously during the administration of Alivardi Khan without any interference from amils. He was well remembered afterwards for his extremely successful administration, during which the Raj underwent tremendous expansion by conquest. After his death his successor Baidyanath had to contend for the zamindari with his cousin Baidyanath. This dispute gave an opportunity to the ambitious and unscrupulous officer Ramnath Bhaduri to seize control of the zamindari with the help of Mir Qasim, to whom he gave an exaggerated accounts of its capacity. Mir Qasim, in his bid to mobilize resources for war against the Company, set aside the zamindar in favour of Kantonath, threw the dispossessed Raja into prison, carried out a survey of this practically unscrutinized zamindari with the aid of Ramnath Bhaduri in the minutest detail of the mauzas, raised the revenue on the basis of this survey from

and other functions which had constituted their local governing power were restored to their authority. Until the great revolution in the administrative structure of the country between 1786 and 1793, the zamindari system still represented an old, not a new, order. Nevertheless, due to the deepening British thrust into the Mughal revenue system from 1757 the government of the local Rajs came to suffer from much the same kind of weakness that had characterized the administration of the countryside by the Nizamat over long periods. By the time of the Decennial Settlement, when the pressure of British rule had stripped the Rajas of much of their coercive authority, the zamindar's control of his establishment in the sadr as well as in the mufassal tended to be lax and he could

Rs 12 lakhs to 26 lakhs, and gave a revenue farm of the zamindari to Ramnath Bhaduri for realizing this amount. In spite of strenuous efforts which ruined the zamindari, Mir Qasim obtained no more than Rs 24 lakhs, which was slightly less than what Raja Ramnath himself had collected on the average each year (Rs 24-25 lakhs). The exhaustion of its resources led to a decline of collections to Rs 19 lakhs afterwards. Reza Khan restored Baidyanath to the zamindari but placed an amil at the sadr Kachari for supervising the collections. The zamindari administration was thoroughly undermined and there were great embezzlements by 50 tahsildars (collectors) and their underlings, who collected revenue from petty Ijaradars (revenue-farmers) in the mufassal. Then came the famine of 1770, which desolated and depopulated Baidyanath's zamindari. He reported that for want of seed and implements of cultivation large portions of his zamindari had fallen waste. He calculated the deficiency caused by deaths and desertions of raiyats at Rs 4 lakhs and 76 thousand out of a surveyed capacity of Rs 18 lakhs and 46 thousand. During the quinquiennial farming settlement which followed, Baidyanath was pensioned off with a moshaira (subsistence allowance) of Rs 1 lakh and 50 thousand. Due to these violent changes in the structure of the zamindari, the authority of the zamindar suffered a permanent decline vis-a-vis the dominant village groups of the jotedar class who became extraordinarily powerful in this area. After the end of the quinquiennial farming settlement, Baidyanath was restored, and a reduction was allowed in his zamindari. He even managed to expand the zamindari to some extent. He was succeeded by his minor son Radhanath, whose officers sold up and divided the zamindari among themselves. *Letter Copy Books of the Resident at Durbar*, enclosure on a separate paper to letter from Richard Becher to Harry Verelst and Gentlemen of the Select Committee, dt. 25 April 1769, p. xxvi, *Proceedings of the Controlling Council of Revenue at Murshidabad*, Vol. II, proceedings of 31 December 1770, Vansittart to Becher dt. Dinajpur, 16 October 1770, p. 143 N.K. Sinha, op. cit., pp. 29, 54, 84, 102.

TABLE 2.3
Nabakrishna's account of presents taken by Hastings and others from zamindars, etc., in the suba of Bengal

		Rs.
Dacca		
Ready money		500,000
Mr. Barwell		400,000
Rangpur, etc.		
Ready money	100,000	
Promissory	100,000	200,000
Murshidabad (exclusive of Middleton)		300,000
Dinajpur		200,000
Bhagalpur		150,000
Birbhum, Bishnupur, etc.		100,000
Midnapur		
Vansittart and other Gentlemen		350,000
Raja Krishnachandra (?)		150,000
Burdwan (exclusive of Stewart)		
Through diwan Brajakishor	200,000	
Pulbandi (embankment contract)	150,000	
Mandalghat salt contract	150,000	500,000
Hugli, Hijli, etc.		
Ready money	100,000	
Settlement for salt mahals	600,000	700,000
Jessore, etc.		
On account of salt of Raymangal, etc.		200,000
Farmers of 24 Parganas		50,000
From Raja Huzuri Mal and Mudan Dutta for relinquishing the farm of Purnia		100,000
Profit of batta (exchange), Premium on Bills etc. from Raja Huzuri Mal and Dol Chand		150,000
From servants wages		100,000
		4,200,000

collect the revenue only by working, like the Nizamat, through locally dominant elements.

THE STRUCTURE OF ZAMINDARI ON THE EVE OF THE DECENNIAL SETTLEMENT

The formal structure of zamindari bureaucracy, at least in the bigger zamindaris, had apparently always consisted of a graded hierarchy of local establishments (mufassal kacharis) in mauzas, tarafs (portions of a pargana), and parganas in an ascending order to the head office (sadr kachari) and a regular chain of accounts going up from the patwari at the village level to the chief manager, the diwan or naib of the head office.[59] Starting at the bottom of this chain of command, the mandal or headman of a village held his office at the good-will of the villagers, subject to the approval of the zamindar. He was the mediator between the body of raiyats in the village and the petty collectors of the revenue. Besides the mandal, the village also contained a patwari, theoretically an accountant and a servant of the village, but in reality the lowest officer of the zamindar collecting the revenue from the village. In many villages the zamindars also appointed karmacharisor servants who collected the revenue. The karmacharis and patwaris were seldom changed and the office of the patwaris seems to have been hereditary in many places.[60] The experience and the knowledge which they possessed made them indispensable in the process of collection of revenue, and whether they paid revenue to a zamindar, a revenue farmer or an amil, these village officers continued to hold their offices. Because of their local and hereditary position, the patwaris and karmacharis could not be brought under proper bureaucratic control by the zamindar.

Proper zamindari bureaucracy started at the level of the gomasta, an officer placed as a check on the patwaris. The gomasta was immediately appointed by the person who had settled for the revenue and was frequently changed at the end of the year without any great inconvenience to the collection of revenue. The gomasta of different villages transmitted their accounts and paid their revenues to shiqdars and etmamdars, who were temporary officers appointed to collect the revenues from dihis (collection of villages), tarafs and parganas.

[59]The account of zamindari establishments which follows is based mainly on the report of the Amini Commission appointed by Warren Hastings after the failure of the quinquiennial farming settlement. The Amimi Commission made detailed investigation of zamindari management and revenue arrangements during 1776-1777 and its report can be accepted as a fairly accurate picture of the prevailing system of zamindari management not only during early British revenue administration but also in the Nawabi period. The report is to be found in the Home Miscellaneous Series, V . 206.

[60]Midnapur Collectorate Records, Register of Patwaris.

Over these mufassal establishments stood the sadr kachari situated at the usual place of residence of the zamindar.[61]

The difficulties of managing from the sadr these various mufassal establishments, which at the lowest level were local and hereditary, need little emphasis. The problem of a proper control of affairs in the mufassal was also enhanced by the fact that in larger zamindaris it was the usual practice to farm out the revenues to farmers. When the revenues were farmed out in this way, the mufassal establishments of the zamindari were placed under the authority of the farmers. The farmers were often specifically prohibited from changing the mufassal establishments, but such restraints were seldom very effective. At the time of the British takeover of the revenue administration under Warren Hastings, zamindari management in the big zamindaris of Burdwan, Bishnupur, Birbhum, Rajshahi, Dinajpur, Nadia, etc. consisted of a long chain of farms and sub-farms (taken by the local gentry who also staffed the zamindari establishments) going down to the village level where the system was confronted by the village heads—a class of superior raiyats variously known in different regions as mandals, pradhans, or Busnias. This revenue-farming system in the bigger zamindaries was sometimes an alternative to the chain of sadr and mufassal establishments we have just described, but very often—as in the case of the zamindari of Dinajpur—the regular zamindari establishments and the revenue farms and sub-farms continued to co-exist. The farms and sub-farms would be interposed between the sadr and mufassal establishments so that each mufassal establishment would hand over the revenue to a revenue-farmer in the interior who in turn would pay the revenue to a superior revenue-farmer directly under the sadr establishment.

A zamindar of a large district, having made a settlement with the government, farmed his zamindari in portions (ijaras) to several sadr farmers called mustajirs and ijaradars. These again made over their leases in whole or in part, to renters of inferior denominations in a descending order down to the revenue-farmers of the villages (qutqinadars) who were given

[61]Home Miscellaneous, Vol. 206, Amini Commission Report; Francis MSS Eur. E 28, 'On the different modes of settlement' (no date, probably 1774).

the charge of collecting the revenue from the village establishments of the zamindari. If we look at this same hierarchy from the other end of the scale, the cultivators paid the revenue, in the first place, to village officers manning the village establishments of the zamindars. They, in turn, paid to a qutqinadar or a small local renter of perhaps two or three villages, he to a farmer of a taraf or a division comprehending several villages, and so on through farmers of a pargana to the zamindar.[62] This was the condition in all big zamindaris where revenue-farming seemed to prevail almost invariably.[63] In the medium-sized zamindari, if the zamindar happened to be sufficiently energetic to look after his establishments in the interior, the farming system would be dispensed with. But even if such an energetic zamindar appointed his own officials, little reduction in the revenue-collecting chain resulted. Only in the smaller zamindaris and taluqs did the holders collect—and by no means invariably—directly from the raiyats. The zamindars and their sadr officers knew little of what passed beyond the first degree of revenue-farmers.

Even at the sadr office, however, it was not often that the zamindar had a firm control of affairs. In the large zamindari of Birbhum, for instance, where the Raja died before the Permanent Settlement leaving his son a minor, Lala Ramnath, the diwan, and other officers divided the zamindari among themselves, holding mahals as renters. The young Raja was put in possession of the zamindari before he became a major by the interested parties who could get any paper signed by him. Great embezzlements took place and the zamindari was ruined by the Raja's rapacious servants who were involved in court intrigues, taking advantage of the fact that the Raja was both ignorant and reluctant to conduct business.[64] The Collector of Rangpur, describing the notorious incapacity of the zamindars of his district to look after their own interests, observed:

[62]Shore's minute of 18 June 1789. Appendix No. 1 to Fifth Report, *Parliamentary Papers*, sess. 1812, Vol. VII.

[63]In Nadia for instance, subletting of farms to the third or fourth degree only added to the machinery of mismanagement. Nadia, Old English Correspondence, Collector Redfearn to BR, dt. 16 March 1787.

[64]BRP, 17 February 1789. Petition of the Ryotts and Inhabitants concerned in the Revenues of the District of Birbhum, BRC, 9 October 1795, No. 21.

> The Zemindars of this district either from sex, age or long habitual indolence are never known to interfere in public business and are in such a state of dependence on their gomastahs that I have known a zemindar Day after Day attend the Durbar of his own Gomastah thereby reversing the distinction of their respective ranks in life.[65]

Fundamental to the problem of controlling a zamindari was the dichotomy between the sadr and the mufassal. As the Collector of Rajshahi reported, the people in his district had

> continually in their mouth the necessity of distinguishing between sudder and mufassil; by which they mean, in this instance, the difference between the general knowledge that can reach the Governing Power, compared with the real state of things in Detail. The Naib if he never leaves his Pergunah Cutcherry will form a very defective judgement of the state of his villages. The Zemindar if he relies on his Naibs or his Diwans, will know as little of his Pergunahs.[66]

By the custom of the country, mufassal officers enjoyed considerable power which made them in a sense independent of the control of the sadr kachari. Pattas (leases) granted by naibs and karamcharis (village revenue collectors under the command of the naibs) to a raiyat did not require the zamindar's authority, and as the granting of the pattas was exclusively vested in these officers, pattas granted by them were necessarily valid and could not be set aside consistently with the raje-ul-mulk (law of the land).[67]

---

[65]*Bengal District Records, Rangpur,* Walter K. Firminger, ed., 1786-1787, Vol. VI, No. 54, pp. 41-42, Collector to BR 24 April 1786. The gomastas, taking full advantage of the situation oppressed the country by their exactions and instigated the raiyats to create disturbances and hamper collections. By acting together they increased their own power. Four gomastas of Rangpur combined to foster intrigues in the revenue business of the district. One gomasta named Rajmohan Chaudhuri acted as gomasta for four zamindars and this wielded extraordinary power.

[66]Home Miscellaneous, Vol. 385. Speke's report on Rajshahi, 23 May 1788.

[67]BRP, 22 May 1787, No. 50. Report of the Qanungos of Mahmudshahi, 19 February 1787.

In the interior, the practice of every mufassal officer becoming a farmer in his own right was well established.[68] They obtained annually considerable remissions from the fixed jama of their lands on the ground that much of them had fallen out of cultivation. These lands, being brought back again into cultivation, yielded considerable profits as they were now virtually revenue-free. Sadr amlas (officers) held taluqs or farms in collusion with mufassal officers. They fed the zamindars with false reports of the capability of land in order to avoid payment of the full revenue. Lower down the revenue-paying hierarchy substantial local people holding leases of jote[69] and qutqina[70] invariably possessed themselves of more land than specified in their leases. By these collusive means villagers of substance managed to obtain under-assessed raiyati holdings and the lower classes of raiyats had to make up for the deficiency by paying irregular cesses.[71] The process of collection was a constant struggle between fraud, exaction, and concealment.[72]

In this struggle the advantage lay with the local men who knew the real state of things in detail rather than with the governing power at the sadr. Harrington's survey of the Swaruppur pargana of the Natore Raj (bought by Darpanarayan Tagore of Calcutta in 1789) clearly showed this.[73] In this pargana the village officers of the zamindari—38 amins and 53 karmacharis—received only a small allowance from the zamindar. Their wages, diet, and private expenses were paid by the raiyats. Thus, although they were supposed to prevent any encroachment by the raiyats on the rights of the zamindar, they were dependent on the influential raiyats for their livelihood. Most of the amins and patwaris were natives of the pargana and held raiyati lands themselves, from which they derived a profit. Some of the amins came from neighbouring

---

68*Bengal District Records, Dinajpur*, Walter K. Firminger, ed., to John Shore dated 17 March 1787, No. 124, p. 72.

69Large raiyati holdings granted directly by the zamindar.

70Revenue farm of a village held by an influential local man under a superior farmer of the revenue.

71BRP, 28 May 1790, No. 8, Enclosure from Collector.

72Shore's minute of 18 June 1789, Appedix No. 1 to Fifth Report, *Parliamentary Papers*, sess. 1812, Vol. VII.

73Home Miscellaneous, Vol. 385, Seroopore.

Bhaturia and supported themselves by the established allowance given by the zamindar and the contributions raised by the raiyats. While the naib of the zamindari appointed all the amins and gave them sanads, generally the raiyats appointed the patwaris and the naib merely gave approval. The raiyats could remove the patwaris appointed by themselves, but not the patwaris and amins appointed by the naib without his permission. If, however, ten raiyats were dissatisfied with an amin or a patwari, he was removed at their request unless he was a favourite at the head office. The disorder and partiality in the mufassal settlement which Harrington found in Swaruppur was due to the fact that the mufassal officers were dependent on the leading raiyats in a very large measure. According to the prescribed pargana rates, each raiyati holding should have been equitably assessed on the basis of size, quality of soil, and nature of the crop but, in fact, these pargana rates were simply swept aside and assessments were fixed arbitrarily over villages in a manner which favoured the powerful and oppressed the weak. Venality and fraud vitiated all the standard arrangements of revenue in the mufassal and the sadr authorities could exercise no detailed control on the affairs of the villages.

Though in theory the revenue of the raiyats should have been fixed directly by the governing power at the sadr according to equitable economic principles, in practice the fixation of the assessment and the collection of it was determined by a whole set of political relations between the village, the mufassal establishment, and the head office. The political character of the relations between the village and the zamindari (complementing the political relations between the Rajs and the Nizamat) was clearly illustrated by the method of collection—by quartering footmen on recalcitrant village—to which the naib of Swaruppur had frequent recourse.[74] Payment of

[74]Describing these methods the naib of Swaruppur said to Harrington 'First a Pyke carries the Chitta (or Demand for the monthly Kist) if there be any delay another Pyke is sent and then a Peudah. If it be judged necessary more Peudahs are sent but in general only one is sufficient. When the Rents are all remitted the whole are withdrawn, and sometimes when a Peudah is sent the Pykes are recalled'. The paiks (village footmen) and piadas (sadr footmen) quartered in the villages were maintained at the

the jama was like the rendering of tribute, which awaited the demonstration of sufficient force by the superior power to overawe the village oligarchies. The control of the Bengali zamindar over his villages stood on an altogether different basis from the control of the English landlord over his tenants.

villagers' expense. 'If I have reason to think that the Ryots misbehaved I send over Mohussils to the Head Ryots and summon them to the Sudder, where after hearing any Complaints I oblige them to pay what is due and if necessary to borrow it from the Mahagans. The means of enforcement are either that of confining them, or that of chastising them with the Rattan. First, however, I chastise the Aumeen & Putwarree, because they are Zemindarry Servants after which if the Ryots are not awed by the punishment of the Aumeen & Putwarree & the Rents be still in arrear I chastise the Ryots. If however the Aumeen & Putwarree represent the Arrears to be owing to the misbehaviour of the Ryots, these are summoned, & after an Enquiry they are punished, but if they are not expressly charged with misbehaviour Rigour is used in the first Instance towards the Aumeen and Putwarree.' Ibid.

3

Evolution of Pre-modern Agrarian Society in Bengal: Jotedars

The Village Oligarchies

At the base of the revenue-collecting pyramid stood the bedrock of all social institutions—the village. Each village was in itself a small pyramid, unless it happened to be an equal community of simple tribal folk like the Santhals in the inaccessible jungle mahals of the western border. The dominant village groups could be regarded from two aspects: from the economic point of view, as a rich peasant or (more appropriately) village land-holding class who cultivated their lands by using share croppers and agricultural labourers; and from the political point of view, as a village oligarchy (a term much more suitable than that unhappy expression 'village republic') which decided the affairs within the village and controlled its relations with the outside world through its headmen. There was also a ritual and social angle from which it would often appear that the ruling class or faction in the village was drawn from a single dominant caste or a few influential castes who employed and controlled the untouchables and tribals living in a separate quarter of the village. Each village had its own peculiar caste structure; and while it might appear that in the province as a whole the Brahmans, Kayasthas, and Vaidyas were the privilege castes, in each village there might be a dominant agricultural caste rated quite low in the provincial ritual ranking. In areas of high-caste concentration there were, of course, Brahman and Kayastha villagers who participated in agriculture and controlled the production of their villages. But more typically such controlling groups came from locally dominant agricultural castes. In the villages of Midnapur, they would be quite likely to be Kaivartas and Sadgops; in Burdwan, Sadgops and Aguris; in Rangpur and Dinajpur, Muslims; in Kuch Bihar, Rajbanshis; in Jessore, Faridpur, and Bakarganj, Muslims and Namasudras; in Bishnupur, Brahmans.[1]

There were different local terms, derived from local categories of land tenure, for these groups : in North Bengal, jotedar; in Jessore, gantidar; in Bakarganj haoladar; in Midnapur, mandal.[2] The tenures under which the village land-holding groups held their lands thus varied a good deal from district to district, and even from locality to locality.[3] But due to the

[1]In each local study, the caste composition of different social strata will be examined.

[2]*Report of the Rent Law Commission*, Vol. 1 (Calcutta 1880), pp. 6-9.

[3]Jote, in the strictly technical sense of the term, was a raiyati lease held direct from the zamindar; there might be under-raiyats, share croppers or agricultural labourers below the direct raiyatwari holder, or he might himself be the cultivator if the jote was small. Hamilton-Buchanan Manuscript, Mss. Eur. D. 75, Account of Ronggopur, part II, p. 110.

Ganti was a lease of land given direct by the zamindar, either for a term of years or in perpetuity, but always at an under-rated assessment. The gantidars were also farmers of revenues for the villages in which their ganti lands were situated and were expected to pay in the whole collections of their revenue farms as they would be compensated by the profits from their gantis. Home Miscellaneous, Vol. 385, Decennial Settlement Report on Jessore from Tilman Henckell, 25 June 1788.

Haola was a lease of land given by a taluqdar under the zamindar usually for clearance of forest, at a very low, and sometimes permanently fixed, revenue. There might be karshadars (actual tillers) under the haoladar, but often there would be an under-tenure holder called osat haoladar, in which case the haoladar would become a mere rent-receiver; many actual cultivators of the soil might also hold small haolas. Ibid., pp.244-245.

Mandali tenures in the jungle mahals of Midnapur were given by zamindars to people who contracted to clear forest by employing tribals; he mandal would pay revenue on behalf of the tribal cultivators to the zamindar, who would have no jurisdiction to collect directly from the occupiers of the cleared land. *Final Report on the Survey and Settlement Operations in the District of Midnapur, 1910-1918*, by A.K. Jameson, pp. 40-41.

It should be borne in mind that many high caste gentry held jotes and haolas which they leased out to other holders, treating the tenures simply as revenue-collecting jurisdictions, just like taluqs.

basic similarity of their social and economic roles in village life, the village land-holding class came to be known in the Bengali language of the late nineteenth century as jotedars. This specific social meaning of the term as an identifiable class in village society was not, of course, unknown in the eighteenth century; and in the revenue records of this period, there are instances in which Bengali zamindars used the term in exactly this sense.[4] But there was a strictly technical and legal meaning of the term jote—direct raiyati lease from the zamindar—which made it possible for even a poor peasant holding five acres on a direct lease from the zamindar to describe himself as a jotedar. At the other end of the scale, there were in the native state of Kuch Bihar many big jotedars, cultivating by means of chukanidars (under-tenants) and adhiars (sharecroppers), who gave up their jotes by a legal deed called ikrar-nama to powerful officers of the state and placed themeselves under the latter's protection as their chukanidars (in which case the existing chukanidars became dar-chukanidars). The former jotedars, in this case, were the real land holders, and the high officers who nominally enjoyed the jotes were more annuitants who collected tribute from the land-holding chukanidars.[5] From the jotedar class in the social sense of the term, both poor peasants holding a few acres on direct lease and annuitants holding nominally raiyati tenures were excluded; and since this social meaning of the term had already come into a limited currency in the eighteenth century, we shall use jotedar as a term synonymous with village landlord.

How this class, whose existence the collectors noted in almost every district at the time of the Decennial Settlement,[6] came into existence is not known. The ascendancy of a superior tenantry has been dated by a modern economic historian of Bengal to the year 1772 as a consequence of the farming experiment introduced by Warren Hastings which dissolved existing relations in agrarian society and enabled village

[4]See the petition of small zamindars of Dinajpur in 1799 in pp. 215-216.

[5]See pp. 228-229.

[6]N.K. Sinha, op. cit., p. 133, concludes that a privileged tenantry existed all over Bengal on the eve of the Decennial Settlement.

headmen to become under-farmers of the revenue.[7] Henry Thomas Colebrook, in a treatise on agriculture written in 1794, also argued that an intermediary tenantry cultivating through under-tenants and share croppers arose from the government's practice of raising large contributions by appointing farmers in place of regular collectors like amils or zamindars but he back-dated this process to the beginning of Mir Qasim's administration—the year1760. In his view, the practice of farming out collections did not become universal, nor its ill consequences fully felt, until Mir Qasim obtained a sudden and large increase in revenue by appointing farmers who disregarded usage and engagements and imposed taxes at pleasure which they collected by force.

> Favouring a few leading cultivators, they obtained, through their influence, general agreements to authorize exactions and imposts. Peasants became farmers of revenue, with the view of granting, on their own authority, reductions in the rent of the lands occupied by themselves; and continued to farm the revenue that they might perpetuate their undue advantages. The peasants at large were discouraged by an unequal assessment; and the favoured few did not use to the best advantage the lands which they held,[8] but formed that class of intermediate tenantry which has already been mentioned in another place.[9]

There is no evidence from contemporary literary or revenue sources to lend substance to the speculation that a rich tenant class sprang up suddenly in 1760 or 1772. The power of the rich tenantry had its roots much deeper in the social and economic structure of the village than is allowed by the theory which ascribes it to their crucial position in a decaying revenue-collecting hierarchy. Certainly the anarchy in revenue administration during the decline of the Nizamat (1757-1765) and the rise of the Company (1765-1786) gave much greater room

[7]Ibid., pp. 131-132.

[8]That is because they resorted to the wasteful practice of share-cropping.

[9]H.T. Colebrook, *Remarks on the Husbandry or Internal Commerce of Bengal*, (Calcutta 1804), p. 85.

for manoeuvre to the village oligarchies. Even more important, perhaps, the great depopulation, desertion, and increase of waste lands caused by the famine of 1770 gave splendid opportunities to villagers with capital to increase their holdings by employing their capital to bring the waste lands under their own cultivation. There is evidence from Purnia, Rajshahi, and Birbhum that they even forcibly drove out inferior raiyats in order to get hold of more land. Having secured the lands of the expelled raiyats at a low rate on the ground of 'desertion', these rich villagers then employed their dependents as share-croppers in order to bring the lands under cultivation again.[10] There was no lack of such dependants, for the famine had swelled the army of vagrant, destitute peasants who migrated from place to place in search of employment, taking cash or grain loans for subsistence from any rich villager seeking to attach their labour power by giving credit.[11] William Wilson Hunter, the great annalist of rural Bengal, oversimplified the situation when he wrote that after the famine of 1770 the advantage lay with the cultivators on account of excess of land and shortage of labour. After the calamity, which affected

---

[10]The Collector of Purnia wrote in 1788: 'Many of the Ryots have taken villages for one or two years with no other view than that of lowering their own rents by granting Pottahs to themselves and their Relations, and that of forcing other Ryots to abscond. On their first advance into the farms of the absconded Ryots they suffer their Land to lie uncultivated for the first year, but in the 2nd they occupy it themselves under Pottahs of a very low rate. At the expiration of the lease they relinquish the village, [i.e. the revenue farm of the village] and by the Inattention of the Zemindarry Amlah are not only allowed to continue in possession of what they have fraudulently obtained, but are also permitted to cultivate those lands by Malguzarry Ryots, with whom they divide the Harvest (i.e. (adhiars or share croppers). Home Miscellaneous, Vol. 385. Purnia, Report from Collector Hartley, 7 March 1788; See also BRP, 28 May 1790, No. 8, enclosure from Collector of Rajshahi containing seven articles by Raja Ramkrishna to be sanctioned by the Board, and Home Miscellaneous, Vol. 385, decennial Settlement Report on Birbhum including Bishnupur.

[11]But if Colebrook is to be believed, attached labour was by no means secure, for being oppressed by usury and rack-renting, the dependents fled from the yoke, migrating to further lands and swelling the streams of vagrant labour. Colebrook, op. cit., p. 103.

districts like Birbhum laid four-sevenths of the land waste,[12] the premium was not so much on labour as on the capital which was employed for maintaining destitute labour and clearing extensive waste. Merchants and bankers who lived in towns, and territorial magnates who ruled over extensive zamindaris, were in no position to engage in the enterprise of reclaiming waste, for it needed personal and on-the-spot supervision. It was the class of rich villagers with experience of agriculture who represented the capital and enterprise for reclamation. In contemporary despatches from the collectors, this class was usually referred to as mandals and paikast raiyats, and was universally condemned for turbulence and conspiracy (with a view to reducing the jama on reclaimed lands).[13] Hunter identified the paikast (i.e., non-resident, as opposed to khudkast or resident raiyats) raiyats with the growing body of 'vagrant' peasants after the famine of 1770, who exploited the scarcity of labour by obtaining lower rates of rent than the resident tenants.[14] But, as a matter of fact, many paikast raiyats were 'non-resident' only in name—they were an extremely influential and violent class of villagers who had compelled the zamindars to give them under-rated tenancies so as to employ their capital in clearing the waste lands in their own or neighbouring villages. Those who had obtained possession of the deserted lands in their own villages were called nij gaon paikasts, and those who had committed their resources to reclamation of waste in other viliages were known as baje gaon paikasts. The nij gaon paikasts paid a lower rate of jama than the khudkast raiyats, and the baje gaon paikasts paid even less. In Burdwan, both categories of paikast raiyats belonged to the dominant castes, while the ordinary khudkast raiyats were of lower ritual status and were compelled to make up in irregular cesses for any deficiency caused in the jama by the privileges of the

[12]Hast-o-bud accounts of Birbhum for the Bengali year 1183 in the district manuscript records, referred to by W.W. Hunter, op. cit., p. 51. Also Home Miscellaneous, Vol. 815, Rennel Letters, latter dated Dacca 6 April 1772 and Francis Manuscripts Mss. Eur. E. 28.

[13]Bengal Revenue Consultations, 25 February 1789, Collector of Birbhum to BR, 13 February 1789.

[14]Hunter, op. cit., pp. 62-63.

mandals (superior khudkast raiyats) and paikasts.[15] After the famine of 1770 the commodity for selling which the raiyats, or rather a small section of the raiyats, were in a bargaining position, was not labour, but capital.

But while the revenue-farming under Mir Qasim and Warren Hastings and the increase of waste land after the famine of 1770 undoubtedly gave the village oligarchs greater power vis-a-vis both the poor population of the village and the subordinate government of the country, there is no evidence to show that the jotedar class was a formerly non-existent class which sprang into existence between 1760-1790. A solution to the problem of their origin must await further research in the medieval rural history of Bengal.[16] But, at any rate, it seems likely that they had for long been a prominent element in traditional agrarian society for at least two reasons. First, land distribution was closely related to caste stratification in all villages which had undergone the transition from tribal to 'Aryan' or 'Dravidian' society. Forms of agrestic servitude, such as slavery, share cropping, and hired or attached labour, have been shown by recent research to have arisen from the traditional relationship between ritually pure and untouchable village groups in pre-British South Indian society.[17] In Bengal also the same relationship between land-holding and caste status was revealed in early British revenue records, and the caste structures of the existing villages certainly went further back in time. Secondly, the mode of production based on the

---

[15]Describing the categories of raiyats, the Collector of Burdwan wrote in 1788 '. . . the first are the Khod Kast or aborigines being Ryots of inferior cast (sic) who pay a House rent, a greater Revenue for the lands. . . than the Pykhast who are Ryots of a superior Rank that neither pay Rent for their dwelling house nor do they pay so high a revenue for their lands. The last are again distinguished by the appellation of Nishgong Pykhast who cultivate the lands of their own village and the Baziegong Pykhast who pays a still lower rate of revenue . . . BRP, 24 June 1788, No. 23, Collector of Burdwan to BR, 20 May 1788.

[16]It seems that over an indeterminable period in medieval times, there was a transition from revenue fixed per hoe or plough to revenue rated on land according to quantity, quality, and article of produce, followed by a growing substitution of payments in kind by payments in cash. A solution may be found in these periods of transition.

[17]See Dharma Kumar, op. cit., pp. 30-32, 47-55.

relationship between the jotedar-rich farmer and adhiar-agricultural labourer which Colebrook and Hamilton Buchanan commented upon in 1794 and 1808 respectively was very well-established and quite widespread in their time. Had this relationship come into existence in this short span of thirty years, it could only have been produced by a revolution on a scale, intensity, and pace which would surely have attracted the attention of contemporary observers. The jotedars were an integral part of a complex village economy described in the early revenue records of the Board of Revenue with an amplitude of detail which must, inevitably, disappoint the seeker of a simple and virtuous rustic society. Within this economy, the relationship between those who controlled land and capital and those who sold labour power was a great deal more contractual than has so far been allowed. It was not merely a matter of caste and ritual status which condemned some to performing menial service and debarred others from holding the plough, as has been argued in the case of South India. By the middle of the eighteenth century it was more than a matter of 'land and caste' in a status-bound society; already there was a question of land and the means to cultivate it (i.e. capital) in a society differentiated by complex economic laws (and not merely by status) into those who held the means and those who did not.[18]

The Village Economy and the Role of the Jotedars

Due to an unprecedented inflow of specie[19] in Bengal on account of the growing East India Company trade between

[18]Carrying the speculation about the medieval origins of agricultural labour and landlordism further, it now seems possible to distinguish two phases of development: an earlier state of status-bound society and self-sufficient subsistence economy in which caste was the crucial economic divider, and a later stage of more contractual society in which commercial links were developing and reinforcing the existing differences of caste. This later stage coincided with the transition from produce rents to cash rents. Certain highly commercialized regions like Gujarat, Malabar and Bengal had reached the later phase by the eighteenth (and possibly seventeenth) century.

[19]Prior to 1757 the annual bullion import was estimated to be Rs 2 crores. Home Miscellaneous, Vol. 434, 'Plan for the conservation and augmentation of current specie of Bengal, 1785'.

1700-1756, the impact of which was heightened by the stoppage of tribute in specie to Delhi from about 1700,[20] there was a considerable degree of monetization of the rural economy and stimulation of commerce in the countryside in the first half of the eighteenth century. The economic isolation of the villages was broken by the rapid expansion of the East India Company's trade, the total value of which exceeded the land revenue of Bengal at the beginning of British rule.[21] On account of the greatly increased volume of currency, the Mughal government was able to insist on the payment of the sadr jama from all zamindaris in the standard sikka rupee; and it is clear from the early revenue records of the Board of Revenue that the mufassal jama was also collected from raiyats and renters in almost every zamindari mainly in cash, though here a great many varieties of depreciated currency (such as arcot rupee) were used in revenue transactions. The large amount of cash which was necessary for payment of the revenue was acquired by peasant households by the marketing of grain, mulberry, cotton, sugar cane, salt (important in Midnapur where salt workers were peasants) and other marketable crops. Before the growth of indigo plantation, was sugar cane and mulberry cultivation and sugar and silk manufacture which flourished; it was estimated that between 1726-1756 export of sugar to other provinces in India brought in an annual 60 lakhs in specie.[22] Rice, also was exported to other provinces; its importance might be judged from the fact that in 1790 export of rice to other parts of India was estimated to be worth Rs 36 lakhs.[23] Rice was exported in

[20]From the beginning of Murshid Quli Khan's administration, the tribute to Delhi was paid in banker's drafts on the Delhi branch of Jagat Seth, which stopped the annual drain of specie which depressed commerce in Bengal. After the Maratha invasions Alivardi Khan stopped the tribute altogether.

[21]In 1769 the 'Investment' (i.e. the goods purchased for export) of the Company was £2,901, 194; the revenues of Bengal, £2.467,846. Home Miscellaneous, Vol. 766. 'Of a free trade in Bengal',

[22]MSS. Eur. D. 281, 'Historical Review of the External Commerce of Calcutta from 1750 until 1830', entry under the year 1776.

[23]Since the total rice produced in the Presidency was estimated to be Rs. 219 lakhs, the export to other parts was 16.47 per cent of the total. Home Miscellaneous, Vol. 434, 'Estimate of the fertility of Bengal, Bihar and Orissa, March 1791'. Much earlier than this, in fact throughout the

bulk from Dinajpur to Murshidabad and Calcutta, and all metals except iron were imported to Dinajpur from Calcutta. Iron, used mainly for agricultural implements, came from Birbhum via Murshidabad. Thus, bulk of the trade was in necessities, not in luxuries.[24] Even a backward agricultural district like Rangpur exported rice, oilseeds, betel nut, ginger, tobacco, opium, lac, silk sugar, indigo, paper, bamboo, timber, hemp, cattle, fish, elephants, etc.; and imported pulses, salt, cotton, copper, tin, iron, shells, lime, fruit, coconuts, stone-plates, blankets, shawls, perfumes, horses, etc.[25] There were 512 market centres in Rangpur (1 per 14.5 square miles) at the time of Buchanan-Hamilton's survey in 1808 and the total value of the exports and imports from this backward district amounted to as much as 24 per cent of the value of its agricultural produce.[26] In the more highly commercialized neighbouring district of Dinajpur, the hats (weekly fairs) and bandars (riverine trade centres) numbered 635 (1 per 8.5 square miles) and the value of exports and imports was as high as 30 per cent of the value of the agricultural products of the district.[27]

The needs of this ramified economy were complex and production would not have been possible without certain facilities which are not to be found in a self-sufficient subsistence economy, such as a well-developed marketing structure and credit network. Monetized commercial and revenue transactions facilitated the concentration of wealth in the hands of a

---

Mughal period, Bengal stood out for a large surplus in the provisions of export. There was a regular coastal trade in rice, sugar and butter with Coromandel and Kerala, and a riverine trade up the Ganges in rice and silk with Patna, and in rice, raw silk and sugar with Agra. From Agra Bengal silk was carried to Gujarat and from the seventeenth century the Dutch also developed a sea-borne trade in silk from Bengal to Japan and Holland. Irfan Habib, *The Agrarain System of Mughal India (1556-1707)*, pp. 71-72.

[24]Francis Buchanan (Hamilton), *A Geographical, Statistical and Historical Description of the District, a Zilla, of D najpur in the Province, or Soubah, of Bengal* (Baptist Mission Press, 1883), pp. 314-317.

[25]Montgomery Martin, *The History, Antiquities, Topography and Statistics of Eastern India* (London 1838), pp. 710-711.

[26]Ibid., pp. 710-713.

[27]Buchanan, *A Geographhical Description of Dinajpur*, statistical appendices.

few men in village society. It was achieved by the economic complex of money-lending, money-changing, and grain-dealing. Both production of crops for the market and collection of revenue for the government was financed by money-lenders; raiyats and renters took money from them—at exorbitant rates of interest—to pay their instalments. Indeed, as the Naib of Swaruppur told Harrington, they were compelled by the officers of the zamindar to borrow from mahajans whenever any difficulty arose in the payment of the jama.[28] The mahajans supplied essential rural credit without which cultivation would not have been possible. Production of cash crops like oil seeds, mulberry and sugar cane was more than usually expensive and was almost entirely based on advances from the traders to the cultivators.[29] Rice production was also based on advances in the surplus districts which exported rice in bulk.[30] In the zamindari of Nadia, situated very near Calcutta and linked with the metropolitan market by river, cultivation was almost entirely carried on with the grain and seed advanced to the peasants by petty mahajans dispersed all over the mufassal.[31] The money-lenders were at the same time grain merchants and advanced money for the future crops at the commencement of the sowing season. By such activities they were able to establish such a local monopoly of grain that many early British Collectors were compelled by scarcity of food (which hit the weavers in particular and therefore affected the Company's 'Investment') to take stern measures against the monopolists.[32] Money-changing was also very profitable

---

[28]See p. 56, footnote 74.

[29]Buchanan, *A Geographical Description of Dinajpur*, pp. 212, 276, 304.

[30]Thus in Dinajpur, which exported much more rice than Rangpur, the system of advances for grain was carried to much further extent. Buchanan Hamilton Manuscript, MSS, Eur. D. 75, Account of Ranggopur, Vol. 11, p. 106.

[31]BRP, 7 April 1789, No. 13, Collector of Nadia to BR, dt. 1 April 1789.

[32]*Bengal District Records*, *Dinajpur*, Vol. 1, No. 29, George Udney, Resident, to Collector of Dinajpur, dt. 19 January 1788, pp. 89–90; Ibid., Vol. 11, No. 367, Collector of Dinajpur to Shore, dt. 14 June 1788, p. 231.

because of the circulation of various kinds of currency which were depreciated in relation to the standard sikka rupee in which revenue payments to the state had to be made. The rates of batta (exchange) were constantly fluctuating and were manipulated from the towns by the big sarafs (bankers and money-changers). Below them were the poddars (money-changers) in the villages, a very numerous class of men who possessed no shops but attended the weekly fairs from morning till evening with bags of currency.[33]

Who were the people who ran this complex of money-lending, money-changing and grain-dealing? The mention of a numerous body of village poddars with no shops and petty mahajans dispersed all over the mufassal gives us a clue to their identity. They did not form an urban commercial class distinct from the body of villagers. Of course there were established bankers; currency manipulators and grain monopolists, but they were not numerous and operated in towns and cities only. Money-lending, money-changing, and grain-dealing in the interior centred around rich villagers who combined these activities with agriculture. In Rangpur the grain-dealers or beparis were large farmers with more than five ploughs (i.e., more than 33 acres) who kept cattle for transporting the grain collected from the village to the nearest market.[34] In Dinajpur even middling farmers with three to five ploughs (20-33 acres) who occupied stiff clay land (which required only six months of the year for cultivation as opposed to rice clay bearing cash crops) employed their six idle months in purchasing grain from the village and carrying it to the market, by which they made a considerable profit.[35]

Each large jotedar, it might be said, held an economic empire which dominated his village in all aspects. During his

---

[33]*Bengal District Records, Dinajpur*, Vol. 1, No. 29, George Udney, Resident, to Collector of Dinajpur, dt. 19 January 1788, pp. 89-90; Vol. 11, No. 367, Collector of Dinajpur to Shore, dt. 14 January 1788, p. 231; No. 153, Collector of Dinajpur to Shore, dt. 10 July 1787, p. 89; No. 260, Collector of Dinajpur to Shore, dt. 29 December 1789, p. 162; BRP, 8 May 1178, No. 37, enclosure from Collector of Rangpur.

[34]Buchanan-Hamilton Manuscript, Account of Ronggopur, Vol. 11, P. 103.

[35]Buchanan, *Geographical Description of Dinajpur*, p. 235.

surveys of Dinajpur district in 1808, Hamilton-Buchanan found that 6 per cent of the cultivating population enjoyed 36.5 per cent of the land leased by raiyats from the zamindars, whereas 52.1 per cent of the agricultural work force had no land at all and worked for the rich farmers as hired labourers or sharecroppers (see Table 8.4 on page 212). With this concentration of land-holding went another remarkable feature of the village economy—the combination of grain-dealing and money lending with land-holding, which gave the jotedar families enormous economic and political power within the village. According to Buchanan-Hamilton, at least half of the cultivation of the country was carried on with grain or money advanced by the jotedars, to whom small farmers and sharecroppers were indebted for more than the whole value of their agricultural stock.[36] Through the credit mechanism the jotedars were assured of the labour power of the village and political control over the villagers. The marketing structure gave them, in addition, command over the produce of the village. The poor farmers and sharecroppers, lacking holding power and means of transport to the market, sold their produce, to the local grain-dealer immediately after harvest when the ruling prices of grain were lowest during the year. The grain-dealing jotedars, who were equipped with stores (golas) and bullock-carts, were under no pressure to sell their produce after the harvest and could afford to wait until the prices rose again in the middle of the cultivating season, when they could either send their produce by bullock-carts to the nearest market or lend it as seed or food to poor villagers who had exhausted their supplies of grain. The latter received grain at the high rate which prevailed for six months before the harvest and were compelled to pay it back at the low rate after harvest when the market was glutted with corn sold by needy peasants. The turn of the agricultural cycle thus resulted in considerable invisible losses to the poor, and corresponding profits for the affluent.[37] Economic concentration in the village could not, therefore, be measured only by the amount of land and

[36]See pp. 289-290.

[37]Hamilton-Buchanan Manuscript, MSS, Eur. D. 75, Account of Ronggopur, Vol. 11, p. 103; Buchanan, *Geographical Description of Dinajpur*, p. 236.

number of employees of the jotedars. Indirectly, through credit and marketing, their domain extended over the whole work force and the whole produce of the village.

POLITICS AND EXTERNAL AFFAIRS OF THE VILLAGE OLIGARCHIES

To preserve their domain within the village the jotedars had to take account of the possibility of interference from the zamindars and the local officers of the government in village affairs. The ruling factions in the villages were continually engaged in the conduct of policies designed to fight off external pressures—by the offer of collaboration where possible and resistance where necessary. The Collector of Birbhum noted in 1788 that the mandals or head raiyats derived from their number and mutual support such influence that the success of a settlement depended on their pleasure.[38] The jama to be paid from the village might be settled by negotiations between the mandals and the zamindar's local representative but the mandals would try, as far as possible, to prevent interference with the detailed distribution of the demand among the villagers.

According to the prescribed mode of settlement there was, in theory if not in practice, an asal jama on each piece of land, assessed after a measurement of every pargana, at different rates according to the article cultivated and the quality of the soil. After the measurement had taken place, an annual survey was to be made in order to ascertain the quantity of land under cultivation and the kind of crop cultivated, and the asal jama was to be adjusted accordingly; there were to be no abwabs or irregular cesses. Such a mode of settlement implied very detailed control of the economic affairs of the village from the seat of government. But, as the survey of Swaruppur by Harrington in 1788 revealed, for a long time past little attention had been paid in the pargana to the quantity of land under cultivation and the article of produce. The settlement had come to be made for the villages in the pargana collectively and the amount due from each cultivator had been

[38]BRP, 6 May 1788, No. 1, Collector of Birbhum to BR, dt. 18 January 1788.

left to the influential villagers. A few of the principal raiyats signed the engagement for the jama on behalf of the villagers. If there was any individual settlement, it was concluded with big huzuri jotedars (direct raiyatwari holders under whom existed the actual tillers of the soil) or with revenue-farmers of villages who executed separate engagements.[39] The zamindar or his local representative, therefore, had no direct relations with the raiyats, unless the zamindari happened to be small enough for raiyats to pay direct to the sadr establishment. In Jessore, if the zamindari happened to be large, then the daul bandobast or the settlement register of the zamindar entered only the farmers or gantidars, and not the raiyats, for most raiyats held under a gantidar or farmer paying a fixed sum to the zamindar. It was the gantidar who collected revenue from the raiyats in occupation (hazira), resettled the lands of those who deserted (ferari), and disposed of unappropriated lands. The zamindar had nothing to do with the raiyat's contracts. Whatever the actual state of land and whatever the amount paid by the raiyats, his daul bandobast continued to show the unvarying sum fixed with the gantidars.[40]

As the price of their collaboration in the collection of the jama, the village leaders thus demanded the right to settle the details of the revenue in the village without outside interference. Their aim was to secure virtually unfettered power for transferring the incidence of revenue from their own holdings to those of inferior raiyats. The yearly revenue thus fell with the heaviest weight on the class of people least able to support it.[41] In the course of settlement operations in 1793, the Collector of Burdwan discovered that the poorer raiyats were overburdened with rates of assessment while head raiyats not only enjoyed a greater quantity of land than what was stated in their leases but did not pay half as much per bigha as the common raiyats did.[42] In some areas no better terms

[39]Home Miscellaneous, Vol. 385, 'Seroopore'.

[40]Report from Collector of Jessore, dt. 12 January 1793, referred to by J. Westland, *A Report on the District of Jessore, its Antiquities, its history and its commerce*, (Calcutta 1874), pp. 89-90.

[41]BRP, 6 May 1788, No. 1, Collector of Birbhum to BR, dt. 18 January 1788.

[42]BRP, 9 July 1793, No. 57, Collector of Burdwan to BR, dt. 31 May 1793.

could be obtained by the zamindars than what the head raiyats were willing to offer. In Bishnupur there was a combination among the mandals for securing the revenue farms of the villages, so that there was no competition when the farms were put up to auction by the zamindar.[43] From time to time the zamindars tried to interfere in the revenue affairs of the village by survey and measurement with a view to obtaining an increase of jama. This was considered a drastic and unusual measure since it necessarily hit at the roots of the power of the mandals—usually it was proposed merely as a threat to obtain better terms in the negotiations with the mandals. In 1781 the zamindar of Birbhum, Muhammad Wali Khan, directed an actual measurement of his zamindari as a means of imposing an equal and general settlement. But the mandals of Birbhum diverted him from this proposal by promising to raise a new cess from the villages. From this new cess the zamindar was easily persuaded to exempt the principal raiyats, so that a plan for relief of the inferior raiyats by equalization of the assessment was converted into a means of increasing their hardship.[44]

After the famine of 1770, which fundamentally disturbed the rural economy due to an increase in the amount of waste-land, the need for capital, and the number of migrant labour, there were frequent confrontations in the villages between the mandals and the zamindars. The richer section of the peasantry all over the affected parts of the province seized the opportunity for obtaining more lands at lower rates. Since the zamindars (on whom the Company began to impose new demands on the assumption of the diwani in 1772) naturally tried to resist the process of reduction of village assessments as far as possible, new tensions built up in the agrarian economy, and there were frequent revolts in the villages against the local establishments of the Rajs. These village outbreaks did not represent a general rising of the peasantry against the existing order but merely a pursuit of diplomacy by violent means on the part of the village oligarchs in order to force the

[43]N.K. Sinha, op. cit., p. 132.

[44]Home Miscellaneous, Vol. 385, Decennial Settlement Report on Birbhum (including Bishnupur).

principalities to come to terms. Whenever there were any village commotions, the mandals were instrumental in fomenting them.[45] Instigated by the village heads—who were themselves responsible for the impositions on them—the raiyats would gather in arms at the time of the actual collections until the revenue-farmers came to terms—which were designed to benefit the superior raiyats. The usual method was for mandals to assemble a few hundred raiyats and make them take an oath not to pay the revenue, whereupon footmen sent in to collect the revenue would be beaten up. Farmers and tahsildars, the local collectors of revenue, would be molested and driven away from local offices of the zamindari and the collections would be stopped until the mandals obtained satisfaction.[46] Often the common raiyats had no interest in these commotions but the richer raiyats who were trying to preserve the low rates on their holdings insisted on violent confrontation. In Birbhum the common raiyats proved eager to pay the revenue according to the jamabandi formed for the Decennial Settlement but the mandals and paikast raiyats who had got hold of much deserted land at low rates objected to the assessment imposed by the dominant official faction of Lala Ramnath in the sadr kachari. They informed the collector that they could at their will and pleasure carry off the raiyats and cause them to pay or not to pay the revenue. 'Dismissing the Lala Ramnath clique from office, they 'appointed' their chosen representatives from the opposite clique as officers for settling the lands. There were riotous combinations of villagers all over Birbhum and the British government was obliged to intervene with military force in order to prevent disturbances.[47]

---

[45]Referring to the insurrection of Rangpur raiyats against the revenue-farmer Debi Singh in 1783, the Collector of Rangpur commented: '. . . the poorer Ryotts in Insurrections of this kind are only a deluded multitude led on by their more designing Busneahs' (headmen). *Bengal District Records, Rangpur*, Vol. IV, p. 133, No. 180, Collector of Rangpur to Lt. McDonald, dt. 13 February 1783.

[46]BRP, 72 May 1788, No. 23, from Governor-General-in-Council to BR, dt. 21 May 1788; BRP, 27 November 1787, No. 1, Collector of Birbhum to BR, dt. 21 November 1788; BRC, 15 March 1793, No. 16, Translation of an arzee of Raja Ramkishan (of Rajshahi) to BR.

[47]BRC, 25 February 1789, Collector of Birbhum to BR, 13 February 1789; together with petitions of Lala Ramnath and the raiyats of Birbhum.

Often dissatisfied zamindari officers would be at the root of the disturbances instigated by the mandals.[48] In such typical agrarian disturbances, farmers, qutqinadars and local officers of the zamindar along with the zamindari paiks confronted assembled raiyats who were led by their mandals, controlling whom was a rival faction of dissatisfied zamindari officers.

Did these conditions, described by various collectors in their reports on Decennial Settlement operations in the respective districts, prevail all over Bengal? Professor Sinha, who has methodically summarized evidence of this nature emanating from Birbhum, Bishnupur, Rajshahi, Dinajpur, Buldacaul, and Nadia feels 'justified in generalising' and concludes that on the eve of the Decennial Settlement 'this domination by the privileged tenantry' which very much aggravated the plight of the lesser raiyats extended over the whole of Bengal. It is, however, significant that the violent tumults instigated by the village leaders against the zamindars at the time of the Decennial Settlement seem to have occurred mostly in the areas devastated by the famine of 1770, such as Birbhum and Rajshahi. In Burdwan, which was less affected than the neighbouring zamindaris of Bishnupur and Birbhum, no revolts took place in the villages against the ambitious and energetic Raja Tejchand, though his neighbours Chaitan Singh and Muhammad Zaman Khan did not manage nearly so well. In the district

---

[48]The Collector of Rajshahi wrote in 1788 that frequent commotions in the parganas of Bhaturia and Bhusna since 1781 had their origin in the intrigues of a *clique* of zamindari officers to effect the ruin of their rival Nandalal Ray, which was fully obtained. In Bhaturia, an English officer was obliged to fire on the mob. The raiyats had themselves maintained barkandazes (footmen), contributing either voluntarily to the cost or being compelled to defray the expenses by the mandals. The object was to obtain a reduction of the jama. In 1788 the raiyats of Bangong, instigated by the leading mandals, dispossessed the farmer, and maltreated the footmen sent by the magistrate to restore him. BRP, 24 December 1788, No. 27 Collector of Rajshahi to BR, dt. 15 December 1788. Disturbances were also very frequent and widespread in Birbhum and were reported to have taken place in 1781 (Home Miscellaneous, Vol. 207, Disturbances in Birbhum) 1787, 1788 and 1789. It is significant that both Birbhum and Rajshahi had been devastated by the famine of 1770, and in both areas leading raiyats were continually trying to obtain more and more 'deserted' (real or fictitious) land at low rates.

of Dacca, where the famine made practically no impact, collectors did not report any village revolts against zamindars or taluqdars and in old settled parganas like Bikrampur the domination of the Hindu taluqdar class apparently faced no challenge at this point of time from Muslim villagers, though conditions might have been different further south on the borders of the Sunderbans. It is likely that the disbanding of the armies of the big Rajas in North and West Bengal by the British caused a reduction of their coercive authority which led to the conditions of spasmodic village revolts reported by the collectors from Birbhum and Rajshahi, two districts especially devastated by the famine. The progressive breakdown of government during the period of transition when the Nawabs were being deprived of their means of administration and the Rajas were being stripped of their means of coercion, naturally led to a shift of the centre of political influence from the sadr to the mufassal. Widespread rural violence in the early years of British ascendancy, of which the best known examples were the chuar rebellion in Midnapur, the peasant insurrection in Rangpur, and the depredations and robberies by bands of sannyasis and dacoits in many districts of North, East, and West Bengal was symptomatic of the breakdown of the superior administrative structures over the village oligarchies. During the full vigour of the Nizamat under governors like Murshid Quli Khan and Shuja Khan, when ambitious and energetic zamindars built up new principalities by conquest and aggression, the villages and their dominant cliques were apparently quiescent for the Persian chronicles mention no agrarian disorders at this time apart from individual revolts by powerful zamindars like Sitaram Ray. Before the famine of 1770 powerful resident zamindars presumably carried out, from time to time, a measurement and survey of their villages which resulted in some measure of equalization in the revenue rates and imposition of jama on concealed holdings, so that the economic margin of the ruling village cliques over the body of common villagers was not necessarily great in all villages at all times. Even after the famine of 1770, hast-o-buds were carried out in the zamindaris of Jahangirpur, Jessore, government khas taluqs, Lasskarpur, Mahmudshahi, Mahisadal, Midnapur, and

Nadia[49] though the particulars of these surveys preserved in the Revenue Department give no clear picture of the impact on the village oligarchies.

It is now clear that 'traditional' society in Bengal cannot be treated as a fixed yardstick by which to measure change under the Permanent Settlement. Many of the characteristic features of the nineteenth century agrarian scene in Bengal could be detected in eighteenth century rural society: a considerable market for export and import of commodities, a relatively high degree of monetization, payment of revenue in cash, rural credit supplied by money-lenders, brisk sale of property rights in land, and a certain fluidity in the composition of the hereditary revenue-collecting classes. The rural society which had evolved on the basis of this complex agrarian economy was constituted at the base by economically and ritually stratified villages ruled by a creditor-employer class of peasant landlords and, at the apex, by a revenue-collecting and tribute-sharing structure which supported numerous upper caste local gentry who supplied the needs of a developed civilization and government built up over the extended revenue-collecting and peace-keeping jurisdictions of the territorial magnates. Pre-modern agrarian society in Bengal, at least in its upper levels, was always shifting, and never more decisively than from the time of Murshid Quli Khan to the advent of Cornwallis. The village base adapted gradually to these changes instead of undergoing decisive structural change in a very short period. This pre-modern historical process—constant change at upper levels and imperceptible adjustment at the village base—continued after the Permanent Settlement which, by sweeping away the Mughal revenue structure that had persisted up-till 1786 in modified forms, introduced a more recognizably modern fiscal and administrative framework for rural society in Bengal. Though substantial fiscal, administrative, and economic changes had already been effected under early British rule, the older Mughal system had still supplied the basis of land revenue administration. It was not until 1772 that the British assumed

[49]Revenue Department, Hast-o-bud accounts of Jahangirpur, Jessore, Khas Taluks, Lashkarpur, Mahmudshahi, Mahisadal, Midnapur and Nadia districts from 1179-1183 B.S. or 1772-1776 A.D.

the diwani from Mughal revenue officers; and from 1772 to 1786 various revenue experiments were tried without really transforming the older basis of rural administration. Under the temporary revenue-farming experiment from 1772 to 1777, the zamindars survived as under-farmers below the Calcutta merchants who took many of the biggest revenue farms. The failure of the experiment once again led to a reversion to revenue management through zamindars from 1777 to 1786. The zamindars lost many important powers in this process but until the proper establishment of the collectorate system in 1786 for concluding the Permanent Settlement, their traditional jurisdictions continued to be the basis of rural control.[50] It is, then, to the new order established between 1786 and 1793 which abolished the Rajs and transformed the basis of zamindari that we must now turn.

[50]The period of transition from Mughal to British systems of revenue management between 1757-1793 has received detailed treatment from N.K. Sinha, op. cit.

4

The Permanent Settlement

A Case of Mistaken Identity

The head mandals, a collector reported from Rajshahi during the operations leading to the Permanent Settlement, 'are become the real Masters of the Land, and the first object of a zamindar should be a gradual reduction of their Power'.[1] How successful were the zamindars in implementing this object after the Permanent Settlement? Time, for the moment, was certainly on their side. The growth of population and increase of cultivation was repidly correcting the imbalance in the ratio between land, capital, and labour which led to the growth of extraordinary power of the jotedar class in the countryside. In the districts where most of the land had been under cultivation before the famine, resettling of the depopulated villages and recovery of the deserted lands was quite rapid and, if we are to believe the impressionistic reports of contemporary officers, by the end of the eighteenth century the ratio between the factors of production prevailing before 1770 had been restored. Though the jotedars had in the meantime consolidated the privileges which they had seized, the zamindars were now in a better position to exert pressure. In the districts where, in contrast, much of the land had never been cultivated and was covered by virgin forest, the settling of villages and extension of cultivation was a much more arduous, dangerous, and time-consuming task

[1]Home Miscellaneous, Vol. 385, Decennial Settlement Report on Rajshahi, letter from Speke dt. 23 May 1788.

and the advantage still lay with professional agriculturists able to supply the capital and enterprise for the clearing of forest.

But for all lands, whether cultivated or uncultivated, the zamindars had been declared proprietors in 1793. Did this proclamation of law help the zamindars to become in practice landlords on a firmer basis? By means of local studies of developments in the revenue-collecting and land-holding structures, in which variations in local conditions produced by the amount of waste, nature of land tenures, caste composition of different categories of landlords, etc., will be taken into account, we shall explore the problem in depth. But at the outset, we shall have to be clear about the exact implications of the legal rights conferred on the zamindars by the Permanent Settlement. For contrary to the general impression, the regulations of 1793 did not give the zamindars the legal rights possessed by English landlords, though the architect of the regulations, Lord Cornwallis, certainly had in mind the model of an improving English landlord class.

The framers of the Permanent Settlement did not set out to engineer new social forms and categories conceived from abstract doctrines. Their object was to give a shape and definition to existing circumstances that would be more conducive to the interests of the East India Company and the productive enterprises of its subjects. Physiocratic radicalism or aristocratic prejudice might shape their conceptions of the order they wanted to impose on the facts; but the facts, in all their complexity, were explored in depth and accepted as the foundation on which to build. The Decennial Settlement, which was subsequently declared Permanent, was based on reports from collectors on the spot on three questions which were addressed to them by the Board of Revenue:

1. What was to be the amount of revenue to be fixed for each collectorate?
2. Who were the class of people with whom this sum was to be settled?
3. What were the regulations necessary for the protection of various rights in the soil?

On the basis of these reports, the government of Calcutta

sent certain general directives to the collectors but each collector was left very much on his own to make arrangements suitable to the local circumstances. Thus a distinctive settlement, arising from local compulsions, emerged in each district.

This being the actual process by which policies were formulated and implemented by a sprawling government which had as yet no time or opportunity to acquire the means of becoming absolute master in each locality, there was no question of conferring on the zamindars rights which did not exist. All that was contemplated was to give a more exact definition to the confused mass of existing rights—to confirm by law the undefined privileges which the zamindars enjoyed by custom. Had the newly-founded government of the East India Company been more established and powerful than it was, it might have tried, like Munro's government of Madras fifteen years later, to bypass the magnates and reach the villages. But even the relatively established Mughal government of Bengal at the height of its power under Murshid Quli Khan had not been able to sweep the zamindaris entirely aside. And, as it turned out, it was not until the British handed over power to the Congress and the Muslim League that the governments of the two Bengals gathered sufficient resources to wipe the zamindaris off the map. Yet the policy outlined by Cornwallis, of carrying out agricultural improvement through a landlord class, might undoubtedly have pointed in the direction of a settlement with the actual controllers of land in the villages (i.e. the jotedars) rather than with those who collected revenue from them by hereditary right.[2] Any form of raiyatwari settlement would have established a direct relationship between the supreme government and the village landlord class. But raiyatwari management through government servants (appointed in place of hereditary zamindars) was ruled out because, as Shore put it, 'it presumes a degree of knowledge, experience and application in the collectors, which is rarely to be found or attained'.[3] Unavoidably, the collector would have to rely

[2]It was calculated by Shore that the land in the actual control of the zamindars—such as khamar, nankar, and nij jote— never exceeded 3% upon the jama. N.K. Sinha, op. cit., p. 214.

[3]Shore's minute of 18 June 1789 in Appendix to the Fifth Report, *Parliamentary Papers*, sess. 1812, Vol. VII.

on native subordinate agents with local interests incompatible with those of the government, and if he was not sufficiently skilled in detecting fraud in revenue accounts, public loss would be considerable. The zamindars would take to intrigue in their idleness and would apply themselves against the success of the collector. The government would have no security of revenue and would have to stand losses and accident of seasons.

In short, the exigencies of revenue collection compelled a weak government to settle with people who ran a government of their own. The most important task of government, collection of the land revenue, was contracted out to them on a perpetual basis. But a weak government could only give away that it possessed: the right to collect revenue. It could not seize and give away what it did not possess: the land occupied by the village landlords. Nor did it intend to. The perpetual assignment of the right to collcct revenue did not mean, either in law or in practice, that other rights in land were extinguished. All it meant was that the government could hence demand no more than the sum contracted for by the zamindars and taluqdars in 1793. This sum was assessed on the basis of the jama fixed on lands under cultivation at the Decennial Settlement, after deducting from it a percentage (theoretically 10 per cent from the government demand of revenue but in practice varying between 10 and 50 per cent) as the proprietary right of the zamindars. To this percentage on the produce of the lands in cultivation, the zamindars were at liberty to add what they could obtain from new lands brought under cultivation without paying anything further to the government.[4] The proportionate claim of the government on the produce of the land was so large in 1793 that the Bengali zamindars, compared with English landlords, could but claim to be imperfect landlords. The margin of their property was so narrow that in the next

[4]Whether they could obtain the whole economic rent of the new lands or only a portion of it as tribute depended on whether they undertook extension of cultivation themselves or leased jungle lands out to the jotedars. Unless the social basis of production changed, it was likely that the crucial component of capital and enterprise necessary for the clearing of forests at the most economically competitive rates would continue to be supplied by professional agriculturists possessing men and money.

sixteen years, as calculated by Islam, nearly seven-tenths of their 'properties' changed hands. By means of local studies, we shall try to explore the effects of these transfers in depth. It should be borne in mind that these properties were not actual lands, but perpetual rights in revenue management subject to the payment of government dues. In an interesting minute on the rights of the zamindars under the Permanent Settlement, Cumming observed:

> The rights conferred upon the Zemindars with whom the Permanent Settlement was concluded, consisted of the perpetual assignment of a portion of the Circar dues from the land, which was payable by the royts, at the period when the arrangement took place, and what would be the Circar dues from the lands then waste, when brought into cultivation; in consideration of which, the Zemindars undertook to pay a fixed annual sum to government, subject neither to increase nor abatement. The rights granted to the Zemindar on the above condition are proprietary rights in the Circar share of the produce of the land and not in the land itself; and these he can sell, mortgage, and bequeath, in any way he pleases, subject to the performance of the tenure under which they were granted. If the Zemindar be not the actual proprietor of the lands within his Zemindarry, they are not his landed Estate, nor is it correct to describe as "lands" the Zemindarry property derived from the Permanent Settlement, which may under the Regulations be sold by the government for the liquidation of arrears on the part of a Zemindar; for that which is sold, is not land, but a portion of the rights and advantages accruing from a given portion of land, which are vested in the Zemindar by that Settlement .... The restrictions and limitations of the rights of Zemindars, under the Permanent Settlement as prescribed by the Bengal Reg VII. 1793 . . . are irreconcilable with their being proprietors of the land within their Zemindarries and of the Zemindarries being distinct landed estates. . . .[5]

[5]Home Miscellaneous, Vol. 530, pp. 493-500, 'Rights Conferred on Zamindars by the Bengal Regulations (i.e. the Permanent Settlement), Cumming's Observations on a Memorandum from the India House'.

The regulations of 1793 specifically limited the rights of the zamindars by the rights of the raiyats. The government reserved the right of legislation to regulate their relations, and the importance of this reservation was proved by the passing of the Rent Act of 1859 and the Bengal Tenancy Act of 1885. The rights that the Governor General-in-Council and the Court of Directors proposed for the raiyats under the Permanent Settlement were very different from those of tenants under English landlords and quite inconsistent with the existence of the proprietor of the land in the person of the zamindar. The zamindars were not landed proprietors before 1793, nor were they constituted as such by the Regulations of 1793.[6] In the absence of any radical change in the social basis of production after the Permanent Settlement,[7] the zamindars were afforded no opportunity for converting their title to revenue collection into actual possession of land. The state of agricultural technology did not permit large-scale farming directed from estates. As Justice Phear observed in an address to the Bengal Social Science Association in 1872, the zamindar

> never did, and he does not to this day, stand towards the ryot in the position which the English landlord occupies relative to his tenant. The area of his zemindary covered large districts of country, and was reckoned not in *beegahs*, but in communities of men (mouzahs). The money-proceeds of his zemindary were not spoken of as rent, but as village collections (the jumma of the mouzah). The *assets* of a zemindary made up of the jummas of sub-tenures and of mouzahs very little resembled the *rental* of an English estate. The zemindar himself was a superior lord, enjoying personal privileges, and through officers exercising some powers of local administration. The population of the villages in his zemindary were his subjects (ryots). And it is not until you get within the mouzah itself that you find any one concerned with the actual land.

[6] Ibid., pp. 505-537, 'Rights of Zemidars and Ryots, Notes prepared by Cumming for the Board of Control'.

[7] Cultivation continued on the basis of small plots of raiyati land worked by the raiyats themselves or by their under-tenants, sharecroppers and hired labourers.

> How little the two cases of zemindar and landlord were parallel to each other in those older days may be perceived from a comparison which may be made even now. If an English landlord says, I have fine estate in such and such a country, he mentally refers to the amount of the acreage, the fertility of the soil, the beauty of the landscape, and so on, not at all to the tenants, the labourers, or the dwelling-houses, which may be on the land; whereas if a zemindar makes a like remark, he has in his mind the number and importance of the villages, which form the zemindary, and their respective jummas, but he takes no thought about the actual land.[8]

The mistake about the identity of the zamindars did not, therefore, bring about an actual change in their role. Lord Cornwallis might persuade himself that he was conferring a great boon on the magnates of Bengal by calling them landlords. But the magnates disagreed in no uncertain terms and their fierce resistance to several features of the Permanent Settlement (which ultimately forced the government to add Regulation 7 of 1799 and Regulation 5 of 1812 to make the package acceptable) was due to real loss of important powers. For while there were ample grounds for doubting whether the zemindars had grown more like landlords under the Permanent Settlement, there was no room for doubt that they had become less like the territorial lords they had been before.

Abolition of the Principalities

The real changes brought about by the Premanent Settlement in the position of the zamindars lay in an altogether different direction from that intended by Cornwallis. The role of the zamindars, after all, lay in the governance of the country; and it was here that Cornwallis' judicial and administrative reforms brought about a great transformation. The whole structure of government was altered in such a way that the arena of the zamindars shifted from principalities to localities. They had represented government to the people at large, for government

[8]J.P. Phear, 'On some Features of Litigation in Bengal', *Transactions of the Bengal Social Science Association*, Vol. VI, 1872.

had been built on and fused with revenue collection. Now police and judicial functions were made into a separate category from revenue collection and converted into a branch of the supreme government through the newly built machinery of district administration. From a public organization administering the country by customary right, zamindari became a private establishment collecting revenue on a permanent contract. The structure of zamindari was distorted, its social necessity (as distinct from the political and administrative need of a weak government) destroyed. As long as the supreme government had not maintained a direct presence in the districts, zamindari had rested deeply and solidly in the needs of the community. Once the supreme government began to establish a presence in the countryside, the social reason for the existence of zamindari disappeared.

The most revolutionary innovation in the field of governance in the history of British administration in Bengal was the establishment, by Cornwallis, of a network of collectorates and magistracies (later fused into a single unit under a district officer keeping peace and collecting revenue). Under the Nawabs of Murshidabad there had been, in theory, a roughly comparable unit of territory called the sarkar; but as we have seen, in practice it had no administrative substance. Insofar as the Nizamat had a machinery of district government, it was controlled on a hereditary basis by the big Rajas. All this was changed by Cornwallis. Each big zamindari of Bengal—Burdwan, Birbhum, Nadia, Jessore, Rajshahi, and Dinajpur—were constituted as separate collectorates and smaller zamindaris and taluqs were amalgamated into collectorates of similar size. Each Raja now found a British officer who was permanently stationed in the sadr breathing down his neck, examining his accounts, ordering his officers, selecting his farmers, receiving petitions from his raiyats, in short telling him how to run his zamindari.[9] For the Board of Revenue had 'deemed it expedient

[9]In Nadia Collector Redfearn, discovering in 1786 that the Raja had received from his farmers the previous year sums of money beyond the amount specified and had collected through them unauthorized taxes from the raiyats for his religious ceremonies, ordered the farmers not to pay revenue larger than the sum engaged for, or else they would be dismissed.

ent to revert of Ancient Usage, and to consider the zemindarry cutcherries as offices of Government, where the business shall be conducted by the Zemindarry Amlah, but under the Superintending Control of the Collector whose orders they must obey and furnish him with all such accounts as he may require.'[10]

It was no easy task that the Board of Revenue assigned to the collectors. From Rajshahi Peter Speke wrote to the Board:

> In my situation in Rajshye, what between the pleas of the revenue, the evasions, delays and at last Disobedience of the Rannees Paishkar and Amlah, I have been constantly baffled in the most essential part of my duty—In spite of unwearied and very willing Exertions to give Redress to the Ryots, all the relief that they have yet got from me, is the conviction that I wanted but could not effect it for them.[11]

No collector could intervene effectively in the mufassal business for the protection of the raiyats from exactions without impairing the authority of the zamindar and endangering the collections. If exactions were proved on enquiry, who was to make redress to the raiyats—the zamindar or his karmacharis? If it was to be the zamindar, then the Raja of Rajshahi was in balance himself, and when the collector could not get the public revenue, would he make the Raja repay the raiyats? If it was to be the Raja's officers, then the karmacharis were produced—if they were produced at all—in irons, 'in the most miserable and squalid appearance'. The zamindar would insist that they had collected for themselves and were largely in

Hearing complaints of exactions by the Raja, he summoned the farmers and had them refund the money unjustly collected from the raiyats. Nadia Old English Correspondence, Issue 1786-1787: Vol. 2, letter no. 105, collector Redfearn to BR, 19 August 1786, and letter no. 110, Collector Redfearn to BR, 30 August, 1786.

[10]To make the order effective, the Board of Revenue continued: 'The collector shall also station officers in the Zemindarry Cutcherry to take an account of the daily Receipts of Revenue the allowance to whom shall be degraded from the present Establishment of the Zemindarry Amlah.' BRP, 8 May 1787, BR to Collector of Rangpur, D.H. Macdowall.

[11]BRP, 13 April 1787, Collector of Rajshahi to BR, dt.31 March 1787.

balance to him. The karmacharis, flatly denying this, would plead that the engagement (tahud) had been taken from them by force, that the country did not produce the amount, that some villages had been taken from their jurisdiction without being deducted from their undertaking, that they had been put to expenses without reimbursement and that they had not been fully credited for the revenue they had sent. 'These pleas, or some of them are made by all, in the midst of Clamours of Hundreds of Ryots, shoal succeeding shoal, in the months of April and May, the hottest months in the year, while contention with the zamindar for his Balance is strongest—How is it possible for the Collector to do anything effectual?' asked Peter Speke in despair.

But however ineffectual he might feel, it was the very presence of the British officer, on a permanent basis, that slowly but surely altered the framework of governance. When the Committee of Revenue (the Board's predecessor) sent Vansittart to Nadia after Raja Krishnachandra fell into balance in 1783, his instruction was 'to take charge of the District, and to use the most effectual means to destroy all the Influence and the Authority of the Rajah, and his officers'.[12] As the collectorate system became organized for the first time in the course of the settlement operations of the Decennial and Permanent Settlement, a flood of regulations began to sweep away the regional power of the Rajas.[13] The troops of the Rajas were disbanded, police was taken out of their hands, customs duties were abolished from their jamabandi, taluqs were separated from their zamindaris, embankments (pulbandi) were made over from them to contractors, and rent-free grants to their dependents and servants were resumed as far as possible. From

[12]To give effect to this instruction, Vansittart was 'empowered to resume all grants of lands and alienations from the Revenue and annex them to the Jumma'. Home Miscellaneous, Vol. 205, Vansittart's Nuddea Deputation, 1783.

[13]So decisive did the policies of the collectors become for the zamindars that the diwan of the Raja of Nadia promised to give 200 bighas of rent-free brahmottar land to the collector's Bengali writer to be kept informed of the collector's correspondence with the Board of Revenue. Nadia Old English Correspondence, Issue 1785-86, Vol. 1, Collector Redfearn to BR, 24 February 1786.

1786 to 1793 a great revolution in the structure of government led to the replacement of the Rajs by the collectorates as the units of district administration. And as the Rajs broke up one by one after 1793 under the hammer blows of the Permanent Settlement, the collectorates which presided over their disintegration emerged as the decisive centres of power and decision-making. The zamindars continued by right to collect revenue and by practice to exercise local government; but only at mauza or pargana level, and that too under competition with local agents of the supreme government like the darogas of police, with whom they had to strike bargains in order to achieve the ends of local power.

The organization of local establishments of regular police under government-appointed darogas was, indeed, as fundamental a revolution in the structure of rule as the creation of collectorates and magistracies at district level. Under the police reforms of 1792 zamindars and farmers were ordered to discharge their police establishments and were prohibited from entertaining them in future. The following year the newly-established magistracies were divided into police jurisdictions (thanas) of 20 square miles[14] and were committed to darogas with establishments of policemen[15] paid by the government. The village watchmen (paiks) who had so long served the mufassal kacharis of the zamindars were placed under the orders of the darogas.[16] The efficiency of zamindaris

[14]But this prescribed limit of the thana was often exceeded in practice.

[15]Usually the local thana would include a daroga, a muhrir (writer), one or more jamadars (leaders of detached police parties on assignments) and 10 to 40 barkandazes (matchbockmen). Home Miscellaneous, Vol. 692, pp. 173-208, 'Police in the Territories under the Supreme Government, March 1811'.

[16]Nevertheless, the authority of the zamindars over the paiks was not altogether abolished, for the zamindars were required to replace dead or removed paiks. The archives of the Church Missionary Society contains an interesting Bengali manuscript muchleka (written undertaking) to an ijaradar (farmer) in Burdwan, Gourikanta Mukherjee, by the paiks of Kalna market, Kriparam Sardar, Haridas Paik and Gangaram Paik, dated 1831, by which they undertook to be present for watch in the watch-posts (chowkis) of Ambikanagar, Kalnar Ganj, Laksmiganj and Chakchandni. to obey all orders, to inform the local naib of the zamindar and the

as police jurisdictions was thus impaired in such a way that when the government decided to obtain the aid of the zamindars for the suppression of robbery in 1800,[17] not much help could be secured from the zamindars who naturally avoided responsibility without power. Whereas formerly they had enjoyed unfettered authority as arbiters in local disputes and affrays, now the darogas, who came to control the decisive means of physical coercion in the localities, established an oppressive hold on the country from which the zamindars could not expect to be exempted without offering favourable terms in the bargains of local power.[18] In the traditional order of things, people expressed good wishes by pronouncing 'Be ye a raja'. Under the new order of the Company, they began to say, 'Be ye a daroga'.[19]

---

daroga of police at once upon any theft, murder or arson, to pay fines decided upon in the court of the ijaradar upon failure to inform and to carry out instructions by the ijaradar for collection of the revenue. They undertook not to try to escape from these duties on the plea that they were under the orders of the official police and promised to keep a watch on strangers in the markets and to keep out all branded persons among strangers from other jurisdictions. In the strictly local arena, therefore, the zamindars and their farmers and officers apparently continued to exercise considerable police powers. Church Missionary Society Records, CI 1/022/9/1, muchleka to Gourikanta Mukherjee by Kriparam Sardar, Gangaram Paik and Haridas Paik, 25 Agrahayan 1237, B.S.

[17]Birbhum Old English Correspondence, Letters Received, No, 830, Secretary to Government to Magistrate of Birbhum, dt. 1 April 1801.

[18]As early as 1793 the the zamindar of Chitwa complained against unwarrantable exactions from himself and his raiyats by the daroga of police, Durlabh Ram, who exacted Rs 85 from raiyats as salami, Rs 25 from a father by accusing his son of theft, and Rs 5 from another householder for having an illicit connection with a woman. The daroga was dismissed by the government, but such dismissals were rare and did nothing to check the rapacity of the darogas. Bengal Criminal and Judicial Consultations, Criminal Branch, 23 August 1793, No. 11, Collector of Midnapur to Governor-General-in-Council, dt. 15 August 1793.

[19]A vernacular newspaper commented in 1830: 'In the realm of the company the police daroga may be pronounced to be a "man-lion" (a sarcastic allusion to a Sanskrit verse which extols the enterprise of those lion-like men who are embraced by the Goddess of Wealth) inasmuch as by his own wits he becomes invested in such a great post where he feathers his own nest by pure fraud and deceit and after performing his service for a few years accumulates so much wealth that becoming a superior or resigning his post he spends his whole life in the happiness of a rich man—

HAPTAM, (REGULATION 7 OF 1799) AND PANJAM (REGULATION 5 OF 1812)

Because of these fundamental changes in the structure of rule, the zamindars found their authority vis-a-vis the village oligarchies considerably weakened in the 1790s. The new judicial regulations of the Company prohibited flagellation and confinement in irons for the realization of dues from the raiyats,[20] and though the zamindars continued to have recourse to these methods in the mufassal, the presence of courts, collectorates and magistracies in the sadr hindered the free exercise of coercion, especially in respect of those influential raiyats whose ready wits enabled them to manipulate the new structure of rule to protect their village power from interference by the zamindars. During the period from 1770 to 1799, until Regulation 7 was passed in order to strengthen the hands of the zamindars, the ruling village cliques exploited both economic and administrative changes to acquire powers and privileges which they had never enjoyed before, nor were destined to enjoy for a long time afterwards.

The zamindars, on the other hand, encountered unprecedented difficulties in the collection of revenue which, for the moment, seemed to render the acquirement of permanent proprietary rights a hollow gain. Large balances of revenue stood against every important zamindari, caused by refractory conduct of underrentersand raiyats; and these balances had to be realized by the selling of 'lots' of mauzas and mahals prepared by the collectors. In Burdwan alone the number of suits for arrears of revenues from raiyats, which the civil court with its extensive jurisdiction could not possibly deal with in the lifetime of a judge, was thirty thousand in 1795. From Bishnupur the sarbarakar appointed by the government to take charge of the zamindari complained in the same year that the qutqinadars (village farmers who in this district, it will be remembered, were mandals) were deliberately withholding payments, taking advantage of the delay in the judicial process.[21] From Birbhum the collector wrote that in his

wealth which God-fearing and respectable man cannot accumulate even if they work their whole lives. *Samachar Chandrika,* 14 June 1830.

[20] BRC, 20 July 1729, No. 15, Harrington, Commissioner of Rajshahi, to BR, dt. 29 June 1792.

[21] Bengal Judicial Proceedings, Civil Branch, 27 March 1795, No. 17.

opinion the balance in his district arose from the refusal to discharge kists (instalments of revenue) by raiyats and farmers, who knew that the zamindar had no further power over them than that of prosecuting them in the district court.[22] It was not that all raiyats had suddenly been emboldened by the new rule of law to defy their zamindars; the problem was that under-farmers and head raiyats were collecting and pocketing the instalments, testing the power of their masters to make them punctually discharge revenue under the new dispensation.

There was, moreover, about this time a temporary economic depression which made matters worse in the business of revenue collection. Immediately after the famine of 1770, inflationary conditions had prevailed for some time and the prices of grain, sugar, and raw silk had risen very greatly.[23] But in the 1790s the ruling prices of agricultural produce proved to be much lower than in the previous decades, and it was not until the beginning of the nineteenth century that the depression fully lifted.[24] During this decade, therefore, the zamindars found it difficult to pay the revenue, as the raiyats found the cash prices obtained by marketing produce with which they paid revenue rather lower than before. At the same time, the zamindars were required to discharge every instalment of revenue with unprecedented punctuality, on pain of the dismemberment of their estates. Many zamindars were hit hard by these simultaneous happenings; those who survived through the stormy nineties were finally rescued by Regulation 7 and a lift in prices from 1800.

Because of the accumulating arrears of revenue and the heavy sale of estates, the government was ultimately forced to pursue the modifications in the structure of rule to their logical end. The zamindars lost their regional power in relation to the govern-

---

[22]Birbhum Old English Correspondence, Issue Register 1799-1801, Collector of Birbhum to BR, dt. 26 August 1799.

[23]Francis Manuscripts, Mss. Eur. E. 28, Vansittart to Governor-General-in-Council on Burdwan Settlement, 20 January 1775; and the Account of the State of the Country given by Middleton, Dacres, and Vansittart in reply to queries of the Council, 1775; Home Miscellaneous, Vol. 766, 'Of a Free Trade in Bengal'; Mss. Eur. D. 281 'Historical Review of the External Commerce of Calcutta from 1750 until 1830'.

[24]Bengal Commercial Reports 1795-1802, Thomas Brown to Board of Trade, 8 August 1801.

ment but acquired more local power in relation to the raiyats. By Regulation 7 of 1799, the new legal and judicial machinery of the British government was ranged squarely behind the zamindars in their endeavours for realizing the revenue. This regulation empowered them, on the ground of arrears of revenue from raiyats, to summarily distrain and sell the latter's property through munsifs and qazis without going through the delaying procedure of the courts. Under the regulation the raiyats had no redress against unjust distraint and sale of property on fictitious charges of arrears of revenue except a tedious and uncertain prosecution by appeal to the civil court which generally completed his ruin. By Regulation 5 of 1812 the law was modified slightly in favour of the raiyats conferring on them the right to contest the demand by giving security and executing bond to the amount of the demand, whereupon the cases would be referred to the collector for summary decision.[25] In other ways, however, Regulation 5 took away important privileges from the raiyats, for it was based on a minute from Colebrooke which suggested that there was no need, in view of altered economic and social relationships to regulate engagements between zamindars and raiyats and that the zamindars should be given full liberty to make contracts with the raiyats to their mutual advantage.[26] Accordingly Regulation 5 rescinded the earlier regulations of the Permanent Settlement which entitled the raiyats to ten-year renewable leases and give the zamindars and raiyats liberty to come to any agreement they might reach.[27] In such a freely adjustable relationship, the advantage naturally lay with the zamindars who had the resources to utilize the courts and the police.

In effect, then, the zamindars, while losing the pomp and power of the local princes, obtained access to the means of coercion acquired by a centralizing and bureaucratic state. But the power of the state now stood impersonally and independently

---

[25]Home Miscellaneous, Vol. 775, Judicial Nuddea, 1816.

[26]Bengal Civil and Judicial Proceedings, Civil Branch, 1 May 1812, No. 17, Colebrooke's minute of 1 May 1812.

[27]T. Sisson, Late Judge and Magistrate of Rangpur to W.B. Bayley, Acting Secretary to Government, Judicial Department, 2 April 1815, printed in Appendix A No. 3 in E.A. Glazier, *Further Notes on Rungpore Records*, Vol. II (Calcutta 1876).

of its local beneficiaries and might in time be utilized to effeet changes in the balance of power in the localities. For the moment the zamindars were able to utilize the official means of coercion for their unofficial and private ends by forming local alliances with the darogas of police.[28] With this newly acquired power they sought to appropriate the increasing rents of the country arising from the rise of prices of agricultural produce, extension of cultivation and introduction of more cash crops. But since the social basis of production was still the small raiyati holding cultivated from generation to generation by the same family, and as the raiyats continued by custom to regard themselves as the owners of their holdings, a contest followed between different categories of landholders over the sharing of the increased economic rent value. In each case the issue of the contest depended on local circumstances and can best be examined by local studies.

[28]Birbhum Old English Correspondence, Issue Register October 1808 to March 1811, Magistrate of Birbhum to Secretary to Government, Judicial Department, dt. 15 August 1810. The Magistrate wrote: 'I have ascertained that the great body of the People are entirely subject to their (zamindars) influence and power; that it is the first object of every zamindar to establish an interest with the Police and Sudder officers; and that they keep agents both at the Thanah, and the magistrate's Cutcherry, to afford them early notice of the orders, and Proceedings of those authorities, to counteract their operation, when adverse to their Interest'.

5

Burdwan

The area comprising the zamindari of Burdwan—an extensive river-intersected tract of old alluvial deposit—consisted for the most part of rich rice-producing plains. Its population consisted of Rarhi Brahmans and Kayasthas (a large number of whom, unlike the more prosperous Vangaja Kayasthas and Varendra Brahmans of East and North Bengal respectively, were agriculturists, though not actual holders of ploughs) as well as of dominant cultivating castes like the Sadgops, Aguris and Kaivartas, below whom stood untouchable landless castes like the Bagdis and the Bauris. The Sadgops were the largest agricultural caste in the area and dominated many of its villages before as well as during the administration of the Rajas of Burdwan. Before the rise of the house of Burdwan, their political power in the region—based on the dominant position of Sadgop agriculturists in the villages—was reflected in the existence of Sadgop principalities in the Gopbhum tract immediately north of Burdwan town. The Sadgop Rajas of Amragarh, with the subordinate houses of Kanksa and Bharatpur, ruled over Gopbhum before the rise of the house of Burdwan.[1] When the regional political power of the Sadgops was eclipsed by the expansion of the zamindari of Burdwan, the domination of the Sadgop groups at the village level continued as before.

The Burdwan Raj was a deliberate creation of Mughal official policy, which promoted its growth as a means of bringing the

[1]Hitesranjan Sanyal, 'Continuities of Social Mobility in Traditional and Modern Society in India: Two Case Studies of Caste Mobility in Bengal," *Journal of Asian Studies*, February 1971.

area under government control through a loyal princely house. The existence of semi-independent kingdoms like those of Chitwa and Amragarh was a threat to the security of the Mughal state in Bengal, as was amply demonstrated by the rebellion of Sobha Singh of Chitwa in 1696. As a means of destroying these principalities the Nizamat created and expanded the zamindari of Burdwan, which was held by an upcountry immigrant Khatri family with no local military base and therefore deemed to be worthy of trust. In 1694, the Rajas of Amragarh were reduced to the position of feudatories of the Burdwan family which secured zamindari rights over Gopbhum under the orders of Aurangzeb.[2] Three years later the rebellious house of Chitwa was also reduced to the position of feudatory under the Burdwan family. Feeding on state patronage the zamindari of Burdwan grew steadily in the first half of the eighteenth century. The expansion of the Burdwan Raj profoundly changed the political superstructure in the area, leading to the destruction of powerful principalities outside the political orbit of the Nizamat, the extension of government control through a reliable local power, and the realization of a much greater amount of land revenue. But the superimposition of the Burdwan family over this huge area does not seem to have changed the realities of economic and political power lower down the hierarchy of social organization, especially at the village level. In each village, the Raj faced an intricate set of superordinate-subordinate relationships based on crop-sharing, credit-giving and rent-collecting. Without coming to terms with these village relationships, the Raj would not have been able to collect the revenue: dominant agriculturist groups of Sadgops, Aguris, Kayasthas, Brahmans and Muslims who enjoyed most of the village lands continued to exercise control over their respective villages. Higher up the social hierarchy, there existed in the area a solid local gentry who continued to hold and acquire landed rights under the Burdwan Raj—and whom the Raj had to accommodate in its structure of revenue collection and zamindari administration. This was the country of Rarh, the home of the ancient and ritually high-ranking Rarhi section of the Brahmans and the Kayasthas. The

[2]Ibid.

revenue-collecting rights which these high caste gentry enjoyed over groups of villages all over Rarh could not be abolished by the growth of the Burdwan Raj which, therefore, accommodated them by granting revenue-free lands, temporary farms and high positions in the zamindari administration. The ancient rights in the land were overlaid by a new political super-structure but by no means abolished.[3]

At the time of the British takeover, the Burdwan Raj was thus of a fairly recent growth when compared to other existing landed rights which had been subordinated to it in the course of its expansion. This fact becomes evident upon a close examination of the history of the Raj prior to the British take-over. Although the original possessions of the family were acquired as far back as 1680, it was only during the rule of Maharaja Kirtichand (1701-1739) that the family came to possess the premier Raj in Bengal, paying the highest revenue among all Bengal zamindars. The founder of the family, an enterprising upcountry Khatri (a trading caste of Punjab claiming Khatriya status) named Abu, who helped the faujdar of Chakla Burdwan with foodgrains and transport at a critical time, was appointed chaudhuri in 1680 to a few mahals. His ancestors lived in Kotli until his grandfather settled down in Baikantpur near Burdwan and engaged himself in commerce and money-lending. Abu's son, Kishen babu, obtained possession of pargana Burdwan on the dismissal of its zamindar Ram Ray. At this stage, the family had only four mahals in its possession. Kishen babu was succeeded by Ghanashyam and the latter by Krishnaram, who obtained possession of the zamindari of Azmatshahi and two or three other parganas and was honoured with a farman from Emperor Alamgir. He was killed in 1696 by the zamindar of Chitwa, Sobha Singh, who rose in rebellion against the Mughal government. After the suppression of this rebellion, Krishnaram's son Jagatram was not only reinstated in his father's zamindari but obtained an additional four mahals.

[3]There are few contemporary sources of evidence on the social impact of the growth of the Burdwan Raj, but the nature of this impact can be deduced retrospectively from the records which become available from the early years of British rule, which contain ample evidence of the influence of dominant land-holding village groups and high caste gentry.

His son Kirtichand was a warrior prince who immensely enhanced the zamindari by his wars against neighbouring magnates. With the favour of the faujdar of Hugli, Kirtichand acquired the zamindaris of Naranarayan and Shibchand, zamindars of Manoharshahi and Bhursut, who fell into disfavour with the faujdar. Kirtichand also got pargana Mandalghat from Murshid Quli Khan when the chaudhuris of the pargana were dispossessed because of their notorious conduct. Kirtichand fought against the Rajas of Chandrakona and Bardah and dispossessed them of their petty kingdoms. He also seized the possessions of the Raja of Balghara near the famous temple of Tarakeswar. His boldest military expedition was directed against the Raja of Bishnupur whom he defeated in war. Kirtichand's son Chitrasen Rai (1739-1744) added Arsa to the Burdwan Raj from Narsing Deb Roy by working in collusion with an officer of Nawab Sarfaraz Khan. He also defeated the last Raja of Amragarh and annexed Gopbhum as an integral part of his zamindari without intermediary vassals. At its fullest extent, the Burdwan Raj covered the whole of the future collectorates of Burdwan and Hugli and parts of Midnapur. It was smaller in area than the Natore Raj, but much more compact and considerably richer.[4]

However, the administration of the Burdwan Raj was no more centralized than that of the zamindaris of Rajshahi and Dinajpur and at the time of the British takeover it was at least as riven by faction at the top as the other two zamindaris. The tussle between diwan Brajakishore and the dowager Rani Bishnukumari fed the disputes in the highest councils of the Company's government, which was divided into the two hostile camps of Warren Hastings and Philip Francis. Brajakishore ruled the zamindari of Burdwan with the help of Warren Hastings' party against the active opposition of Philip Francis and his followers who backed Rani Bishnukumari. Brajakishore ultimately lost

[4]N.K. Sinha, *Economic History of Bengal*, Vol. II, 'Territorial Aristocracy of Bengal', No. 1, 'The Burdwan Raj', *Calcutta Review*, Vol. LIV, 1872, *Bengal District Gazetteer*, *Burdwan*, J.C.K. Paterson, p. 193; Santosh Chakravarty, 'The History' of the Relations of the Rajas of Burdwan and the East India Company, 1760-1832, unpublished thesis, University of Burdwan.

Genealogical tree of Burdwan Raj

Sangam Rai
Banku Bihari
Abu Rai (founder)
Babu Rai
Ghanashyam Rai
Krishnaram Rai

Jagatram Rai

Kirtichand — Mitrasen Rai
Chitrasen Rai — Tilakchand

Tilakchand = Bishnukumari, Rupkumari

Tejchand = Jaya, Prem, Sitab, Tej, Nanki, Ujjal, Kamal, Basanta

Pratapchand and Mahtabchand (adopted son of Pranchand Kapur, brother of Kamalkumari).

Source: Santosh Chakravarty, The History of the Relations of the Rajas of Burdwan and the East India Company, 1760-1832, unpublished thesis, University of Burdwan.

the battle as he could not discharge revenue arrears and Bishnukumari was vested with the management of the zamindari on behalf of her minor son Tejchand.[5] The elimination of Brajakishore did not end the struggle for power within the Burdwan Raj as the relations between Bishnukumari and her young son, Maharaja Tejchand, were poisonous. Tejchand, at the instigation of his followers, tried to dispossess the dowager Rani from the Dewry Mahals traditionally made over to the Ranis by the Rajas of Burdwan. For a time, Bishnukumari's ungrateful servants brought Tejchand to Calcutta, lived with the powerful diwan of the Company, Gangagovinda Singh, and had the young Raja at their disposal.[6]

At the time of the Permanent Settlement the whole of the Burdwan Raj, measuring 4,800 square miles according to Rennell's map, was let out in 92 revenue farms of the first grade (sadr ijaras).[7] An attempt by the collector in 1793 to sell parts

[5]Santosh Chakravarty, op. cit.

[6]BRP, 16 June 1787, No. 61. Arzee of Rany of Burdwan.

[7]BRP, 24 June 1793, to BR from Collector of Burdwan.

of the zamindari in lots to recover arrears revealed how loose was the structure of management of the Burdwan Raj. The Raja himself possessed no information as to the relative assessment of the lots in his zamindari. All information relating to these matters was the monopoly of four sadr officers of the Raj who were away at the time in Calcutta: Nandakumar Ray, diwan; Gangaram Mitra, karkun; Debnath Singh Chaudhuri, keeper of records; and Budden Mitra, principal counsellor and manager of different departments. These four officials, moreover, were all farmers of the first degree.[8] These farmers were called sadr mustajirs, who in turn let out their farms to sub-farmers called qutqinadars. Many of the sadr mustajirs, who were mostly relations and dependents of the Raja, had held their revenue farms almost as ancestral estates and their attachment to their farms was such that out of fear of dispossession they were prepared to bid higher than the real value of the farms.[9] The collector could not find in the sadr office of the zamindari, records pertaining to mufassal affairs from which a detailed knowledge of village assessments (on the basis of which he was to fix the assessment of the lots to be sold) could be gathered.[10] The Raja of Burdwan objected to the roughly estimated assessment of the lots (hudas) proposed for sale, for the sadr mustajirs sometimes intentionally underlet portions of their farms at a very low rate to their friends and dependents as qutqinadars. As the assessments assigned by the collector to the lots were founded on the qutqina jama (assessment of under-farms), the assessment of a lot fell below the standard of the zamindari as a whole in every case in which the qutqinas were under-assessed. The Raja feared that, in consequence, the mahals left to him would be over-assessed. This whole situation arose from the fact that the Raja in his sadr office possessed no effective information that would enable him to check fraud in the mufassal. The sadr mustajirs virtually excluded the Raja from the possession of information, and

[8]Ibid.

[9]H. Verelst, *A View of the Rise, Progress and Present State of the English Government in Bengal*, (London 1771), p. 214-216.

[10]BRP, 24 June 1793, to BR from Collector of Burdwan.

manipulated the apportionment of the assessment in the mufassal in their own favour.

In the mufassal, qutqinadars and zamindari servants knew nothing of the engagements between the Raja and the sadr mustajirs. The mufassal staff of the zamindari and the village farmers stood at a great distance from the Raja and his sadr farmers. The village farmers were in real possession of the villages, and the Raja's shiqdars, who were appointed only to collect revenue from the farmers, did not have the least pretension to interfere.[11] A qutqinadar was given a whole village in farm, including paddy, cotton, mulberry and salt land; no separate farms were created for these products for fear that if raiyats in a village were placed under more than one master, they would soon be left without any.[12]

Having obtained possession of a whole village, a farmer advanced loans to raiyats in the hope of purchasing from them grain, salt and other produce in preference to any other purchaser. Loans were also given in the hope of turning uncultivated lands, which raiyats ordinarily would not have cultivated, into cultivated lands. Usually the raiyats could dispose of their produce to anyone they liked and the farmer received his dues according to prevailing rates per bigha specified in the raiyati leases. But if the raiyats refused to work a particular piece of land, as happened often for lack of funds or accidents of season, the farmer could improve the ground at his own cost and let it to other raiyats on more advantageous terms for himself. Many farms throughout the zamindari of Burdwan paid less to the farmer than he paid to the zamindar owing to the former ijaradars having, for present or future advantage, granted leases to raiyats on easy terms below valuation. It was only because the village farmers could make up this deficiency by giving advances for the

[11]Rupnarayan Chaudhuri, Shiqdar for pargana Mandalghat, never interfered in village affairs until 1861, when he and Hugli merchants associated with him intervened only in order to ensure fulfilment of a fair contract which they had made with the ijaradars and their tenants, the raiyats, for the supply of produce.

[12]Home Miscellaneous, Vol. 47. Burdwan-lands upon which salt is made—extract of letter from Johnstane to Governor-General-in-Council, 22 Augus 1762.

cultivation of uncultivated lands and thereby obtaining enhancements of rates that they were induced to take farms from the sadr mustajirs.

Under such a system, substantial peasants could obtain permanently under-rated holdings by giving a lump sum to temporary ijaradars who were going to give up their farms next year. Outgoing ijaradars could create such under-rated tenancies for their own future enjoyment or for the benefit of their dependents. New ijaradars in turn had to make up the losses resulting from the fraud of their predecessors by bringing waste lands into cultivation through loans, which always resulted in enhanced rates of revenue. A whole range of political and economic relations in the mufassal thus lay outside the control of the central office of the zamindari, the sadr.[13]

With regard to the distribution of physical force also, the force under the direct command of the Raja was smaller in comparison with the village militia, the paiks, who remained outside the orbit of immediate palace influence. The hereditary militia, maintained by service lands, were mostly under the command of the village and pargana officers of the Raj, and only a small portion of them were huzuri, that is, directly under the order of the Raja and his relations (see Table 5.1). Since this large local militia of about thirty thousand men did not constitute a force readily available

TABLE 5.1

THE MILITIA OF THE BURDWAN RAJ

	Servants	*bighas*
1. Huzuri or servants attending the Raja and his relations, also mutsuddis (officers for collection)	4710	81840
2. Guards in different forts and passes	4793	82332
3. Pargana saranjami or servants in the high roads and head kacharies in each pargana	2683	38038
4. Gram saranjami or servants such as paiks, peons and kotwals allotted for the service of the several villages throughout the province	19846	156906
	32031	358516

Source : Santosh Chakravarty, The History of the Rajas of Burdwan and the East India Company, 1760-1832, unpublished thesis, University of Burdwan. Ch. V.

[13]Ibid.

to the Raja, the Burdwan Raj maintained by cash payments a considerable body of household troops (nagdian troops), whose cost in 1761 was Rs 33,000,[14] by means of which the Burdwan Raj had grown into the premier zamindari in Bengal during and after the administration of Murshid Quli Khan. In spite of his distance from the mufassal farmers and officers, a powerful Raja could keep the holders of under-rights within his jurisdiction under control with the help of his infantry. Thus, Tejchand arbitrarily levied a tribute (salami) of Rs 1,000 from Haider Ali, a dependent taluqdar[15] of Doabashee, and ordered the preparation of a new survey (hast-o-bud) in order to increase the latter's assessment.[16] On another occasion, he forcibly collected Rs 5,000 from Niamutulla, Fate Muhammad, Muhammad Jaffir, etc., nazirs (military officers) who enjoyed whole villages in parganas Arsha and Mandalghat for military service in protecting the inhabitants from Magh incursions. Since no depredations had taken place for some time under the early British government, the Raja considered himself entitled to resume the revenue of these villages and carried out the resumption in spite of the strong complaints made by the nazirs.[17]

With the establishment of the British collectorate in Burdwan, the Raja's authority as a supreme power in the district began to decline. As early as 1767, the cost of the nagdian corps was reduced by the government to Rs 8,660, at which sum Raja Tilakchand was allowed to maintain 149 horses and 690 foot.[18] On the eve of the Decennial Settlement this household corps was totally abolished and only a part of the former military establishment remained under the zamindar[19] who was allowed

[14]Santosh Chakravarty, op. cit., Ch. V.

[15]Dependent taluqs, which contained all the features of zamindari property except the right to pay revenue directly to the government, were not created in any large number by the Rajas of Burdwan, who preferred to integrate the influential local men within the structure of the zamindari by giving them revenue farms which were sometimes hereditary in practice but were technically resumable at will.

[16]BRP, 27 February 1789, No. 17, Report from Rayrayan.

[17]BRP, 13 September 1793, No. 32, to BR from Collector of Burdwan, dt. 25 April 1793.

[18]Santosh Chakravarty, op. cit. Ch. V.

[19]BRP, 3 April 1787, No. 4, to BR from Governor-General-in-Council, dt. 30 March 1787.

a sum of Rs 50,000 for the maintenance of paiks necessary to protect the district.[20] Even this force, nominally under the Raja, was placed at the disposal of the collector for the purpose of revenue collection and peace keeping. As the regular police became organized in Burdwan (which was divided into sixteen thanas with an establishment of one daroga and several constables for each),[21] the Burdwan Raj lost its police functions. Increasingly the village paiks came under the authority of the darogas of the thanas and were removed from the control of the zamindar and his farmers or lessees.[22]

The diminishing status and authority of the Raja under this new structure of rule was accompanied by the establishment of a uniform law of sale for revenue arrears which brought the zamindari close to dismemberment in the first few years of the Permanent Settlement. The loose structure of the Raj was a source of potential danger in this period of crisis, for the considerable sadr mustajirs like Nityalal, Basantalal, Raghuram Mitra, Lala Dayachand and Banarasi Ghose were in the habit of making irregular payments,[23] and the zamindari servants, farmers and qutqinadars were constantly intriguing to reduce the assessment of the mahals under them.[24] Between 1791 and 1816, 93.28 per cent of the revenue-paying landed rights (in terms of the total assessment on lands in Burdwan) changed hands. Of these transferred rights, 50 per cent belonged to the Raja and 43 per cent to other independent proprietors in the district who had settled for the revenue at the Permanent Settlement or had become proprietors later on by purchase. Thus, on paper, the greater part of the zamindari of Burdwan was put up for sale including the private lands like Nankar and Dewry Mahals.

Capitalists from Calcutta were by no means prominent among the purchasers, although many of them worked in the capacity of sezawals (attaching managers on behalf of the government), sadr mustajirs and farmers under the Raja of Burdwan. Nearly

---

[20]BRP, 8 June 1787, No. 25, to BR from Collector of Burdwan, dt. 1 June 1787.

[21]Home Miscellaneous, Vol. 775, Report on the district of Burdwan by N.J. Halhed, Acting Judge and Magistrate 1814.

[22]BRP, 28 May 1819, Nos. 5, 6, Petition from Raja of Burdwan.

[23]BRP, 13 March 1793, No. 6, Petition from Raja of Burdwan.

[24]BRP, 31 October 1794, No. 73, Petition from Bishunkumari.

two-thirds of the rights sold (74.99 per cent) circulated among the inhabitants residing within the districts of Burdwan and Hugli, both of which were included in the zamindari of Burdwan. Purchases made by inhabitants of other districts were practically negligible (3.88 per cent).[25]

However, the Burdwan Raj which had apparently disintegrated at the beginning of the nineteenth century emerged in the twentieth century not only intact but also paying most of the revenue in the district, a fact which demonstrates how misleading the paper transfers were. During the survey and settlement of Burdwan district from 1927 to 1934, over 70 per cent of the entire area in the district was found to be included within the estates of the Raj.[26] Soon after the heaviest sales, the Raja appeared to be solvent enough to buy a market (bazar) in Calcutta and to invest considerable money in Company securities.[27] Reporting on the town of Burdwan in 1830, Reverend W.J. Deerr of Church Missionary Society wrote that the town was flourishing on account of the residence of an opulent Raja whose presence had attracted a great number of persons from different places.[28]

The reason behind the survival of the Burdwan Raj lay in the fact that during the period after the Permanent Settlement, the zamindari came under the expert management of a series of extremely clever administrators who invented a variety of ingenious techniques to fight off the new pressures of British land revenue policy. Raja Tejchand's first move to preserve the zamindari was to transfer it to his mother Rani Bishnukumari by a deed of sale. As collector Davis wrote to the Board of Revenue:

> As far as the Raja's object can be inferred from his conduct in the late transaction, it appears to have been to embezzle

[25]As much as 21 per cent of the purchases were made by people whose residence is not known.

[26]*Final Report on the Survey and Settlement Operations in the District of Burdwan 1927-1934* by K.A.L. Hill and Phanindra Kumar Banerjee, p. 20.

[27]BRP, 18 Juue 1819, No. 12, to BR from Collector of Burdwan, dt. 27 May 1819.

[28]Church Missionary Society, General Information respecting Burdwan and Culna by Rev. W.J. Deerr, CI 1008/46 dt. 22 February 1830. The number of the inhabitants of Burdwan in 1830 was estimated by Reverend Deerr at 40,000.

> as much he could of the rent, and leave government to look to the Ranny for the balance which would happen in consequence. This would not subject the Ranny to any inconvenience, for being by her sex exempted from imprisonment or coercion of any kind, she would remain undisturbed, till the end of the year, while the rajah, no longer subject to restraint, would be at full liberty to try every means he might think conducive to the reduction of the assessment on the district, which appears to me to have been his aim, ever since he entered into his decennial engagement; and should this scheme fail, he might then speculate in regard to any land that might be sold to realize the balance, by repurchasing any mahals offered at an advantageous jumma, leaving the rest to the risk of government, as in the case of Mundulghaut, by the exchange of which disadvantageous mehaul for the one he at the same time purchased in Bishenpore, he has undoubtedly gained very considerably.[29]

As a next successful move, both the Raja and his mother took to rigging the auction sales. They managed to conceal from the collector the relevant papers regarding the mahals to be sold.[30] They deliberately fell into arrears and when their mahals were put up for sale, their agents outbid other purchasers but ultimately did not pay up the purchase money. Repeated sales took place which restrained other people from buying those mahals which had earned the bad reputation of having deficiency of resources.[31] Ultimately, the Raja family succeeded in buying them up at a greatly reduced assessment in fictitious names.

Among the other purchasers, the principal men were Dwarakanath Singh of Singur, Chhaku Singh of Bhastara, the Mukherjis of Janai, and the Banerjis of Telinipara who were all inhabitants of Hugli and rose rapidly to prominence and affluence after the Permanent Settlement. Apart from these big purchasers who

[29]BRP, 14 March 1794, No. 44, to BR from Collector of Burdwan, dt. 27 February 1794.

[30]BRP, 24 April 1794, No. 1, to BR from Collector of Burdwan, dt. 25 April 1794.

[31]Burdwan Old English Correspondence, Issue May 1799—July 1800, Statement of 24 May 1799.

came to constitute a new class of magnates in Hugli and Burdwan, a great number of high caste smaller gentry in these districts bought small lots. Many of the auction purchasers were farmers of the Burdwan Raj, and were fully acquainted with the resources of the lots, while others had been in the service of the Maharaja, and from their long association with zamindari administration knew the ins and outs of the mahals offered at public auctions.[32]

TABLE 5.2

THE SALE OF THE ZAMINDARI OF THE RANI OF BURDWAN, 1797

Purchasers	*Sadr jama*	*Identification*
Ramchand Mukherji Ramprasad Mukherji	133720-12-6-2 30967-13-6-2 }	Relation of Ramkanta Ray who was confident to the Rani
Rupchand Palit	10,016-11-6-2	Vakil (agent) of the Rani stationed in Calcutta and included in the list of her zamindari officers
Sarapchand Ray	334,720-1-18	Zamindari Khazanchi (treasurer) and diwan (manager) of the lots sold
Ramchandra Sein	104,985-3-6	Vakil of the Rani residing in Calcutta
	614410-10-13-2	
Panchanan Sarkar	10401-13-14	A sherista vakil (legal agent) in the Burdwan court. Purchased on his own account
Kesabram Ray	9790-15-6	A farmer of several villages in Burdwan and a man of property. Purchased on his own account
Nilmony Haldar	9721-11-2	Resident of Calcutta and proprietor of Taraf Jagdispur
	29914-8-12	

Source: Miscellaneous Records, Board of Revenue, Registers etc. relating to land and land revenue, Account of Sales, Vol. I, Burdwan, 1794-1800.

[32]'The Burd wan Raj', *Calcutta Review*, p. 180.

The biggest auction purchaser, Dwarakanath Singh of Singur, was a trader as well as a sadr farmer of the Burdwan Raj,[33] and purchased 25 lots bearing an assessment of Rs 489,438.

Many zamindari servants of the Burdwan Raj, besides making purchases on their own account, fictitiously bought lands for Maharaja Tejchand and his mother Maharani Bishnukumari. In 1797, as the Collector discovered later, very few of the mahals sold were actually purchased by individuals on their own account. The genuinely transferred mahals bore an assessment of Rs 29,914 while the mahals sold in name but really bought up by Maharani Bishnukumari under fictitious names were assessed in Rs 614,410.

Raja Tejchand, using the same tactics, saved his lucrative mahals by purchasing them in the names of his wife Kamalkumari and his agents (vakils) Nandakumar Ray, Ramsebak Mallick, Vallabhikanta Das, Brindaban babu and others.[34] The profitable mahals were later transferred to his own name while the unprofitable mahals were held in the name of members of the family like his wife Rani Kamalkumari and his brother-in-law Pranchand Kapur. In case of arrears to be recovered, he got rid of the unprofitable mahals by sale and retained those standing in his own name.[35]

The most striking innovation of the Rajas of Burdwan for the preservation of their zamindari was the notorious sub-infeudatory tenure called patni. Within a few years after the Permanent Settlement, the patni system altered the whole structure of the Burdwan Raj, which became 'one of the largest zamindaries in the Country paying *rent* to Government without the Zamindar having a right to the *actual property* of one Begah scarcely in the

[33]Burdwan Old English Correspondence, Issue 1811, the darkhast of Babu Mahendranath, eldest son of Babu Dwarakanath deceased of Singur and zamindar of pargana Mandalghat; BRP, 8th February 1790, No. 36, to BR from collector of Burdwan dt. 2 February 1790.

[34] Burdwan Old English Correspondence, to BR from Collector of Burdwan, dt. 5 May 1799; BRP, 5 February 1796, No. 10, Petition of Ramsebak Mallick; Ibid., 10 November 1795, No. 13, to BR from Collector of Burdwan; Ibid., 11 November 1794, No. 61 B, Secretary's report to BR.

[35]BRP, 16 May 1800, No. 7, to BR from Collector of Burdwan, dt. 12 May 1800.

soil, but merely a title to the Rents'.[36] Sub-infeudation of the landed rights, however, was not a phenomenon which arose after the Permanent Settlement. In the Burdwan Raj, as we have seen, zamindari management had always consisted in giving out farms and subfarms held by a chain of sadr mustajirs, ijaradars and qutqinadars. The change that occurred in zamindari management in the Burdwan Raj after the Permanent Settlement was simply the increasing substitution of temporary farms (ijaras) by permanent leases (patnis, darpatnis, daradarpatnis, etc.).[37] In effect, the patni system led to greater articulation of the existing intricacies in the revenue-collecting structure of the Burdwan Raj, cutting off the Raj from the land more visibly than ever before.

Soon after the Permanent Settlement, Maharaja Tejchand, finding it impossible to realize revenue from his farmers in time to pay the government dues punctually, resorted to the expedient which 'rendered his estate the most productive in the Company's provinces.'[38] He divided his zamindari into portions, denominated patni taluqs and sold these taluqs to individuals with his rights as zamindar. These were perpetual leases, the conditions being punctual payment of dues and liability of the tenure to summary sale in case of default. The patnidars in turn sold perpetual leases within their taluqs to others who again resorted to the same device, and thus a chain of patnis, darpatnis, daradarpatnis and chowpatnis sprang up in the Burdwan Raj. The patni system was legally recognized by the Government by Regulation VIII of 1819, under which the Raja was authorized to sell patni taluqs twice every year on default of payment of revenue after having secured the permission of the civil court.[39] From a statement made by Tejchand's son, Pratapchand, it appeared that by 1819 there were 1,495 patni taluqs comprising 8,738 villages and paying a yearly jama of Rs 32,25,494.[40] Big houses became

[36]Judicial Proceedings, Civil, Minute of the first Judge dt. 16 September 817 No. 7.

[37]Ibid., Petition of Maharajadhiraj Pratapchand Bahadur, zamindar of Burdwan.

[38]Home Miscellaneous, Vol. 775, Report on the district of Burdwan by N.J. Hhed, Acting Judge & Magistrate, 1814.

[39]Ibid.

[40]Judial Proceedings, Civil, 8 October 1819, Nos. 28, 37.

established on the patnis of the Burdwan Raj, such as the Mukherjis of Uttarpara in Hugli and the Singh Roys of Chakdighi in Burdwan.[41] But it was the smaller local gentry, who had traditionally taken many of the farms of the Burdwan Raj, who secured the greater number of smaller patni taluqs.[42]

The patni system naturally involved speculators who gambled with the possibility of raising large sums by putting pressure on the peasants. Describing the vicious effects of the patni system, the Magistrate of Burdwan wrote in a report on the district in 1814:[43]

> The Putneedar by means of his power and oppression having increased the rent of the estate he has bought from the Rajah sells a proportion of it to the Durputneedar at an assessment which will realize the revenue due to the Rajah for the whole, and keeps the remaining part in his own hands (as it is the interest of the Putneedar to gain as much as he can, he never specifies any Leases he has granted to the Raeets who are consequently tenants at will). The Durputneedar having annulled the leases of the Putneedar proceeds on the same principle and sells a proportion of the Estate to the Dur Durputneedar, having first increased the rent to such an extent as will enable him to hold what he keeps in his own hands rent-free. The Dur Durputneedar sells it to a 4th and he to a 5th person, and so on, till a bad year makes the over-assessed Estate fall in balance and the whole of the parties from the Rajah to the last person in possession file suits against each other. The Rajah resells the lot at an assessment equal to the rate realized by the last person to a new Putneedar who proceeds in the same mode that those before him have done. In this way the rents paid by the Raeets are more than double what was realized from them 10 years ago.

[41]Burdwan Raj Estate Bundles, Burdwan Collectorate, Tauzi No. 2.

[42]S.B. Chaudhuri, 'Pattani (Putni) Tenures', *Calcutta Review*, Vol. 62, 1876, pp. 348-354.

[43]Home Miscellaneous, Vol. 775. Report on the district of Burdwan by N.J. Halhed, 1814.

By the 1850s, the rates of assessment in Burdwan had increased nearly three-fold since the Permanent Settlement, and by the 1870s by four or five times (see Table 5.3). The benefit of this increase of assessment went not to the Burdwan Raj but to its patnidars. Thus, although the patni system saved the Raj,

TABLE 5.3

RATES OF ASSESSMENT IN BURDWAN FROM THE PERMANENT SETTLEMENT TO 1872

Kind of Land	*Rates of Assessment at the Permanent Settlement*	*Rates of Assessment in 1852*	*Rates of Assessment in 1872*
1st class sona	Rs 1-0-0	Rs 2-8-0	Rs 4 to 6-0-0
2nd class sona	,, 0-12-0	,, 2-0-0	,, 3-0-0
3rd class sona	,, 0-8-0	,, 1-8-0	,, 2-4-0
4th class sona	,, 0-6-0	,, 1-0-0	,, 1-12-0
1st class sali	,, 1-0-0	,, 2-8-0	,, 4-0-0
2nd class sali	,, 0-12-0	,, 2-0-0	,, 3-0-0
3rd class sali	,, 0-8-0	,, 1-8-0	,, 2-0-0
4th class sali	,, 0-6-0	,, 1-0-0	,, 1-8-0

Note: Sona lands grew aus, paddy, potatoes, mustard, sugarcane, etc.
Sali lands grew aman paddy, boro paddy and jute.

Source: 'The Burdwan Raj', *Calcutta Review*, p. 187.

subordinate lease-holders reaped the profits of the new system. It would appear that in Burdwan the sale of lots at public auctions and the creation of patni taluqs by private contracts gave a decisive advantage to the smaller local gentry. In 1871, there were 6,532 'estate' holders in Burdwan, nearly all of whom resided on their estates or within the district. Only 20 among them were absentees.[44] The number of patni taluqs had by this time grown to 2,446 and there were 876 under-tenures under the patnis.[45]

[44] *A Statistical Account of Bengal*, Vol. IV by W.W. Hunter, p. 105.
[45] Ibid., p. 82.

Before the advent of British rule the local gentry in Burdwan, composed of the well-off sections among the higher castes—Brahmans, Kayasthas, high Muslims, etc.—had existed as a class politically and economically subservient to the Burdwan Raj and dependent, to a great extent, on its favour. They held rights of collecting revenue from villages, but these rights, usually in the form of temporary farms, were inchoate. After the Permanent Settlement the political and military authority of the Rajas of Burdwan over these local gentry was removed, and in place of their former vaguely defined customary rights of revenue collection, they acquired legally recognized estates and patni taluqs and managed to intercept the greater part of the increasing jama of the district.

This process is clearly revealed by a comparison of the family histories of Bharatchandra Ray, the famous Bengali poet of the latter half of the eighteenth century, and Rammohan Ray, the father of Bengali prose and reformist Hinduism, both of whom came from land-holding Rarhi Brahman families under the jurisdiction of the Burdwan Raj. Bharatchandra's father Narendranarayan Ray, a landholder in pargana Bhursut under the Burdwan Raj, was expelled from his ancestral village because of a land dispute by Maharani Bishnukumari who appropriated his rights. Bharatchandra fled to Mandalghat, learnt Sanskrit, but finding it useless from a worldly point of view, learnt Persian from a Kayastha in Hugli. Meanwhile, his father had taken an ijara from the Raja of Burdwan. On account of his knowledge of Persian, Bharatchandra was sent to the court of Burdwan as muktar (agent) to safeguard the family interests in the ijara, to ensure prompt payment of revenue, and to prevent all trouble. He was imprisoned by the Raja of Burdwan for failure of payment but managed to make good his escape. Ultimately, he became the court poet of Maharaja Krishnachanrda of Nadia, an equally big magnate, and obtained for this maintenance the ijara of Mulajore at a revenue of Rs 600 a year.[46]

[46]See Iswarchandra Gupta's biography of Bharatchandra Ray reproduced in the introduction to Bharatchandra's poetical work 'Annadamangal' in *Bharatchandra Granthabali*, ed., Brajendra Nath Bandopadhyay and Sajani Kanta Das, (Bangiya Sahitya Parishad, Calcutta, n.d.).

Rammohan Ray's family also started as dependent farmers under the Burdwan Raj, but became independent proprietors after the Permanent Settlement. Rammohan's father, Ramkanta Ray, who held ancestral land in the village of Radhanagar in Burdwan had for a time served in a low post under the Nawab of Murshidabad. Ramkanta returned to his village to look after his own property and undertook the management of the neighbouring mahals of Maharani Bishnukumari. He took the farm of parganas Balia and Begri from the Raja of Burdwan, but the revenue of this farm fell into arrears. Raja Tejchand had him imprisoned on charges of arrears of revenue and for claim of restitution of mahals purchased by Ramkanta Ray with money advanced by Rani Bishnukumari and fraudulently transferred to his elder son Jagamohan Ray and others. But Rammohan Ray saved some of the family property by fictitiously transferring his own share to Rajiblochan Ray, an influential landholder in Burdwan. By learning English, Rammohan Ray was able to enter the service of the collectors of Dacca and Rangpur and reinvested the profits of his office in landed properties in the district of Burdwan. He came to acquire a number of estates registered in the collectorate of Burdwan, as well as quite a few patni taluqs under the Burdwan Raj. By the time Rammohan Ray moved permanently to Calcutta he had become a very substantial independent landholder in Burdwan.[47] It was a typical example of social mobility among high caste grihastha families formerly existing as a dependent landed gentry under the magnates.

The patni system, which permanently fixed the dues payable by the patnidars to the Burdwan Raj in the nineteenth century, ensured that the smaller landed gentry would intercept the considerable increases of mufassal jama. The foundation of a thriving so-called middle class was thus laid in Burdwan. The economic impact of this social development was a great increase in the pressure exerted by the revenue-collecting hierarchy over the villages. But it does not appear that this increased pressure

---

[47]Brajendranath Bandopadhyay, ed., *Sambad Patre Sekaler Katha*, (Calcutta 1340 B.S.; Vol. II, pp. 349-352); Iqbal Singh, *Rammohan Ray, A Biographical Inquiry into the Making of Modern India*, (Bombay 1958), pp. 15-67.

brought about any fundamental changes in the structure of land-holding at the village level. By the repetitive annulment of the raiyats' leases by a succession of sub-infeudatory landholders, the amounts realized from the villages were greatly increased, but the intermediary landlords did not supplant the village landed elites who constituted a body of principal raiyats led by the village headmen (mandals). The mandals continued to settle the accounts of the raiyats in their villages with the collecting agents (gosmastas) of the zamindars and patnidars.[48] The purchase of a zamindari or a patni taluq would give a title to revenue collection from specific villages but not to the lands appertaining to these villages. Such lands continued to be held by the dominant village families which had traditionally enjoyed the lion's share of the village lands and very often these families ensured their possession of land by acquiring the lowest grade of tenure in a chain of sub-infeudatory patnis. The collector of Burdwan wrote to the Board of Revenue in 1820:

> It has been a common practice for the Munduls and headmen of Villages to take their village in dur or Seputny and to exclude from the date of their purchase a certain number of begahs of land from their maal[49] accounts keeping a separate account for the alienated portion as Mohattran[50] Dauvuttran[51] etc. After keeping the village account in this way for 3 or 4 years and after destroying those of former years a fictitious putny sale of the Village is made after which the former man falls in arrears and the Village is sold again. The purchaser then finds it difficult to discover the trick and if he does he has hitherto had as much difficulty to prove his right of resumption.[52]

We have seen earlier how, in the 1760s, outgoing ijaradars and qutqinadars whose farms were about to expire made a

[48]Burdwan Old English Correspondence, Issue December 1819—March 1820, to BR from Collector of Burdwan, dt. 22 February 1820.

[49]Revenue.

[50]Rent-free land for the 'relief of the great' (mahattran).

[51]Rent-free land for the support of the idols (devottar).

[52]Burdwan Old English Correspondence, loc. cit.

regular practice of granting leases on easy terms below the standard rates of revenue to the principal landholders (i.e., principal raiyats). Often these village landholders themselves took the lowest grade of farm in the chain of farms coming down from the sadr office of the Burdwan Raj—the qutqina—and utilized their position as farmers to under-assess their jotes. It appears that the same practice was continuing in the 1820s: instead of securing qutqinas the village landholders were now securing darpatnis or sepatnis, as the case might be, in order to ensure their continued possession of the village lands. At the contact point between the revenue-collecting structure and the village, the dominant upper level of the village population sought to fight off pressures on their own position by acquiring a position in the lowest rung of the hierarchy of revenue-collecting rights. By utilizing this crucial position they managed in many cases to shift the incidence of increased assessments to the body of poor villages. The main element among the body of village landholders continued to be the rich Sadgop agriculturists.[53] The purchasers of superior proprietary rights thus did not invariably succeed in setting aside the landed elites of the villages. On the contrary the very purchase of such proprietary rights could often be utilized as a tactic to bolster an existing dominant position in the land.

[53]Lal Behari Day, *Bengal Peasant Life*, ed., Mahadevaprasad Saha (Calcutta 1969), p. 11.

6

Bishnupur

The Bishnupur zamindari, which is now comprised within the present Bankura district, was included in the district of Birbhum under early British administration and was transferred in 1793 to the district of Burdwan. The zamindari formed the connecting link between the plains of Bengal in the east and the mountains of Chotanagpur in the west. In the eastern portion of the zamindari adjoining Burdwan, the land was alluvial and flat, bearing the aspect of ordinary paddy lands of Bengal. In the north and west, the land was rocky and interspersed with jungle.[1] Rice formed the staple crop of the area, but the district was not surplus in foodgrains and was more exposed to famine and starvation than any other district of Bengal. In 1863, the revenue surveyor reported that the general condition of the people, as compared with that of the adjoining districts in the east, was one of poverty, which was especially apparent in the jungle tracts.[2] The district of Bankura was a Brahman-dominated area where many of the Brahmans were not only landholders but also cultivators of the soil. The Bankura Brahmans, mostly belonging to the Rarhi section, took part in all actual operations of cultivation except holding the plough. Apart from them, the agricultural land was occupied mainly by cultivating castes like the Sadgops and a military class called Ghatwals who were formerly guardsmen of the passes on the western

[1] *A Statistical Account of Bengal*, W.W. Hunter, Vol. IV, p. 207; *Bengal District Gazetteer, Bankura*, L.S.S. O'Malley, p. 123.

[2] *A Statistical Account of Bengal*, Vol. IV, p. 245.

border under the Rajas of Bishnupur. The untouchable castes like the Bagdis and the Bauris and the aboriginal tribes like the Santhals, all of whom formed a considerable part of the population of the district, served as a landless labour class on the land occupied by the Brahmans, the Ghatwals and the cultivating castes.[3] As a result, Bankura never lacked sharecroppers and hired labourers. These were essential to an agrarian economy in which 42.2 per cent of the land was in direct possession of the tenure-holders, who were mostly Brahmans holding rent-free lands which they cultivated by hired labour or on the half produce system.[4]

Unlike the relatively 'new' zamindaris of Rajshahi, Burdwan, and Dinajpur, the zamindari of Bishnupur was a truly ancient principality which Murshid Quli Khan did not attempt to bring under full subjugation because of the inaccessible nature of the territory—full of woods and adjoining the mountains of Jharkhand. The Nawab calculated that the cost of direct administration would far exceed the revenue of the country, which was poor in produce.[5] Thus the Bishnupur Raj continued to exist under the Mughal empire as a relic of antiquity. Originally a chieftaincy over the Bagdis and the Mals (aboriginal peoples), it was founded by Adi Malla (Original Wrestler) who was born, according to tradition, in 715 A.D. Although upon his investiture Adi Malla assumed the Sanskritized Rajput name of Raghunath Singh he was almost certainly, as legends long current in Bishnupur regarding his birth indicate, of aboriginal stock. His family continued to use the aboriginal patronymic of Malla (along with the Rajput surname of Singh) down to the fiftieth lineal prince, Gopal Singh, who dropped the name of Malla and adopted the exclusive title of Singh, along with the definitely Hindu cult of Vaishnavism.[6] In medieval times, therefore, the Bishnupur Raj was an independent Rajput kingdom, which acknowledged a vague Muslim suzerainty for the first time in

[3]*A Statistical Account of Bengal*, Vol. IV, p. 219-222.

[4]*Final Report on the Survey and Settlement Operations in the District of Bankura 1917-1924*, F.W. Robertson, p. 66-69.

[5]Charles Stewart, *History of Bengal*, pp. 370-372.

[6]W.W. Hunter, *Annals of Rural Bengal*, Appendix E, 'The Pundit's Chronicle of Bishenpore"; *A Statistical Account of Bengal*, Vol. IV, pp. 230-238.

1586 under the forty-ninth prince, Raja Bir Hambir, who agreed to pay an annual tribute of Rs 1,07,000.[7] In 1715, Nawab Murshid Quli Khan granted a diwani sanad (title deed) to the Raja of Bishnupur[8] which bestowed the territory on him by virtue of office rather than hereditary right. In reality, the Raja continued as an autonomous border chief. The territory of the zamindari was measured by Rennell in 1779 at 1,256 B. square miles,[9] but the provenance of surviving Bishnupur inscriptions proves that the family ruled at some indeterminable point in history over a much more extensive territory stretching to Damin-I-Koh in the Santhal Parganas in the north, and including parts of Midnapur in the south, Burdwan in the east, and Chhota-nagpur in the west.[10] Much of this territory, it seems, was seized by the rival Rajas of Burdwan, so that in the eighteenth century the Bishnupur Raj was somewhat shrunken in size.

The decline of the house of Bishnupur may be said to have started from the reign of Raja Gopal Singh (1728-1743) who, incidentally, wrote the family history of the Bishnupur Raj which Hunter found in the Bankura collectorate. The rising house of Burdwan under Maharaja Kirtichand expanded at the cost of Bishnupur until both houses were threatened by the Marathas and had to combine in common defence. The Maratha horsemen made Bishnupur their base of operations against Burdwan and Murshidabad.[11] On account of the devastation caused, Alivardi Khan had to reduce the jama of Bishnupur from Rs 1,29,803 to Rs. 1,11,803.[12] But the resources of the Raj suffered a much more fundamental and catastrophic decline during the famine of 1770, for the poor soil of Bishnupur lacked the recuperative power of that of the zamindari of Burdwan. The misfortunes of the Raj were multiplied by what is described by Grant as the 'constitutional mode of Settlement, a regular hustabood (investigation and survey) by which the British supervisor increased the revenue of the zamindari to Rs 3,93,750 immediately after the famine in 1772.[13]

[7]*Bengal District Gazetteer, Bankura*, p. 25.
[8]*Parliamentary Papers*, sess. 1812, Vol. VIII, p. 268.
[9]Ibid., p. 393.
[10]*Bengal District Gazetteer, Bankura*, p. 21.
[11]*Riyazu-s-Salatin*, pp. 340-344.
[12]*Parliamentary Papers*, 1812, Vol. VII, p. 394.
[13]Ibid., p. 394.

Meanwhile, the effects of depopulation spread and the land relapsed more and more to the jungle. Hesilrige, who carried out a hast-o-bud (detailed inquiry) of the zamindari in 1788-89, found that it was not flourishing and ascribed this state to a decreasing population. Due to the diminution of the agricultural labour force, the country was not cultivated as well as it had been before.[14] The uprooted rural population had taken to violence the arrangements for law and order maintained by the Raja in the countryside had broken down, and British troops had to be called in to restore tranquillity and impose peace.[15]

In the midst of this turmoil, Chaitanya Singh became the Raja of Bishnupur. Hesilrige described him in the following terms: 'A man of the weakest intellect, he is governed and imposed upon by all around him, and on no occasion is equal to the giving of a denial; hence arises his private distresses, and to this cause must be attributed the difficulties he has so long laboured under'.[16] He was used as a tool in court intrigues by his first Rani, 'a woman of the loosest principles', and by a slave girl 'as prone to intrigue as her mistress'.[17] Taking advantage of the situation, Damodar Singh, a cousin of the Raja and head of the junior branch of the family, ousted the latter by force with the help of the Nawab of Murshidabad. A costly litigation followed which reduced the family fortunes to such an extent that Chaitanya Singh had to raise money by pawning the family idol of Madan Mohan to Gokul Mitra, a merchant of Bagbazar in Calcutta. He secured the aid of diwan Gangagovinda Singh, a high revenue officer of the Company, by greasing his palm and the British thereafter reinstated Chaitanya Singh to the throne of Bishnupur. By a decree of 1787, Chaitanya Singh became the possessor of the entire Raj while Damodar became entitled only to maintenance. In 1791, when the government proposed a division of the zamindari between the two claimants, Chaitanya instituted a suit in the court. The protracted litigation

[14]*Burdwan District Record, Letters Received,* to Sherburne, Collector of Burdwan, from Hastings, dt. 14 July 1788, pp. 1-2.

[15]A vivid description of these turbulent times may be found in Hunter's *Annals of Rural Bengal.*

[16]*Burdwan District Records, Letters Received,* to Collector Keating from Hesilrige, dt. 6 September 1789, p. 49.

[17]Ibid., 18 October 1789, p. 49.

which resulted from the family feud ruined the finance of the house.[18] The zamindari suffered a considerable loss as the idol of Madan Mohan which had formerly contributed to the resources of the zamindari by attracting the offerings of pilgrims, was withheld by Gokul Mitra.

The district records of Birbhum and Bishnupur in 1786 open with the Raja of Bishnupur in confinement for non-payment of revenue, even his personal allowance being attached as security for payments. Under conditions created by the famine and internal quarrels, revenue arrears went on accumulating even after the assessment was reduced in 1775; and in 1788, collector Sherburne despatched his assistant Hesilrige to Bishnupur with the object of raising the collections to the reduced assessment of 1775. The detailed investigation of Hesilrige throws considerable light on the structure of the zamindari and the causes of heavy balances of revenue. The ruling zamindar himself had no talent or sense of responsibility with regard to the management of his zamindari, which was left to his favourite minister Kamal Biswas. As a result, large scale misappropriations of revenue were committed by Darpanarayan Kar, the peshkar of the government, Chandicharan Mukherjee, the zamindari's diwan and other officials.[19] There was no record of revenue-paying lands and the raiyats, except in the case of Byntul and Barahazari, possessed no leases. The accounts were deliberately kept confused, intricate, and unintelligible to the raiyats.[20] As in Burdwan, the revenues were farmed out to sadr farmers, who were mostly relations of the Raja and were extremely irregular in payments. Real control of the revenue-collecting business lay with the mufassal farmers, who were mainly mandals or village heads. They had such a complete hold over the land that their terms, whether high or low, had to be accepted. The raiyats of Bishnupur had no close ties with Chaitanya Singh unlike the raiyats of the

[18]Ibid., *Letters Issued.* to BR from Collector of Burdwan, Davis, dt. 12 February 1794, p. 102.

[19]BRP, 23 March 1789, No. 28, to BR from Collector of Birbhum.

[20]*Burdwan District Records, Letters Issued,* letter from the Collector of Burdwan, dt. 10 November 1789, p. 53.

Jungle Mahals who were closely bound to their zamindars.[21] So little control had the Raja over his zamindari, and so extravagant was fraud in the mufassal, that about half of the land was alienated from the revenue, causing a permanent decline in mufassal collections while the sadr jama remained unchanged on paper.[22] The Raja had made grants of rent-free lands and had relinquished part of his demands on the police officers.[23] The zamindari officers also secured considerable grants, while the finest lands were appropriated by the mandals as rent-free holdings.[24] The Raj family, unable to check alienations of revenue-paying lands by officials and mandals, themselves resorted to the device of increasing the family lands (Bhitarjote Mahals) as a security against the attachment and sale of the whole zamindari for arrears of revenue. On enquiry Hesilrige found the quantity of revenue-free land (baze zamin), exclusive of what was contained in the Bhitarjote Mahals, as follows:[25]

[21]'Bankura Old English Correspondence, to the Acting Register of the Nizamat Adalat from Ernst dt. 30 September 1806. The jungle zamindars were mostly tribal chieftains (who had Sanskritized themselves as Rajput or Kshatriya Rajas) ruling over aboriginal tribes with whom their ethnic and ritual association was close. Presumably the Rajas of Bishnupur, suspected to have been Bagdis in origin, at one time belonged to this jungle Raja type. But in historical times their claim to Kshatriya status was well established, probably due to their patronage of the large number of Brahmans who were encouraged to settle in their country and civilize its inhabitants. The basis of their power had shifted from chieftaincy over tribals to Kshatriya kingship over a settled agricultural population of Brahman and other castes. Under such circumstances, personal ties characteristic of a tribal situation could not survive. Correspondence, Vol. I, 1800-1808.

[22]*Burdwan District, Records Letters Issued,* letter from Collector of Burdwan, dt. 5 August, 1788, p.3; Home Miscellaneous, Vol. 385, Birbhum including Bishnupore, Collector Joseph Sherburne to BR, dt. 12 June 1788.

[23]*Burdwan District Records, Letters Issued,* to Keating from Hesilrige, p. 49.

[24]Ibid., to Sherburne from Hesilrige, dt. 5 August 1788, p. 4.

[25]Ibid., 11 September 1789, pp. 42-43.

	Bighas
Held by sanad previous to the diwani grant of the company	15,548
Held by sanad since the date of the diwani grant	11,506
Held without sanad and of which the period of obtaining possession was not ascertained	77,582
Total	104,636

The structure of landed rights in the Bishnupur Raj thus exhibited the same pyramidal form, and the same fundamental distinction between revenue collection rights and actual possession of land, as in the rest of Bengal. At the top of the structure was the ancient house of Raghunath Singh, whose right might best be described as 'territorial' rather than 'land-owning'. The Raj family, together with the farmers of the Raj who were mostly relations of the Raja, exercised tribute-collecting rights over the whole territory of Bishnupur. It was only in the Bhitarjote Mahals, recognized during Mughal rule as the private land of the zamindars of Bishnupur, that the Raj family enjoyed an actual title to the land itself. In other mahals the Raja and his farmers stood as a body of rent-sharers over the holders of land at the village level. The land-holding class in the villages was composed of a numerous body of Brahmans who possessed rent-free tenures, a chain of Ghatwals who enjoyed military dominance in their areas, and a large number of rich cultivators of agricultural or priestly stock led by their village headmen. Over this whole structure of landed rights, the authority of the ruling house stood as an administrative umbrella, until it was taken over by the local representatives of the East India Company, which divested the Raja of his rulership and conferred on him instead a doubtful 'proprietorship' of the land.

In this process of centralization of government under the East India Company, its local agent, Hesilrige effectively replaced Chaitanya Singh as the source of administrative authority and action in Bishnupur during his stay in that district. He made arrangements for the resumption of a large part of the alienated lands, reduced the establishment of the Raja on the ground that the latter was no longer the revenue collector and abolished the caste kacharis (courts for caste disputes) in the

Kullatha Mahals which the Raja's son, Nimai Singh, had turned into a source of big profit. Even under the direct collection of Hesilrige, however, the collector's accounts in 1789 revealed a balance amounting to Rs 50,000. Nevertheless, Chaitanya Singh accepted the settlement offered by collector Keating who succeeded Sherburne—a settlement for ten years at an annual assessment of Rs 4 lakhs—rather than risk losing the zamindari to his bitter rival Damodar Singh, who, he feared, might supersede him by agreeing to the full amount.[26] The settlement, though looked upon as an equitable one by the Board of Revenue, was pronounced by Keating's successor, Davis, as vitiated by over-assessment. Davis granted an abatement of more than Rs 20,000.[27] This reduction did not prevent the disintegration of the Bishnupur Raj, which was further hastened by the new judicial regulations and the delays involved in the judicial process which encouraged the under-farmers in the mufassal to withhold the revenue. The suits pending in the courts numbered 36,913. The collector estimated that it would take a lifetime to dispose of all the cases. Meanwhile, failures, deaths, and desertions increased the balance of revenue to an irrecoverable amount.[28] As the difficulties of the Raja increased and his mahals were exposed to public sale, the Bishnupur zamindari was taken over step by step by Tejchand, Maharja of Burdwan.

Before we move on to consider the effects of the public sales under the Permanent Settlement we must pause for a moment to consider the social structure of the Bishnupur Raj in order to determine the exact impact which the transfer of the zamindari was to produce on the pattern of land control in the area. As we have seen, the control of the Raj family over the land of the kingdom was by no means absolute and there were other important interests below the Raj family. Bishnupur had been in historical times a Hindu kingdom and as such maintained especially large military and religious establishments which were supported by land grants. The military nature of this border

[26]BRP, 12 August 1791, Petition of Raja Chaitan Sing.

[27]BRP, 18 August 1795, No 15, to Governor-General-in-Council from BR.

[28]BRP, 10 March 1795, No. 13, to BR from Collector of Burdwan.

principality is proved by the existence of a large number of service tenures held by the commanding officers of the army, the guards of Bishnupur fort, military paymasters, gunners, drummers and musicians who paid a panchaki or quit rent for their lands. The kingdom was guarded from the Chuars (tribal 'savages') and Marathas by a long chain of Ghatwals who held lands under a panchaki jama and protected the passes on an open area.[29] Under British administration, the political power of the Bishnupur Raja was reduced to a considerable extent by the new police arrangements which placed the Ghatwals under police darogas. The Ghatwals, so long as they were under the control of the zamindar, regularly paid a quit rent amounting to about Rs 12,000. Freed from the obligation of service to the zamindar and encouraged by the police darogas, the Ghatwals refused payment of the panchaki to the ruling family.[30] The Raja, finding the Ghatwals more a liability than an asset, relinquished his claim over them and was given an abatement of revenue. Although this represented a significant reduction in the political power and the social authority of the Raja, the Ghatwali establishment itself survived and in 1807 the magistrate of the Jungle Mahals (a newly constructed magistracy to which the criminal jurisdiction over Bishnupur was made over) estimated that there were nearly 3,000 Ghatwals in Bishnupur, holding lands which were capable of yielding a revenue at least eight times the amount of the quit rent at which they were assessed.[31] Thus, while the military character of the kingdom disappeared, the military servicemen of the kingdom largely retained their hold over the land.

Even more important than the military establishment was the especially large religious establishment in Bishnupur. Being ruled by Hindu kings, the city of Bishnupur was embellished with beautiful terracotta temples, which represented a distinguished school of architecture known as the Bishnupur style.

---

[29] *A Statistical Account of Bengal*, Vol. IV.

[30] *Burdwan District Records, Letters Issued*, to BR from Collector Davis, dt. 12 February 1794, p. 102.

[31] Bankura Old English Correspondence, Vol. I, 1800-1808, to Dowedswell, Secretary to the Government, Judicial Department, from Collector Blunt, dt. 25 April 1807.

Hesilrige found within the boundaries of Bishnupur no less than 360 thakurbaris or temples. Considerable rent-free lands were granted for the upkeep of the temples to numerous Brahmans who resided within Bishnupur.[32] Hesilrige advised the Board against resumption of these lands because the step was liable to provoke native religious sentiment and to invite trouble from influential classes whose interests were directly involved.[33] Though he concluded that much land had been made devottar (for the gods) or brahmottar (for the Brahmans) without proper authority by the village headmen, revenue farmers, and zamindari officials, his resumption proceedings affected only a small portion of the lands endowed ostensibly for the religious establishment. While the Bishnupur family at the top of this huge military and religious establishment might thus well be displaced from its position of pre-eminence, its overthrow did not mean necessarily that the land control system based on the military-religious establishment would disintegrate.

Such, indeed, proved to be the case. Ghatwals, Brahmans and temples continued to dominate the land in Bishnupur although the princely house of Bishnupur ceased to rule over them. By 1806, the whole of the ancient Bishnupur Raj had been sold at public auctions in lots from which originated the ten revenve-paying estates of the Bishnupur subdivision of Bankura in the late nineteenth century—Bishnupur, Barahazari, Karisunda, Jungle Mahals, Kuchiakol, Panchal, Jamtara, Shahjora, Kismat Shahjora and Maliara. When the government regulation of 1791 declared the subordinate taluqs as independent, separate engagements were made with the taluqdars of Bishnupur. The taluqs of Shahjora, Kismat Shahjora, and Maliara were detached from the parent Raj prior to the declaration of the Permanent Settlement.[34] During the subsequent years Bishnupur was sold piecemeal, the largest part falling into the hands of Maharaja Tejchand. Unlike Bishnupur which was being sold after the Regulations of 1793, the zamindari of Burdwan acquired new

---

[32]The censuses of Bengal revealed Bankura as the district with the highest concentration of Brahmans in the province.

[33]*Burdwan District Records, Letters Received,* to Keating from Hesilrige, p. 43.

[34]*Bengal District Gazetteer, Bankura,* pp. 123-136:

territories in the aftermath of the Decennial Settlement. The methods pursued by Tejchand in order to preserve and enlarge the Burdwan Raj under the challenging conditions of the

TABLE 6.1

Name of the estate	*Origin*	*Area in acres*	*Revenue (Rs)*
1. Bishnupur	Purchased by Raja Tejchand in 1806	2,06,471	1,35,989
2. Barahazari	Purchased by Raja Tejchand in 1791	1,31,943	1,92,633
3. Karisunda	Purchased by Raja Tejchand	13,129	23,395
4. Jungle Mahal	Purchased by Raja Tejchand in 1798	1,22,354	3,499
5. Kuchiakol	Purchased on behalf of Nimai Singh (son of Chaitan Singh) by Krishnamohan Aich in 1798	8,542	8,237
6. Panchal	Purchased in 1798	493	408
7. Jamtara	Purchased by Harisprasad Pantik in 1798	9,575	6,310
8. Maliara	Separated as an independent taluq in 1791	32,043	5,202
9. Shahjora	Separated as an independent taluq in 1791	16,623	3,110
10. Kismat Shahjora	Separated as an independent taluq in 1791	4,665	1,156

Source: *Final Report on the Survey and Settlement Operations in the District of Bankura*, F.W. Robertson, (Calcutta 1926), p. 28. Bankura Collectorate Records, General Register, A Part 1, Tauzi roll of revenue paying estates, in Bankura (1924); Sale Account of Lands in Burdwan, Miscellaneous Records, Board of Revenue.

Permanent Settlement were extremely ingenious. Finding several of his parganas in Burdwan over-assessed, he made collections which he withheld from the government, let the revenue arrears accumulate on the over-assessed mahals, made over the Burdwan zamindari to his mother Bishnukumari (who could not be confined on account of her sex) and himself retired to that part of the Bishnupur zamindari which he had bought in 1791. While Bishnukumari lost the over-assessed pargana of Mandalghat in consequence of her son's devices, Tejchand himself acquired pargana Barahazari (1791), which formed nearly half of the zamindari of Bishnupur.[35] Tejchand benefited particularly from this transaction because Keating made an unfair division of the sadr jama of the Bishnupur Raj between pargana Barahazari and pargana Bishnupur. Some Rs 20,000 which should have been fixed on Barahazari, according to Keating's successor, Davis, was imposed on Bishnupur, which in consequence became grossly over-assessed.[36] While Tejchand bought Barahazari, Durgacharan Pakrasi, an inhabitant of Calcutta, bought pargana Karisunda at the same auction.[37] Durgacharan having defaulted, the pargana was later bought by Raja Tejchand. Tejchand also came into possession of the Jungle Mahals of Bishnupur in 1798, a valuable property for its jungle products which under its farmers had yielded considerable revenue to the Raja of Bishnupur.[38] Finally, in 1806, Tejchand bought pargana Bishnupur, the remaining part of the zamindari. He benefited from this purchase too, because Collector Davis had a few years earlier reduced its assessment in consideration of the poverty of the house of Bishnupur.

An analysis of the above sales reveals that, in opposition to the accepted view that landed rights were transferred wholesale to 'new men', in Bishnupur the chief beneficiary was another old zamindar of nearly the same dignity and status. As the purchaser of 93.57 per cent of the late zamindari of Bishnupur, the Raja of Burdwan paid an annual revenue of £35,973 in Bankura district, the total land revenue of the district in 1870 being £45,110.[39] Proprietor of the four most important estates in Bankura, namely Barahazari, Karisunda, Jungle Mahals, and

---

[35]BRP, 14 March 1794, No. 44, to BR from Collector of Burdwan, dt. 27 February 1794.

[36]*Burdwan District Records, Letters Issued,* to BR from Collector Davis, p. 102.

[37]BRP, 18 July 1791.

[38]*A Statistical Account of Bengal,* Vol. IV, pp. 252-253.

[39]*A Statistical Account of Bengal,* Vol. IV, pp. 256-279.

Bishnupur, the house of Burdwan enjoyed a position in the district nearly as superior as it held in Burdwan itself. Bishnupur provided a striking case of the circulation of landed rights within an older class of magnates, and the supplanting of one traditional landed magnate by another. A hereditary enmity between the rival houses of Bishnupur and Burdwan, going back to Gopal Singh and Kirtichand in the early part of the eighteenth century, was brought to a dramatic denouement by the operations of the Permanent Settlement. This settlement finally enabled the third descendant of Kirtichand to take over in 1806, without a battle being fought, the kingdom which Kirtichand had sought to conquer by arms a century earlier.

The outcome of the public sales in Bishnupur seems to suggest that in organized zamindaris possessing the characteristics of a 'kingdom' (Raj), outside adventurers—in this case native capitalists from Calcutta—were not in the best position to convert purchases into effective rights. Families of standing, wealth, and influence such as the house of Burdwan stood a much better chance of making their auction purchases effective. Jaynarayan Ghoshal, a big capitalist of Calcutta, who had lent money to Damodar Singh, tried to take over the Bhitarjote Mahals in satisfaction of his claims, but without success.[40] Other outsiders, such as Durgacharan Pakrasi of Calcutta, and Kasinath and Biswanath Banerjee, purchased Bishnupur mahals at public auctions but could not take effective possession. This failure was due to the stiff resistance of the Bishnupur family, which made it impossible for them to collect revenue. As Kasinath and Biswanath Banerjee complained in a petition to the government, Madhab Singh, the grandson of Chaitanya Singh, 'having assembled 2,000 Chuars plundered and burnt 50 villages in Tong mahal and Khamar area of our Zamindarry. He also plundered several villages, and robbed our amlah[41] of Rs 500 (which they had collected) with their papers and furnitures—The Ryotts have all absconded . . .'[42] Durgacharan Pakrasi, the purchaser of Karisunda, had the same complaint:

[40]BRP, 2 November 1787, No. 40; and 25 March 1788, No. 19, Petitions of Jaynarayan Ghoshal.

[41]Officers.

[42]BRP, 5 March 1798, No. 33, Petition from Kasinath and Biswanath Bonnagees.

> This year in the month of mag 1205 B.S. people on the part of Raja Chyton Sing, the former zamindar, assisted by the jungle zamindars in the boundary of Midnapur with a gang of some thousands of Fighting Choars having come into Bishenpur and plundered the Pergunnah purchased by your Petitioner have set on fire and reduced to ashes the houses of the Ryotts in the said pergunnah so that the whole of the Ryotts and mustajers belonging to your Petitioners pergunnah have fled—relinquishing their crops and other property—And the plunderers say openly, we have been deprived of this zamindary until it is restored we will not suffer a Ryott's house to remain.[43]

Unable to collect the jama, purchasers like Durgacharan Pakrasi failed to pay the revenue for their estates and Maharaja Tejchand, with his far greater influence and resources, took over these mahals.

How far did the Raja of Burdwan succeed, where other outsiders had failed, in giving effect to the title he had purchased at auction? Upon his purchase of Bishnupur, Tejchand dismissed all the farmers and officers of the Raja of Bishnupur and appointed his own officers who collected revenue from the raiyats.[44] He then resorted to the method of raising money on the estate by selling patni taluqs within it. The patni taluqdars, again, sold their rights to darpatnidars, and they in turn to daradarpatnidars, at increased assessments until the estate was no longer divisible and admitted no further enhancement.[45] Describing these intermediaries as 'those numerous adventurers' and as 'men for the most part of very indifferent character and of no responsibility', the Judge and Magistrate of the Jungle Mahals wrote: '. . . very few of these persons reside in the Talook or employ any local agent therein or are ever known in the Talook—

[43]BRP, 5 March 1798, No 34, Petition of Durgacharan Talukdar of Pargana Karisunda.

[44]BRP, 13 March 1807, No. 45, to BR from Collector of Burdwan.

[45]Bankura Old English Correspondence, Vol. I, covering 1800-1808, C.R. Blunt, Judge of Birbhum to Bayley, Register of Sadr Dewani Adalat, 1808; Ibid., Blunt to George Dowedswell, Judicial Secretary, dt. 28 August 1809.

A fixed resident of Burdwan or perhaps of Hooghly, Nuddeah or some other adjacent zillah purchases of the Zemindar of Burdwan a Putney Talook in Bissenpore. . . .'[46] Being absentees, the patnidars were not in a position to get the most out of their properties and as a result the patnis were continually changing hands.[47] To retain control over the Bishnupur estate and its patni taluqdars, Tejchand resorted to a characteristically devious transaction. In 1813, he made over the Bishnupur estate by private deed of sale to Ramsebak Mallik, who happened to be his muktar (legal agent) in Calcutta. Tejchand remained the real proprietor as the patni taluqdars continued to settle accounts with the Raja and not with Ramsebak Mallik. In case of a public sale of the whole estate for the recovery of revenue arrears, the Raja was thus in a position to repurchase it in his own name and to dispossess the patni taluqdars, if he so wished, on the ground that their engagements with the former proprietor were null and void.[48] Whenever it suited him, the Raja ejected individual patni taluqdars on the fictitious ground that they had failed to pay the revenue,[49] and the patni taluqdars in their turn resorted to the same practice with regard to their under-renters.[50]

While the Raja and his intermediary taluqdars thus continually fought among themselves for the rent of the land, they combined against the Bishnupur family and its dependents to eject them from the private and rent-free lands which the latter occupied. Tejchand obtained favourable court decisions in disputes relating to several lands which he resumed—thakurseba (temple) lands for the support of religious institutions, babuan (personal) lands for the support of branches of the Bishnupur family, and Senapati (militia) and Ghatwali (frontier guard) lands for the maintenance of police officers.[51] Yet the task was by no means easy.

[46]Ibid.

[47]There were 288 patni taluks in Bishnupur under the Burdwan Raj during the survey and settlement of Bankura from 1917-24. Of these, no less than 54 were sold during a ten-year period. *Final Report on Bankura*, p. 61.

[48]BRP, 23 November 1813, No. 17, from Collector of Burdwan to BR.

[49]Ibid.

[50]Bankura Old English Correspondence, Vol. I, 1800-1808, Blunt to W.B. Bayley, Register to Sadr Dewani Adalat, dt. 8 May 1809.

[51]Ibid., Magistrate of Jungle Mahals to Bayley, Register of Sadar Nizamat Adalat, dt. 10 June 1808.

As Tejchand himself wrote in several petitions to the government, his predecessors who had purchased Bishnupur mahals had failed to take possession of villages as they had been violently ousted by members of the Bishnupur family who claimed them as babuan lands; and Tejchand encountered the same difficulty.[52] In 1807, Tejchand complained that Madhab Singh and other members of the Bishnupur family had taken violent measures for retaining possession of the zamindari in concert with the jungle Raja of Pachet, who was violently opposed to the sale of the neighbouring zamindari of Bishnupur. Tejchand claimed that members of the Bishnupur family had burnt down the houses of several raiyats in order to stop them from paying revenue and had also collected Chuars in the jungles to intercept payment to the treasury.[53] Ernst, the collector, refused to lend credence to these complaints against the Bishnupur family and pronounced that the threat to peace had been exaggerated.[54] The provocations, in fact, came from the Raja of Burdwan who was deliberately planning to dispossess the Bishnupur family and their numerous dependents from the remaining lands which they held. But the attempt of Tejchand and his dependent taluqdars to call on the newly established police officers for help in resuming lands proved futile because the police lacked the support of the Ghatwals and paiks whose lands were being resumed.[55]

The ill-judged attempt of Tejchand to resume the militia land called Senapati Mahals provoked widespread disturbances in Bishnupur in 1808. The holders of the Senapati Mahals formed a very large body of men dispersed throughout Bishnupur pargana. Daring of character and experienced in the use of arms, they possessed a thorough knowledge of the jungles and looked upon the Senapati Mahals as their hereditary lands by immemorial custom. Tejchand's action threatened to deprive them of

---

[52]Ibid., Vol. 2, 1809-1810. Petition of Maharajadhiraj Tezchund, dt. 13 July 1810; Burdwan Old English Correspondence, Issue October 1808-October 1809, Darkhast of Maharaja Tezchund.

[53]BRP, 10 February 1807, No. 54, Collector to BR.

[54]Bankura Old English Correspondence, Ernst to Dowedswell, Secretary to Government, Judicial Department, dt. 4 February 1807; Correspondence, Vol. I, 1800-1808.

[55]Ibid., Blunt to Dowedswell, dt. 9 March 1808.

their sole means of subsistence. A sardar of the Senapati Mahals conducted 500 chuars from the Raipur jungle estate through the Dalbhum zamindari to the fort of Bishnupur. Failing to capture the fort, they plundered the towns in the vicinity.[56] Once the disturbances had been suppressed, the Raja of Burdwan, in his vindictive pursuit of the house of Chaitanya Singh, demanded that the members of the Bishnupur family should be banished altogether from Bishnupur and their family residence in the fort of Bishnupur made over to himself in virtue of his right as purchaser of Bishnupur.[57]

In this project, Tejchand did not wholly succeed, but his great resources enabled him to break the hold of the Bishnupur family over the district more or less completely. Madhab Singh, the head of the senior branch of the Bishnupur family, was banished to Hugli in 1808 and was prohibited from returning to Bishnupur on pain of forfeiting his pension. However, other members of this branch and members of Damodar Singh's branch continued to live in the Bishnupur and to occupy the Bishnupur fort.[58] Many of the descendants of Chaitanya Singh were violently dispossessed of their private and rent-free lands by the Raja of Burdwan and his patni taluqdars. The poverty of the house of Bishnupur prevented them in these cases from seeking judicial redress effectively. Suits instituted for the recovery of their rent-free lands were carried in appeal from one court to another till the

---

[56]Holding the Raja of Burdwan responsible for the disturbances the Magistrate of the Jungle Mahals wrote to the government in Calcutta: 'It is to be lamented, that instead of gradual increase of rent, or reannexation of these lands to the assets of the Estate, which might in time be affected without hazard to its tranquillity, or without any permanent or material sacrifice of the interests of the Zemindar, he should be impelled by an inordinate desire of accumulation, to persevere in an inconsiderate, unprofitable, and inflexible severity against these people, the object of which, even on its attainment, will not be attended with any material advantages and may in its execution be productive of serious ill consequences to the peace of the Pergunnah.'

Bankura Old English Correspondence, Blunt to Dowedswell, dt. 9 March 1808.

[57]Bankura Old English Correspondence, Vol. I, 1800-1808, Blunt to Dowedswell, dt. 10 September 1809.

[58]Bankura Old English Correspondence, Vol. I, 1800-1808, Blunt to Ernst, Magistrate of Hugli, dt. 30 August 1808.

Bishnupur party were obliged to drop their claims.[59] A few small rent-free mahals were all that was left to the Bishnupur family in the way of personal possession.[60] But the family continued to receive supplementary incomes from the temple lands assigned for the maintenance of 168 idols of which the Raj family of Bishnupur remained sebaits (caretaking worshippers). With all their economic and political power gone, they still retained a considerable degree of social prestige as the former rulers of the country and the present sebaits of the temples.[61]

It would appear, therefore, that at the top of the hierarchical structure of landed interests in Bishnupur, the Rajas of Bishnupur and their farmers were effectively replaced by the Rajas of Burdwan and their patni taluqdars. But did this revolution in landed interests at the top of the structure go down to the village level? The manuscript records preserved in the Bankura collectorate show that there was a strong attempt by the Raja of Burdwan and his patni taluqdars to dispossess the holders of lands endowed for military and religious purposes. Unfortunately for the tranquillity of Bishnupur, the zamindari was supposed to

---

[59]Burdwan Old English Correspondence, Issue 1820, July 1820-October 1820, Collector to BR, dt. 26 August 1820.

[60]The Bishnupur family continued to hold the resumed lakhiraj estate No. 72 on the tauzi roll comprising 107 bighas and yielding Rs 145 in 1840. Bankura Collectorate Records, Tauzi (estate) Bundles, No. 72.

[61]In 1835, the Reverend J.J. Haberlin visited Bishnupur and made the following entry in his journal: 'Our way led us thro' Jungle to Bishenpore (Vishnupur) a large town with above 7,000 houses. In the evening we went into the old fort, now a heap of ruins, with the exception of a few houses, belonging to the Rajah's family. Formerly this was one of the wealthiest and strongest provinces in Bengal. The Rajah's family are all Rajputs; they coun 57 generations thro' a period of 1,100 years the greater part of which they were independent sovereigns with an annual income of more than 400,000 Rupees; their present monthly income is 400 Rupees. The fort must have been very strong in former times, the whole filt (sic) with temples, all dedicated to Vishnu . . . Only a few of the one hundred and eight temples in the fort are kept in a tolerable state of repair. 360 Gods are once a year carried to a temple outside the fort and deposited there for several days in as many stalls for the gaze and worship of the people. All the inhabitants of the fort are camouous (sic), tho' weak, enemies against the English; from the door-keeper up to the Rajah, you hear nothing but complaints.' Church Missionary Society, CI 1/0127/3 Rev. J.J. Haberlin, Journal, January to November 1835, 10 January 1835.

possess resources infinitely exceeding the settlement made by government officers when it was taken under direct government management in 1806. This impression enabled the Raja of Burdwan 'to rent it out in numerous small Talooks at a vast increase of Jumma, to persons who possessed no permanent interest in the welfare of the Estate and whose only object is the exaction of the utmost rent which can be realised'.[62] It was the conduct of these taluqdars that gave rise to the disturbances in the Senapati Mahals in 1808. Further disturbances were only avoided by the promise of the government that the complaints of the dispossessed would be dealt with in court.[63] Tejchand and his patni taluqdars attained some measure of success in resuming the Senapati Mahals and other rent-free lands. The extent of this success can be gauged from the fact that Tejchand made a mufassal settlement of the zamindari at Rs 2,52,000; before the estate passed to Tejchand, gross collection under government management, exclusive of the Senapati Mahals, had amounted to Rs 1,71,589.[64]

Although higher rates were imposed on under-rated or rent-free mahals after 1846, it does not seem that there was physical dispossession on a large scale; otherwise disturbances would have continued. In accordance with the advice of the government, many of the dispossessed took their cases to the law courts, and the available evidence indicates that many of them attained success in their suits.[65] The courts in Bishnupur were flooded with innumerable suits between the patni taluqdars of the Burdwan Raj (or, as the case might be, darpatnidars) and raiyats who claimed their lands to be rent-free.[66] Being absentees, the taluqdars could not always prosecute their cases successfully. The fact that in the twentieth century, 42.2 per cent of the land in Bankura is held in direct cultivating possession by tenure-holders —mostly Brahmans enjoying rent-free lands—proves conclusively that the Burdwan Raj and its taluqdars did not succeed in

[62]Bankura Old English Correspondence, Blunt to Dowedswell, dt. 9 March 1808. Correspondence, Vol. I, 1800-1808.

[63]Ibid., Blunt to W.B. Bayley, Register of Sadar Dewani Adalat, dt. 9 May 1809. Correspondence, Vol. I, 1800-1808.

[64]Ibid., Vol. I, Blunt, Magistrate of Jungle Mahal, to Ernst, Magistrate of Hugli, dt. 30 August 1808. Correspondence, Vol. I, 1800-1808.

[65]BRP, 17 January 1815, No. 8, Petition of Durpnarain Roy, inhabitant of Kotulpore in Pergunnah Bishenpore.

[66]See for instance serial No. 196 in Tauzi 1 Estate Bundles, Bankura Collectorate.

getting any tribute from large portions of the land in Bishnupur. The house of Burdwan, for all its reputed piety, did its level best[67] to resume lands given to temples and Brahmans but, in a Brahman dominated area, this attempt at resumption did not make much headway.

The patni taluqdars of the Burdwan Raj were in a weak position especially with regard to the powerful body of Ghatwals, who often held revenue-paying (malguzari) lands for which they refused to pay rates on the pretext that these were Ghatwali lands.[68] The Ghatwali lands, of course, remained outside the orbit of control by the Burdwan Raj and its taluqdars. In the 1870s, there were 43 estates in Bankura which were held by Ghatwals and measuring over 33,000 acres.[69]

If the patni taluqdars attained only indifferent success in their effort to bring under their revenue-collecting jurisdiction the whole of the land under cultivation in 1806, they were not rewarded with much greater success in the task of bringing under their control the lands which were brought under cultivation later on. As landed property rose in value, large portions of the waste lands were cleared and cultivated in Bankura in the 1820s and the 1830s. These improvements were not undertaken by the patni taluqdars. Sometimes they were undertaken by the Ghatwals who secured control of the new lands. More often the extension of cultivation was undertaken by migratory tribes of Santhals. As soon as the lands had been brought under cultivation in this way, the Santhals were ejected, and the rival parties of patni taluqdars and Ghatwals laid claim to the lands. Such disputes were frequent and the issue depended on the relative strength and means of the rival parties.[70] As a rule, however, patnidars

---

[7]See the complaint of attempted dispossession by Brahmans against the Raja of Burdwan in Bankura Old English Correspondence, Vol. I, Darkhaust of the Brahmins, Pundits, Gosains and Mohunts of Pergunnah Bishenpore, dt. 14 Bysack 1214 B.S. Vol. I, 1799-1808.

[68]Bankura Old English Correspondence, Vol. covering 1818-1847; Extract from a letter dt. 17 April 1833 from the Commissioner of Circuit for the division of Burdwan to the Court of Nizamat Adalat.

[69]*A Statistical Account of Bengal*, Vol. IV, pp. 254-255, 264.

[70]Bankura Old English Correspondence, Vol. covering 1818-1844, letter cited 17 April 1833.

did not succeed in building up a position of sufficient local influence to convert their patnis into actual possession of lands for they were a fluid class of transitory revenue collectors whose tenures were repeatedly sold by the Burdwan Raj for realizing arrears of jama.

The complete displacement of the Rajas of Bishnupur and their farmers by a big zamindar and patni taluqdars from outside the district did not, therefore, bring about a transfer of the land itself from its occupants to outsiders. At the higher levels, the revolution in landed interests in Bishnupur seemed more complete than in any other district; but lower down the hierarchy, the people who had actually held lands under the Rajas of Bishnupur and their farmers continued to enjoy them.[71]

[71]The Sahana family of Bankura town, a cultivating Aguri family whose ancestor got some lands from the Rajas of Bishnupur in the eighteenth century, have continued to hold these lands to this day. John Broomfield, 'The Rural Parvenu' typescript report on research under progress. I am indebted to Prof. Broomfield for supplying this information.

7

Midnapur

Midnapur, a faujdari jurisdiction on the border of Bengal included in the province of Orissa at the time of its cession to the East India Company in 1760, was later organized by the British as a Bengal collectorate and expanded by the inclusion of the salt producing chakla of Hijli, which consisted of the salt agencies of Tamluk and Contai. In the south (Contai) and east (Tamluk), where the soil was called jal (wet), the land was extremely liable to inundation by sea water against which an intricate network of embankments had been set up by the zamindars. Here the largest quantity of the salt of Bengal was manufactured by malangis (salt workers) who were practically serfs to their zamindars.[1] In the central portion of the district, where jal alternated with kala (black loam) land, the country was open and cultivated with rice, like the rest of riverine Bengal. In the western part of the district, the soil was a thin layer of red laterite over rock and the country was covered by jungle. The district could thus be naturally divided into the forest parganas, the ordinary cultivated parganas and the salt parganas.

[1]The British took over the manufacture of salt as a monopoly, giving the zamindars compensation by reducing their revenue. Two salt agencies were established at Tamluk and Contai, which formed the collectorate of Hijli. In 1836, when the collectorate of Hijli was merged with the neighbouring collectorate of Midnapur, the district assumed its present shape. Soon after this, salt ceased to be manufactured due to destructive competition from Liverpool and jalpai (salt manufacturing) lands began to go under rice cultivation.

The composition of the population of Midnapur differed according to the natural divisions of the district. The forest parganas were inhabited by turbulent tribes under refractory zamindars who paid only a nominal tribute to the Mughals. The other parts of the district were inhabited by a mixed Oriya and Bengali population.[2] The peculiarity of this population was that Bengali Brahmans and Kayasthas were comparatively few in number and did not enjoy the degree of power and influence which was characteristic of other districts in Bengal proper. Unlike other districts where the population was much divided by caste and religion, the great body of the population of the southern and eastern parts of Midnapur was formed by the dominant agricultural caste of the Kaivartas or Mahisyas. The only other big cultivating caste in Midnapur was the Sadgop caste.[3] While the Kaivartas and Sadgops formed the main body of cultivators,[4] the bulk of the zamindars and taluqdars in this district, unlike the neighbouring areas of Bengal, also came from these peasant castes.

---

[2]The Oriya population was older. As part of the ancient Hindu kingdom of Orissa, Midnapur was formerly dominated by the Oriya military class called Khandait. From Abul Fazl's account of the parganas of Midnapur, it appears that the Khandaits were the principal zamindars of the district in the sixteenth century, though it is possible that this designation was merely adopted as a sign of status by aboriginal Bhuiyas who are today known as Kaivartas or Mahisyas [see *Ain-i-Akbari*, Vol. II, translated by H.S. Jarrett, (Calcutta 1949), pp. 155-156.] The great prevalence of Oriya family names among all classes of the population (especially Kaivartas), such as Bera, Giri, Mahapatra, Maiti, Patnaik, etc., show that the Bengalis were comparatively recent immigrants in the district, who probably settled there in the trail of Pathan and Mughal conquerors as revenue collectors and civil administrators. This fact explains why in Midnapur, unlike other districts of Bengal, the dominance of Bengal Brahmans and Kayasthas was confined to government office and did not extend to land. *Memoranda of Midnapur* (Calcutta, Bengal Secretariat Press, 1902), written in 1852 by H.V. Bayley, Collector of Midnapur, pp. 4-5; hence, Bayley, op. cit.

[3]In 1872, the main communities in Midnapur were the following: Kaivarta (27%), Sadgop (6%), Muslim (6%), Brahman (4.5%), Tanti (4%), Kayastha (4%), aboriginal tribes (5.5%), Semi Hinduized aboriginals (9.5%). *A Statistical Account of Bengal*, Vol. III by W.W. Hunter, pp. 49-51.

[4]Agricultural labourers and Krishans (bonded sharecroppers), on the other hand, were recruited from the Semi Hinduized aboriginals and aboriginal tribes, although the Kaivartas and Sadgops also figured prominently among this class of people.

The caste identity of zamindar and raiyat so peculiar to Midnapur was a result of the pattern of agricultural settlement and subsequent organization of political power in the district during (and before) Mughal rule. The homeland of the agricultural Sadgops, who were originally part of the pastoral Gop caste, was Gopbhum in Burdwan district. The section of the caste which adopted agriculture became in the course of time a separate and ritually purer caste (Sadgop=pure Gop) which spread out from Gopbhum over a thickly forested lateritic tract stretching from the south-western part of Bankura to the western half of Midnapur.[5] This region, as we have seen, was inhabited by jungle tribes like Santhals and Mahatos, contemptuously referred to by the Bengalis as 'chuars' (savages). The Bengali Sadgops imposed themselves over the aboriginals as the dominant agricultural caste and in the course of this colonization seized the jungle Rajs held by tribal chieftains in the area, such as the Midnapur and Narayangarh zamindaris, and became zamindars.[6] The new Sadgop Rajas, surrounded by Sadgop agriculturists who settled around their forts, ruled over much of western Midnapur, the basis of their power being the caste identity between the usurping Rajas and the colonizing agriculturists. In the eastern and southern half of Midnapur also, the same process of colonization and seizure of power occurred, but here the colonizers and usurpers happened to be the Kaivarta caste who probably spread from Orissa into Midnapur as a military-agricultural class (Khandait) employed in the service of the kingdom of Orissa. By the time of the British occupation of Midnapur, virtually every cultivator in Tamluk (eastern part of Midnapur) was a Kaivarta. The kingdom of Tamralipta (Tamluk), ruled from time immemorial by the Mayura dynasty, was seized by the Kaivarta house of the Bhuiya Rays who became the zamindars of Tamluk.[7] Other Kaivarta

[5]Hitesranjan Sanyal, 'Continuities of Social Mobility in Traditional and Modern Society in India: Two Caste Studies of Caste Mobility in Bengal', *Journal of Asian Studies*, February 1971, pp. 321-326.

[6]See the history of the Mdnapur and Narayangarh zamindaris below.

[7]Prakash Chandra Sarkar, *Mahishya Prakash* (Calcutta 1912), pp. 382-387.

adventurers founded similar Kaivarta Rajs in the area and powerfully encouraged the settlement and colonization of Midnapur by Kaivarta agriculturists. The ritually top-ranking Kaivarta farmers of Mainachoura colonized this pargana after its conquest by Govardhanananda Bahubalindra, a Kaivarta general of the King of Orissa, who provided incentives for settlement by his caste men.[8] These gentlemen-farmers of Mainachoura and other parganas usually maintained a number of servants and slaves of their own caste for use as agricultural labourers. They also commanded the labour of small Kaivarta farmers in the area whose holdings were too small to support them and who, therefore, worked as sharecroppers on the farms of richer-Kaivartas in their spare time.[9] In Tamluk, Contai, and the adjacent areas of Midnapur all classes of agrarian society from zamindars, rich farmers, and small peasants down to sharecroppers and agricultural labourers, thus, came from the Kaivarta caste.

As a border march between Bengal and Orissa, which had witnessed centuries of conflict between Oriya and Pathan, Pathan and Mughal, and Mughal and Maratha, Midnapur came to develop a structure of government peculiar to this district, and its land tenure bore the imprint of the military character of its faujdari administration. There was no single powerful Raja or zamindar who was allowed by the Mughals to exercise jurisdiction over the whole district, as in Burdwan or Nadia. As a border chakla it was placed under a faujdar who was responsible not only for keeping the peace but also for collecting the revenue, a task never assigned to the faujdars in the interior of Bengal. Under the faujdar was his diwan, the chief revenue administrator of the district, and an officer called the sadr chaudhuri, who was the chief collecting officer.[10] Alongside the diwan and the sadr chaudhuri was a sadr qanungo (chief record keeper of the district) who was responsible not to the faujdar but to the Qanungo of the Bengal suba, and was meant to serve as a check to fraud by the district authorities in the revenue administration. Just as

[8]Harish Chandra Chakravarti *Bhranti Vijaya*, Part 1, *Brahman Kanda* (Andul Howrah 1319 B.S.), pp. 158-159.

[9]*Selections from the Correspondence on the Resettlement of the Majnamuta and Jellamuta Estates in the District of Midnapore* (Calcutta 1881), p. 42.

[10]*A Statistical Account of Bengal*, Vol. III, p. 192.

there were chaudhuris in each pargana under the sadr chaudhuri for collecting the revenue, there were qanungos in each pargana who preserved records for the information of the sadr qanungo. So, unlike many other areas in Bengal, Midnapur had a district administration, though it hardly constituted a centralized bureaucracy. The office of the sadr qanungo and the sadr chaudhuri had become hereditary, and the local families which held these two offices from generation to generation were allowed to hold considerable taluqs at reduced rates. From the nature of his office and the lands which he held rent-free in every pargana, the sadr qanungo had great influence on the collecting (gomasta) and accounting (patwari) staff in each pargana. This influence, however, was exerted not in the interest of the government but in favour of local interests opposed to it. The qanungos in Midnapur enjoyed taluqs at a very low rate charging the deficiency upon other taluqdars, and acted in collusion with the gomastas of the zamindars and the taluqdars to reduce the mufassal assessment of the district.[11]

Nevertheless, the very existence of a district administration,[12] however light its penetration to the pargana or village level, affected the nature of land tenure in the district. The patwari and gomasta establishments in the villages were under the control not merely of the zamindar of the pargana but also, in some measure, of district revenue officers like the diwan, the sadr chaudhuri, and the sadr qanungo, who had a say in the appointment of these establishments.[13] When a cultivator wished to leave one taluq and settle in another, he had to secure permission

---

[11]BRP, 22 June 1787, No. 78, from Collector of Midnapur to BR.

[12]The apparatus of district government under the Mughals which we have described for Midnapur certainly did not exist in the more settled areas in the interior of Bengal proper such as Dinajpur, Rajshahi, Burdwan and Nadia. The Mughals seem to have built up a regular apparatus of district government only in border faujdari areas like Midnapur, Chittagong, Rangpur, and Purnia. There were faujdars also in the more centrally situated areas, such as the faujdars of Hugli, but they were merely military officers who played no part in revenue administration.

[13]The sadr qanungo apparently had come to enjoy the power of fixing nine-tenths of the zamindari servants and gomastas in each pargana. BRP, 22 June 1787, No. 78, from the Collector of Midnapur to BR.

not from his taluqdar but from the diwan of the faujdar.[14] Unlike Burdwan, Bishnupur, Birbhum, Nadia, Dinajpur, and Rajshahi where the payment of the revenue to the government was controlled by a single Raj family which administered its territory in a more or less autonomous manner, the land revenue collection of Midnapur was shared by a large body of zamindars and taluqdars of varying size. As a collector of Midnapur wrote to the Board of Revenue in 1787:

> There are very few zamindars, who hold a whole pergunnah in their own person, and who are singly accountable to the government for the rents of such pergunnah—The pergunnahs here have been divided and sub-divided into a vast number of talooks, in as much as several of their talookdars act as Ryots in their own talooks, and pay separately their own rents: and again in those pergunnahs held solely by zamindars, these give farms to their own Vassals and Dependants accountable to them alone, and excepting these farmers there are none in this Chakla but those who held the lands lately Rent free resumed in this and the preceding year.[15]

As these remarks indicate, there was a wide variety of land tenure in Midnapur; this variety was due not only to the diverse origin of landed rights but also to the differing degrees of control exercised by the district revenue authorities over various kinds of landholders. There were, in the first place, the zamindars in the Jungle Mahals, who were practically independent of the Mughals[16] and were brought under British control only by regular military expeditions into the jungle after 1760;[17] a few big zamindars holding several parganas in the more settled parts

[14]*Final Report on the Survey and Settelement Operations in the District of Midnapur, 1910-1918*, A.K. Jameson, pp. 35-36.

[5]BRP, 22 June, 1787, No. 78, from Collector of Midnapur to BR.

[16]The zamindar of Kalyanpur, for instance, paid only the nominal sum of Rs 30 as tribute to the Mughal government. *Midnapur District Records* 1763-1767, W.K. Firminger, ed., No. 115, Fergusson to Graham, 3 February 1767, pp. 87-88; Ibid., No. 117, Graham to Fergusson, 4 February 1767, pp. 88-89.

[17]Even then the jungle zamindars were persuaded to pay only a very light sum as revenue to the British.

of the district who also enjoyed some measure of authority and independence and affected the title of Raja; a vast body of small zamindars, taluqdars, chaudhuris and qanungos on whom the district revenue authorities could practise oppression with impunity and among whom the majority of the parganas were divided into minute shares; and, finally, the mandals, baruas (village heads in Tamluk and Contai), and jotedars who physically occupied the lands along with cultivating taluqdars and rent-free tenure-holders.

The number of small zamindars and taluqdars in Midnapur before the Decennial Settlement was about 3000.[18] Some of these small proprietors were of considerable antiquity and had at one time held whole parganas. The zamindars of Birkul and Kakrachour, for instance, originated as feudatories of the Raja of Mayurbhanj in the sixteenth century. These two parganas had formerly been managed by sardars (vassals) of the Raja of Mayurbhanj to whom they paid the revenue. But the cultivators revolted against the Raja and established Sagar Ray in the zamindari of Birkul about 1500. Sagar's great grandson, Narahari Ray, made his eldest son zamindar of Birkul, his second son chaudhuri (hereditary local official for collecting the revenue, theoretically distinct from the zamindar but often identical in practice) of the same pargana, and his third son zamindar of Kakrachour. In 1760, one Sarveswar Ray purchased a nine-anna share of Birkul, whereupon the zamindari became nominally divided into a nine-anna and a seven-anna share. In reality, however, these large portions were further subdivided into various small tenures by sales, executions of decrees, and foreclosures of mortgages under the British.[19] A large number of taluqs were created even before British rule because many zamindars, being unable to pay the revenue, were compelled to sell their rights to petty taluqdars. In 1741, the zamindar of Jalkapur, who could not pay the revenue, had to sell his zamindari to fourteen taluqdars. However, he managed to retain a

[18]N.K. Sinha, *The Economic History of Bengal*, Vol. II.

[19]Bayley, op. cit., pp. 31-32. *A Statistical Account of Bengal*, Vol. III, p. 194. Hunter's account of the establishment of the Birkul zamindari differs slightly from that of Bayley. I have relied on Hunter because he refers directly to a report by Collector Hewett, dt. 15 June 1787.

share in the zamindari through his servant Tikaram who purchased a Taluq in his master's name.[20]

The taluqdars in Midnapur were almost without exception independent.[21] Each taluqdar paid his revenue separately to a government officer but, by custom, only certain individuals signed the engagement for the whole lot of inferior taluqdars in a pargana. The head renters remained responsible for making up losses resulting from the defalcation of the taluqdars. The taluqdars usually continued to exist as under-renters even where a superior zamindar established his right to a whole pargana. In 1760, immediately before the cession of Midnapur to the East India Company, the Raja of Mainachoura conquered pargana Sabang in a regular military campaign lasting three months. This pargana was held by about a hundred petty taluqdars and qanungos, who after the expedition acknowledged his overlordship and became under-renters of the Mainachoura Raj.[22] However, the Raja was able only to levy a quasi-tribute, not a regular revenue, from the occupiers of the land in Sabang.[23]

The chaudhuris and taluqdars in the divided parganas being small proprietors were easy prey to the cupidity of the superior revenue officers of the district. An instance of this was provided in 1789 by a petition of the chaudhuris and taluqdars of chakla Jalasore. They complained that the sadr qanungo Rajnarayan Ray was laying unjust increases of revenue upon them, while at the same time he had suspended Rs 2,50,000 of the previous year's balance in revenue in his own chakla, Midnapur, where he enjoyed taluqs in almost every pargana. Acting in concert with the collector's diwan, the sadr qanungo sold the houses, grain, cattle, and jewels of the Jalasore chaudhuris and taluqdars, and pushed them into a state of indebtedness to

[20]Board of Revenue, Miscellaneous Records, Land and land revenue, Survey of parganas in Midnapur with geneology and succession of zamindars—1788: Survey of pargana Julcapore.

[21]In 1792, there were only eleven dependent taluqdars in Midnapur. BRP, 13 March 1792, No. 6., Collector to BR.

[22]Home Miscellaneous, Vol. 47, Midnapur, Zamindari of Mynachoura, John Johnstone to Committee of New Lands of Fort William, dt. 8 January 1760.

[23]Bayley, op. cit., p. 20.

mahajans.[24] Usually, however, the taluqdars and chaudhuris were able to secure the favour of the sadr qanungo against the interests of the government by means of bribery, and such collusion between landholders and qanungos resulted in the dissipation of large sums of government revenue.[25]

The bigger zamindars who ruled over whole parganas were not so exposed to petty exactions by revenue officials, but they suffered from a different kind of weakness arising from the internal structure of their zamindaris. The large body of vassals and dependants who were invariably attached to the train of a big Raja were usually rewarded with farms and subfarms within the parganas controlled by the Raja. Collusive leases were granted by the head farmers to qutqinadars and other under-renters at rates lower than the pargana rates.[26] Many of these farmers in effect held their farms on a hereditary basis, though their leases had to be renewed periodically. In the zamindaris of Majnamuta and Jalamuta, there was a class of sabek ijaradars existing prior to the Permanent Settlement who were farmers of portions of these zamindaris nominally on a temporary basis but in reality permanent.[27]

The big Rajas in the salt and ordinary cultivated parganas of Midnapur at the time of the Permanent Settlement were mostly Kaivartas, though a few belonged to other castes. The local genealogy of Gadadhar Bhatta, a Brahman bard of Midnapur, records the foundation of five kingdoms in Midnapur and Hijli by Kaivarta chiefs at different times. These kingdoms were

---

[24]*Midnapur District Records*, Letters Received, 1777-1800, Harington to Collector of Midnapur, 11 June 1789, p. 328.

[25]BRP, 22 June 1787, No. 78, from Collector of Midnapur to John Shore.

[26]Midnapur Old English Correspondence, Letters Issued, Collector to BR 22 February 1796. The big zamindari of Kasijora Shahpur, for instance, was in the period before Permanent Settlement almost without exception let to farm. After the collector attached the zamindari for revenue balances in 1793, the zamindari was partly in the hands of etmamdars (charge-holding farmers) appointed by the collector himself, partly in the hands of farmers who got their lease directly from the Raja of Kasijora in 1789, and partly in the hands of a class of permanent (mokarari) farmers. BRP, 11 Jan. 1793, from Collector of Midnapur to BR.

[27]*Final Report on Midnapur*, p. 36.

Tamluk, Balisita, Turka, Sujamuta and Kutubpur.[28] Of these, only Tamluk, Mainachoura (formerly Balisita) and Sujamuta retained anything of their former size at the time of the Permanent Settlement. Kutubpur had become divided into four shares of ten annas, three annas, one and a half anna and one and a half anna respectively. In Turkachour, the Kaivarta family of Raja Panchanan Gajendra Mahapatra still remained the biggest proprietor at the time of collector Bayley, but much of the pargana had passed to new proprietors.[29] Among big zamindars belonging to other castes, the Sadgop family of Narajole held the biggest zamindari of the district — that of the Midnapur Raj. Another big zamindari, the Mahisadal Raj, had passed long before the coming of the British from a Kaivarta dynasty to a Brahman family. Table 7.1 shows the big zamindars of Midnapur, as mentioned by James Grant, when the British took over Midnapur.

TABLE 7.1

BIG ZAMINDARIES IN MIDNAPUR UNDER EARLY BRITISH RULE

Zamindari	*Caste*	*Jama*
Midnapur	Sadgop	1,79,378
Narajole	Sadgop	13,724
Kasijora	Unknown	2,21,881
Jalamuta	Brahman	1,64,224
Majnamuta	Kayastha	1,27,481
Mahisadal	Brahman	1,01,565
Tamluk	Kaivarta	59,358
Sujamuta	Kaivarta	25,314
Mainachoura	Kaivarta	59,491

[28]Gadadhar Bhata's Kulaji as quoted in Harish Chandra Chakrabarty. *Bhranti Vijaya*, Part I, *Brahman Kanda* (Andul, Howrah, 1319 B.S.) pp. 154-162.

[29]Bayley, op. cit., pp. 20, 23-24. The Turka family, for all its reputation of antiquity, was not really very old, and supplanted an older family ruling over parganas Turkachour and Mirgoda from the fort of Turka as a feudatory of the king of Orissa. Sometime in the seventeenth century, the feudatory Raja refused to pay the revenue to the king of Orissa who, thereupon, sent his sardar, Krishnachandra Gajendra Mahapatra of Khurdarthipur, to subdue the rebel. Krishna Gajendra killed the rebel and was

The district records of Midnapur contain no information about the history of the zamindari of Kasijora though this was the largest revenue paying zamindari in the district. In 1777-78 the zamindar of Kasijora, Raja Sundarnarayan Ray, held a 14/16th share of the pargana, the rest being held by others.[30] Besides the fourteen-anna share of pargana Kasijora, Sundarnarayan also held the whole of pargana Shahpur. The zamindari of Kasijora and Shahpur was a highly assessed zamindari for, though it was liable to frequent inundation and measured only 108,448 acres as compared with the 309,613 acres of the Midnapur zamindari,[31] it paid a higher revenue than the latter.

The Midnapur Raj consisting of the parganas of Banjbhum (Midnapur), Bahadurpur, Denkiabazar, and Manohargarh was the principal zamindari of the district, lying partly in the forest parganas, partly in the ordinary cultivated parganas. A large part of the zamindari was held at quit rent by a turbulent militia (paiks). The tribute of the zamindari was drawn in kind. A portion of the zamindari of Midnapur originally formed a part of a feudatory state under the king of Orissa. The ruler of this feudatory state, Raja Surat Singh (commonly called Khaira Raja, Khaira being a jungle caste) ruled over most of Midnapur and the whole of Narayangarh, Balarampur, Kedar, and Kharagpur. The Khaira Raja was slain in a conspiracy formed between his diwan, his garh sardar (commander of the fort), and his deputy garh sardar who divided the kingdom among themselves. The diwan and commander-in chief, Laksman Singh, became the founder of the Midnapur Raj. The garh sardar seized Balarampur, Kedar, and

---

appointed zamindar of the two parganas by the king of Orissa. His grandson Rajvallabh obtained a zamindari sanad from the Diwan of Bengal, Shuja Khan, possibly in 1720s. Rajvallabh's son Jasodanandan Gajendra Mahapatra, fourth in descent, was the zamindar of Turka when the British took over Midnapur. Bhagabati Charan Pradhan, *Aryaprabha* (Tamluk, 1318 B.S.); pp. 126-127.

[30]James Grant, 'Analysis of Bengal Finances', Appendix to Fifth Report, *Parliamentary Papers*, Vol. VII, Session 1812.

[31]*A Statistical Account of Bengal*, Vol. III, pp. 203, 209-216.

Kharagpur while his deputy made himself Raja of Narayangarh.[32] The zamindari of Midnapur underwent considerable expansion during the time of Ajit Singh, who seized pargana Bhanjbhum from the ruling Bhanjas of the pargana, a subdivision of the forest race of Bhumij. Ajit Singh died in 1755 without a son and was succeeded by his widow, Rani Siromoni, who settled for Midnapur at the time of the Decennial Settlement. At this settlement pargana Bahadurpur, so long a separate zamindari, was attached to the Midnapur Raj, the zamindar of Bahadurpur having fled after having been in arms against the British government.[33] Rani Siromoni was unable to manage the zamindari because of Chuar disturbances instigated by the robber baron, Govardhan Dikpati, a Brahman of pargana Bagri. The coffers of the Midnapur Raj were empty and its infantry had dwindled in number. Rani Siromoni, therefore, appointed as her agent the Raja of Narajole, Trilochan Khan, who was a maternal relative

[32]Tradition records that the Khaira Raja's seven wives burnt themselves, predicting at their death that after seven generations the families of the three treacherous servants would be heirless and the properties would go to others. This prediction was not fulfilled in the case of the Raja of Narayangarh who was the principal zamindar in the Jungle Mahals at the time of the British takeover and assisted the British actively against the Marathas. In spite of the curse, the Narayangarh family survived well into the twentieth century and continued to enjoy a very profitable and lightly assessed zamindari, proving themselves to be 'model' landlords highly regarded by the collectors of Midnapur. In the case of the Balarampur family the alleged curse came true; at the time of the Decennial Settlement the sadr chaudhuri of the district, Birprasad Das, took the settlement for parganas Kedar, Kharagpur, and Balarampur. The prophecy was fulfilled also in the case of Midnapur, which passed into the hands of the Narajole Rajas. The story, though in part plainly legendary, does illustrate in a striking manner the evolution of land tenure in a traditional society, leading to the creation of three zamindaris from a feudatory kingdom. The new Rajas of Midnapur and Narayangarh were Sadgops and the legend seems to recall the migrations as a result of which the Sadgop agriculturists established their domination over the jungle tribes in the western part of Midnapur.

[33]The dispossessed family of Bahadurpur were, however, kept on as farmers of Bahadurpur at a very low rate by the Midnapur Raj till 1847. They were finally ousted in that year when the Midnapur Raj itself became the property of the Nawab Nazim of Murshidabad, whose agent stopped the practice of giving the farm to the Bahadurpur family. Bayley, op.cit., p. 17.

of her husband. With the death of Rani Siromoni the dynasty of Ajit Singh came to an end and the zamindari of Midnapur passed to the Narajole family.[34]

The Maina Raj, one of the five Kaivarta kingdoms recorded in tradition, was a practically autonomous zamindari under the Mughals and was brought under proper government control for the first time by the British Residents of Midnapur. The ancestor of his family, Raja Kalindiram Samanta, ruled from the fort of Balisita in pargana Sabang as a feudatory of the king of Orissa. His sixth descendant, Govardhanananda, captured the fort of Maina from Sridhar Hui, another Kaivarta chief of the area, and was rewarded with the title of 'Bahubalindra' by the king of Orissa for his services. When the British took over the district, Jagadananda Bahubalindra, twelfth in descent, was ruling from the fort of Maina over the parganas of Mainachoura and Sabang.[35] He was esteemed a formidable and very rich Raja and kept a body of about 3,000 men in his pay. Before Midnapur passed to the British, he was a great favourite at the court in Murshidabad and scarcely paid anything for his pargana of Mainachoura. 'Notwithstanding the Encrease which has been laid on his Rents by the Company...' wrote the Resident of Midnapur to Warren Hastings in 1773. "he has continued the same expenses and indulged the same Extravagancies (sic) of Pomp & Show as when he was possessed of a plentiful Estate—but even at that time he was not able to support himself without plundering, & borrowing from every Body who would lend him...."[36] He did not prove to be a peaceful subject of the British. On apprehension of any disagreeable order he shut

[34]The above history of the Midnapur Raj is based on Bayley, op. cit. Raja Mahendralal Khan, *The History of the Midnapur Raj*, (Calcutta 1889), Ambika Charan Gupta, *Hugli* (Calcutta 1321 B.S.), pp. 186-195.

[35]The latter pargana was conquered by Jagadananda in 1760 from its petty taluqdars. The Maina family apparently possessed a taluq and a fort (Balisita) in this pargana before his time, if tradition is to be believed, but the pargana was controlled by petty taluqdars. These taluqdars became under-renters of the Maina Raja in 1760, but for all practical purposes they continued as the real masters of Sabang. His authority was supreme only in pargana Mainachoura.

[36]*Midnapur District Records*, Vol. IV, 1770-1774, No. 153, to Warren Hastings from Edward Baber dt. 6 January 1773, p. 99. Jagadanande Bahubalindra in fact borrowed from all available sources—from the East India

himself up in his fort of Maina which was surrounded by two ditches filled with alligators and closely planted with bamboos making it inaccessible to any unwelcome messenger from the government.[37] Jagadananda died in 1773 and was succeeded by his son Brajananda Bahubalindra who accepted the Permanent Settlement for pargana Mainachoura. Pargana Sabang was, however, taken out of his control and was settled on the taluqdars of the pargana who became independent once again.

Like the Maina Raj, the Mahisadal Raj also belonged at one time to a Kaivarta family. It was founded by Bhuiya Ray Mahapatra whose sixth descendant, Kalyan Ray, could not realize the revenue and had to furnish Janardan Upadhyaya, a Brahman of substance, as his security. Janardan soon supplanted Kalyan in the zamindari but his successor, Durjan Upadhyaya, was killed in a skirmish with Kalyan Ray. The Mughal governor of Bengal, however, confirmed his son, Ramsur Upadhyaya, in the zamindari of Mahisadal in 1659. The zamindari was held for over a century by this Brahman family in uninterrupted possession. From 1765 to the era of the Permanent Settlement, the zamindari was administered with great ability by Rani Janaki, the widow of Anandalal Upadhyaya who died in that year.[38] It was a flourishing zamindari consisting of six parganas,[39] which were divided into 18 mahals comprising in all 438 villages.

The oldest family in Midnapur was of the Tamluk dynasty which had held the kingdom of Tamluk from time immemorial. Abul Fazl mentions in the *Ain-i-Akbari* that in the time of Akbar it was a zamindari held by a Khandait family. The actual caste of the family was Kaivarta, Khandait being merely a term indicating the feudal military class at the service of the kingdom of

---

Company, from the faujdar of Midnapur, from European Company servants and their native banians to keep up his state. Ibid., 1763-1767, No. 233, translation of a letter from the Mainachoura Raja to Jagatram Dutt, dt. 5 July 1767, p. 169.

[37]Ibid., Vol. IV, 1770-1774, No. 162, to Warren Hastings from Edward Baber, dt. 6 February 1773, p. 105.

[38]BRP, 18 September 1787, No. 94, The Hereditary descents of the Zamindars of Mysadul etc. Sarkar Maugettea Chuckla Hijli agreeable to the records of Canungoe's office.

[39]Mahisadal, Tiyarpara, Gomoi, Aurangnagar, Kasimnagar, Goomghar.

TABLE 7.2
CONSTITUTION OF THE MAHISADAL RAJ

	Rs
Revenue of lands occupied by raiyats	142473
Baze mahal or lands on quit rent	2178
Taxes upon lands held and cultivated by zamindar	2593
Lands held by qanungo	63
Lands held by qazi	90
Total hazeera or actual sources of revenue	166119
Plateka or rated revenue of lands deserted but still kept on the hast-o-bud	25527
Sayer revenue	3800
Lands held by servants	14920
Total hast-o-bud jama	191647

Orissa. Containing the famous ancient port of Tamluk, this kingdom was in antiquity ruled by the Mayura dynasty from which it passed to the Kaivarta Bhuiya family long before Mughal rule, in the 38th generation of the Rajas of Tamluk. The earliest Raja whose date was mentioned in the genealogy of the dynasty was the 42nd Raja Bhangar Bhuiya Ray, who died in 1404 A.D. Although according to the *Ain-i-Akbari*, this zamindari was supposed to furnish the empire with 1,000 infantry, 50 cavalry and cash to the amount of 2571,430 dams,[40] it would appear that the zamindars of Tamluk acknowledged only a nominal suzerainty of the Mughal Emperor. In 1757 the zamindari was seized by a Muslim adventurer called Mirza Didar Beg. In 1767 the zamindari reverted to the dispossessed Kaivarta family, which secured this favourable decision from the government by bribing the principal officers, Nandakumar Ray and Gangagovinda Singh, who obtained as their reward respectively the taluqs of Basudebpur (consisting of six villages) and Gopalpur (consisting of eight villages) in the south of the zamindari.[41]

[40] *Ain-i-Akbari*, Vol. II, p. 156.

[41] Taluq Basudedpur was subsequently transferred from the descendants of Nandakumar Ray (the famous Nuncoomar hanged during the administration of Warren Hastings) to the Rajas of Mahisadal. Taluq Gopalpur was retained by the descendants of Gangagovinda Singh, the zamindars of Paikpara and Kandi, well into the twentieth century. Prakash Chandra Sarkar, op. cit., p. 391-392; Bayley, op. cit., pp. 33-34.

The Hijli portion of Midnapur consisting of the zamindaris of Sujamuta, Jalamuta, and Majnamuta was originally a Kaivarta kingdom which was seized by a Pathan adventurer—Masnad Ali—who acknowledged the suzerainty of the Mughal Emperor Akbar in 1556. Subsequently a descendant of the dispossessed Kaivarta family recovered a portion of the Hijli Raj which became known as the zamindari of Sujamuta. The rest of the kingdom of Hijli was constituted by the Mughals into the zamindaris of Jalamuta and Majnamuta which were settled respectively on a Brahman cook and a Kayastha clerk serving the ruling Kaivarta family. At the time of the Permanent Settlement only the Kaivarta family of Sujamuta accepted permanent settlement in Hijli. The Brahman and Kayastha zamindars of Jalamuta and Majnamuta agreed to settle only on a temporary basis since the area was specially liable to inundation.

We have discussed the history of the zamindaris in the settled agricultural parts of Midnapur at some length in order to explore the variety of the origin of landed rights and the evolution of zamindari tenure. Many of the older zamindaris originated as feudatory kingdoms created by the king of Orissa and, in a few cases, by the Raja of Mayurbhunj. The Mughals tried to regularize the position of these chiefships, comprising considerable stretches of territory ruled from mud-and-stone forts,[42] by giving such military-administrative jurisdictions the name of zamindaris and compelling their masters to take zamindari sanads from the Mughal government. Not all zamindaris, however, originated in this way in Midnapur. Some were created through the administrative action of the Mughal faujdar in Midnapur, who appointed chaudhuris for different parganas to collect the revenue. By long practice all important officials connected with revenue administration tended to acquire landed rights. Then again there was a numerous body of taluqdars and revenue-farmers some of whom got their mahals as dependents of the big Rajas while others had existed for long in their own right. They formed the gentry of the countryside, enjoying actual possession of land and labour while Rajas, zamindars, and

[42]Abul Fazl in 1654 mentions the forts of Tamluk, Turka, Sabang (Balisita), Kharagpur, Kedarkund (3 forts), Midnapur (2 forts), Kutubpur and Khundar. *Ain-i-Akbari*, Vol. II, p. 156.

chaudhuris over them administered the country and collected the revenue.

To fit all these different grades of landed rights into an administrative framework subservient to the supreme government of the Mughals, the possessors of all these rights were designated as zamindars and taluqdars appointed by official sanad to collect the revenue. But such a systematic grouping and organization of landed rights under the effective authority of the Mughal government did not extend over all parts. Even in the settled agricultural areas, as we have seen, the Rajas of Maina and Tamluk were able to resist successfully the extension of government authority over their jurisdiction. In the Jungle Mahals, this attempt at systematization was much less effective. The territory was nominally divided into 17 parganas, and each of these was governed by a 'zamindar' (so-called by the Mughal government), who was dignified among his subjects with the title of Raja. The jungle chiefs were freebooters who habitually plundered their neighbours as well as their subjects. After the harvest, there was scarcely a chief who did not call his subjects to his standard to defend his territory or attack his neighbours.[43]

Whereas in the Jungle Mahals the zamindars were aboriginal Bhuiya or Bhumij chiefs who had assumed the status of Rajput or Khandait, in the settled agricultural areas the forts from which the country was dominated were usually held by 'royal' Kaivarta lineages having extensive blood or matrimonial ties with the Kaivarta land-holding gentry of the surrounding countryside. In pargana Mainachoura, the respectable Kaivarta families had long had matrimonial connections with the Bahubalindra family of Killa Mainachoura. This family acted as the social leader (samajpati) of the Kaivarta samaj (local society) of Mainachoura. On the eve of British rule Sanskritized rites were introduced among the respectable Kaivarta families of Mainachoura by their samajpati, Jagadananda Bahubalindra, the then Raja of Maina.[44] It would appear that most of the

---

[43]*Midnapur District Records*, Vol. IV, 1770-1774, No. 163, to Warren Hastings from Edward Baber, dt. 6 February 1773, p. 106.

[44]Prakash Chandra Sarkar, op. cit., p. 329.

ruling Kaivarta lineages were founded by generals in the service of the kingdom of Orissa. The family titles of the respectable land-holding Kaivartas of Midnapur at the time of the Permanent Settlement leave no doubt that they had originally formed a military class (Khandait) in the service of the king of Orissa.[45] They had at the same time carried on agricultural operations with the help of servants who were also of the Kaivarta caste. In all Kaivarta samajs of the area, the respectable families maintained a number of farm servants. This servant class, called shiqdar and sudra, intermarried among themselves and were not allowed to have any matrimonial relations with respectable agricultural Kaivartas.[46]

Besides these Kaivarta families, usually bearing aboriginal or Oriya names, many Bengali Kayastha families also carved out landed rights in Midnapur under Mughal rule. The Quinquennial Register of landed rights in Midnapur for 1795, which lists 928 proprietors, mentions at least 121 proprietors whose names are definitely identifiable as Kaivarta and 80 proprietors whose names indicate them to be Bengali Kayasthas. Significantly, 228 among the proprietors had as their surnames Mughal official titles which were customarily adopted by families which boasted sons in government service.[47] Most of the revenue officials employed by the government of the Mughal faujdar in Midnapur —diwans, chaudhuris, and qanungos—were Bengali Kayasthas and Brahmans. This was how Bengalis--particularly Kayasthas— carved out a share in landed rights which were formerly enjoyed by a Kaivarta gentry predominantly Oriya in culture. However, by the middle of the nineteenth century, the landed gentry in Midnapur of all castes were insensibly approximating to the manners of the same category in Bengal proper.[48]

---

[45]Midnapur Collectorate Records, Quinquennial Registers, 1795; Basanta Kumar Ray, *Mahisya Bibriti,* (Babur Bazar, Dacca, B.S. 1322), pp. 191-192.

[46]Ibid., p. 253.

[47]Kaivartas—121, Oriya surname holders—68, Mughal official title holders —228, Bengali surname holders of unidentifiable caste—186, Bengali Kayasthas—80, Bengali Brahmans—24, Sadgops—2, Upcountry Khatri—1, Muslims—14, Unknown—204, Total—928, Quinquennial Register, Midnapur Collectorate, 1795.

[48]Bayley, op. cit., p. 5.

Although the Rajas, chaudhuris, and taluqdars in Midnapur were all made to feel in some measure the weight of authority imposed by the government of the Mughal faujdar—an authority far more effective than the former system of rule through feudatories by the king of Orissa—there remained, as we have seen, considerable scope for local adjustments or personal arrangements with individual revenue officials which enabled the various categories of landholders in Midnapur to arrange matters suitably in their localities within certain limits without constant interference from the faujdar's government in the town of Midnapur. Over such a state of diffused and varied jurisdiction, the British attempted to establish a centralized structure of rule with new methods of collection of revenue and with greater power to interfere in the locality from an upper level of authority. The essential feature of this new structure of rule was that a European officer, at first called resident and subsequently collector, was placed in sole charge of revenue collection in the district under regular supervision from the government in Calcutta. The impact of the new district administration on the mode of land control was clearly demonstrated in the zamindari of Kasijora. Once the machinery of district government was fully set up in connection with the Decennial Settlement, the collector took over and streamrolled the estate administration of Kasijora in a way that could hardly have been conceived by the faujdar of Midnapur. In 1796, the collector of Midnapur divided the parganas of Kasijora and Shahpur into zillas (units of collection), the zillas into hudas (lots or portions) and the hudas into villages, appointing his own patwaris in each village since those appointed by the zamindar used to maintain two sets of accounts—an authentic one for their master and a false one for the government.[49]

[49]BRP, 29 December 1795, No. 55, Ibid., 3 May 1796, No 29. The collector at first ordered the patwaris appointed by the zamindar to submit five years' papers of assessment and collection (jama hasil) quickly so that they did not get time to alter the records. Where the patwaris absented themselves, he demanded these accounts from the sarbarakars appointed by the Raja to collect the revenue from the villages. But both patwaris and surbarakars proved disobedient and sent evasive answers. The collector, determined to execute the business in spite of all the machinations of the zamindar, appointed his own patwaris. Midnapur Old English Correspondence, Letters Issued, December 1795, Collector to BR.

Having completed the allotment of the parganas of Kasijora and Shahpur in 50 lots, the collector sold the zamindari, destroying its very identity.

The zamindars did not of course submit tamely to the unfamiliar exercise of authority by the collector and sought to fight off the pressure exerted by him in various ways. Whenever the collector issued an order for the sequestration of a zamindar's mahals or an examination of village accounts, the zamindar immediately removed the qualified patwaris and sarbarakars and appointed new officers without the necessary knowledge.[50]

The continuous pressure exerted by the new district administration during the Decennial Settlement began to produce for the first time a sort of combination among the zamindars of Midnapur. Two officers, Rajnarayan Ray (sadr qanungo) and Ramlochan Mukherjee, were appointed to investigate the resources of the district and carry into effect a proposed increase of revenue. In order to foil this attempt, the zamindars of Midnapur combined in a manner never seen in the district before and lodged a general complaint that the above-mentioned officers of the government were oppressing them.[51] Under the faujdar's government, such a combination among the zamindars of Midnapur had never been necessary, for the faujdar's government had never followed a general revenue policy applied without exception to all areas. Revenue transactions had been made locally and the scope for individual arrangements between the various grades of landholders and revenue collectors had been considerable. The general pressure of the British district system began to produce a new unity among the zamindars as a class as they were all people equally affected by government revenue policy.

Very few landholders escaped from the increased incidence of the revenue in the settled parts of the district. From Rs 8 lakhs in 1787, the revenue rose to Rs 11 lakhs in 1793, a sum finally

---

[50]The patwaris frequently complained of their unmerited ejection by the zamindar. Midnapur Old English Correspondence, Letters Issued, 1797, Collector to BR, dt. 11 February 1797.

[51]Midnapur Old English Correspondence, Letters Issued 1788, Collector to acting preparer of reports, Revenue department, dt. 8 November 1788.

and permanently assessed on the district.[52] This sudden increase of 37 per cent in the revenue of the district in the course of five years, combined with the frequency of floods in Midnapur, led to heavy selling of zamindaris and taluqs in the next few decades.

Transfer of revenue-collecting rights in Midnapur was not, however, a new phenomenon ushered in by the Permanent Settlement. Under the Mughal faujdars of Midnapur, zamindaris changed hands continually on account of failure to pay government dues. Such transfer of zamindari rights could take place in several ways. The chaudhuri or zamindar, unable to pay the revenue, might sell portions of his zamindari to several taluqdars.[53] Defaulting zamindars might be asked by the government to furnish securities who would often take over the zamindari right supplanting the older families.[54] Alternatively, the government might dismiss a defaulting zamindar and appoint to the zamindari an officer of the former zamindar, a process which occurred often and was usually engineered by the machinations of interested zamindari officers.[55] Another process which occurred often was the takeover of zamindaris by the revenue officers of the

---

[52]*Final Report of Midnapur*, pp. 78-79.

[53]Pargana Bhuiyamuta was in the possession of two chaudauris who held eight annas each as their respective shares. One of them, Raghunath, sold 7.10 annas to 18 taluqdars who agreed to pay him rasum (zamindar's allowance) and dastur (customary percentage) amounting to Rs 146. The other chaudhuri, Govindram, kept to himself 2.18 annas and sold 5.2 annas to the same taluqdars, receiving from them Rs 131 as rasum and dastur. Miscellaneous Records, Board of Revenue, Land and land revenue, Survey of Parganas in Midnapur with genealogy and succession zamindars—1788: Survey of Pargana Bhuiyamuta. In pargana Jalkapur, the zamindar sold his land to 14 taluqdars in 1741, retaining for himself only one taluq in his slave's name. Ibid., Survey of Pargana Julcapore and the genealogy of the zamindars of Julcapore.

[54]Ramchandra and Bhupat Ray, zamindars of Hijli, became securities for the zamindars of Bhuiyamuta. The latter absconded and the securities succeeded to the zamindari in 1720, possessing it till 1730 when the zamindars got back their patrimony by complaining to the Nawab. Ibid., Genealogy of the zamindars of Pargana Bhuiyamuta.

[55]In the middle of the seventeenth century, Uttar Ray Chaudhuri became the zamindar of Uttarbihar by the sanction of the government upon the dismissal of his employer who had absconded after failing to pay the revenue. Ibid., Genealogy of the zamindars of Uttarbihar.

district or the creation of taluqs in their favour within these zamindaris.[56] The zamindari of Khundar, which became divided in the course of time into numerous taluqs and chaudhrais, (jurisdictions of chaudhuris or hereditary revenue managers) witnessed several of these processes. In 1588 the zamindar was obliged, in order to pay the revenue, to sell an eight-sixteenth share (eight annas) to the sadr qanungo and a six-sixteenth share (six annas) to the sadr chaudhuri reserving to himself only a two-sixteenth (two annas) share. The sadr qanungo and the sadr chaudhuri were, in turn, unable to pay the revenue and sold their shares to the vilayati chaudhuris[57] in 1645. The zamindar himself had to sell his two-sixteenth share in 1645 when he fell into arrears of revenue, but later he purchased his two-anna share back. The rest of the pargana became divided among 147 taluqdars, among whom stood the vilayati chaudhuris. By virtue of their purchase, the vilayati chaudhuris stood in the position of zamindar, receiving the rasum and the dastur of the pargana proportionate to their shares.[58] The immense opportunities for acquirement of permanent revenue-collecting rights by revenue officials which existed within the Mughal system was seen in the fact that Rajnarayan Ray, the sadr qanungo of Midnapur under early

---

[56]In 1756, the zamindars of Kharagpur, Kedar, and Balarampur unable to pay the revenue, sold a 2 annas 15 gandas share to Govinda Das, the diwan of the faujdar of Midnapur. This share came to constitute the zamindari of Tappa Jamna which Govinda Das registered in the name of his son Abhiram Harichandra. Ibid., Survey of Tappa Jamna and genealogy of the zamindars of Kharagpur and Tappa Balarampur.

The zamindar of Pratapban sold shares to the sadr qanungo, the vilayati qanungo, and taluqdars keeping a 9.9 annas share for himself before his death in 1696. Ibid., Genealogy of the Pratapban and Survey of Pargana Pratapban.

In 1716, the zamindari of Jalkapur was purchased from its defaulting zamindar by the vilayati chaudhuri Shaturghna. From the family of the vilayati chaudhuri, in turn, the zamindari passed to the family of the gomasta to the sadr chaudhuri, who had at first stood as farmer of the zamindari. Ibid., Genealogy of the zamindars of Julcapore.

The zamindar of Dattamuta sold a 15 gandas share to the sadr qanungo and one anna to the vilayati qanungo before his death in 1681. His heirs sold 4 annas to one Nayanchand and 5 annas to taluqdars, keeping 5 annas in the family. Genealogy of the zamindars of Dattamuta.

[57]Chauduris appointed to parganas in Orissa.

[58]Ibid., Survey of Pargana Khundar.

British administration, enjoyed valuable ancestral taluqs in several parganas which were conferred on his family by zamindars in order to purchase the favour of the keeper of records.[59]

After the Permanent Settlement, the pace of transfer of zamindari rights became much faster, at any rate for the first two decades, than had ever been witnessed under the administration of the Mughal faujdar. But the direction of this transfer did not change radically: the bigger zamindars continued to lose their right to smaller taluqdars, zamindari servants, revenue securities, and government officers. There was, thus, a continuity of change in agrarian society, of which contemporary British administrators in India, in their descriptions of a melancholy revolution in landed rights, showed no comprehension.

Ten years after the Permanent Settlement, Henry Strachey, the Judge and Magistrate of Midnapur, wrote to the government that the older land-holders in Midnapur, for the most part were ruined very few having survived 'the almost universal destruction of zamindars'. The former ruling classes, the Muslim nobles and the Hindu zamindars, had given way to a new urban class rising in association with the East India Company, whom Strachey characterized as 'Hindoo Mahajens and Banyans of Calcutta'.[60] But Henry Strachey himself supplied weighty evidence in his list of 'persons of greatest rank and opulence' in Midnapur which did not substantiate his speculations regarding the nature of change in agrarian society under British Rule. The persons included in his list were:

---

[59]List of taluqs enjoyed by Rajnarayan Ray: (a) Meerpur taluq in pargana Midnapur granted by the Mughal government to the qanungo; (b) Taluq Shahpur in pargana Shahpur granted 100 years earlier to his ancestor, the then qanungo Ramjiban Ray, by the Raja of Kasijora as gratuity for deciding a dispute between the latter and another claimant to the pargana; (c) Taluq Nagra in pargana Kharagpur granted to his ancestor as a bribe for recording the name of the new zamindar of the pargana in the register. Midnapur Old English Correspondence, Letters Issued 1792, 'Account of taluqs in zamindari mahals'.

[60]Judicial Proceedings, Civil, 8 July 1802, No. 55, Report from the Judge and Magistrate of Midnapur.

1. Darpanarayan Ray, late qanungo of Midnapur.
2. Chandrasekhar Ghose, a considerable taluqdar, formerly diwan of Mr. Peirce, judge and collector of the district.
3. Lakhicharan Satpathi, taluqdar.
4. Kanai Poddar, a merchant in the town of Midnapur.
5. Chaitan Poddar, a merchant in the town of Midnapur.
6. Darpanarayan Bose, a merchant residing at Brahmanbhum.
7. Kishen Singh, a merchant at Brahmanbhum.
8. Raja Anandalal Khan, zamindar of Midnapur and Narajole.
9. Raja Krishnaballabh Chaudhuri, zamindar of Narayangarh.
10. Raghunath Chaudhuri, zamindar of Amarsi.
11. Raja Anandanarayan Ray, zamindar of Tamluk.
12. Rani Janaki, zamindar of Mahisadal.
13. Raja Naranarayan, zamindar of Hijli (Jalamuta).
14. Raja Gopalindra Ray, zamindar of Sujamuta.
15. Birprasad Chaudhuri, zamindar of Kharagpur and Balarampur.
16. Jagannath Dole, zamindar of Gatshila.
17. Lakkhinarayan, zamindar of Chatna.
18. Baidyanath Chaudhuri, a considerable merchant and landholder in Kharagpur.

Among the wealthy zamindars and taluqdars listed by Strachey, there were only two—Chandrasekhar Ghose (No. 2) and Baidyanath Chaudhuri (No. 18)—whose connection with land was not traditional. The zamindars of Midnapur, Narayangarh, Amarsi, Tamluk, Mahisadal, Jalamuta, Sujamuta, Ghatshila, and Chatna belonged to old zamindar families while Darpanarayan Ray and Birprasad Chaudhuri, sadr qanungo and sadr chaudhuri respectively, were also traditionally connected with the land. It is significant that none of the big merchants of Midnapur and Brahmanbhum had become zamindars in the district, the only exception being Baidyanath Chaudhuri, a merchant of Kharagpur who bought taluqs in Sabang.[61]

[61] The above information about the fortunes of opulent men listed by Strachey is drawn from Quinquennial Register of 1795 and accounts of land sales sent to the Board of Revenue by the collector of Midnapur.

The model of change conceived by Strachey—transfer of property from an old zamindar aristocracy to a new urban class of banians and mahajans based in Calcutta—did not become effective in Midnapur because the market for revenue-collecting rights after the Permanent Settlement was very imperfect and tended to discourage outsiders. There was no free and open competition at the public auctions of zamindaris and taluqs in Midnapur. The whole mechanism of sale was manipulated by a ring of local speculators in such a way that a practical monopoly was established at these public auctions.[62] The systematic way in which fraud was practised at the public auctions held at the collectorate was described by the collector of Midnapur in 1800 in the following terms:

> Several persons in this district appear to have made it a sort of profession to speculate and commit all sorts of frauds in the purchase of lands at public sales. They have bought them in the names of their relations and dependants or in fictitious names, and having embezzled the greater part of their collections and caused the lands to be brought to sale again for the recovery of the arrears which in consequence arose while the mahals stood in those names, have purchased them a second time in other names, and sometimes having again fallen in arrear have repeated the same practice three or four times in the course of the year, by which means, as the names in which the arrears have accumulated have been fictitious, or the nominal proprietors possessed of no property whatever and were not to be found, Government have in numerous cases been defrauded of a very considerable part of their revenues.[63]

The speculators constituting the ring which had established a monopoly at the public auctions were about 25 in number. They acted as agents (vakils) for half the zamindars in the district.

[62]The best proof that there was no free and open competition at these public sales was that zamindars preferred to sell and mortgage their mahals privately. Such private transactions invariably fetched better prices than public sales for revenue arrears. BRP, 3 April 1789 No. 28.

[63]Quoted in *Final Report on Midnapur*, p. 80.

They regularly attended the collector's office, particularly, at the time of public auctions, where almost all the valuable purchases were made by them either for themselves or for their patrons. This was especially true for sales in the parganas of Kasijora, Shahpur and Mainachoura where the rights sold for defaults (committed by the Rajas of Kasijora and Mainachoura) were by far the greatest. Being agents for the zamindars who intended to bid for their own mahals at public auctions, the speculators knew exactly who were their competitors and what villages were being purchased fictitiously by the zamindars. The Raja of Mainachoura who had contracted a very large debt persuaded these 25 men to stand collectively as his securities for the debt in consideration for a large sum of money. In 1799, the securities were all put into the diwani jail when the Raja of Mainachoura absconded in order to avoid paying his debt to the Rani of Mahisadal. Undaunted by this reverse, the securities continued their speculative bidding and revenue farming from the diwani jail. The collector wrote to the Board of Revenue in 1802:

> Most of the frauds in the purchase and management of lands in this district which have come to my knowledge appear to have been planned or matured within the precincts of the Dewanny Jail by several persons who have been in confinement there since the year 1205. These persons were formerly Vakils to most of the landholders and having had their hands full of business some time ago when they were sued for a large debt for which in consideration of a considerable premium they had jointly become securities, they did not choose to preserve their liberty and lose their livelihood by running away, but they deliberately resolved to go to jail and there pursue as well as they could their customary operations. They have now been in jail more than four years; during this time they have been very extensively engaged in farming and in buying and selling lands either for themselves or other persons in other names, real or fictitious, and have acquired such a reputation for their skill and address in the transaction of business that the jail have been for some time a common place of resort for the purpose of consulting them when expedients to make encroachments on the

rights of others or to evade the penalties of law and the regular course of justice are required.[64]

Among the ring-leaders of the faction operating from the diwani jail were Samirchand babu, Gokul Bhuiya, Bostam Charan Bhuiya, and Shankar Bose. Samirchand babu, who was put into the diwani jail for arrears of revenue, held mahals on behalf of the Raja of Mainachoura in the name of Chaitan Das.[65] Gokul Bhuiya and Shankar Bose, the two principal securities for the Raja of Mainachoura, had purchased mahals on their own account which were put up for sale in 1802 for the recovery of the amount of the decree against the Raja of Mainachoura obtained by the Rani of Mahisadal.[66] Bostam Charan Bhuiya, who was also in the diwani jail for arrears of revenue, purchased several taluqs in the names of his nephew, Lakkhinarayan Bhuiya, and his agent, Dharanidhar Das.[67]

The structure of the market for revenue-collecting rights in Midnapur determined the composition of the class of people who purchased these rights in the district. Experience showed that zamindari mahals in Midnapur, when exposed to sale in small lots, sold at a much higher price at the collector's office in Midnapur than in Calcutta under the auspices of the Board of Revenue.[68] This implied that men of capital in Calcutta were not often to be seen making purchases of large zamindaris in Midnapur. Local speculators tended to buy up the small lots prepared by the collector, through the agency of the eminently corruptible amins, which offered opportunities of making splendid profits on particular purchases to men possessing inside information. As the ring of speculators operating in Midnapur was closely connected with the Rajas of Kasijora and Mainachoura, these older magnates whose zamindaris were brought

[64]BRP, 8 October 1802, No. 39, from Collector of Midnapur to BR, dt. 29 September 1802.

[65]Ibid.

[66]BRP, 20 December 1802, No. 45, Register of Midnapur, from Secretary to BR. Ibid., 28 December 1802, No. 46; Decree passed on 23 February 1797.

[67]BRP, 28 October 1796, Nos. 19,20. A Darkhast and a petition of Rajnarayan Ray Chaudhuri in pargana Sapochour in Jellasore.

[68]BRP, 28 October 1794, No. 21, to John Shore from BR.

under the hammer of the Permanent Settlement were able to manipulate the public auctions in such a way as to salvage some of the most valuable parts of their former possessions.

The sale accounts recorded in the Board of Revenue registers relating to land and land revenue[69] indicate that between 1794-1816, 53 per cent of revenue-paying rights in Midnapur[70] were sold at public auctions, conducted either by the collector at Midnapur or by the secretary to the Board of Revenue in Calcutta, in order to realize arrears of revenue from defaulting proprietors and to satisfy decrees against them passed by the law courts in private suits for debts and mortgages.[71] These public auctions did not affect zamindari rights in the Jungle Mahals, except in two small parganas.[72] It appears, too, that in the salt parganas, which were then comprehended in the collectorate of Hijli, virtually no properties were sold at public auctions. Revenue-collecting rights were affected by bublic auctions mainly in the ordinary cultivated parganas of Midnapur. Even in this area, the majority of the parganas were not seriously affected. Of the landed rights sold at public auctions in Midnapur 79.60 per cent lay in the contiguous parganas of Kasijora, Shahpur, Mainachoura, and Sabang.[73]

---

[69]These statistics are somewhat incomplete as some sales are not recorded in these registers.

[70]This percentage is calculated in terms of assessment and not area for which figures are not available. Midnapur as defined here excludes Tamluk and Hijli, which constituted a separate collectorate at this time, but includes the zamindars of Mahisadal and Tamluk which although situated in the collectorate of Hijli and Tamluk, paid revenue to Midnapur.

[71]Miscellaneous Records, Board of Revenue, Resisters, etc., relating to land and land revenue—Midnapur Account Sales, Vol. I, 1794-1799, Vol. II, 1799-1816.

[72]These were Tappa Dharinda and Kakrajeet, where landed rights were sold over and over again. In Kakrajeet 327.70% of the landed rights were sold and in Dharinda 159.40%. These percentages, as well as those which follow, are calculated in terms of the assessment.

[73]Only in six ordinary cultivated parganas were landed rights sold over and over again: Mainachoura, Sabang, Kasijora, Shahpur, Lapuchour, and Gugnapur. 116.50 per cent of the landed rights were sold in Lapuchour and 111.95 per cent in Gugnapur, in terms of the assessment fixed on the lands in these parganas. But since Gugnapur and Lapuchour were comparatively small parganas, the heavy portion of salese in thes two parganas constituted only a small part of the total sale in Midnapur.

The purchasers of revenue-collecting rights, as might have been expected from the way in which the public auctions were manipulated, were mostly local inhabitants of Midnapur and not adventurers from outside the district. Out of 53 per cent of revenue-collecting rights sold in Midnapur only 9.65 per cent went to purchasers outside the district, residing mostly in Burdwan, Hugli, Nadia, and Calcutta, while 29.86 went to inhabitants of Midnapur. Revenue-collecting rights tended to circulate within the neighbourhood, for 13.04 per cent of the rights went to purchasers who resided within the pargana in which the sale was taking place. Purchasers residing in other parganas bought up 16.82 per cent out of the 53 per cent rights sold, but these purchasers belonged mostly to neighbouring parganas. It was significant that the heaviest sales took place in Kasijora, Shahpur, Mainachoura, and Sabang and that the largest number of purchasers came from these same parganas.

TABLE 7.3
REVENUE-COLLECTING RIGHTS SOLD IN MIDNAPUR BETWEEN 1794-1816
(AS A PERCENTAGE ON THE ASSESSMENT OF THE DISTRICT)

Sold to purchasers within the pargana	13.04
Sold to purchasers outside the pargana but within the district	16.82
Sold to purchasers outside the district	9.65
Sold to purchasers whose place of residence is unknown	13.49
Total amount sold in Midnapur	53.00

In the parganas of Kasijora and Shahpur, constituting the zamindari of Raja Sundarnarayan, 95.16 per cent of revenue-collecting rights (in terms of assessment) changed hands between 1794 and 1816, and Raja Sundarnarayan apparently lost his whole zamindari. But during the time the collector of Midnapur attached the zamindari appointing his own patwaris and amins in order to prepare 'lots' for the sale of the zamindari for revenue arrears, the Raja was able to conceal a large amount of land from the lots. The concealed or chapee lands, which might have yielded to the government a revenue of Rs 30,000, continued in the possession of his son, Bastinarayan.[74] Bastinarayan himself acquired two of the lots sold by the collector while his brother-in-law, Durlabhchand, purchased three lots.[75] A large portion of the zamindari consisting of 75 villages, which bore an assessment of Rs 27,550, was purchased in 1789 from Sundarnarayan by his creditor, Kasinath babu, an upcountry Khatri banian of Calcutta who had earlier stood as his security.[76] The rest of the zamindari was sold in lots to small taluqdars who by 1798 numbered 204.[77] These were mostly local inhabitants, residing in Kasijora, Shahpur, or in neighbouring parganas like Kharagpur, Midnapur, Khundar, Narajole, and Sabang. Typical of this new class of smaller taluqdars was a former subject of Sundarnarayan, Gokul Bhuiya, who resided within his zamindari and purchased some of its most valuable lots.[78]

The rise of petty taluqdars was a well-marked phenomenon also in the zamindari of Mainachoura though, in this case also, the Raja managed to retain some of his most valuable possessions and much of his social prestige as the samajpati of the Kaivarta gentry of Mainachoura. By various artifices the intrusion of outside purchasers was successfully resisted in this pargana, but nevertheless, the social structure of this Kaivarta-inhabited area was significantly changed by the circulation of revenue-collecting rights within the pargana. Due to the machinations of his dishonest servants, Raja Brajananda of Killa Mainachoura fell into arrears after the Permanent Settlement and had to borrow a large sum in 1795 from Rani Janaki of Mahisadal by a mortgage of his zamindari providing for its conditional sale to the Rani. The interesting feature in this transaction was the attempt to take over an old zamindari not by new urban capitalists but by an almost equally ancient zamindar. Nevertheless, Rani Janaki's designs upon pargana Mainachoura were frustrated by

[74]BR, 17 June 1814, No. 20, Collector to BR, dt. 13 June 1814, Ibid., 26 July 1814 No. 10, Collector to BR, dt. 13 July 1814.

[75]Account of sales in Midnapur, op. cit.

[76]*Midnapur District Records*, Letters Received, 1777-1800, to Collector from Secretary to BR, p. 329-330.

[77]Midnapur Old English Correspondence, Collector Imhoff to BR, 31 December 1798.

[78]But the biggest number of these 'lots' was purchased by Samirchand babu, the agent for many of the Zamindars of the district.

a systematic rigging of public sales arranged by Raja Brajananda in association with the ring of speculators operating in Midnapur. Finding himself deep in debt which he could not possibly discharge, the Raja deliberately defaulted and let his arrears of revenue go on accumulating. Subsequently, when his mahals were exposed for sale, he either prevented the sale by bidding very high in the names of other persons and not paying up the purchase money, or purchased the most valuable mahals in fictitious names thus taking them out of the reach of Rani Janaki. Rani Janaki pleaded with the collector not to proceed with the public sale of this zamindari and promised to pay up all balances—on her taking possession of the whole zamindari—but to no effect. In a frantic effort to avoid losing the benefit of her mortgage, Rani Janaki joined the collector in his search for fictitious purchases by Raja Brajananda, so that the mahals mortgaged to her could be exempted from sale and the mahals pointed out by her be put up to auction instead. With her assistance the collector was able, in 1800, to detect 20 villages bought up by Raja Brajananda in the names of his servants and dependants.[79] Not all villages fictitiously purchased or fraudulently alienated by the Raja could be detected in this way, and collector Bayley found, in 1850, that undiscovered purchases in the names of Lalmohan Das and Sabitra Dey were still held by the Rajas of Mainachoura and had proved very profitable.[80] Some of these fictitiously purchased mahals, sold over and over again in the game of deception played by the Raja, were fixed with a revised lighter assessment the benefit of which went to his descendants.[81] The Rani of Mahisadal thus failed in her object of taking over

[79]The above account has been constructed from the following sources: Midnapur Old English Correspondence, Collector to BR, 30 June 1800; BRP, 3 February 1795, No. 41, Petition from Raja Brajananda Bahubalindra; Ibid., 10 March 1795, No. 11A, Petition of Rani Janaki; Ibid., 4 December 1795, No. 2, BR to Collector; Ibid., 5 April 1796, No. 41, Collector to BR; Ibid., 10 September 1799, No. 50, Collector to BR; Ibid., 7 January 1800, No. 29, Collector to BR; Ibid., 25 February 1800, No. 17, Collector to BR.

[80]Bayley, op. cit., p. 19.

[81]Ibid.

the Mainachoura Raj,[82] and although on paper 185.11 per cent of Mainachoura was sold at public auction the Maina Raj family continued as a prominent, though no longer predominant, zamindar in the pargana. The real beneficiaries of this transfer of rights in Mainachoura were the local Kaivarta gentry of the pargana.[83] The fact that out of 185.11 per cent as much as 72.17 per cent of the purchases were made by local residents of Mainachoura indicates that control over land was largely retained by local people although practically the whole zamindari was sold.[84] Urban penetration in the revenue-collecting structure would appear to have been a negligible factor in this area. There was no big Calcutta merchant who could edge his way into this pargana occupied by a solid local gentry. Like Kasijora, Mainachoura also was transformed from a single zamindari into a number of small taluqs held by petty proprietors. As the fortunes of the big zamindar declined, his place was taken up by numerous local men of small fortunes who had formerly existed as his dependants and subjects. As regards their occupation, nothing definite can be said as the collector provided no indication in that direction. Since they came from local families living in the countryside and belonged mostly to the agricultural Kaivarta caste, their connection with land can be inferred as traditional.

It must be emphasized that the smaller local gentry, whose rise was so marked in Kasijora, Shahpur, and Mainachoura were not a new social class in the district. In other parganas there were countless petty taluqdars who sometimes paid their revenue through the zamindar but mostly they were independent and dealt directly with the government without an intermediary zamindar. In such parganas, the change in the social scene after the Permanent Settlement was hardly striking. Bordering on Mainachoura was the extensive pargana of Sabang, the sale

[82]But she recovered the money lent by her to Brajananda through the public auction of his rent-free lands in satisfaction of a decree in her favour.

[83]The surnames of purchasers of taluqs in Mainachoura indicate that they were mostly Kaivartas, although there was quite a number of Kayastha purchasers also.

[84]See statistical table.

accounts of which show the fate of smaller taluqdars as contrasted with the fate of big zamindars. Since 1760, as we have seen, the Raja of Mainachoura had been overlord of the taluqdars, chaudhuris, and qanungos of this pargana. At the time of the Decennial Settlement, the pargana was settled by the government with the taluqdars and the Maina Raja, thus, lost his position as the overlord of the pargana. Whereas in Mainachoura, the dominant land-holding element was of Kaivarta extraction, in Sabang, where a large number of families holding service under the Mughal government had settled, Kayasthas were also an important element among the taluqdars.[85] During the years after the Permanent Settlement, quite a number of taluqdars in Sabang fell into arrears and their rights were sold at public auctions. Between 1794 and 1816, 67.93 per cent of the revenue-collecting rights of the pargana were sold in this way. Out of this, 44.94 per cent was purchased by 87 local residents of Midnapur of whom 51 lived in Sabang itself.[86] The purchasers were mostly Kayasthas, since Sabang was one of the Kayastha colonies in Midnapur.[87]

Proprietors in other parganas, whether large or small, do not seem to have suffered to the same extent as the Rajas of Kasijora and Mainachoura and many of the taluqdars of Sabang. It would appear that for the majority of proprietors in Midnapur there was considerable continuity of possession even in the decades of turmoil after the Permanent Settlement. In the Jungle Mahals the Raja of Narayangarh, the Raja of Silda, the Raja of Jhargram, and the Maharaja of Mayurbhanj continued to be the principal zamindars after the Permanent Settlement and benefited greatly from light assessment and rising rent. The

[85]Quinquennial Register of Midnapur for 1795 indicates the following caste distribution among the taluqdars: Kayastha—301; Kaivarta—23; Brahman—4; Mughal official title holders—39; Muslim—8; unidentifiable Bengali caste—56; unidentifiable Oriya caste—3; and entirely unidentifiable —43.

[86]Local residents of Sabang purchased 19.23 per cent; inhabitants of other parganas in Midnapur 25.71 per cent; and inhabitants of other districts 6.21 per cent.

[87]Of the auction purchasers 23 were Kayasthas, 11 Kaivartas, 6 Brahmans, 2 Muslims, 13 Mughal official title holders, 39 unidentifiable Bengali castes, 7 unidentifiable Oriya castes, and 26 were entirely unknown.

Narayangarh Raj, assessed only at Rs 70,000 per annum, had acquired by the twentieth century an annual collection value of Rs 177,000.[88] The Rajas of Narayangarh proved good and prosperous zamindars always ready to assist the district administration. In the course of the nineteenth century, however, new men broke into the landlord classes in this region, for instance, the government vakil Harinarayan Datta who acquired Gunissar and the Nawab of Murshidabad who purchased Nayagram and Khelagram. The principal agency oJ social change in the forest parganas proved to be Messrs Watson & Co., later converted into the Midnapur zamindari Company, who obtained patni leases from various zamindars of the area, dispossessed the jungle tribes and cultivated the land with date-sugar, indigo, and other cash crops.[89]

Bordering on the jungle parganas was the important estate of the Midnapur Raj which came into the possession of the Narajole family after the death of Rani Siromoni. The Narajole Raj hence became the biggest zamindari in the district. The family continued in this pre-eminent position within the district for a long time but ran into heavy weather in 1841 when Asutosh Deb of Calcatta obtained the Midnapur zamindari in execution of a decree for debt. The property then passed from Asutosh Deb to Mr Abbott and from him to the Nawab of Murshidabad. The Narajole family eventually recovered possession of the Midnapur zamindari by a prolonged suit in the Supreme Court in 1852, only in the very next year to lose its ancestral property at Narajole which was sold, for arrears of revenue at public auction, to the Maharaja of Burdwan. The Rani of Burdwan magnanimously restored the property to the Narajole family in 1879.[90] From this time the Narajole Raj entered its prime. Mahendralal Khan, who became Raja in 1895, entered politics in the Swadeshi era and was arrested in connection with the Midnapur Conspiracy Case in 1908. His son, Debendralal Khan,

---

[88] *Final Report of Midnapur*, p. 84.

[89] Bayley, op. cit., pp. 14-15. *Bengal District Gazetteer, Midnapur* p. 195.

[90] Bayley, op. cit., pp. 17-18. *Bengal District Gazetteer, Midnapur*, pp. 214-215.

became one of the most important Congress leaders of Midnapur in the mass phase of politics from 1920 onwards.

Such continuity of possession was not uncommon for other older zamindars in the ordinary cultivated parganas of Midnapur. In pargana Turkachour, containing the ancient fort of Turka from which one of the five traditional Kaivarta chiefs had ruled Midnapur, Raja Panchanan Gajendra Mahapatra of this ancient Kaivarta lineage was still the principal zamindar in the 1850s, though a new proprietor named Mahendralal Pal had also acquired considerable property in the pargana. For such new proprietors it was no easy matter to dislodge dominant local families from effective control of a zamindari. This same Mahendranath Pal, no inconsiderable taluqdar, could not get possession of certain mortgaged mahals under an eleven-year-old decree against Abhayram Chaudhuri, the principal zamindar of Jalasore, Danton, Rajgarh, and Chakismailpur. 'It is stated', wrote collector Bayley in 1852, "as a curious fact that, although many bond-debts have been decreed against Oberam Chowdri and his family, and execution ordered upon his landed property, no one could obtain possession on the spot of any such landed property; the ryotts being so completely under his influence, from his profuse liberality to them, that they swear their master's villages are not *his*; and no property can be identified or a decree successfully sued out."[91]

The five large and old zamindaris which constituted the Hijli district at the time of the Decennial Settlement—Jalamuta, Majnamuta, Sujamuta, Mahisadal, and Tamluk—were not adversely affected after 1793. It was only in the middle of the nineteenth century that the zamindaris of Jalamuta and Majnamuta were brought under government administration on account of gross mismanagement and farmed out under the supervision of tahsildars to Sambhuram Mirda, a rich mahajan, Ramnarayan Giri, the diwan of Mahisadal, and Raghunath Das, the muktar (lawyer) of the Jalamuta family.[92] The zamindari of Sujamuta, described by Bayley as a fairly profitable zamindari, remained in the possession of its ancient Kaivarta zamindars

[91]Bayley, op. cit., p. 24.
[92]Ibid., pp. 66-72.

(one of the five traditional chieftains of Midnapur) until the 1870s, after which it was sold for arrears of revenue to the Maharaja of Burdwan. Tamluk, an even more ancient Kaivarta kingdom, continued in the possession of the Kaivarta family till the middle of the nineteenth century. Then a family quarrel between two brothers, Laksminarayan and Rudranarayan, ruined the zamindari and led to its entire alienation. Laksminarayan's share was first obtained by Asutosh Deb, a Calcutta mahajan who had the former deep in debt,[93] and Rudranarayan's share was purchased by Madhusudan Mukherjee of Hugli, a marine contractor.[94] Ultimately, both shares passed to the Mahisadal Raj which had been expanding throughout the eighteenth and nineteenth centuries. Rani Janaki who had been managing this zamindari successfully from 1765 added Goomghur to it in 1771 because of a defaulting zamindar[95] and some valuable mahals from the Raja of Mainachoura after the Permanent Settlement. Lokenath Ghose,[96] the historian of the Indian Chiefs, Rajas, and Zamindars reported in 1881 that the Mahisadal estate was generally improving. By the beginning of the twentieth century, it had become a very large estate, covering an area of 323 square miles and comprising almost the whole of the parganas of Mahisadal, Tiarpara, Kasinagar, Gomai, Aurangnagar, Goomghur, Natshal, and Tamluk.[97] In direct contrast with the nationalist Rajas of Narajole, the equally ancient Rajas of Mahisadal, who were surrounded by rebellious Kaivarta tenants aided and abetted by the Midnapur District Congress, consistently helped the British district administration during the mass uprisings of the Non-Cooperation, Civil Disobedience, and Quit India movements in Midnapur.

A noticeable fact about the sale of zamindaris and taluqs in Midnapur was that most of the wealthy and influential auction purchasers in this district were not urban capitalists from

[93]The same man who obtained the Midnapur zamindari in satisfaction of a decree against Narajole family.

[94]Bayley, op. cit., p. 34.

[95]Ibid.

[96]Lokenath Ghose, *The Modern History of the Indian Chiefs, Rajas, Zamindars & C*, Part II (Calcutta 1881).

[97]*Bengal District Gazetteer, Midnapur*, pp. 202-205.

Calcutta, but older magnates from within and without the district, such as the Rajas of Narajole,[98] the Rajas of Mahisadal,[99] the Rajas of Majnamuta,[100] the Rajas of Narayangarh,[101] the Rajas of Burdwan,[102] and the Nawabs of Murshidabad.[103] The family of diwan Kasinath and the Tagores,[104] and Seals of Culcutta bought some valuable estates in Midnapur but, as a rule, Midnapur did not attract adventurers from outside. Land tenure remained simple in Midnapur after the Permanent Settlement, and there was no growth of sub-infeudation because the proprietors for the most part continued to live in their zamindaris and taluqs and to manage these with the help of gomastas and farmers. The chief exceptions were the Maharajas of Burdwan, the Nawabs of Murshidabad, and the Seals of Calcutta—the principal outside proprietors recorded by Jameson during the survey of 1910-1918. In any case, these outside proprietors usually let their estates in patni tenures to local men,[105] so that, as far as raiyats were concerned, the immediate revenue-collectors were not absentees.

No statistical information regarding the occupations of these purchasers was recorded by the collectors, but a report from the collector of Midnapur to the Judicial Department in 1802 mentioned that when the great zamindaris were first sold, zamindari servants were very often the purchasers. Since then land-holders, money-lenders, dealers in grain and salt, and a few monied men who had no particular occupation became the purchasers. The price at auction sales was pushed up by the ignorant bidding of traders in salt who did not know anything about the

[98]Bought 'lots' in Govardhanpur in 1807, Kasijora Shahpur in 1808 and 1814, and Midnapur in 1809. Account of Sales of Midnapur, op. cit.

[99]Bought the zamindari of Tamluk.

[100]Rani Sugandha bought a 'lot' in Mainachoura in 1801. Ibid. A successor of the Rani purchased some of the most valuable mahals in pargana Bhuiyamuta. Bayley, op. cit., p. 22.

[101]Bought a 'lot' in Bajerpur in 1794.

[102]Bought the zamindari of Sujamuta.

[103]Bought the zamindaris of Nayagram and Khelagram.

[104]Harakumar Tagore purchased a 10-anna share of the ancient Kaivarta zamindari of Kutubpur. Bayley, op. cit., p. 21.

[105]*Final Report on Midnapur*, p. 38.

management of taluqs.[106] The most valuable purchases were made by the ring of speculators operating from the diwani jail in Midnapur. As agents and securities of the zamindars, these men had access to inside information about the value of particular lots.[107] The farmers of the zamindars also possessed such inside information and in Shahpur Raja Sundarnarayan's farmers figured among the auction purchasers.[108] In the parganas settled with smaller taluqdars, the same body of men whose taluqs were put up to auction in lots very often purchased other lots in which they had formerly no proprietary rights. The zamindars, on the one hand, and the securities, agents, farmers, servants and dependants of the zamindars on the other, thus, constituted the two main classes of auction purchasers. Besides these two classes, there was a third fairly numerous class of auction purchasers—officers and lawyers connected with district administration. Some of these officers had been connected with the former Mughal administration, such as sadr qanungo Rajanarayan Ray[109] who purchased several lots in the name of his son, Darpanarayan Ray. Others were connected with the new British administration in Midnapur in the capacity of revenue officers and government pleaders. This latter element was usually constituted by Brahmans and Kayasthas and was usually not indigenous to Midnapur.[110]

---

[106]Bengal Judicial Department Proceedings, Civil, 8 July 1802, No. 102. Report from the Collector of Midnapur.

[107]Samirchand Babu, agent of the Raja of Mainachoura, bought lots in Kasijora in 1795 in his own name and one lot in the same pargana in 1798 in the name of Choitancharan Das. The assessment on the lots amounted to Rs. 29,818. Gokul Bhuiya, security for the Raja of Mainachoura, purchased one lot each in Sabang, Shahpur, Khutnagar, and Bajerpur in 1794, one lot in Dharinda in 1795, two lots in Uttarbihar in 1795, six lots in Sabang in 1796, one lot in Khutnagar in 1795, one lot in Kasijora in 1798, two lots in Kasijora in 1799, one lot in Shahpur, in 1799 and one lot in an unnamed pargana in 1801. The total assessment on these lots was Rs 5,655. Some of these purchases might have been on behalf of the land-holders for whom Samirchand and Gokul Bhuiya were acting as agents but, on the other hand, they purchased other lots in fictitious names for themselves.

[108]BRP, 3 May 1796, No. 29.

[109]BRP, 26 August 1796, No. 47, Collector of Midnapur to BR.

[110]In the forest parganas, the government vakil, Jadobendra Banerjee, a Brahman, purchased parganas Kakrajit, Barajit, and Kalori which thus passed from the hands of the jungle zamindars. In the Jungle pargana of

Structural change in Midnapur society has to be analyzed with reference to three distinct classes of proprietors in the district—a number of big zamindars exercising authority over a jurisdiction of one or more entire parganas; a larger body of small zamindars, taluqdars, chaudhuris, qanungos, and other superior tenure-holders who constituted a middling landed elite beneath the class of magnates ruling from forts; and the numerous category of headmen and large jotedars among the ordinary cultivators of the Kaivarta and Sadgop caste who actually occupied the lands in Midnapur except the home farms (nij jotes) of the agricultural taluqdars. We may first deal with the question, what happened to the territorial magnates? Except Kasijora, Mainachoura, and Kutubpur all the big zamindaris continued under their traditional zamindars at least until the middle of the nineteenth century. Three zamindaris—Narajole, Mahisadal and Narayangarh—survived not only intact but continued to grow well into the twentieth century and played an important role in the politics and the economy of the district. By the beginning of the twentieth century, the houses of Tamluk, Sujamuta, Jalamuta, and Majnamuta, like those of Maina and Kasijora earlier, had lost their zamindaris while Midnapur had been incorporated with Narajole long before. It was not new men but the older zamindars of Mahisadal and Burdwan who took over Tamluk and Sujamuta respectively. A few old houses benefited from the ruin of other older houses but the 'kingdoms' within the state which had flourished under the Mughal faujdar—ruled from ancient forts like Maina, Tamluk, Turka, etc.—uniformly ceased to exist as political entities under the centralized administration of the British collector. The decay

Gunissar also another government pleader, Harinarayan Datt, a Kayastha by caste, became the principal zamindar. In the ordinary cultivated pargana of Lapuchour where 116.25 per cent of landed rights were sold between 1794 and 1816, the diwan of the Judge and Magistrate of Midnapur became the principal proprietor and his son, Krishnomohan Chaudhuri, who became the treasurer of the district, also augmented the family property though he was dismissed from government service for a defalcation of Rs 30,000. In the salt pargana of Birkul, the government vakil and the Judge's diwan purchased lots. In another salt pargana, Orissa Balsye, the principal sadr amin of the district, qazi Kumber Ali, and a muktar, Darpacharan Das, bought a few lots. Bayley, op. cit., pp. 14, 16, 24, 32.

and ruin of the forts in Midnapur, which had ceased to fulfil the function of guarding against invasions and mounting expeditions, bore witness to the transformation of the political scene in Midnapur.[111] The territorial magnates, whether they decayed or flourished, had ceased to be 'rulers'.

On the whole it was the local middling landed elite, constituted by a great body of Kaivartas and a smaller number of Brahmans and Kayasthas, who gained the decisive advantage as a result of the disintegration of the older kingdoms ruled from forts. Even before the Permanent Settlement revenue-collecting rights in Midnapur had been unusually diffuse for, both outside and within the big zamindaris, there had been thousands of smaller taluqdars. Many of these petty taluqdars, as we have seen, suffered to some extent under the sale regulations of the Permanent Settlement. The revenue-collecting rights thus put up for sale circulated largely within the same class of smaller taluqdars. Those among this class who were dependent on the zamindars, such as the taluqdars of Sabang, were rendered independent under the Permanent Settlement. Petty taluqdars and local inhabitants purchased properties from the bigger zamindars. As a result, a great body of independent proprietors consolidated their hold on the countryside in Midnapur. In 1790, there were 999 estates on the tauzi register of the district. In 1800, there were 1,888; in 1,850, 2561; in 1870, 2,808.[112] It would appear that all over Bengal smaller people with local knowledge—knowledge derived from association with zamindari management and district administration—purchased properties from the defaulting bigger zamindars. In most other parts of Bengal this class seems to have been constituted by Brahmans and Kayasthas, the traditional literate castes forming the literati of the country. The peculiarity of Midnapur seems to have been that in this district the backbone of the class of proprietors of

[111]Henry Strachey wrote in 1812: 'There are several forts in Midnapur of stone and mud; but they are gone to decay. They were all, I believe, except the fort at the station, built long ago, and were well calculated to defend the inhabitants of the district from the incursions of Mahratta horse, but were otherwise useless.' Bengal Judicial Proceedings, Civil, 8 July 1802, No. 55. Report from the Judge and Magistrate of Midnapur.

[112]*A Statistical Account of Bengal*. Vol. III, p. 157.

middling status was constituted by the members of the dominant agricultural caste—the Kaivartas. Kaivarta princes had ruled the country traditionally. After the Permanent Settlement, the Kaivarta caste did not lose this advantageous position in the land; rather, their ownership of property was somewhat more democratized.[113] The main trend in social change in Midnapur consisted in the fact that while the forts of the Kaivarta princes crumbled their Kaivarta subjects who had settled in the countryside around the forts parcelled out among themselves the territory of their masters. Along with them a large number of Bengali immigrants, mostly of the Brahman and Kayastha castes, who had moved into Midnapur in the trail of the Mughals and subsequently the British government, also consolidated their hold over a portion of the territory by utilizing their connection with the supreme rulers.

The new Brahman and Kayastha proprietors who rose through their official connection were seldom agriculturists but many of the Kaivarta taluqdars held jotes of their own which they cultivated by means of agricultural labourers of sharecroppers. The agricultural Kaivarta taluqdars were, thus, part of the larger Kaivarta jotedar class of the area who cultivated their large farms by employing sharecroppers of their own caste. While the Permanent Settlement effected changes in the revenue-collecting structure over the villages, the domination of the landholding structure within the villages by the Kaivarta jotedars of Tamluk and Contai apparently continued unimpaired. Available settlement reports indicate that in Tamluk and Contai the Kaivarta jotedars steadily increased their power vis-a-vis the estates in the course of the nineteenth century and intercepted the profits which resulted from the rising rents of the land.[114] In

[113]The surnames of the auction purchasers between 1794 and 1816 recorded in the sale accounts indicate the following distribution of castes: Kaivarta—118; Bengali-Kayastha—48; Bengali Brahman—29; Sadgop—2; Muslim—11; Marathi—1; unidentifiable Bengali castes—157; unidentifiable Oriya castes—54; Mughal official title holders—104; entirely unidentifiable—174. Total—698.

[114]This did not mean, of course, that all Kaivarta cultivators in the area benefited similarly at the expense of the estates. In fact, the village heads, known in this area as baruas and mukhyas, generally sided with the

the estate of Majnamuta both the productive power of the soil as well as the value of the produce increased between 1845 and 1876 without any action on the part of the cultivators, partly as a result of government embankments for the control of floods and partly as a result of a rise in prices.[115] It was not the zamindars who benefited primarily from the rise of the rents but the bigger Kaivarta cultivators who realized the increased rents without paying correspondingly higher sums to their zamindars. During the survey and settlement of Midnapur from 1910 to 1918, Jameson noted that in the estates in the eastern part of Midnapur tenants had shown 'considerable power of resistance to attempts to raise their rents'.[116] In the zamindari of Sujamuta, purchased by the Raja of Burdwan with the object of enhancing the rates of assessment, the Kaivarta tenants compelled the new zamindar to compromise on the existing rates. In the temporarily-settled Majnamuta and Jalamuta estates under the management of the government, the Kaivarta tenants stubbornly resisted the enhancements which the government sought to obtain at each periodic resettlement. In Mahisadal the sums obtained by the Brahman zamindar remained unchanged for long periods due to the intractable character of the Kaivarta tenants. In the estate purchased by the Seals of Calcutta in Panskura, the tenants paid just what they pleased for the forty years before Jameson's survey. The inability of zamindars who were outsiders, either in geographical or in caste terms, to obtain enhancements commensurate with the increase in the value of produce in Tamluk and Contai can only be explained in the light of the historical fact that the Kaivarta caste had been traditionally dominant in this area. The Kaivarta Rajas of the area were all replaced at the top at one time or another (starting with the replacement of the Kaivarta Rajas of Mahisadal by the Brahman zamindars in the seventeenth century and ending with the

well-to-do raiyats or the zamindars, underlings in order to harass the poorer classes. Correspondence on the Majnamita and Jalemta estates, op. cit., p. 59.

[115]Ibid.

[116]*Final Report on Midnapur*, p. 113. On the other hand, Jameson observed an unmistakable tendency towards replacement of money rents by produce rents, which meant that while the bigger cultivators were improving their position, the smaller tenants were losing out and becoming sharecroppers.

purchase of the Kaivarta zamindaris of Tamluk and Sujamuta by the Rajas of Mahisadal and Burdwan in the latter half of the nineteenth century), but their Kaivarta subjects continued to dominate the villages. The regional jurisdictions were taken over by the government (zamindars of Majnamuta and Jalamuta), the Seals of Calcutta (zamindars in Panskura), the Rajas of Burdwan (zamindars of Sujamuta), and the Brahman zamindars of Mahisadal (zamindars of Mahisadal and later, Tamluk), but these intrusive overlordships from outside the localities did not fundamentally alter the local structures of political influence established by Kaivarta colonizers during the mass migration from Orissa recorded in tradition.

8

Dinajpur and Rangpur

The British collectorates of Dinajpur and Rangpur in the north of Bengal were formed respectively out of the zamindari of Dinajpur and the sarkar of Kuchwara conquered from the Hindu Raja of Kuch Bihar by the Mughals in the seventeenth century. Almost the whole area consisted of flat rice-growing plains covered by alluvial deposits of recent formation. The Barind tract, however, was formed of an old alluvial deposit of stiff reddish clay covered with brushwood which ran in a long narrow strip through Rajshahi, Malda, Dinajpur, and Rangpur.[1] The cultivating classes were composed of Muslims, who formed a substantial majority in the area, and low caste Hindus among whom the Dravido-Mongoloid castes called Rajbangshi and Koch were the most numerous. Most of the revenue-collecting landlords (zamindars and taluqdars) and their agents, as well as the native officers of the court and the collectorate, were Hindus of Brahman and Kayastha castes. The rural high caste gentry of the sub-infeudatory taluqdar class which characterized Dacca, Faridpur, Bakarganj and Mymensingh in East Bengal were not to be encountered in these North Bengal districts; the proportion of high caste Hindus to the population was much lower than anywhere else in Bengal. The dominant element in the countryside was, therefore, the rich Muslim agriculturist class, known in this area as jotedars. While the high caste Hindus dominated the revenue-collecting

[1] *Eastern Bengal and Assam District Gazetteers*, *Rangpur*, J.A. Vas (Allahabad 1911), p. 10; *Eastern Bengal District Gazetteers*, *Dinajpur*, F.W. Strong (Allahabad 1912) p. 7.

structure and the lower echelons of the Company's government, the rich Muslim agriculturists dominated the village land-holding structure and the union and local boards which came to be formed in the twentieth century.

No other region in Bengal demonstrated more clearly the wide and inclusive character of the category conveniently known as zamindar. The term include different classes of proprietors, the origin of whose rights was naturally various in an area which had come relatively late under Mughal rule. There was, in the first place, the Hindu kingdom of Kuch Bihar to the north of Rangpur, inhabited by the Mongoloid tribe of the Koches. Their chief, Viswa Singh, had embraced Hinduism in the sixteenth century. His descendants, who managed to preserve their independence in spite of repeated Mughal aggressions, became protected princes under British rule. In their own territory the Kuch Bihar princes were rulers not zamindars; but in the chaklas of Boda, Patgram, and Purabbhag, conquered from them by the Mughals, they became autonomous zamindars paying tribute to the Mughal government. These three chaklas, and the state of Baikunthapur held by a collateral branch of the family, were semi-feudatory states which the Mughals chose to designate as zamindaris. Secondly, there were the sub-feudatory states, or the rest of Kuchwara consisting of the chaklas of Kankina, Fathipur, and Kazirhat where the Mughals left in possession, as chaudhuris and zamindars, the officers of Kuch Bihar state who enjoyed the hereditary right of collecting the revenue on behalf of the state. Thirdly, there were the large zamindaris, such as Idrakpur and Dinajpur, which the proprietors held by sanad from the Mughal Emperor. Lastly, there were the small taluqs which had been separated from the larger zamindaris.[2] It was the position of the third category of large xamindari holdings by sanad that determined the question of the position of zamindars in general under the Permanent Settlement. For this reason, it will be appropriate to take a closer look at the origin and nature of the zamindari of Dinajpur which was typical of this category.

[2]*Report on the Statistics of Rungpore for the Year 1872-73*, Gopal Chunder Dass, Special Deputy Collector of Rangpur (Bengal Secretariat Press 1874).

The Dinajpur Raj was a principality built up by successive generations of powerful Rajas through extensive warfare against neighbouring zamindars.[3] By the public use of violence, permitted under a central power which was either unable or unwilling to suppress the independent use of violence by native chiefs, existing landed rights over a large territory were either reduced or extinguished by the warrior Rajas of Dinajpur, who brought under their administration a territory of 4,119 square miles between c. 1682 and 1780.[4] The core of the zamindari consisted of six parganas which were acquired by the founder of this Kayastha family, Sukdev Ray, by inheritance from his maternal grandfather, Srimonto Datta , a deputy of the qanungo of Bengal. Sukdev Ray, who was an officer under the zamindar of Khetlal, acquired a seven-sixteenth share of the Khetlal zamindari on the extinction of the Khetlal family. The nine-sixteenth share was obtained by another officer who founded the Idrakpur zamindari. Sukdev died in 1677 A.D. His youngest son, Prannath (c. 1682-1733 A.D.), enormously expanded the zamindari by seizing all the smaller zamindaris in the neighbourhood, some twelve in number, as also Maligaon and a large area in Malda. His son Ramnath (c. 1733-1760 A.D.) proved even more warlike and conquered parganas Santosh, Sultanpur, Apaul, Khatta, etc. The next ruler, Baidyanath, acquired pargana Rajanagor and died in 1780 A.D., leaving the zamindari to his minor adopted son, Radhanath, who lost the zamindari after the Permanent Settlement in five years between 1796 and 1800 A.D. At its greatest extent, measuring over 4,100 square miles, the Dinajpur Raj comprised 61 parganas, of which 26 were shared with other zamindars and 35 possessed exclusively by the family. The successful expansion of the Dinajpur Raj during the administration of Ramnath brought it recognition from the Mughal State, which sought to bring the growing principality into the political orbit of the Nizamat by confirming his right by sanad and by conferring on him the title of 'Maharaj Bahadur'.[5]

---

[3]Francis Buchanan (Hamilton), *A Geographical, Statistical & Historical Description of the District, or Zilla, of Dinajpur in the Province of Soubah, of Bengal,* Baptist Mission Press, 1883.

[4]Appendix to the Fifth Report, *Parliamentary Papers.* sess. 1812, Vol. VII, p. 353. As calculated by Rennell.

[5]Ibid, p. 352-356; Francis Buchanan, op. cit., pp. 254-257; *Eastern Bengal District Gazetteer, Dinajpur.*

However simple the whole structure seemed at the top as a isemi-autonomous Raj confirmed by the Mughal state and adminstering a considerable territory by means of its own bureaucracy and local militia, a closer look reveals an intricate pattern of landed rights and extreme diffusion of the local basis of power within the zamindari. Although the Raja, from his palace in Dinajpur, exercised a political, administrative, and military jurisdiction over the territory, under him there were innumerable surviving proprietary and intermediate revenue-collecting rights which were annexed during the course of the expansion of the Dinajpur Raj but could not be wholly liquidated. The dispossessed proprietors continued to enjoy rent-free properties in their localities. There was intermixture of lands belonging to different families in the parganas shared by the Dinajpur Raj with the zamindars of Idrakpur, Jahangirpur, Rajshahi and others. The mauzas, or villages constituting each pargana within the Raj, were so intermixed with those of other parganas, and there were so many confusing shares possessed by different families in each of the shared parganas, that there was no compactness or homogeneity in the constitution of the parganas of the Dinajpur Raj. Pargana Apaul, for instance, belonged to four families: first, the Dinajpur family, who in the time of Ramnath seized the whole pargana; second, the family of Ekhlas Khan, a Muslim, some of whose descendants remained and continued to enjoy a small rent-free estate; third, the family of Indrajit Chaudhuri of the milkman caste whose descendants stilll enjoyed 300 bighas of rent-free lands and an annual pension of Rs 360 from the Dinajpur family; and fourth, the family of Lokhymon Bollobh, a kayastha, which became extinct.[6] In the parganas inherited from the zamindar of Khetlal, the zamindars of Dinajpur and Idrakpur, instead of dividing the lands, each retained a share in every village, which caused much inconvenience when during British rule one estate was administered by the collectorate of Dinajpur and the other by Rangpur.[7]

Diffusion of the means of administration was, moreover, built into the management of the zamindari itself. There was no

[6]Buchanan, *Geographical Description of Dinajpur*.

[7]*Dinajpur District Gazetteer*, p. 28.

effective integration of the different levels of the zamindari bureaucracy. Lines of communication between the sadr kachari (head office), presided over by the diwan of the Raja, and the various mufassal kacharis at different local centres of the zamindari were tenuous, and at all times the mufassal servants of the Raj carried on the local business of the zamindari on their own initiative, without much control by the Raja. Within the head office itself, the diwan and other officers in crucial positions often formed factions for controlling the resources of the Raj excluding the Raja from detailed knowledge of its affairs. A powerful Raja like Ramnath kept the factions well in hand and maintained his autonomy by paying the Nawab a private sum in return for which the public demand of revenue was fixed at a very moderate pitch by the Nizamat. Inevitably, factions raged rampant whenever the controlling hand of the Raja grew weak, and the Nizamat then exploited these internal factions in order to promote its own control over the zamindari. Ramnath died in 1760 leaving behind two sons, Baidyanath and Kantonath, who immediately engaged in a dispute for succession to the zamindari. This was a great opportunity for Mir Qasim who, having succeeded to the Nizamat in the same year, proceeded to make a regular hast-o-bud of the resources of the Raj, which was carried out during 1761-62 through the agency of Ramnath Bhaduri in the minutest detail of all the villages. Kantonath was temporarily appointed to the zamindari and the assessment on it was increased enormously. The overthrow of Mir Qasim, however, led to the regular investiture of Baidyanath and the assessment was once again reduced under the administration of Muham ad Reza Khan.[8] After the death of Baidyanath there was, once again, a loss of control of the zamindari bureaucracy and rival factions contending for power were formed at the head office since his adopted son, Radhanath, happened to be a minor. The young Raja was deliberately excluded from all knowledge of the mufassal affairs of the Raj.[9]

---

[8] *Dinajpur District Records*, Vol. I, No. 152, letter from James Grant to John Shore, President of BR, pp. 105-108.

[9] Bengal Revenue Consultations, 11 April 1794, No. 9.

In the mufassal it was the established practice of the Raj to farm out the collections of revenues to ijaradars and qutqinadars, who were vested with control of the local offices of the zamindari. Even where the zamindari bureaucracy retained direct control of the collections, the distance between the head office and the local officers of the Raj encouraged embezzlement of large sums of revenue by the local collectors (tahsildars). The Raja's naibs and local agents connived with the farmers and qutqinadars in the fabrication of accounts to reduce the assessment of particular lands. The jama was reduced also by the manoeuvres of mandals, paramaniks and other principal inhabitants of the village, who under the plea of fictitious or real desertions of raiyats obtained possession of considerable tracts of land at an underrated assessment.[10] The patwaris, the village officials appointed by the zamindar to check the accuracy of the accounts, connived in the whole process.[11] The fact that the entire structure of the Raj was loose and unconnected rendered all its transactions vague and indefinite. Knowledge of the ostensible and secret resources of the Raj was possessed only by mufassal officers, who became ijaradars in their own right.[12] Regular collection of revenue by the mufassal officers, renters, and village heads depended on the impression of the permanency of management of the faction in power at the centre, for people in the interior were guided mainly by this circumstance. When they had reason to entertain a suspicion that the faction was liable to be dislodged from power, they never failed to benefit by delaying or withholding payments, thus becoming themselves the agents for bringing into disrepute the existing management.[13]

Just as the Nazims (governors) in their suba (province) never succeeded in concentrating the means of violence and administration in their hands, the Rajas of Dinajpur within their zamindari could not centralise the instruments of exercising power. The revenue-collecting staff and the militia in the mufassal remained village-based and the process of their bureaucratization,

---

[10]*Dinajpur District Records*, Vol. II, No. 277, to BR from Collector, dt. 15 June 1788, pp. 171-183.

[11]Ibid., No. 121, to Shore from Collector, dt. 9 March 1787, pp. 69-70.

[12]Ibid., No. 222, to Shore from Collector, dt. 25 October 1787, pp. 142-143; Ibid., No. 125, to Shore from Collector, 17 March 1787, p. 72.

[13]Ibid., Vol. I, No. 353, Collector to BR, dt. 25 May 1789, pp. 223-225.

that is, their direct control and supervision by a central authority, did not go far. Two kinds of guards were maintained in the zamindari to protect the revenue and preserve the peace—the barkandazes (matchlockmen) and the paiks. The barkandazes were fewer in number and were a more recent establishment commanded by dafadars and jamadars and were paid in money. This was the only force under the direct control of the Raja. The far greater body of local militia, called paiks, were a more ancient and unwieldy body commanded by mirdhas (head of spearmen) and sardars and were paid in paikan lands in their respective villages. Although liable to carry out the orders of mufassal officers, they were an organic part of the village and remained outside the sphere of direct control by the Raja.[14]

The local bases of power underwent considerable modification with the organization of a proper collectorate system under British rule. Dinajpur was not organized into a functioning collectorate until the coming of collector G. Hatch in 1786. Under Hatch, the collectorate replaced the Raj as the local unit of power. Unlike the Mughals, the British centralized the means of violence in the hands of the government. With the coming of the collector, it was no longer conceivable for the Rajas of Dinajpur to wage wars against the neighbouring zamindars as they had done under the Mughals. The huge militia of the Raj were mostly disbanded and were replaced with a regular police which became the instrument for intervention used by the collector or magistrate in major local disputes formerly decided by the Rajas. The collectors and magistrates took over the police and judicial powers of the Rajas over the territory of Dinajpur. The revenue administration of the Dinajpur Raj was also brought under government control to an unprecedented degree by Hatch.

On coming to Dinajpur, Hatch immediately became involved in a bitter struggle for control of the zamindari with the widow of the late Raja Baidyanath, Rani Saraswati, who, with the help of her brother Janakiram Singh, the diwan of the Raj, was administering its affairs on behalf of her minor son, Radhanath. The first act of Hatch was to remove Janakiram Singh from the

[14]BRP, 16 August 1787, Collector G. Hatch to BR, dt. 15 July 1787; Buchanan, *Geographical Description of Dinajpur*, p. 251.

management on account of a failure to discharge instalments of revenue punctually. He then took over the zamindari under the direct management of the collector against the active opposition of the Rani and invested his own man, Ramkanta Ray, as diwan of Dinajpur in 1787 on the condition that the business at the sadr kachari would be conducted by zamindari servants under the collector's supervision, that the collector's officers would be stationed at the kachari to take account of receipts of revenue, that the manager would provide the collector with the names and duties of all zamindari officers and disburse their salaries with his consent, that the collector would have the right to send amins to hear complaints at the sadr kachari and to call on the mufassal farmers for an account of their transactions.[15] The management of the zamindari was thus practically retained by Hatch who publicly attended the sadr kachari to hear complaints. Rani Saraswati and Janakiram Singh struck back by concealing the Raja's seal and confining the young Raja during the annual revenue-collecting ceremony (Punyaha). Ramkanta Ray dismissed the officers of Rani Saraswati's faction and appointed his own men in the zamindari. The dismissed officers, many of whom were harassed and confined by the new manager, carried on intrigues behind the scenes with the aid of Rani Saraswati; their aim was to obstruct the collections as far as possible. This rival faction, led by Janakiram Singh and Sadananda Sen (both of whom had been dismissed), opposed the dominant faction of Ramkanta Ray, which was really the faction of collector Hatch. The young Raja, who was excluded by Ramkanta Ray from the management of his zamindari, grew up with a long-nourished sentiment of hostility towards the manager, whose officers embezzled large sums with impunity.[16] When Hatch left Dinajpur to join the Board of Revenue in Calcutta, Ramkanta Ray was removed from his office. Manikchand, the personal diwan of the

[15] *Dinajpur District Records*, No. 73, 19 June 1787, to Hatch from BR, pp. 55-58; Ibid., No. 38, to Hatch from BR, dt. 29 December 1786.

[16] BRC, 11 April 1794, No. 9; An extract from the proceedings of the mahal kachari of Dinajpur dt. 19 September 1793; *Dinajpur District Records*, No. 375, to BR from collector, dt. 28 June 1788, pp. 236-237; Ibid., No. 22, to BR from Collector, dt. 25 Oct. 1787, pp. 142-143; Ibid., No. 159, to BR from Collector, dt. 15 July 1787, pp. 93-94; Ibid., No. 178, to BR from Collector, dt. 10 August 1787, p. 115.

new collector Eliot, was appointed in the place of Ramkanta, and Manikchand's grandson, Phulchund, assumed his grandfather's office of diwan to the collector. A plot was now hatched between the officers of the Raj, led by Manikchand, and the officers of the collectorate and the court, led by his grandson, Phulchund, to sell the zamindari of the young Raja, who had hardly as yet assumed control of its affairs. Between 1796 and 1800, almost the whole zamindari was sold up for arrears of revenue at fantastically low prices. Ramkanta Ray also shared in the spoils of this conspiracy.

In the district of Dinajpur as a whole, 74.29 per cent of the revenue-collecting rights changed hands between 1796 and 1819.[17] This included, besides the properties of the smaller proprietors, almost all of the 61 parganas of the vast zamindari of Dinajpur, with the exception of one. This pargana, bearing a jama of Rs 96,584, paid land revenue to the amount of Rs 81,591. Besides this pargana, the Raj retained 8 lots sold up for arrears of revenue, which were purchased at auction by the young Raja's mother and wives. These lots bore a jama of Rs 110,000 and paid Rs 79,000 in land revenue. At the time of the Decennial Settlement the land revenue of the Dinajpur Raj was fixed at Rs 14,80,000; by the time of Buchanan Hamilton's survey in 1807, the zamindari paid a revenue of only Rs 1,60,000, According to the calculations of Buchanan Hamilton, the Raja of Dinajpur still enjoyed a net income of Rs 28,017 per annum and was the third biggest proprietor in the district.[18] Two other older big zamindars in the district, Idrakpur and Jahangirpur, apparently retained their possessions, and the zamindars of Jahangirpur even added to them by auction purchases. The older zamindars, therefore, retained a considerable hold in the district.

Fragmentary statistics of the regional distribution and professions of the purchasers of revenue-collecting rights in Dinajpur district are available from sale accounts submitted by the collector of Dinajpur to the Board of Revenue. The collector did not mention the place of residence or profession of all purchasers.

[17]See Table 8.1.

[18]Buchanan, *Geographical Description of Dinajpur*, pp. 247-248.

TABLE 8.1

REGIONAL DISTRIBUTION OF AUCTION PURCHASERS IN DINAJPUR

Region of purchasers	*Percentage of jama bought*
Dinajpur	47.72
Calcutta	4.46
Rangpur	4.73
Burdwan	4.01
Patna	3.60
Rajshahi	2.71
Murshidabad	2.27
Purnia	0.80
Mymensing	0.69
Dacca	0.56
Kuchbihar	0.29
Malda	0.62
24 Parganas	0.17
Nadia	0.07
Farasdanga	0.06
Unknown	1.48
Total	74.24

Source: Miscellaneous Records, Registers etc., relating to land and land revenue, Account Sales, Dinajpur, 1793-1817.

It is still possible to draw some striking conclusions from his accounts.

With the enervation of the zamindari of Dinajpur, it might have been expected that once the sales were under way the native capitalists who had lent considerable sums to the impoverished Raja of Dinajpur would take over the zamindari. Raja Baidyanath bequeathed to Radhanath, a debt of Rs 3 lakhs. The principal claimants were the bankers Ganesh Das Ratanchand and Anupchand Jagat Seth of Murshidabad and the merchant capitalists Baranasi Ghose and Darpanarayan Tagore of Calcutta.[19]

[19]*Dinajpur District Records*, No. 143, to BR from Collector, dt. 13 May 1787, p. 83.

TABLE 8.2

PROFESSIONS OF AUCTION PURCHASERS IN DINAJPUR DISTRICT

Professions of purchasers	*Percentage of jama bought*
Zamindars	10.07
Dinajpur Raj servants	4.18
Dinajpur collectorate officers	3.93
Calcutta banker	2.81
Dinajpur Raj family	2.66
European officer's servants in Dinajpur	0.36
Money-lenders of Dinajpur	0.30
Merchants	0.10
Dinajpur court officers	0.04
Unknown	49.79
Total	74.24

Source: *Dinajpur District Records,* No. 143, to BR from Collector, dt. 13 May 1787, p. 83.

Even after the zamindari had been sold the debts of its creditors were cleared. The brick-built houses and other buildings of the palace (rajbari) were sold in satisfaction of a decree passed in favour of Baranasi Ghose,[20] and even the horses, elephants, cows and buffaloes of the Raja were sold at auction to satisfy his creditors.[21] Yet the strange fact was that neither the Murshidabad bankers, nor Baranasi Ghose and Darpanarayan Tagore, figure among the new purchasers of the Dinajpur Raj. Transfer of properties under the operation of the Permanent Settlement failed to revolutionize the rural society of Dinajpur as it took place largely within the classes which already lived off the land. The new bourgeoisie which seemed to be emerging in Calcutta failed to establish its hold on the agrarian society of Dinajpur. Although 74.24 per cent of the revenue-collecting rights in Dinajpur were sold, only 4.46 per cent of these properties are known to have passed into the hands of men of capital from Calcutta.

[20]BRP, 18 March 1800, No. 35, to BR from Collector, dt. 7 March 1800.

[21]BR, 4 November 1800, No. 14. Raja's petition to Governor-General-in-Council.

The Permanent Settlement did not create a free market for revenue-collecting rights operating under conditions of perfect competition. The intrusion of the bourgeoisie of Calcutta into the revenue-collecting structure was checked by local combinations among zamindars' agents and government servants who succeeded in rigging the sales. The combination between the officers of the Dinajpur collectorate, the Dinajpur court, and the Dinajpur Raj led by Manikchand and Phulchund distorted the whole mechanism of revenue sales. It was a combination to promote their own interests and exclude outsiders. During the sale of the zamindari of Dinajpur, the assessment of the lots was divided very unequally by the native officers of the collectorate who had, thus, an opportunity of informing their friends where a valuable bargain was to be found. Therefore, while the profits of some purchasers were great, others made little more than what discharged the revenue.[22] In the sale of to two lots, Sindurhatty and Balabhadrapur, the record keepers reduced the assessment of the fertile villages of Sindurhatty and increased the assessment of the insufficient mahals of Balabhadrapur. The lots were constituted in such a way that only local men with inside knowledge could make the right purchases.[23]

In the hope of reward, Baburam Roy, a lawyer (vakil) of the civil court of Dinajpur, revealed a series of fictitious purchases made at auction sales by government and zamindari officers with the help of their inside knowledge. No action, however, was taken against these officers, who had powerful allies among European servants of the Company, such as G. Hatch who had become by now a member of the Board of Revenue. Mr. Fernandez, writer for fourteen years at the collectorate, bought properties in the name of his son and in the name of Krishnamohan Sharma, a relation of his private manager (sarkar)—Krishnagovinda Sharma. He was charged by the collector of having violated Regulation 2 of 1793, which prohibited the purchase of lands by government officers. Hatch, however, brought round his fellow members of the Board of Revenue in

[22]Buchanan, *Geographical Description of Dinajpur*, p. 250.

[23]BRP, 27 July 1804, No. 3, to BR from Collector, dt. 19 July 1804. Ibid,, 28 August 1804, toNos. 18-19, BR from Collector, dt. 18 August 1804;

TABLE 8.3

FICTITIOUS PURCHASES BY GOVERNMENT AND ZAMINDARI OFFICERS

Name and occupation	Fictitious (benami) purchases
Walimuhammad, Nazir of the collectorate, bought properties in	the names of his sons Ruknuddin & Babullah.
Babullah, employed in the court, bought properties in his brother's name	Ruknuddin.
Dindayal, formerly employed as tahsildar by Raja for 3 yrs, purchased	8 annas 'share of Hejulgurry which belonged to the Raja.
Baidyanath Chaudhuri, sheristadar (head) of excise (abkari) mahals, bought	lands in the names of his brothers, Lakhinandan (who was employed as the zamindar's amin, Muhrir & tahsildar) and Kalicharan. Baidyanath himself was at one time a tahsildar of the Raja.
Brajamohan Bose, muhrir in the collectorate, bought properties in the name	of his brother Rajmohan.
Mr. Fernandez, born at Nacas of parents who though of European descent	were considered natives of China. He was writer at the collectorate for 14 years. He bought properties in the name of his son.
Bhawani Taluqdar, sheristadar (presiding officer) of the zamindar, bought	properties in the names of his sons Guruprasad & Ganganarain and his nephew Gourikanta.
Guruprasad Sharma, was employed by collectors Hatch & Elliot at a salary	of Rs 15 a month, bought properti s in the name of his father, Bhawani taluqdar.
Gaurikrishna Sharma, employed at Bhaturia in the house of Brindaban	Tagore. He was manager of taluq ijara and devottar in parganas Kosambi for 10 years and was employed as ekji novis for 5 years and as jama novis (assessment scrutineer) for 4 years by Mr Hatch. He purchased 8 annas of lot Busbhaneja.

(*Contd.*)

TABLE 8.3 (*Contd.*)

Radhakanta, a muhrir in abkari department.

Phulchund, Collector's diwan and grandson of Manikchand, bought properties in the names of his brothers Kirtichand, Metteenlal, Sangamlal.

Manikchand, diwan of Dinajpur Raj, bought properties in the names of his grandsons.

Sources: BRP, 4 Nov. 1800, No. 23-27, letters from Collector of Dinajpur with enclosures, dt. 14 Oct. 1800; Ibid., 4 Nov. 1800, No. 26, to Acting Collector from I. Fernandez, dt. 9 Aug. 1800; Ibid., 3 Feb. 1801, No. 7, to BR from Collector, dt. 26 Jan. 1801; Ibid., 4 Nov. 1800, No. 24; Proceedings held in the Collector's kachari of Zilla Dinajpur on 22 July & 11 Aug. 1800; Ibid., 12 June 1801, No. 45, to BR from Collector; Ibid., 12 June, 1801., No. 46, to Collector Smith from Fernandez, Ibid., 29 July 1800, No. 2. Petition of Sri Baburam Roy, vakeel of the diwani Adalat of Dinajpur.

favour of Fernandez, and the collector, unable to fight against pressure from high quarters, was induced to undertake a 'mature reconsideration' and to let off Fernandez with a fine.[24] Fraudulent benami purchases were detected also against Phulchund, the collector's diwan; Walimuhammad, the nazir of the collectorate; and others, but the collector's enquiry into these fraudulent transactions did not make much headway as he received little assistance from the officers of the collectorate.[25] In concert with the officers of the court and the collectorate, the servants of the Dinajpur Raj put up the zamindari for sale by misappropriating the collections and allowing the arrears of revenue to accumulate. The members of this league then bought up the mahals themselves in fictitious names with the money they had embezzled. They purchased their properties at ridiculously low prices after having prevented many respectable merchants from bidding for them at the auction.[26] They bought the most fertile and

[24]BRP, 12 June 1802, No. 47, to Governor-General-in-Council from BR; Ibid., 16 June 1801, No. 1, to BR from Collector, dt. 4 June 1801.

[25]BRP, 4 November, 1800, Nos. 23-27, letters from the Collector of Dinajpur with enclosures, dt. 14 Oct. 1800.

[26]BRP, 13 March 1807, No. 40, translation of an arzee by Maharani Saraswati, mother of late Raja Radhanath, received on 22 September 1806; Translation of a memorial by Maharani Saraswati, manager of Raja Govindanath Ray.

productive mahals, the value of which was artificially depressed by their intrigues.

The imperfect nature of the market, closely affected the outcome of the sales. Out of 74.27 per cent rights sold in Dinajpur between 1796-1819, 47.72 per cent went to men of Dinajpur, 25.04 per cent to men of other districts, and 1.48 per cent to men whose place of residence is unknown. The major share of the mahals offered at public auction was bought by the local inhabitants of Dinajpur who were in a strategic position to exploit the new opportunities because of their long association with the land. The vast Dinajpur Raj was broken up in small lots which laid the basis for the rise of the local gentry as a thriving class of small independent proprietors. The new zamindars were mostly local men—zamindari servants, government officers, smaller taluqdars, money-lenders, and merchants. Of the 74.24 per cent rights sold in Dinajpur, only 24.45 per cent went to men whose professions are known. Among these, the largest percentage of purchasers were zamindars (10.07), zamindari servants (4.18) and collectorate and court officers (3.97). Thus the changes which were effected in Dinajpur as a result of transfer of properties arose from the complexities of the local society itself. This society had never been a simple rural society consisting of lords and peasants, nor had it ever been entirely static. Between the magnates and the villagers, there stood the local gentry—smaller taluqdars, revenue farmers, and the sadr and mufassal officers of the zamindars. Thus, while the turnover in rent-sharing rights did not wholly eliminate the Dinajpur Raj, the class of people who really benefited from it were the local gentry—traditionally connected with the land in their own right and as officers for collecting revenue. Formerly dependent on the patronage of the Dinajpur Raj, the class now grew into a solid social force with independent proprietary rights. But, because the district had never contained any large number of high caste Hindu taluqdars, there did not grow up here, as in many districts of East Bengal, a numerous sub-infeudatory grihastha gentry residing in the countryside.

In Rangpur, unlike Dinajpur, a few big capitalists and merchants associated with the East India Company did acquire some splendid zamindaris, which proved very profitable during the nineteenth century.[27] Rai Danishmand Nityananda, a common weaver who rose to affluence as an assistant of the Commercial Resident, acquired three parganas from the old zamindars of Idrakpur. The net proceeds of Nityananda's estate, after defraying the expense of collection, were said to amount to Rs 3 lakhs. Darpanarayan Tagore, the founder of the house of Tagore in Calcutta and diwan of Mr Wheeler, acquired from the zamindars of Natore the highly lucrative zamindaris of Swaruppur and Patiladaha. Canto Babu (Krishna Kanta Nandi of Kasimbazar), diwan of Warren Hastings, also obtained from the Natore Raj the zamindari of Baharband, the single most valuable estate of the Kasimbazar Raj in the nineteenth and twentieth centuries. It must be noted, however, that the Natore zamindars had only recently come in possession of Swaruppur, Patiladaha and Baharband, so that their passing to big merchants did not really represent a transfer from traditional zamindars. By and large, the old zamindars not only managed to survive, but also did pretty well in the nineteenth century. The Kankina zamindari and the three zamindaris of the kings of Kuch Bihar in Rangpur remained intact and in firm possession of the traditional zamindars after the Permanent Settlement. The Idrakpur zamindars lost many mahals, but repurchased some of them in fictitious names in order to avoid the claims of merchants from whom they borrowed large sums. As in Dinajpur, many purchasers of auctioned mahals—contemptuously called nilamdars (auctioneers)—were native officers in the district, or their relatives, such as Kanai Chakravarti, brother of the diwan to Wordsworth (magistrate of Rangpur), Maulvi Golamshah, diwan of the collector of Rangpur, and Munshi Himayatulla, principal native officer of the courts in Rangpur. The sub-infeudatory taluqdar class of Brahmans, Vaidyas, and Kayasthas so characteristic of Dacca, Faridpur, and Bakarganj in East Bengal, were not much in evidence in Rangpur before the Permanent Settlement, and the district did not acquire a large resident grihastha gentry after the settlement.

[27]The details of sales and purchases which follow are taken from two sources: Board of Revenue, Miscellaneous Records, Account Sale or Statement of Lands Sold for Arrears of Revenue—Rangpur 1795-1815; and Hamilton-Buchanan Manuscript, Account of Ronggopur, Vol. II. pp. 121-215.

The numerical weakness of the high caste Hindu gentry and the non-residence of many of the larger zamindars[28] meant that the jotedar class controlling the villages in Rangpur and Dinajpur had no serious rivals to their power in the countryside. The land-holding structure, which remained apparently unaffected by the changes in the revenue-collecting structure produced by the Permanent Settlement, was dominated, before as well as after 1793, by these rich agriculturists. At the time of his settlement of Dinajpur in 1790, the collector, Hatch, reportedly introduced a regulation by which the size of agricultural holdings was restricted to 50 bighas (25 acres). Like many other regulations which had no conformity with facts, this regulation was constantly evaded and leases for 50 bighas each were frequently obtained by five or six members of the same family.[29] In Rangpur, where no such restrictive regulation was introduced during the operations leading to the Permanent Settlement, the size of some of the largest jotes (raiyati tenures held directly under the zamindar or taluqdar) exceeded 5,000 acres. This concentration of land-holding meant that, at the other end of the scale, at least half of the cultivating population, both in Rangpur and Dinajpur, were landless. The statistics compiled by Buchanan in Dinajpur in 1808 make it clear that the distribution of land was extremely unequal from the very beginning of British land revenue administration in North Bengal (see Table 8.4). The landless villagers worked as sharecroppers and agricultural labourers on the farms of the big jotedars, who commanded their labour-power by giving them loans at high interest and keeping them perpetually indebted. Besides these

[28]Among the wealthiest and largest proprietors who were not resident in Rangpur in 1872 were Maharani Swarnamayi of Kasimbazar, zamindar of Baharband, Lakmipat and Dhanpat Singh of Murshidabad, patnidar of Batasun and Khupi, Kritendra Raychaudhuri of Balihar (Rajshahi), zamindar of Bhitarband; Chaudhuri Zaharul Haq of Birbhum, zamindar of Ganganagar; Rani Rasmani of Calcutta, zamindar of Shampur; Bamandas Mukherjee of Ula (Nadia), zamindar of Shaulmari; and the Maharaja of Kuch Bihar, zamindar of three parganas in Rangpur. *Report of the Statistics of Rangpur*, p. 113. In Dinajpur there were, in 1871, exactly 739 registered proprietors paying the land revenue, of which 45 per cent was paid by absentees. *A Statistical Account of Bengal*, Vol. VII, p. 409.

[29]Buchanan, *A Geographical Description of Dinajpur*, p. 234.

landless villagers, there were poor farmers whose lands were insufficient for subsistence and who, therefore, worked in their spare time as sharecroppers and hired labourers. These part-time labourers, as well as other small farmers who found nearly constant employment on their own farms, were called chengras, and were also obliged, during the lean months before the harvest, to take loans in grain or money from the richer cultivators. The economic control of the village by the jotedar class through their position as creditors and employers[30] was bolstered by the dewania system, a village political device peculiar to North Bengal.[31] Under this system, bands of poor villagers attached themselves to a substantial person in the village called the dewania, who was reputed for his ready wit and who acted as the agent for his followers in their dealings with superior persons from outside the village such as the zamindar's agents or the government officers. Substantial jotedars who acted as dewanias thus held a crucial position as mediators between the village and the outside agencies with which it entered into relations.

---

[30]For a description of this economic control, see Buchanan, *Geographical Description of Dinajpur*, pp. 234-245 and Hamilton-Buchanan Manuscript, Account of Ronggopur, Vol. II, pp. 96-121.

[31]Describing the dewania system in Rangpur, Hamilton-Buchanan observed: 'The small farmers are in this district the most timid creatures imaginable. Being totally illiterate, and afraid to speak even to a common village clerk, 5 or 6 families usually united under a chief man, who manages what they called the Dewanya, that is, settles the whole of their transactions with the agents of the landlord; and they are entirely guided by his opinion. These poor farmers are called Chenggoras, and go nearly naked; the men merely wrap a towel (Gammochcha) round their middle, or pass it between their legs, pulling each end through a chord, that encircles their haunches. . . . The Dewanya wraps round his waist a cloth worth 8 annas, throws round his shoulders a sheet worth a rupee, and encircles his head with a turban worth 10 annas. He seldom does any work, and on all occasions is helped first to tobacco and betel. Ibid.' pp. 96-97. In the course of the nineteenth century, the dewanies came to act as lawyers' touts. During the survey and settlement operations in Rangpur and Dinajpur in the 1930s and the 1940s, the settlement staff were impressed with the power and influence which the dewanias exercised over the villagers, frequently against their true interests though ostensibly helping them in their dealings with the outside world. *Final Report on the Rangpur Survey and [Settlement Operations 1931-1938*, Arthur Coulton Hartley, pp. 1-15.

TABLE 8.4

LAND DISTRIBUTION AMONG CULTIVATORS IN DINAJPUR, 1808

Category of Cultivators	*Percentage of Cultivating Population*	*Percentage of Land*
'Principal farmers' holding 165 *bighas* on an average	1.5	16.5
'Great farmers' holding 75 bighas on an average	2.0	10.0
'Comfortable farmers' holding 60 bighas on an average	2 5	10.0
'Easy farmers' holding 45 bighas on an average	4.5	13.5
Poor farmers' holding 30 bighas on an average	12.5	25.0
'Needy farmers' holding 15 bighas on an average	24.9	25.0
Sharecroppers with no land	34.0	0
Agricultural labourers with no land	18.1	0
	100	100

Source: Buchanan, *Geographical Description of Dinajpur*, pp. 236, 244. Two Dinajpur bighas=1 acre.

The jotedars were of varying size and, in Rangpur at any rate, some of them were so big that they were more like intermediaries in the rent collecting structure than rich cultivators practising large-scale farming. These were the people whose jotes ran into thousands of acres. Obviously, such jotes could not be cultivated under the personal supervision of a jotedar, and the usual practice was to let them out at rack-rent to poor under-tenants (prajas or chukanidars), to whom the jotedar would advance money for the expenses of cultivation at a high rate of interest.[32] These giant jotedars retained in their actual possession only a small part of their jotes, enough to supply their big

[32]However, the possibility must be borne in mind that some of the under tenants themselves might be very big farmers, renting hundreds of acres from the jotedar (direct tenant of th ezamindar) and cultivating with the help of sharecroppers.

joint families with food, and cultivated these home farms by means of adhiars or sharecroppers. Significantly, most of the giant jotedars in Rangpur were not of peasant stock but were Brahmans, Kayasthas, or Qazis (high Muslims) practising, at the same time, professions like religion, learning and judicial service under the government.[33] It must be emphasized that this class of noncultivating jotedars was peculiar to Rangpur, and Buchanan-Hamilton noted in his survey that he had not found a class of prajas or under-tenants in Dinajpur where the jotedars invariably employed sharecroppers and retained actual possession of their jotes.[34] The jotedars proper—rich agriculturists whose jotes were not too large for the inspection of one man—acted as money-lenders (Mahajans) and grain traders (beparis) in Rangpur and Dinajpur. These large jotedars, usually holding from 30 to 100 acres, cultivated a portion of their jotes with the help of dependent relations and two or three hired labourers whom they supplied with ploughs, but the remainder was cultivated by adhiars who received a half share of the produce and normally provided their own ploughs. There were also some middling jotedars with smaller farms, who possessed three to five ploughs. These family ploughs were held by their dependent relatives (seldom by themselves) and hired labourers. It was from this class that the dewanias of Rangpur were usually drawn.[35]

---

[33]Describing this class of giant jotedars, Buchanan-Hamilton wrote in his account of Rangpur: 'In general they are well behaved men, superior by much both in manners and education to the generality of their masters; and many of them live better than landlords of the first families and largest estates in the district. It is true, that they have not the same train of idle followers, and flatterers; but by this means they retain their understanding, and the necessity of application to business sharpens their wit, so that they manage their affairs with economy, and their houses, diet and clothing are at least equal to those of the landlords, and many of them can afford to ride on a horse, or to keep a palanquin. The energy, given to their minds, by the necessity of transacting business, is such, that I found one of them acting also as Kazi for a large district, and another deciding the petty suits of a division; and both seemed fully as qualified for their offices, as any, person that I saw.' Hamilton Buchanan Manuscript, Account of Ronggopur Vol. II, pp. 102-105.

[34]Ibid., p. 104.

[35]Ibid., pp. 102-103.

So thorough was the hold of the rich jotedars over their villages, that if any of them happened to have a dispute with his zamindar he might retire, with all his dependents (i.e. his debtors and employees), to another zamindari with plenty of waste lands which his capital would enable him to clear. The village which he left would then remain unoccupied for some years, until the zamindar could find a fugitive jotedar of the same kind with whom he would have to employ a good deal of solicitation before he could induce the farmer with his dependents to settle. 'On this account', commented Hamilton-Buchanan,[36]

> the landlords do not like this class of men; but it is evident that they are absolutely necessary, unless the landlords themselves would advance money to their necessitous tenantry. In a few places I heard that this is done, but it is only practicable to advantage on very small estates; and having large farmers, who are able to supply the stock, is a vast advantage to all persons that have estate of a respectable size. . . . A clamour, however, as usual, has gone abroad against the wealthy farmers, who are considered as mere flayers of the poor, and no people privately join more earnestly in the cry than the landlords. In public, however, they court the wealthy farmers, and it is alleged often, purchase their assistance to enable them to fleece the poor tenantry. A landlord or his agent assembles his people, and states, that he is in need of money to build a house, to perform a pilgrimage, to celebrate some holiday, to marry a son or a daughter, or to alleviate the pecuniary distress in which he is involved, and solicits the assistance of his tenantry. The rich farmers have been previously gained, and give their consent to a general assessment, and the others follow their example, rather than quarrel with people on whom they depend, but it is the poor only who pay. By this mean rapacity, the landlord always renders himself more dependent on these farmers, as he squeezes from his other tenantry what might enable them in time to cultivate with their own stock.

Payment of land revenue being squarely dependent on the cooperation of this village controlling class, the government

[36]Buchanan, *Geographical Description of Dinajpur*, pp. 235-236.

sought by its Regulations of 1799 and 1812 to subordinate them effectively to the superior landlords. In spite of considerable legal and physical power for attachment and distraint made available by the government to the zamindars in this way, even the most powerful zamindars could not level down the high and low of the villages to the same dead level. The bigger zamindars, because of their distance (they were usually absentees), dealt with the jotedars only through their local agents, giving the rich farmers a wide scope for collusion with the revenue-farmers. The big jotedars were allowed by the agents to occupy much more land than their leases specified and for this privilege the jotedars paid the agents a bribe smaller than the usual rent. The smaller resident proprietors of Dinajpur who bought two or three lots found that the new police and judicial mechanism built up by the British for strengthening the zamindars could be manipulated by large farmers as well. As they complained in a petition.

> The Jotedars who cultivate large Portions of Lands, are very refractory, and know that the Zamindars have no power over them they pay only a few Rupees on Account of their Revenue and then fall in Balance almost every kist, they hold more lands than they were entitled to by their Pottahs. Should the Zamindars officers, in consequence, summon them to the Cutcherry, and detain them for one or two hours with a view to reprimand them, they immediately go and complain at the Fouzdarry Tannah for Imprisonment and at the munsiff's Cutcherry for being dishonoured and whilst the Causes continue unsettled, they instigate the petty Ryotts not to pay their revenue consequently......[37]

These smaller zamindars, whose lands worth Rs 100 were reportedly being sold for Rs 10 at auction sales on account of the machinations of the jotedars, prayed that the cases lodged against them by the jotedars for exactions should be dealt with at the sadr diwani adalat instead of at local faujdari thanas and kacharis of the munsifs to which the latter had easy access.

[37]BRC, 29 August 1799, No. 5, encl. Petition accompanying the letter from the Collector of Dinajpur.

The continuing power of the jotedars in the villages did not, of course, mean that the landlords were not able to increase the weight of assessment on the villages as a whole under the Haptam and Panjam Regulations. In effect, an alliance was formed between the zamindars enjoying the power of the state behind them, and the jotedars, entrenched in local positions of power, and the increased burden on the villages was distributed differentially further deepening the lines of stratification within the villages. The weight of assessment increased on the village as a whole but the dominant village groups succeeded in shifting the incidence of jama to their dependants. For any fresh assessment, the consent of the jotedars was obtained beforehand by the grant of special privileges in matters of tenure and the new levies were paid by the poor of the village. Owing to the smallness of the population as compared with the area of the district and the vast amount of cultivable land still remaining unoccupied, the rates of assessment paid by the big raiyats holding direct from the zamindars (jotedars) remained very low down to the twentieth century.[38] In contrast, the rents payable by under-tenants and sharecroppers to the superior raiyats rose steadily in proportion to the increased value of produce. In 1876 E.V. Westmacott, the collector of Dinajpur, wrote in reply to a query on tenancy rights by the Lieutenant-Governor of Bengal that the under-tenants and sharecroppers paid to their jotedars in money or grain three times what the latter paid to the zamindar. What the actual tillers of the soil paid to their jotedars represented the rent that could be obtained by competition for the land according to the ordinary rules of demand and supply, while the zamindar received a customary rent kept far below the economic rent of land (in the Ricardian sense) by the force of usage. The incidence of rent was, however, complicated by the fact that the jotedar was also the moneylender and supplied capital for cultivation by giving seed, corn, and maintenance, and sometimes cattle and ploughs. Rent was thus inextricably mixed up with interest and what the jotedar received could offer no criterion as to what the zamindar ought to receive.[39] Where the

[38]*Dinajpur District Gazetteer*, p.

[39]Richard Temple Collection, Mss. Eur. F 86. 165, E.V. Westmacott, Collector of Dinajpur, to the Commissioner of Rajshahi and Kuch Bihar Division, 29 June 1876.

zamindars actually provided the capital required for the extension of cultivation to new lands, they did succeed in appropriating the rising rent of land. This happened in the uncultivated Barind tract, where the zamindars actively participated in the extension of cultivation in the late nineteenth century and managed to secure the profits which in other areas were being intercepted by the intermediary jotedar class. A rise in agricultural prices in 1873-74 following a famine encouraged the zamindars of Dinajpur to bring colonies of Santhal tribes from the Santhal parganas to clear the huge Barind tract covered by jungle with the result that the cultivated area of the district was increased by one third by the beginning of the twentieth century.[40] However, this was a somewhat unusual case, and in Rangpur, where most of the new cultivation was extended under the enterprise of the jotedars, it is safe to assume that a relatively much smaller portion of the profits went to the zamindars. As for the lands which were already under cultivation at the time of the Permanent Settlement, it does not seem that the conferment of 'landlord' status on the zamindars by the Regulations of 1793, and the sale of zamindaris to profit-motivated auction purchasers under these regulations, affected the dominant position of the jotedars to any significant extent. The purchasers of zamindaris secured a proprietary right to the collection of jama, but did not obtain possession of the lands which constituted their 'estates'.

The very fact, however, that a set of revenue-collectors rather than the actual holders of land were declared to be landlords implicitly carried a potential of conflict within rural society. Such conflict was likely to occur, moreover, in those estates which had been purchased by new landlords as an investment in future

---

[40] *East Bengal District Gazetteer, Dinajpur*, pp. 60-61. F.W. Strong the writer of the Gazetteer, comments: 'It must not be supposed that these Santal settlers retain possession of all the jungle lands they have cleared. The general practice is for the zamindar to settle the lands to be cleared by them for a period of years at very low rent. At the expiry of the period, the lands having been brought under cultivation and having greatly gone up in value in consequence, the rent is raised to the level of that of similar lands in the neighbourhood, whereupon the Santals promptly move on to some other spot where uncultivated waste lands are to be had, while the native Bengali cultivators take their place.'

profits. The modus vivendi which had been worked out by trial and error between the traditional zamindars and their jotedars could not be expected to continue upon the passing of their zamindaris to auction purchasers who were not bound by time-honoured customary agreements with the raiyats. Inevitably, there was some amount of tension between the new revenue-collecting 'landlords' and the existing land-holding 'tanants'. What was the outcome of these conflicts between two different categories of landed proprietors? The point may be illustrated by the result of the prolonged conflict between the Kasimbazar Raj and the Baharband-Gayabari jotedars, and also the Tagore zamindari and the Patiladaha jotedars. Both estates, Patiladaha and Baharband, were carved out of the traditional zamindari of Natore by members of the new Bengali merchant class which rose in association with, and under the service of, Europeon officers of the East India Company. Interestingly enough, in both new estates the rates of assessment had increased much faster by 1872 than in the neighbouring estate of Kankina under its traditional zamindar, where the increase of the total assessment seemed merely to have kept pace with the extension of cultivation.[41] The new zamindars of Baharband and Patiladaha were collecting more than was justified by the extension of cultivation and by implication were deriving part of the increase from older lands held by the jotedars in 1793.

Patiladaha, as we have seen, was purchased in 1793 for arrears of revenue by Darpanarayan Tagore who amassed great wealth by his commercial venture and became diwan to Mr. Wheeler, a senior member of the Company's government. The Tagores did not resort to the universal contemporary practice of farming out the collections. An efficient bureaucratic management with a collecting agent (gomasta), an accountant (muhrir) and a registrar of lands (amin) was set up in each smaller division (taraf) of pargana Patiladaha.[42] Much of the pargana was uncultivated at this time; there was a long narrow forest in its centre. The remarkable feature of the pargana was the absence of the usual subinfeudatory class of high caste Hindu taluqdars,

[41] *Report on the Statistics of Rungpore*, p. 44.

[42] Buchanan-Hamilton Manuscript, Account of Ronggopur, Vol. II. p. 148.

The pargana was occupied by Muslim jotedars, some of whom held upto 700 acres of land which they let out to under-tenants (chukanidars). The greater number of jotedars held about 50 acres and cultivated their lands by employing share croppers.[43] A rich jotedar, who held a lease for about 1,100 bighas (550 acres), refused to comply with the demads of the new zamindar and applied to the collector for a surveyor; but the measurement by the surveyor revealed the extent of the jote to be 1,500 bighas (750 acres).[44] From the beginning, therefore, there was simmering conflict between the Tagore estate and the big Patiladaha jotedars about rent rates. But cultivation was expanding rapidly—in two decades after the decennial settlement the cultivation was said to have more than doubled—and the scope for further expansion mitigated the conflict of interests. To save the trouble of finding settlers and the expense of collecting jama in small sums, the zamindar leased out extensive jotes in new alluvial formations (chars) to his own raiyats in nearby settlements who had gained his goodwill. By 1840 the area not already cultivated before 1793 by resident jotedars was settled in huge blocks of new jotes with settlers of exactly the same class, origin, and functions. Some of these jotes ran into 800 acres.[45]

It was at this stage, when cultivation had reached the highest point in the pargana, that the government passed its first piece of tenancy legislation, the Bengal Rent Act of 1859, and brought out in the open the fundamental conflict between the Tagore estate and the Patiladaha jotedars. Immediately after the passing of the Act, the zamindar Prasanna Kumar Tagore, who was a renowned lawyer of the Calcutta High Court, recorded the legal characteristics of the jote in his Rule Book of the Estate, in which although admitting the semi-permanent character of the jote to a certain extent, he restricted the privileges which had accrued by custom to the old raiyats of the estate to those specifically conferred on occupancy tenants by the Rent Act of 1859. But the issue remained wide open and during the settlement of 1908-1919 a problem arose as to whether jotedars

[43]Ibid., p. 149.

[44]Ibid., p. 152.

[45]*Finance Report on the Survey and Settlement Operations in the District of Mymensingh 1908-1919*, F.A. Sachse, pp. 69-78.

employing under-tenants were to be given permanent rights. After much discussion the government recognized the permanency of the jote, as otherwise, in its opinion, a prosperous and influential class which represented all that was stable and enlightened in the pargana would be ruined. The Tagores were determined to resist the claim of permanency, since the establishment of such a claim would result in the loss of fees (nazars) derived by the zamindar during the transfer of a jote. The case was taken to the courts, where the jotedars gained a partial victory. During Lord Ronaldshay's tour of Mymensingh[46] in 1918, the local Muhammadan Association, which was controlled by the jotedars, lobbied the Lieutenant Governor on this issue. Ronaldshay promised that the question would be gone into when the next amendment of the Tenancy Act came up. In the Bengal Tenancy Amendment Act of 1928, the jotedars attained their object when landlord's fee for transfer of occupancy rights was abolished.

Like the Patiladaha estate, pargana Baharband, which was acquired by the diwan of Warren Hastings, 'Canto Baboo', from Rani Bhavani of Natore, was settled with Muslim giant jotedars, some of whom held 6,000 acres. More than half of the pargana was held by big jotedars, holding 1,000 acres or more.[47] The new landlord, instead of farming out the collections, introduced an organized, though top heavy estate management, which collected revenue directly from the jotedars. Canto Baboo's son Lokenath Nandy of Kasimbazar, carried out a survey and measurement of the whole zamindari in 1784 on the basis of which he fixed the assessment at Rs 3 lakhs.[48] The jotedars. however, were sufficiently organised to stir up an agitation and, in a petition to the government, the raiyats denied the zamindar's right of measurement. On enquiry the collector found that this was by no means the complaint of all raiyats, but only of the principal raiyats who had possession of much more land than their leases specified. The poorer raiyats, who had so far been

[46]Patiladaha was transferred from Rangpur to Mymensingh in the nineteenth century.

[47]Buchanan Hamilton Manuscript, Account of Ronggopur, Vol. II, p. 158.

[48]Ibid., p. 162-165.

annually assessed with arbitrary taxes to make up for the deficiency caused by the fraud of the jotedars, were actually relieved by the new assessment, in which the zamindar abolished the illegal cesses on them. Nor was the plea of the raiyats supported by custom, since a measurement of Baharband had been made before in 1740.[49] Nevertheless, the Committee of Revenue, on the advice of the native officers, ruled that the measurement carried out by Lokenath Nandy was illegal and the new assessment invalid. In spite of this setback, the zamindar did succeed in collecting the enhanced sum of three lakhs, with a trifling balance. The proposed equalization of rates, putting the big jotedars on par with the smaller raiyats. could not, however, be carried into effect. By bribing the estate officials, some of the principal jotedars were able to hold much more land than was entered in the jamabandi, and to have the lands actually entered in the jamabandi described as third or fourth class though they were really first or second class.[50]

From 1818 to 1839 the Kasimbazar estate had no direct relations with the Baharband-Gayabari jotedars since the zamindari was let out in temporary farms to various revenue-farmers who granted confirmatory leases of their farms to the jotedars for that period.[51] From 1845 the munificient but able and businesslike Maharani Swarnamayi of Kasimbazar assumed personal administration of the estate by granting direct leases to the jotedars, and the privileged tenants were made to feel for the first time in many years the full blast of the enormous power and financial resources of the Kasimbazar Raj, which by successive contracts hedged in the rights of the jotedars. Maharani Swarnamayi in her leases to the jotedars made the right of transfer conditional on payment of arrears of rent and bound the tenants to appear and take fresh settlement after the expiry of their leases. In 1873 an attempt was made to levy a guzasta jama or progressive assessment, but it was seldom realized. When the Bengal Tenancy Act of 1885 was passed, the estate management, seemed in doubt,

[49]BRP, 21 August 1787; late Collector of Ghoraghat to BR, 12 April 1787.

[50]Buchanan-Hamilton Manuscript, Account of Ronggopur, p. 162, 165.

[51]The account which follows is based on *Final Report on the Rangpur Survey and Settlement Operations 1931-38*, Arthur Coulton Hartley, pp. 56-58.

at first, as to its legal implications and, as an insurance policy, the term raiyat which had been given an exact definition in the Act with certain accompanying rights was substituted in the leases by the term praja or subject. At the same time the leases stipulated that the right of transfer could not be enjoyed without the consent of the landlord, in other words, without payment of transfer fee, which was a source of substantial profit for the landlord. From 1911 there was a definite attempt to treat the Baharband jotedars as middlemen tenureholders and not as raiyats, and the term madhya-svatta (middle right) was used in the leases. In 1926, a new clause introduced the condition of non-inheritability. During the settlement operations in Rangpur from 1931 to 1938, the manager of the Kasimbazar estate informed the Board of Revenue that he would treat all jotes which were not actually cultivated by the holders as temporary tenures liable to termination at the end of the period specified in the leases. The jotedars, however, gained the victory when the revenue department, after several hearings, decided that the majority of the jotes, those which were not raiyati holdings cultivated by the tenants themselves, were to be entered as permanent.

The history of the Gayabari jotes was identical with that of the Baharband jotes until 1891 when a new survey was carried out in the pargana. The estate tried to fix rates on the basis of the new survey but, in spite of great pressure by the organized staff of the estate such as filling suits for arrears, no enhancement could be obtained. The struggle continued in the form of suits one of which went in 1907 to the High Court which adjudged the jotes to be inheritable and transferable. The decree alarmed the estate; Maharaja Manindra Chandra Nandy, the successor of Maharani Swarnamayi, paid a personal visit to the place and by granting mokarari or permanent leases to some of the more influential leaders he persuaded the jotedars to execute fresh settlements and accept a progressive settlement every 15 years from the prevailing rate of Rs 9 per bish to the pargana rate of Rs 21 per bish. The jotes were settled for 60 years with the option of renewal for another 60 years, and, although the leases clearly defined them as madhya-svatta asthayi (temporary middling rights), the 120-year leases was really a victory for the jotedars. For all its power and financial resources, the Kasimbazar Raj could not level down the jotedars, who, although to some extent weighed down by successive aggression, continued to hold the villages in their control.

How did the mechanics of rural power work out in areas where the jotedars were not over-arched by a hereditary revenue-collecting class in whom proprietary rights had been vested by the state? As we have seen, property in land had been conferred by what might almost be described as a case of mistaken identity on the local magnates whom the Mughal government had designated as zamindars, some of whom had been independent princes at one time. It happened that in Bengal there was one ruling princely house, the Rajas of Kuch Bihar, who were not brought under Mughal administration and were not reduced from independent rulers to the status of zamindar; consequently, under British rule, there was no question of conferring landlord rights on the Rajas of Kuch Bihar, who continued as subordinate native rulers rather than permanent zamindars. As in the rest of Bengal, so in the native state of Kuch Bihar, the land was held by jotedars; but here, unlike British territory, there was no zamindar class over the jotedars, only the state (i.e., the house of Kuch Bihar) and its temporary revenue-farmers (ijaradars). All revenue-paying lands in the state were included in some jote or other, which was a hereditary, transferable tenure. In greater accordance with reality than in British Bengal, the Kuch Bihar state recognized the right of landownership of the jotedar, subject to payment of revenue according to the stipulated rates.[52] There were three categories of jotedars in the state: the huzuri jotedars who paid directly to the treasury; the sarasari jotedars who paid to ijaradars or revenue-farmers; and the mokarari jotedars whose revenue was fixed. Since there were no zamindari or taluqi rights which might be purchased by persons wishing to stake out a proprietary claim to revenue collection, and since revenue farms gave no such permanent title to a share in the tribute from land, the pressure on the jotedar class in the state assumed a different form. Kuch Bihar was invaded by the urban educated classes of British Bengal in the service of the native

[52]Bengal Revenue Proceedings, Land Revenue Branch, Survey and Settlement, July 1872; No. 210. The following account is based on this particular source.

state, who, in the absence of zamindari or taluqi rights, began to acquire the jotes, turning them from land-holding titles to tribute-collecting rights.

Originally the jotedars were all residents of the state and cultivators of the soil. But with the influx of foreigners from outside the state, usually educated Bengalis from British territory, many of the jotes passed into the hands of the non-cultivating classes in the nineteenth century. In many cases, resident jotedars, unable to protect themselves from the oppression of the ladies of the palace and officers of the state who took most of the revenue farms, gave up their jotes to influential foreigners and became their under-tenants in order to be able to live in peace. Influential foreigners were, in many places, farmers of the state revenue and from this position acquired jotes by unfair means; the ladies of the palace and the officers of the state also utilized their position as revenue-farmers to seize jotes. A revenue-farmer who had influence at the court would quietly enter all jotes in his ijara containing the best lands in his own name and reduce the resident jotedars to chukanidars without their knowledge for many years, until a change of revenue-farmer would bring home to the latter that they were no longer jotedars. In this way 54 per cent of the revenue-paying lands in Kuch Bihar had passed to foreigners by 1872. Of the remaining 46 per cent, less than a third was held by cultivating jotedars and the rest by non-cultivating jotedars who collected dues from their chukanidars.

It must not, however, be concluded from these statistics that the old resident jotedar class of the state was obliterated in the process. They continued, as under-tenants, to hold in servitude the large body of peasants called adhiars who cultivated for them for a half share of the crop. In the jotes which passed to ladies of the palace, officers of the state or influential foreigners, the old resident jotedars continued in effective possession as chukanidars, and their chukanidars became dar-chukanidars. The chukanidars and darchukanidars were residents of the state and their tenures were, like jotes, transferable and heritable though subject to the consent of the jotedar. Many chukanidars, who had presumably been jotedars at one time, enjoyed large holdings. In the jote of Jogendranath Karzi, containing 380 bighas, there were only 6 chukanidars and dar-chukanidars who occupied the whole jote, keeping a large body of cultivators under them. The state itself stepped in to protect the position of the old resident jotedars and an order of the state in 1853 prohibited deeds called istafas and ikrars by which jotedars used to give up their jotes to influential persons. By degrees a rent-sharing superstructure was imposed over the village land-holding class in Kuch Bihar, but here, as in British territory, they continued in effective possession of land and in actual control of landless labour.

The position in the native state of Kuch Bihar might be compared with that prevailing in the estates of the Kuch Bihar Raj in neighbouring British territory, where the task of the Rajas of Kuch Bihar, as 'landlords' rather than rulers, appeared to be one of reducing rather than protecting the jotedars. Wherever the title of landlord was conferred on a class of people who themselves were superimposed over the actual holders of land, there was bound to be an element of conflict in the situation. Relations were strained in the 1870s between the Kuch Bihar estate and its jotedars in British territory in North Bengal. The jotedars had allowed their revenues to fall in arrears for many years past, and the greatest difficulty was experienced in making them pay. There was no open feud between the zamindar and the tenantry, but the jotedars offered strong resistance when the zamindar tried to enhance rates, which were generally very light and had not been enhanced for years. The jotedars had succeeded very largely in enhancing their under-tenants' rents, and had increased their jotes surreptitiously by encroaching on the khas lands of the zamindar, which were steadily diminishing. The jotedar class had, thus, succeeded in appropriating nearly the whole of the benefit arising from the great increase in rent for many years past. The independence of some jotedars was so great that they refused to attend when summoned to the zamindar's office. As they were in a position to compel the zamindar to resort to the court of law on any point of dispute and, moreover, rarely agreed to compromise on any point or settle any difference reasonably, the manager of estate was compelled to institute a very large number of suits against them. Since judicial procedure involved considerable delay, no decision could be obtained in many cases for a long time. In other cases, in which decisions were given in favour of the estate, the manager's difficulties really commenced only after he got favourable decisions for the execution of a decree proved to be a much more difficult matter than the successful conduct of preliminary suit. Because the records of the zamindari office contained no reliable information as to the area or situation of the jotes, in every case in which it was necessary to sell a jote under a decree for arrears of revenue or to obtain possession of a jote under a decree of ejectment, the agents of the zamindar in the interior had to institute local inquiries to discover the boundaries of the tenure. Since the jotes often consisted of scattered plots in different places and as the owners of the tenures and their dependent neighbours combined to withhold information, the estate agents were not often successful in their quest and, consequently, the decree remained unexecuted. The manager reported sorrowfully to the Court of Wards: 'In more than one case I have been informed that a ryot for whose ejectment from his jote I had obtained a decree, has laughed at and twitted the amlah who went to discover, by local inquiry, the boundaries of his tenure, telling him that he would not succeed in finding out the boundaries and therefore that the ejectment decree could never be executed.' It was the established practice of the jotedars in the estate to withhold the money payable as revenue and to lend it out at high rates of interest. In this may they obtained economic influence which enabled them to control large numbers of villagers in their disputes with the zamindar.[53]

It seems, therefore, that the 'landlords' recognized in 1793 did not generally succeed in levelling down the village land-holding class with the rest of villagers, though in many cases they did succeed in obtaining substantial increases of tribute from the jotedars during the course of the nineteenth century. More than a century afterwards, in the 1930s, the scene had still not changed substantially. Such change as occurred (induced mainly by tenancy legislation) lay in the direction of further extension of the influence of the jotedars and greater ramification of their political and economic control over the villages. Whereas Buchanan had spoken of rich farmers renting from 30 to 100

[53]Bengal Revenue Proceedings, Land Revenue Branch, Wards, etc., December 1876, Appendix A.

acres, the next surveyor of Dinajpur, F.O. Bell, described jotedar families holding several hundreds and even thousands of acres of land, who had progressed in the world and had acquired, besides their huge raiyatwari jotes, superior proprietary rights like taluqs and patnis. In many cases they had taken patni leases of whole villages from their zamindars in order to facilitate collection of produce rent from their adhiars, and also to get rid of the rival influence of the zamindars over these villages. Most union board presidents were found to belong to the jotedar class and had from 30 to 300 acres of land. Families which had risen higher, whose acres ran into thousands and who had become taluqdars, included the Chaudhuris of Rajarampur, the Chaudhuris of Govindapur, the Mollahar family of Bangshihari, Ramjan Ali Taluqdar of Dhohara, and, above all, the Shah Chaudhuris of Porsha. Besides these old established Muslim jotedars, there were a few giant Hindu jotedars who were new arrivals of the last two or three generations, such as Jagdish Saha of Birampur and the Bhakats of Nitupur. 'All these men are of a class which may be described as practising large-scale farming, though it is farming not with any large capital sunk in machinery, but through the traditional methods, employing either labourers or adhiars. They are the financiers of the countryside.'[54] These capitalist jotedars let out a certain amount of land on cash rent to under-tenants but tended to prefer grain which they got from the adhiars. Ordinary zamindars usually preferred to collect their dues in cash, providing payment was regular but the big jotedar landlords were taking direct possession and collecting produce rent as far as possible.[55] Not quite so rich but working on the same methods on a smaller scale were a more numerous body of jotedars, with perhaps a hundred acres of land, who were able to collect produce rent from the whole area through exclusive cmployment of sharecroppers. The moneylenders in the countryside were pre-eminently these rich cultivators. Often a rich cultivator might lend money to two or three neighbours who needed cash for sudden unusual expenditure, such as performance of a ceremony, payment of revenue,

[54]*Final Report on Dinajpur*, p.17.

[55]Fully a quarter of the cultivated area of the south and west of Dinajpur was cultivated through sharecroppers (adhiars), Ibid., p. 21,

or purchase of cattle. He would also advance grain to the poor men of the village for subsistence before the harvest. As Bell observed the conception of a village 'bania' which was foreign to the cultivator by caste and tradition, did not fit in the conditions in Dinajpur. If there was blood-sucking it was done by the rich cultivators themselves. People of non-agricultural tradition were few in the countryside—rich Muslim agriculturists formed the majority of rural créditors. Whatever changes the Permanent Settlement effected in the structure of landed interests at a higher level, the economic and political structure of the villages in Dinajpur and Rangpur continued to be characterized by the traditional type of domination that had evolved before 1793.

9

Dacca—Jalalpur

DACCA, FARIDPUR, AND BAKARGANJ

The huge and sprawling collectorate of Dacca-Jalalpur—comprising the present districts of Dacca, Bakarganj, and Faridpur[1]—was an extremely fertile alluvial formation of a low-lying, flat and marshy character, intersected by innumerable rivers and covered in the south by the gigantic forest of the Sunderbans. New alluvial formations—called chars—were constantly springing up as the rivers changed their courses every few years. By reclaiming the forests and bringing the chars under cultivation, the inhabitants, a majority of whom were muslims, were steadily extending the frontiers of agriculture. The main crop was rice, of which Bakarganj produced a big surplus. This surplus rice was transported by river to Calcutta for internal consumption and overseas export.[2]

The preponderance of the Muslims in the population was evident especially in the south, where new land was being reclaimed; as hardy cultivators they were better able than the

---

[1]The impact of the Permanent Settlement in relation to Bakarganj has been recently studied by Tapan Ray Chaudhuri, 'Permanent Settlement in Operation' in R.E. Frykenberg, ed., *Land Control of Social Structure in Indian History* (Madison 1969), pp. 163-175.

[2]Bengal Revenue Consultations, 1 February 1788, Shore's questions put to grain merchants in Calcutta. Bakarganj rice being of an exceptionally fine quality, a great part of it was exported to Calcutta, and the rice needs of Bakarganj were met by imports from Mymensingh, Tippera, and Sylhet. The rice production of the area was highly commercialized. H. Beveridge, *The District of Bakarganj, Its History and Statistics* (London 1876), p. 284.

Hindu gentry to endure the unhealthy climate on the seaboard, especially its salt air. In the older agricultural settlements to the north, and in the towns of Dacca, Hindus were not outnumbered by such vast numbers. The ancient and famous pargana of Bikrampur was thickly settled by the ritually highest ranking Brahmans, Kayasthas, and Vaidyas in east Bengal. Such older settlements were marked by a characteristic gathering of several high caste gentry families in local centres, each family having its small properties in the surrounding countryside. The high caste Hindu gentry of Dacca, Faridpur, and Bakarganj enjoyed revenue-collecting rights over the greater part of the territory although it was inhabited predominantly by Muslims. These high caste East Bengalis had moreover established a long tradition of service under the state. Among them, there was not to be found any large number of poor cultivating Brahmans or Kayasthas, as in west Bengal. They were thus marked off in a remarkably sharp manner from the cultivating classes, composed almost entirely of Muslims and low caste Namasudras. There were a number of immigrant Muslim families of high birth, also enjoying revenue-collecting rights and a tradition of service under the niabat (deputy governorship) of Dacca. But the bulk of the Muslims were native cultivators, whose ancestors had been converted by Muslim missionaries.[3] Islamic revivalist movements were strong among these cultivators, many of whom were Faraizis, a sect led by Dudu Mian who caused great alarm among Hindu zamindars by organizing peasant resistance to the exactions of the Hindu gentry.[4] The hardy and enterprising sections of the Muslim peasantry who were engaged in reclaiming chars and forests formed the main Faraizi settlements along the banks of the great rivers. Vigorous in the defence of their rights to the land which they were bringing under cultivation, they were extremely troublesome from the point of view of the Hindu gentry.

[3]Apart from the sharif Muslims of foreign birth, the Muslims of the area were probably converted descendants of the Namasudras, an especially large peasant caste in Bakarganj and Faridpur. *Final Report on the Survey and Settlement Operations in the Faridpur District 1904 to 1914*, J.C. Jack, pp. 6-10.

[4]Beveridge, op. cit., p. 255.

There were thus upper-caste and high Muslim gentry enjoying revenue-collecting rights and lower-ranking Muslim and Namasudra peasantry enjoying actual possession of land. Although this fundamental distinction was relatively simple, there were endless complexities in the land tenure system which arose from local circumstances. Long before the Permanent Settlement, the revenue-collecting rights in this area had been subdivided and subinfeudated to an extraordinary degree; and these complexities in the rights of the superior landlord classes were increased by the fact that the richer Muslim and Namasudra villagers reclaiming vast acres by settling their relations, dependents, and debtors on chars and forests were in a strong position to claim favourable and permanent tenures which could only add to the chain of subinfeudatory rights.

At the apex of a pyramid of revenue-collecting rights, paying revenue directly to the government, stood the zamindars. Only revenue-collectors who held parganas, or shares in parganas, were entitled to be styled as zamindars. Below them stood a great body of dependent taluqdars, who held smaller revenue units within the parganas and paid revenue to the niabat at Dacca through the zamindars appointed by the government.[5] Parganas were divisible into sixteen parts, corresponding to the divisions of a rupee (sixteen annas), and the holder of a half or a quarter of a pargana was classified under this scheme as an eight-anna or a four-anna zamindar ; a taluq was similarly divisible into sixteen annas, and if the occasion arose, into the divisions and subdivisions of each anna. A zamindar or taluqdar was never conceived as the holder of so many bighas or acres, but always as the holder of so many shares (sixteen annas in the case of an exclusive proprietor) of the pargana or taluq.[6] The land of a taluq, as the collector of Dacca noted in 1790,[7] was seldom 'one continued spot of ground', and was usually

---

[5]There was, however, a number of huzuri taluqdars who paid revenue directly to the government. They were not holders of parganas, but merely of tappas or mauzas within parganas which had been separated from the jurisdiction of the zamindars.

[6]Beveridge, op. cit., pp. 56-57.

[7]*Final Report on the Survey and Settlement Operations in the District of Dacca 1910-1917*, F.D. Ascoli, p. 57.

detached in small and separate parts, scattered through many parganas.[8]

The parganas themselves through rapid changes of proprietorship, detachments, and amalgamations had lost the geographical cohesion that they must have possessed at one time.[9] There were four classes of parganas in Dacca: the original grants, the grants carved out of the original parganas, artificial fusions of parts of several parganas under a new zamindar (called muzafat or agglomerated parganas), and subsequent divisions of the first three classes of parganas. The configuration of the parganas in 1793 showed that prior to the Permanent Settlement, in fact throughout the seventeenth and eighteenth centuries, very heavy transfer of proprietary revenue-collecting rights was taking place. Frequently, an influential revenue officer of the government, or an unscrupulous agent of a zamindar, would seize the areas assigned to him and enter these areas in the revenue records as a new zamindari. The new zamindari might either be entered in the revenue records as a fresh pargana, in which case the pargana would be scattered through the different areas in which its creator held assignments, or the zamindari might be shown as belonging to all the older parganas in which its mahals were incorporated. This process explained the anomaly of the inclusion of a zamindari in two or more disconnected parganas or the dispersal of a pargana in areas which had no geographical continuity. This was by no means the only complication which

[8]A Muslim taluqdar of sharif status, named Saiyad Ali Khan, held as many as 32 taluqs in 32 different parganas. BRP, 7 September 1791, collector of Dacca to BR, 16 July 1791. Another Muslim taluqdar, a notorious dacoit named Ainuddin Shiqdar, held taluqs, haolas (tenures under taluqs) and hisyas (shares) under many zamindars, taluqdars and haoladars in pargana Buzrugumedpur, Shahzadpur, and Selimabad: 11 properties in Buzrugumedpur, 2 in Shahzadpur, 2 in Selimabad. BRP, 3 May 1790, Statement of land revenue and collections in the possession of Ainuddin Shikdar.

[9]This process of subdivision and disintegration, which had been going on throughout the eighteenth century, speeded up after 1793. In 1858 the revenue surveyor of Dacca reported: 'The extraordinary and minute subdivisions of this district into no less than 108 parganas and 63 tappas baffles all attempts to define them in the district or even the 1" block maps. Out of all these, only five or six are said to have defined boundaries the remainder are broken up into minute portions and interlaced with one another in the utmost confusion.' *Final Report on Dacca*, pp. 53-55.

arose in the process of transfer of revenue-collecting rights. The older possessors might retain a share in the alienated pargana or zamindari; the new intruders might sell other shares to fresh co-parcenaries; or the families of the old and new possessors might become divided in various branches, all with a share in the patrimony. In such instances, the zamindari was not divided, each co-parcenary being allowed an undivided share in the whole; but each shareholder maintained a separate zamindari establishment and collected separately from the whole area according to his own specified share.[10]

Formal divisions of parganas and zamindaris thus gave no indication of the complications resulting from such unofficial arrangements but even at the level of recorded subdivisions, the trend from simplicity to complexity was steady. In the time of Emperor Akbar, the *Ain-i-Akbari* showed only 22 parganas having a definite interest in the district of Dacca. By 1728, the number had increased to 70; by 1763 there were 115 'estates' excluding about 150 petty taluqs. In 1793 the number of estates amounted to 394 and on the separation of Kharija taluqs (purchased taluqs dependent on zamindaris) the number rose to 14,500.[11] In many parganas the number of taluqs ran into thousands and zamindars retained only a small area of such parganas under khas (direct) collection (see Table 9.1).

The low proportion of territory under direct zamindari management was due to the fact that in many areas settled from older times by the Hindu gentry, the taluqs were much older than the tenures held by the zamindars, who were merely men of local influence appointed, in place of regular tahsildars (revenue-collecting officers), for collecting the revenue from a

[10]In 1790 the zamindari of Rasulpur was held by 3 different persons who jointly accepted the settlement offered by the government. Afterwards each partner appointed his own mufassal manager with equal powers. This resulted in great harassment of the raiyats, upon whom footmen were imposed at the same time by three different zamindars for identical demands. Home Miscellaneous, Vol. 385. Dacca, Zamindary of Russulpore, Consultations of 18 June 1790.

[11]*Final Report on Dacca,* pp. 53-54. In 1791 the Collector of Dacca reported that there were 30,000 taluqdars in the district, of whom less than half—14,500 to be exact—were separated at the Permanent Settlement. The rest remained as dependent taluqdars. Ibid., pp. 61-63.

TABLE 9.1

PROPORTION OF TALUQS IN DIFFERENT ZAMINDARIS IN DACCA IN 1790

Parganas	*Jama under Khas collection by zamindars*	*Taluqdars' jama*	*Total[12] jama*	*Number of taluqdars*
Jalalpur	11000	76001	87001	2148
Chandradvip	17000	72725	89725	400
Bikrampur	2010	25642	27652	268
Rajnagar, etc.	92555	20148	293673	400
Tappa Mysurdi	4000	14004	18004	561
Isakabad	1700	2000	3700	200
Tappa Hyderabad	1237	750	1985	200

Source: Letter from Collector of Dacca to BR, 26 May 1790, quoted in Beveridge, op. cit., p. 417.

multitude of petty proprietors. Such ancient taluqs, which antedated zamindaris, were often called jangalbari taluqs (taluqs created from forest clearances), which the collector of Dacca described in the following terms: 'Previous to the division of the country into pargannahs and tappahs, . . . many persons undertook to cultivate jungle and waste lands, and when the tuxeembandy (revenue settlement) was made, these new cultivated lands were constituted talooks, and included in the zummabandy (revenue-roll) of the nearest zamindar by the Government of that time . . . .'[13] Pargana Bikrampur, which had

[12]It should be noted that the total of the jama under zamindars and taluqdars as given by the collector does not correspond to the total jama in the case of Rajnagar and Tappa Hyderabad.

[13]Letter from the Collector of Dacca to BR, 26 May 1790, quoted in Beveridge, op. cit., p. 416. A.C. Sen, in his *Agricultural Report on Dacca District* (Calcutta 1885), remarked that whatever the case elsewhere, in Dacca the zamindars had no proprietary rights in land. They were merely tahsildars of the government with more or less local influence who were converted by the Permanent Settlement into landlords. This statement derives some measure of support from a letter from the collector of Dacca in 1790; who observed that the difficulty of collecting the revenue through tahsildars

been held from time immemorial by Hindu taluqdars, was always included under one or other of the zamindaris by the Mughal government, which refused to collect the revenue in minute sums from so many small revenue-payers. The zamindars appointed to the pargana were frequently changed by the government and they had no historical connection with the country for the revenue of which they were responsible. At the time of the British occupation of Bengal, the whole of Bikrampur was seized by the well-known conspirator of Plassey, Maharaja Rajvallabh, whose family appears to have held small properties in or near Rajnagar as one of the many petty taluqdars of the country.[14]

Soon after the battle of Plassey Maharaja Rajvallabh, an ambitious men of the Vaidya caste who then held the high position of deputy to the governor of Dacca,[15] fraudulently transferred the major part of the territory of Bikrampur to the parganas of Rajnagar, Kartikpur, and Buzrugumedpur which together constituted his zamindari. The zamindari of Rajnagar was a new revenue jurisdiction which was imposed over countless petty taluqdars, scattered all over Dacca, Faridpur, and Bakarganj, who were brought under the authority of Rajvallabh and compelled to pay the revenue through him. Pargana Buzrugumedpur alone consisted of 594 dependent taluqs of the jangalbari type. These taluqs and haolas (tenures under taluqdars) were placed under the charge (zimma) of 47 zimmadars, who were principal taluqdars who collected the revenue from the lesser taluqs and haolas and paid it to the zamindar. For the trouble of collection and the risk of being responsible for the revenue, the zimmadar received a rasum (allowance) which was deducted from the taluqdari

---

and the inconvenience of requiring every petty taluqdar to pay at the treasury induced the Muslim rulers to settle with the zamindars, who were fewer in number and persons of some respectability. They had no more property in the estate than the expectation of a renewal of the settlement. *East Bengal District Gazetteer, Dacca*, by B.C. Allen (Allahabad 1912), p. 149.

[14]*Final Report on Faridpur*, p. 21.

[15]Rajvallabh rose rapidly in the service of the Mughal government as the peshkar of the nawara mahals (accountant of the fleet maintaining establishment) and subsequently became deputy to the naib (regent) of Dacca. Beveridge, op. cit., p. 97.

jama payable by him to the zamindar. The acquirement of the zamindari by Rajvallabh did not, therefore, mean that the existing proprietors were dispossessed. Only a fresh revenue-collecting right was imposed over the existing layers of revenue-collecting rights. Rajvallabh's son, Gopal Krishna Sen, however, dispossessed many taluqdars by force or fraud and recorded the seized properties as nij (own) taluqs in the names of his sons, Pitambar and Kalisankar, instead of amalgamating them with the zamindari. The estate of Buzrugumedpur thus came to consist of nij taluq Kalisankar, nij taluq Pitambar and 47 zimmas comprising countless taluqs and haolas. Complex by the very nature of its origin, the estate became even more complicated when, upon the death of Gopal Krishna, it was divided in shares between Pitambar, Kalisankar, and three other shareholders. By this batwara or division, almost every taluq or haola, however inconsiderable, was divided between two or more co-sharers, so that none of the shares in the zamindari consisted of entire mahals.[16]

While the complexity and subinfeudation of revenue-collecting rights in mushroom zamindaris like Rajnagar arose from the prior existence of jangalbari taluqs, there were older zamindaris like Chandradvip and Idilpur where the creation of zur kharid taluqs[17] through the sale of particular mahals by the zamindars led to the same intricacy of revenue-collecting rights. The zamindars of Chandradvip, a high-ranking (kulin) Kayastha family, were Hindu princes ruling over the greater part of Bakarganj before Mughal rule. They were one of the so-called bara bhuiya (twelve lords of the land) whom the Mughal army brought to subjection during its conquest of Bengal from the

[16]There were disputes regarding the two nij taluqs between Kalisankar and Pitambar on the one hand and the other three co-sharers on the other. It was decided that Kalisankar and Pitambar should retain entire management of their nij taluqs, but each should pay to the other four co-sharers a fifth part of the dues. In such a complicated system of landed rights, the changes in proprietorship were kaleidoscopic, and it was virtually impossible to determine who was losing or gaining and how much. BRP, 14 October 1800, No. 21 Collector of Dacca to BR, Account Settlement of Kalisankar's share of pargana Buzrugumedpur

[17]Zur kharid taluqdars were at liberty to sell their taluqs by bill of sale, without the sanction of the zamindar. Beveridge, op. cit., p. 416.

Afghans. Subsequently, twenty-two parganas with different zamindars were formed out of the parent pargana of Chandradvip.[18] In order to meet the demand for revenue, taluqs were sold within the parent pargana itself by the zamindars of Chandradvip, the most important among them being purchased by their servants.[19] By the time of the British occupation, the revenue-collecting structure in Chandradvip had in this manner become quite as complex as that of mushroom zamindaris rapidly built up by officials during the decline of the Nizamat. There were frequent disputes between the zamindars of Chandradvip and their taluqdars some of which led to armed violence in the interior.[20] The zamindars in this ancient pargana enjoyed no more

[18]Bakarganj zamindars thus fell into two main categories, the Hindu princes who were converted by the Mughals into zamindars, and revenue collectors appointed by the Mughal government who turned their jurisdiction into zamindaris. Beveridge, op. cit., pp. 82-158.

[19]In a petition to the government in 1790 the Raja of Chandradvip gave the following history of his zamindari: 'My ancient and hereditary zamindarry of Pergunnah Chunderdeep is in Dacca Jelalpore. Previous to this Country's falling into the hands of the Mogul Conquerors it was possessed by twelve Bhueea or independent princes of which my ancestors were one, to whom the Pergunnah of Chunderdeep etc. belonged. At the Commencement of the Cultivation of the lands of Chunderdeep my predecessors cut down the woods, improved the lands and held possession thereof. When the country fell into the hands of the Mogul Emperors of Hindostan, my Predecessors agreed to pay Revenues to them, in return for being invested with the management, and having the possession confirmed .... In this manner and from that time to the present, my Predecessors held possession of the Zemindarry and paid their Revenues. When the Revenues could not be collected from petty Ryots, the zemindars improved new lands and granted Talookdari Pottahs for certain spaces of land constituting Talookdars and zemindars in the Pergunnah. It was stipulated in these Pottahs that while the Talookdars paid their rents, possession should be continued to them, but on a deficiency the Talooks should either be resumed, or made over to some other Talookdar in order to keep up the Revenues.' BRP, 28 June 1790, Collector of Dacca to BR, dt. 17 June 1790, enclosing petition of zamindars, petition of zamindar of Chandradvip.

[20]The intricacy of relations within the revenue-collecting structure which led to these disputes is well illustrated in the case of the dispute between the Raja of Chandradvip and the Muslim taluqdars of Mir Abdal. The Mir Abdal taluqdars were creditors of the Raja. He had obtained from them a considerable loan by giving them a lease of his nij taluq. The Raja, however, not only seized his nij taluq by force before—it was alleged—the expiration

direct control of their territory than did the family of Rajvallabh in the newly formed zamindari of Rajnagar.[21]

By the time of the Permanent Settlement, it was not at all unusual to find five or six grades of subinfeudation in areas formerly under the control of the niabat of Dacca.[22] Most of

---

of the lease, but he also took possession of taluq Mir Abdal by taking advantage of a dispute between the rival Hindu managers of the Mir Abdal taluqdars. One of the managers, finding that the Mir Abdal taluqdars had given charge of the mufassal collections to his rival, sought the aid of the Raja. The Raja, exploiting this opportunity, fixed the taluqdari kachari (office) in his own house and commenced collections on his own. The two rival managers then combined and secured the appointment of an attaching officer (sezawal) from the government to look into their complaints against the Raja. But the Raja's officers, collecting a mob of 500 people, boldly dispossessed the deputy sent by the sezawal and confined both managers of the Mir Abdal taluqdars. The Mir Abdal taluqdars had also leases of the properties of other taluqdars in the zamindari of Chandradvip who were indebted to them for large sums. The Mir Abdal taluqdars had stood as the revenue security (malzamin) of these indebted taluqdars and had pressed numerous claims for interest, allowance, loss etc., from their position as revenue security. But the Raja's farmer (ijaradar), Ramjay Sen, cancelled the securityship held by the Mir Abdal taluqdars and having made a hast-o-bud (survey) of the disputed taluqs possessed himself of them. The Raja thereafter commenced making collections from the taluqs in the names of the original indebted taluqdars through the agency of his own servants. BRP, 11 May 1787, Acting President's notes on complaints of taluqdars against Raja of Chandradvip.

[21]In order to gain direct control of valuable territory, the zamindars frequently employed the method of acquiring nij taluqs, nij haolas, etc., within their own zamindari. The zamindari right was often the least valuable among the revenue-collecting rights coexisting in one pargana on account of its distance from the actual cultivator paying the revenue. The nearer a tenure was to the actual cultivator, the more valuable it was likely to be. On account of this, the zamindars were eager to acquire tenures within their own parganas. In case of their dispossession from the zamindari, they could thus hold on to the tenures which they had acquired.

[22]The following tenures, in descening order were in existence before the Permanent Settlement: *Zamindari*; *Zimma*; *Taluq; Osat Taluq.* A large grant made by taluqdars to holders who stood in exactly the same relationship to the taluqdars as did the latter with regard to the zamindars. Osat taluqdars could freely sell their tenures; and *Haola*: A smaller grant made

them arose from grants made by the government and the zamindars for the clearance of forest and the reclamation of deserted riverside. The grants, known as taluqs, were obtained mostly by two classes of people living in the neighbourhood of Dacca—high caste Hindus of Bikrampur and Sharif Muslims with direct access to the court. These men had usually no intention of personally reclaiming wastes. They, therefore, sublet portions of the waste as osat taluqs and haolas to individuals who were prepared to take with them colonies of men to clear the forest. In Bakarganj, where the area under jungle was the greatest, not many among the haoladars were natives, they were recruited mostly from Dacca and Faridpur. Since an insecure tenure would not induce them to leave their homes for the arduous job of forest reclamation, these large-scale agriculturists had to be attracted by the grant of heritable and transferable tenures.[23] Many cultivators in Bakarganj possessed haolas and enjoyed the same superior and influential position as that held by the big jotedars in Dinajpur and Rangpur.

Before the Permanent Settlement, therefore, the zamindars in Dacca were not in a strong position vis-a-vis their dependent taluqdars, osat taluqdars and haoladars. The Permanent Settlement further consolidated the advantage enjoyed by the lessees occupying the lower rungs of the revenue-collecting hierarchy. Crucial in this respect was the decision of Cornwallis to allow the taluqdars to separate their taluqs from the jurisdiction of the zamindars and to pay revenue directly to the government.[24] There was an exceptionally large number of taluqdars in Dacca

---

by taluqdars, usually for the clearance of jungle. Its peculiarity was that a haoladar, in case of a dispute between bimself and the taluqdar, could get his haola separated from the taluq and included in the zimma of another taluqdar. This was the well known custom of zimma or transfer of allegiance which caused so many disputes in Bakarganj in the nineteenth century.

[23]*Final Report on the Survey and Settlement Operations in the District of Bakarganj 1900-1908*, J.C. Jack, pp. 46-47.

[24]The privilege of separation was at first withheld from the jangalbari taluqs, but later on, after the purchase of the Buzrugumedpur zamindari by the government in 1799, the large number of jangalbari taluqs in this pargana were allowed separation.

mostly Brahmans, Vaidyas, and Kayasthas holding taluqs at extremely small assessments of a few rupees. The collector of Dacca reported that the decision to separate their taluqs would reduce many ancient zamindars to beggary.[25] Not surprisingly, the zamindars found themselves in a predicament in pargana Bikrampur, where the qanungos and the zamindari officials had by unscrupulous means obtained a greater property than the zamindars themselves. These officials had fraudulently reduced the assessment on their own taluqs as well as on those of other taluqdars who had bribed them. In order to prevent detection of their fraud, they had destroyed or concealed the original papers of the pargana.[26] Such fraud could be committed successfully because the officers of the government appointed for the task of separating the taluqs had no time to make detailed enquiries into the assets of thousands of petty taluqs with minute jamas. Their instructions were to accept as revenue the amount which had been paid as revenue for the past twelve years by any taluqdar entitled to separation. With the connivance of zamindari officials, false evidence was fabricated by numerous taluqdars regarding their past twelve year's payments, with the result that a great number of taluqs were very lightly assessed at the Permanent Settlement. At the same time, a large number of fictitious taluqs—created by the zamindars for themselves—and to which they transferred the most fertile parts of their zamindaris—obtained separation at a low revenue. In this way, zamindaris lost territory and taluqs gained land as a whole after the Permanent Settlement. The position of the smaller gentry holding these taluqs was greatly strengthened, since they now became independent of the bigger magnates[27] and, in many cases, achieved a reduction of their assessments.

[25]BRP, 27th June 1791, Collector of Dacca to BR, dt. 15 June 1791.

[26]BRP, 26 June 1787, Collector of Dacca to BR, dt. 21 June 1787. A taluqdari settlement was made in Bikrampur with an increase of Rs 4,000 but it was certain that the influential taluqdars now paid less than formerly.

[27]The independence gained by the smaller gentry through the separation of their taluqs was an important gain in view of the fact that the zamindars, by virtue of controlling the biggest force within their territory, were formerly in a position to exercise coercion on the taluqdars. The Raja of Chandradvip, for instance, had used force most effectively in his dispute with the Mir Abdal taluqdars.

The public sales for revenue arrears after the Permanent Settlement speeded up the disintegration of the great zamindaris and big magnates like the zamindars of Chandradvip, Rajnagar, Idilpur, and Selimabad[28] lost their position of pre-eminence. Countless petty taluqs, osat taluqs and haolas, with assessments of one rupee or even less, were also sold for revenue arrears.[29] But, in practice, the holders of smaller or dependent properties could not be dislodged from the lower rungs which they occupied in the revenue-collecting hierarchy. Beveridge in 1876[30] and Jack[31] in 1908 both concluded that the descendents of the original proprietors were still controlling the principal shares in the smaller properties recognized at the Permanent Settlement.[32]

In just over five years, from 1797 to 1802, 68.99 per cent of the revenue collecting rights were sold at public auctions in Dacca-Jalalpur, at any rate, on paper. Of these, 36.28 per cent were independent rights consisting of zamindaris and separated talqus, and 32.32 per cent were dependent rights consisting of extremely small taluqs, osat taluqs, and haolas. It is, therefore,

---

[28]In the case of Selimabad, the older zamindars lost most of the zamindari before the Permanent Settlement to the Ghoshal family of Calcutta and lost the rent too after 1793.

[29]The complicated nature of the dependent rights sold under the Permanent Settlement may be illustrated with reference to two haolas which were sold for arrears of revenue:

Pargana Buzrugumedpur. The zamindari of Rajvallabh's family.

Zimma Yasomanta Bagal. Charge of smaller taluqs held by Yasomanta Bagal, a principal taluqdar collecting revenue from these smaller taluqdars for the zamindar.

Muzafat hisya Yasomanta Bagal. Annexed share of Yasomanta Bagal.

Joar Bharatkathi haola nij. Own haola of Yasomanta Bagal within his annexed share.

Muzaffat Buddhimat. Property of Buddhimat annexed to the nij haola.

Haola Ramratan Datta. Haola Rajnarayan Das. Two haolas held respectively by Rajnarayan Das and Ramratan Datta under muzafat Buddhimat which were sold.

Source: Miscellaneous Records, BR, Account Sale or Statement of lands sold for arrears of revenue, Dacca Collectorship.

[30]H. Beveridge, Collector of Bakarganj.

[31]J.C. Jack, Collector and settlement officer of Bakarganj.

[32]'In the smaller zamindaris and the taluks the old proprietors have retained the chief stake until the present day'. *Final Report on Bakarganj*, pp. 97-98. Also Beveridge, op. cit., p. 60.

clear that there was a considerable disturbance of existing rights reaching deep down the hierarchy of revenue collectors. In practice, there was not much transfer of rights from local people to outsiders. Of the 68.99 per cent rights sold, 43.81 per cent was bought by residents of Dacca-Jalalpur, 20.83 per cent was bought by the government for lack of purchasers, and only 3.78 per cent was bought by outsiders. There were practically no outside purchasers of dependent rights, though there were a few prominent outsiders among the purchasers of the bigger independent rights.[33] Some of the bigger zamindaris were transferred to capitalists of Calcutta like the Tagores and the Ghoshals, but the smaller taluqs, osat taluqs and haolas were bought fictitiously by the proprietors themselves or, if the transfer was genuine, by their neighbours.

However, in the case of a huge collectorate like Dacca-Jalalpur—comprising enough area for three further districts—the definition of outsiders as persons who were not residents within the collectorate was too narrow, and a purchaser of a Bakarganj taluq from Dacca city was, in reality, as much an outsider as a purchaser from outside the district. Among the residents within the collectorate who purchased proprietary rights at public auctions, some were urban proprietors living in the city of Dacca who seldom visited the properties which they bought in the interior. Such urban proprietors were often native officers of the East India Company employed in the revenue or judicial establishments.[34] Some, again, were commercial magnates, especially cloth merchants and manufacturers like the Basaks. A few among these commercial magnates were country-

---

[33]In the case of independent rights, of which 36.28 per cent was sold, 17.03 per cent was bought by people of Dacca-Jalalpur, 15.54 per cent by the government and 3.46 by outsiders. Of the 32.32 per cent dependent rights sold, 26.42 per cent was bought by people of Dacca-Jalalpur, 5.26 per cent by the government, and 0.32 per cent by outsiders (see Appendix IV on p. 341).

[34]The diwan and sheristadar of the Dacca-Jalalpur collectorate, for instance, jointly purchased in 1793 the parganas of Nurullapur, Pataspur, and Tappa Haveli Jahanabad and resigned their posts immediately after the purchase to deal with the rebellious taluqdars, whose contumacy they had previously instigated in order to bring about the sale of the zamindari. *Final Report on Dacca*. p. 63.

born Greeks, Portuguese, and Armenians.[35] In a class by themselves stood the family of Nawab Sir Khwaja Abdul Ghani, known in common parlance as the Nawabs of Dacca, who became the founders of the Muslim League. This was an eighteenth century aristocratic Muslim family of Kashmir, employed in the service of the Mughal government, who fled to Sylhet district in East Bengal after the sack of Delhi by Nadir Shah. Khwaja Abdul Hakim, the founder of the line, settled in Sylhet as a trader but after his death his two brothers moved to Dacca. Up to this time the family was engaged in trading in gold-dust and skins, but the next heads, Maulvi Hafizulla and Khwaja Alimulla, started investing in landed properties after the Permanent Settlement and acquired magnificent properties in Dacca, Bakarganj, Tippera, Sylhet, and Mymensingh.[36]

There was, thus, a number of auction purchasers from Dacca city who were outsiders in the mahals purchased by them, but by far the greatest number of auction purchasers came from rural centres of gentry habitation like Bikrampur, Rajnagar, Bangrora, etc. These gentry were mostly Brahmans, Kayasthas, Vaidyas and a sprinkling of respectable Muslims who were small taluqdars in their own right or were employed in the service of the zamindars and the bigger taluqdars.[37] The highly

[35]Among these were the Greeks, Alexander and George Panioty, Dominigo de Dilva from Goa who made a large fortune in the rice trade, and the Armenian merchants, Khwaja Michael and Khwaja Aratoon.

[36]F.B. Bradley-Bart, *The Romance of an Eastern Capital* (London 1906). pp. 282-285; *East Bengal District Gazetteer, Dacca*, B.C. Allen (Allahabad 1912), pp. 181-182.

[37]In a complaint typical of the times the zamindar of Baikunthapur wrote in a memorial to the government that an enemy of his, Shibnarayan, made representations to the collector against his naib (manager) Rinodram and obtained the naibship himself. The zamindar opposed this arrangement, but the collector took no heed. Shibnarayan dispossessed the zamindar, and his own signature as naib alone was of any effect in the mufassal in the business of revenue collection. Because of his oppressions, raiyats were absconding and the land was becoming waste. He also appropriated the small quantity of land in the zamindar's private cultivation for the maintenance of his family. Old zamindari officers acquainted with business were dismissed and new people were appointed. The naib's intention was to let the zamindari fall into arrears and purchase it himself. BRP, 5 April 1790, Memorial of Ramkishore Bose, son of Lala Kirtinarayan, Zamindar of pargana Baikunthapur.

intelligent, literate, and mobile Hindu gentry of Bikrampur were conspicuous among the auction purchasers. So, if on paper, a great many small taluqdars of good caste lost their mahals, an equally great number of gentry belonging to the same rank in life managed to buy up the properties offered for sale.[38] On the whole, this class of people gained most from the Permanent Settlement since they not only separated their taluqs from the jurisdiction of the zamindars but also acquired many of the mahals of the bigger magnates who fell from pre-eminence after the Permanent Settlement.

To be sure, not every member of the smaller gentry (a category inclusive of the smaller zamindars, taluqdars, and revenue-collecting haoladars) showed the aptitude for seizing new opportunities that was exhibited typically by those employed in the service of the government and the magnates. The accounts of the public sales sent by the collectors to the Board of Revenue also prove conclusively that a great many among them lost small parcels of revenue-collecting rights, usually to neighbours of similar social status and less often to speculators from Dacca town. Although evidence is hard to find regarding the ultimate fate of small proprietors who lost their rights in public auction, there are good grounds for believing that few among them were entirely dispossessed of their properties.[39] Striking evidence of continuity of possession in spite of public auctions is available regarding the zamindari of Bikrampur, which after the separation of 268 dependent taluqs, was settled in 13 shares with several co-sharing zamindars for the small sum of Rs 2,050 at the Permanent Settlement. In 1801, the collector wrote to his government: 'Between these (the 13 shares) and the fractional parts of them

[38]For a confirmation of these conclusions, see Appendix IV on Dacca Sales.

[39]Rajkrishna Sen, a Vaidya taluqdar, possessed two taluqs, one in Jalalpur and another in Bikrampur, which were sold at public auction in 1796 to the Armenian merchant of Dacca, Khwaja Aratoon. Khwaja Aratoon received a warrant (parwana) putting him in possession of these taluqs, but his men were assaulted by the dependents of the taluqdar when they sought to obtain possession. As a result, wrote Khwaja Aratoon pathetically in a petition to the government, he was now paying the revenue from his own pocket. BRP 16 February 1798, No. 9, Petition of Khwaja Aratoon.

that have been sold at public auction, the pargana is now divided and subdivided into so many minute portions, as to be unsaleable, and the proprietors, notwithstanding the various sales that have been made of their estate, have as full possession now as they had on the day they concluded the Novennial Settlement.'[40] Speaking more generally for Dacca as a whole, the collector observed in 1800: 'I believe there are but few instances in which original Proprietors have not got possession of their Lands again either by purchasing them in the first instance under fictitious names or causing the Purchasers by some means or other to relinquish their purchases.'[41]

In Bakarganj, where the fate of the smaller zamindars can be traced with unusual detail from the pargana reports culled by Beveridge from the collectorate records, the zamindars of the smaller parganas of Haveli Selimabad, Shaistabad, Shaistanagar, Arangpur, Syedpur, and Krishnadebpur retained a principal stake in their properties, although in some cases large shares passed out of their hands. The Raychaudhuris of Ponabalia, an old Vaidya family who had held six annas of the pargana of Haveli Selimabad (a pargana consisting of seven annas instead of sixteen annas on account of its having been separated from Selimabad)

[40]*Final Report on Dacca*, p. 55.

[41]BRP, 22 August 1800, No. 9, Collector of Dacca to BR, dt. 12 August 1800. Describing in picturesque detail the methods employed by the proprietors to frustrate public auctions, an earlier collector gave an account of the resale of Idrakpur, which has been previously purchased by Kanai Babu in benami (fictitious name) for the zamindar. 'Amongst the number attending at the Cutcherry there were as is customary on these occasions—Vakeels on the part of the Zamindar who are ever deputed to frustrate and impede if, possible, a Sale; the sum having regularly risen to Rs 4,000 a person from a distant part of the Cutcherry offered a sudden increase of Rs. 4,000 more, no further sum being then mentioned, the Lands were knocked down, the Bidder called for in due course, one Bungshey was brought forward.' As the collector knew this person to be a servant of the zamindar, he ruled that payment of the balance of unpaid revenue would be sufficient. When this offer was refused, he resold it again to Rokunuddin at Rs 5501 in place of Rs 8,000 offered by Bangshi Badan. It was noted by the collector that the zamindars' agents could outbid other purchasers as the excess amount over the balance was by law returned to the former proprietors. BRP, 30 October 1787, Collector of Dacca to BR, dt. 28 Sept. 1787.

from about 1605 A.D., lost four annas out of six annas to the Nawab family of Dacca in the course of the nineteenth century, but they retained their two annas share in the zamindari and were in effective possession of Ponabalia down to 1947 in spite of their frequent and prolonged suits with the powerful Nawabs of Dacca.[42] Pargana Syedpur, which was formed out of Haveli Selimabad by the qanungo Bhagirath Singh in the same way as Haveli Selimabad was detached by the Ponabalia Raychaudhuris from Selimabad, was settled at the Permanent Settlement with his descendent, Lala Jait Singh. The family retained ten annas of the pargana and the other six annas passed to Briju Ratan Das. A dispute between Lala Mitrajit Singh and Briju Ratan Das caused widespread riots in Bakarganj in 1854, of which more will be said later.[43] Pargana Krishnadebpur, formed out of Uttar Shahbazpur, was obtained by a Brahman pandit in the house of the famous revenue officer of the East India Company, Ganga Govinda Singh, who secured it as a reward for his pandit, Krishnadeb Vidyabagish. The Brahman descendants of Krishnadeb sold a part of the pargana to the Shahs of Baliati, and made over the remainder of their zamindari in patni to a Mymensingh zamindar.[44] Parganas Shaistanagar and Arangpur were also held at the time of the Permanent Settlement by two branches of the same Brahman family, and they retained the principal shares in their parganas after the Permanent Settlement, though many other co-sharers obtained a footing later on.[45] Pargana Shaistabad belonged at the time of the Permanent Settlement to a very highly honoured Muslim family of Saiyada, descended from the Prophet. This flourishing old family not only retained their pargana, but acquired other properties during the nineteenth century in association with the

[42]Beveridge, op. cit., pp, 123-124; Rohini Kumar Sen, *Bakla* (*Bakarganjer Pratna-tattva o Adhunik Itihas*), published by Sudhangshu Kumar Sen (Kirtapasa, Barisal, 1915). Beveridge, in the latter part of the nineteenth century, found the Ponabalia Raychaudhuris in a somewhat reduced condition. Nevertheless their domination in Ponabalia was symbolized by its two temples, Kalachand, possessed by the senior branch, and Durgamandir possessed by the junior branch.

[43]Beveridge, op. cit., pp. 157-158.

[44]Ibid., p. 143.

[45]Ibid., pp. 153-157.

Nawabs of Dacca.[46] Beveridge found many of these smaller zamindars, especially those of Haveli Selimabad, Krishnadebpur, and Shaistanagar in somewhat reduced circumstances in the 1870s; but there can be no doubt that within their own limited areas, they remained dominant families in spite of the invasion of new co-sharers.

The fall of the bigger zamindars from power was more dramatic though even in their case their descendants continued to hold small parcels of land or revenue-collecting rights. The descendants of Rajvallabh lost his zamindari on account of disputes between five co-sharers who maintained five establishments, which naturally increased charges of collection.[47] In 1799 the government bought the zamindari of Buzrugumedpur, but the taluqs and haolas within the zamindari were not affected by this transfer. Even after the transfer, Pitambar Sen, one of the five co-sharers of Rajnagar, retained his nij haola in parganas Rajnagar and Buzrugumedpur, a large property bearing an assessment of Rs 38,117.[48] In the case of the Rajas of Chandradvip, two shares in their zamindari passed out in 1799 to absentees in Dacca, the Greeks George and Alexander Panioty, who bought Rs 5-10-0 share, and one Dal Singh of the town, who bought Rs 1-17$\frac{1}{4}$-1. The largest share, Rs 8-12$\frac{1}{2}$-2, was bought by Ram Manik Mudi, Durgaprasad, Rajiblochan, etc., who were servants and dependents of the Raja. Ram Manik Mudi, a petty shopkeeper in the Madhabpasha bazar, was the Raja's gomasta (agent) and pretended to buy the share on his master's behalf but he soon turned around and claimed to be the real purchaser. Ram Manik's descendants, contemptuously spoken of as the

---

[46]Ibid., pp. 152-153.

[47]BRP, 28 March 1800, No. 8, Arzee of Sheikh Mahomed Zakir, naib of pargana Buzrugumedpur.

[48]BRP, 13 May, 1800, No. 4, Petition of Pitambar Sen. The largest taluq in Buzrugumedpur, known as Joar Ramna Bamna, was obtained by the Bamna Chaudhuris, a flourishing Muslim taluqdar family. Muhammad Shafi, the founder of the family, was leader (jamadar) of the footmen employed by the salt department. Another large and extremely valuable taluq in Buzrugumedpur, Aila Tiarkhali, and Phuljhuri were obtained at a very low rent by the naib of Buzrugumedpur, Kali Prasad Majumdar, from whom it passed in 1812 to Maulvi Hafizulla, the founder of the landed estate of the Nawabs of Dacca. Beveridge, op. cit., pp. 110-118.

'grocer's line' (mudi vamsa), became powerful zamindars at Madhabpasha living side by side with the impoverished family of the old Rajas. The Rajas, however, managed to retain the lands around Madhabpasha as their khanabari (rent-free homestead land), which was of considerable extent, being bounded by a stream called the Raja's Moat said to have been constructed by one of the Rajas as a defence of the palace-fort, now in ruins.[49] The turbulent Kayastha zamindars of Idilpur, who were notorious robbers, lost their zamindari in 1812 to the Tagores of Calcutta. Three years later there were affrays between the auction purchaser and the old proprietors when the manager of the Tagores sought to resume some taluqs, but the Tagores slowly consolidated their hold over the pargana by virtue of their enormous resources.[50] The Tagores also purchased, in 1819, the large zamindari of Tappa Nazirpur from a Muslim family of great antiquity founded by Altaf Ghazi of Ghazipur, a courtier of the Great Mughals who came to Dacca in the time of Jahangir. Dispossessed of their zamindari, the descendants of Altaf Ghazi became very poor and were degraded by a misalliance contracted for the sake of gain.[51] The large zamindari of Dakshin Shahbazpur, also possessed by a Muslim family of some standing, passed before the Permanent Settlement to the Armenian merchant Khwaja Michael. In 1788, a three-anna share in the zamindari was restored by the collector to the Muslim zamindars, who managed to retain it after the Permanent Settlement. The newer co-sharers of the zamindari, the descendants of Khwaja Michael and others like the Basaks of Dacca to whom the former sold shares, were residents of the town of Dacca; and like them, the older zamindars, the Mir Sahibs, also took up residence in the town.[52]

Though the Permanent Settlement brought about the ruin of many big zamindars in Dacca-Jalalpur, it must be emphasized that their decline had started much earlier in the turmoil

[49]BRP, 3 May 1803, No. 7, Collector of Dacca to BR, dt. 28 April 1803; BRP, 26 June 1801, No 15, darkhast of Alexander Panioty, George Paniotty and Dal Singh; Beveridge, op. cit., pp. 81, 87-88.

[50]Beveridge, op. cit., pp. 125-133.

[51]Ibid., pp. 130-132.

[52]Ibid., pp. 135-143.

surrounding the last years of Mughal rule in Dacca. This was especially evident in the case of Selimabad, the largest zamindari of Bakarganj, which had been held from time immemorial by the Rais of Raikati, the ruling Kayastha house in the area whose family idol dated back to 1643 according to a Sanskrit temple inscription. During the administration of Alivardi Khan the zamindari was seized by the Mughal governor of Chittagong, Aga Bakar, who stood as the wadadar, or farmer, of the pargana. After he was put to death for rebellion in 1753, Maharaja Rajvallabh, deputy to the governor of Dacca, attached the property and retained possession until 1758, when Sib Narayan Rai of the old Kayastha family recovered the paternal zamindari with the assistance of Gokul Ghoshal, diwan of the Provincial Council of Chittagong and a big capitalist of Calcutta. Gokul Ghoshal obtained a share in the zamindari as his reward and later, when Sib Narayan fell into arrears of revenue, the Ghoshal family obtained another share, which gave them possession of more than half of the pargana before the Permanent Settlement. The descendants of Sib Narayan continued to live at Raikati with a considerable property in the pargana, but the Ghoshal family of Calcutta became the principal zamindars. Gokul Ghoshal, who held the zamindari in the pseudonym of Bhavani Charan, resided in Calcutta and, being in need of cash and not receiving regular remittances from the manager, took to selling the office of the manager every year to the highest bidder. Thus, each year the manager was changed and the new manager, holding his tenure for only one year, practised every kind of oppression on the raiyats. For a pecuniary consideration, he also gave taluqs at undervalued rates to powerful salt merchants (beparis) who oppressed the salt workers (malangis) in their taluqs and threatened to stop their salt business whenever the Company proposed to measure their taluqs. In the course of the nineteenth century, however, the Ghoshal famfly consolidated their position in the pargana and became mild zamindars who drew favourable notice from Beveridge, the collector of Bakarganj, for keeping their accounts in an orderly way, managing the zamindari in a peaceful manner, and carrying out public works which made the bazar at Jhalakati the most flourishing in the district. The Rais of Raikati, and the old dependent families connected with them, continued as big proprietors in the pargana. The Sens of Kirtipasa and the Mahalavavises of Basanda, descended from old officers of the Rais of Raikati when they were zamindars of Selimabad, held the biggest taluqs in the pargana. The numerous co-sharers of Raikati also held considerable mahals but all in names of their relatives and servants owing to most of them being in debt.[53] Whether it was a Muslim governor of Chittagong, a Vaidya officer of the niabat of Dacca, or a Brahman capitalist of Calcutta who managed to get hold of their zamindari, the Rais of Raikati continued to hold the mahals which they had occupied since long.

The major changes resulting from the Permanent Settlement in Dacca-Jalalpur occurred within the ranks of the gentry, where an internal circulation of revenue-paying rights took place but there were also some sweeping changes which affected the position of the bigger magnates. The consolidation of the position of the gentry after the Permanent Settlement at the expense of the large zamindaris was reflected in the further complexity of the land tenures of the collectorate. As the Settlement Officer of Dacca observed, the result of the sales, public or private, in the twenty years of fiscal disorganization succeeding the Permanent Settlement was:

> Firstly to increase the number of estates, not in compact blocks but in scattered units, in each of which the interests of the proprietor were likely to differ, secondly to divide the lands of a single estate into the joint property of a series of new estates, or finally to retain the original estate as the unit under a rugged system of coparcenary, in which the interests of each coparcener might differ in each block of the estate, and remain subject to continual fluctuation according to the varying strength of each coparcener.[54]

---

[53]Ibid., pp. 118-123; BRP, 28 February 1791, Collector of Dacca to BR, dt. 14 January 1791.

[54]*Final Report on Dacca*, op. cit., p. 57. The classic example of this process was the zamindari of Rajnagar which, settled in five shares with the

In this process the estate was cut off more and more from the land and the problem of maintaining control over the cultivators only increased over time with the growth of subdivision, aliquotization, and subinfeudation within the estate. By the beginning of the twentieth century the position of the holders of 'estates' was very difficult indeed, as the settlement operations carried out by J.C. Jack in Bakarganj showed clearly. An ordinary Bakarganj village, noted Jack.

> . . . will form part of several estates paying revenue to Government, but the land of these estates will be jumbled in a hotch-potch of small parcels throughout the village. The proprietors of these villages will have no connection with the cultivators of the land, but will have sublet to talukdars at a peppercorn rent the whole of their interest in the village with the exception of a few rent-free grants made to Brahmans . . . . Between the cultivators and the talukdars there will be a vast sea of middlemen's tenures . . . . The owners of the various tenures will be usually not a single person but a

---

descendants of Rajvallabh at the Permanent Settlement, became divided into 36 estates within eight years in this manner:

Share (hisya)	*Transferred to Tippera*		*Private Sales*		*Public sales*		*Total*
	No.	*Revenue*	*No.*	*Revenue*	*No.*	*Revenue*	*No.*
Hisya Raikrishna Sen	1	609-4	1	1266-8-12	5	7436-8-14	7
,, Kebalram Sen	1	609-4	1	100-0-0	5	8603-1-12	7
,, Kalisankar Sen	1	609-4	—	—	2	8703-1-12	3
,, Nilmani Sen	1	609-4	2	1214-4-18	4	7488-12-14	7
,, Pitamber Sen	1	609-4	1	100-0-0	10	8603-1-12	12
	5	3046-0	5	2680-13-16	26	40834-10-4	36

The 5 estates of 1793 thus became 36 by 1801, but the trouble had only commenced, and by 1832 the original 5 estates were split up into as many as 126, the only relatively compact blocks being those which emerged from sales made by the government. Ibid., pp. 55-56.

> group of partners, originally members of the same family but often including purchasers. Most of the tenure-holders will be resident in different parts of the country and not in the village, many will be moneylenders and many will own several tenures in several estates. The tenure-holders will come personally or by agent to the village to collect their rents in February, but will otherwise take no interest and have no part or lot in its affairs . . . . On the other hand, a considerable portion of the tenure-holders will be prosperous cultivators who live in the village . . . . Such men will in many cases be middlemen in respect of some portion of their lands and cultivators of the rest. Most of the cultivators and many of the tenure-holders will be unable to explain the title of their landlord or the chain of tenures which connect him with the proprietors of their estate. No one in the village will be capable of pointing out the land of different estates, still less of the different tenures in the village.[55]

It was the increasing complication of revenue-collecting rights which led to the curious state of affairs observed by Jack in which many zamindars and taluqdars found themselves helpless in enforcing their legal rights against powerful cultivators. The prolonged dispute between the Nawabs of Dacca and the Ponabalia Raychaudhuris for the possession of Haveli Selimabad may be taken as a typical instance of the development of the complex land tenure in Bakarganj. The seven-anna pargana of Haveli Selimabad had from the beginning consisted of two separate estates, a one-anna share which became detached from the main estate and a six-anna share acquired by Rambhadra Ray of Ponabalia, which came to be known as 'seven-anna Heveli Selimabad muzafat (annexed) zamindari 6 annas'. The muzafat zamindari six annas of seven-anna Haveli Selimabad in turn became divided after the Permanent Settlement, into the four-anna hisya (share) Srikrishna Ray (elder son of Rambhadra Ray) and the two-anna hisya Manohar Ray (son-in-law of Rambhadra's younger son, Harekrishna Ray). The zamindars of 'two-anna hisya Manohar Ray, muzafat zamindari 6 annas, 7-anna zamindari

[55] *Final Report on Bakarganj*, p. 58.

Haveli Selimabad', began to flourish after the Permanent Settlement, although they inherited only a two-anna share. In order to consolidate their hold over the pargana, they began systematically to acquire the under-rights which existed below them, such as taluqs, osat taluqs, haolas, osat haolas, and nim haolas.[56] In this process in 1832 they acquired haola Prankrishna Das under nij taluq Premnarayan Ray which had been granted to him in 1770 when the muzafat zamindari six annas had not yet been divided into hisya Manohar Ray and hisya Srikrishna Ray.[57] The descendants of Manohar Ray of the two-anna hisya thus began to pay revenue to the holders of the four-anna hisya of Srikrishna Ray for haola Prankrishna Das from 1832. The descendants of Srikrishna Ray, in spite of possessing a four-anna hisya, did not flourish and in 1849 the four-anna hisya of Srikrishna Ray was sold for revenue arrears to the Nawabs of Dacca.[58] This proved ruinous for the Ponabalia Raychaudhuris of the two-anna hisya, who became involved in a series of judicial disputes for more than half a century with the four-

[56]The zamindari papers of the Ponabalia Raychaudhuris contain many documents showing the steady acquirement of under-rights by the two-anna zamindars. They acquired taluq Ganga Govinda Chakravarti in their zamindari, but finding other under-tenures within this taluq, started purchasing them in order to come into direct contact with the cultivators. In 1883 they purchased a nim haola of less than two bighas from Krishna Chandra Mitabbar, belonging to osat haola Gurunath Chakravarti within haola Lakshminarayan Ray under taluq Ganga Govinda Chakravarti. Deed of sale dated 1289 B.S. addressed to Ramdhan Ray etc., Ponabalia Zamindari Papers. Ramdhan Ray of Ponabalia also purchased the osat haola of Gokulkrishna Saha within taluq Ganga Govinda Chakravarti and thus came into direct contact with nim haoladar aminaddi and his brothers, who were actual cultivators holding a tenure. Case No 429-430, 1889, Ponabalia Zamindari Papers.

[57]In 1825, by which time muzafat zamindari six annas was divided into four-anna and two-anna hisyas, Prankrishna Das was paying a tribute of Rs 1,513 for his haola, of which Rs 1,009 was being received by holders of the four-anna hisya, and Rs 252 each by the senior and junior branches of the two-anna hisya. Letter dated 21 Asharh 1233 B.S. In 1832 the senior and junior branches of the two-anna hisya obtained possession of the haola jointly. Letter dt. 1239 B.S., Ponabalia Zamindari Papers.

[58]Bengali manuscript describing particulars of haola Prankrishna Das, Ponabalia Zamindari Papers.

anna possessors, the Nawabs of Dacca, over various issues including the possession of haola Prankrishna Das. The Ponabalia Raychaudhuris of the two-anna hisya had by now become divided between a senior branch (bara hisya) and a junior branch (chhota hisya) and their disputes prevented them from presenting a united front to the Nawabs of Dacca.[59] Immediately on taking possession of the four-anna share, Khwaja Abdul Ghani seized haola Prankrishna Das, but in 1851 the Ponabalia Raychaudhuris recovered possession of the haola by a judicial decision. Two years later the Raychaudhuris quarrelled among themselves over the division of the profits from the haola and in accordance with a decree obtained by one co-sharer against another for arrears of revenue the haola was sold in 1853 to one Chandra Kumar Guha. The real purchaser, however, was Khwaja Abdul Ghani and soon Chandra Kumar Guha transferred the haola to him. Before the purchase of the haola, Khwala Abdul Ghani had brought a suit for rent enhancement against the Raychaudhuris in their capacity as haoladars of haola Prankrishna Das and he succeeded in raising the dues from the haola from Rs 1,000, payable to the four-anna co-sharer, to Rs 3,942.[60] When the haola passed to Khwaja Abdul Ghani, the senior branch of the two-anna zamindars of Ponabalia used this judicial decision as a lever for increasing jama from the haola, and claimed an increase to Rs 985 from Rs 252, payable to their one-anna share, which was proportionate to the increase obtained by Khwaja Abdul Ghani.[61] Interminable judicial disputes continued between the Nawabs of Dacca and the Ponabalia

[59]Relations between members of the senior and junior branch were apparently good, but difficulties were caused by intriguing employees of both sides. Govinda Das, an employee of the junior branch, was a deadly enemy of the senior branch. Case No. 102, dt. 1902, Ponabalia Zamindari Papers.

[60]Bengali manuscript describing particulars of haola Prankrishna Das; English manuscript (partly torn) on suit for enhancement of rent brought by Khwaja Abdul Ghani, Ponabalia Zamindari Papers. It should be noted that the family of Khwaja Abdul Ghani were not yet known as the Nawabs of Dacca. Khwaja Abdul Ghani obtained knighthood and the title of Nawab for his services in Dacca during the mutiny of 1857.

[61]The following document in the Ponabalia Zamindari Papers is a translation of the Bengali letter from the Ponabalia Raychaudhuris to Khwaja

Raychaudhuris until the end of the nineteenth century and a considerable strain on family finances compelled the petty zamindars of Ponabalia to branch out into government service and the liberal professions in the early part of the twentieth century.[62]

The frequent disputes between co-sharing zamindars, whether belonging to entirely alien groups (as in the case of the Nawabs of Dacca and the Ponabalia Raychaudhuris) or to the same extended kin group (as in the case of the senior and junior branches

Abdul Ghani claiming enhanced rent: 'There is in station Jhalakati within the under-mentioned limits a haola named Prankrishna Das in Joar Baraiya under nij taluq Premnarayan Ray in seven-anna Tappa Haveli Selimabad muzafat six-anna zamindari. This haola bears an assessment of Rs 1513-2-8, collected more or less in each year. We are proprietors of a one-anna hisya in the names of the late Durgaprasad Ray, the late Guruprasad Ray and Sriyut Rajkumar Ray in the two-anna zamindari Manohar Ray within the above-mentioned six-anna zamindari, as also of 50 bighas of land. According to our share, Rs 252-3-1-6 out of Rs 1513-3-8 has been collected separately so long. In accordance with a decree for revenue arrears on the above-mentioned haola, it was sold at auction and purchased by Chandra Kumar Guha, who sold it to your father, so that you are now in possession of the haola by inheritance. Since according to the custom of the parganas in this district the rent of your haola, is liable to enhancement and since your previous haoladars paid a low rate, we demand a higher rent from you. It is possible to pay this enhanced rent from your haola. Previously according to a suit brought by your father for determining rent, it has been decided that the rent of the haola is liable to increase and has been increased by two-thirds. The amount collected from the haola for our share of the zamindari is proportionably less to that collected for the four-anna share, and is also less than that collected from other haolas in the pargana. In your father's suit for rent determination, the rent for the two-thirds share from this haola was fixed according to amount of land and nirikh (rates) at Rs 3942-5. Proportionately the due amount for our share is Rs 985-15-3. So we are hereby notifying that within 15 days of this notice you in person or your empowered agent will attend at the office of our zamindari and pay the above-mentioned Rs 985 according to instalments. Zamindars Ramdhan Raychaudhuri, Rajkumar Raychaudhuri, etc. versus Khwaja Abdul Ghani, haoladar, 1281 B.S. (1874).

[62]The first zamindar of the senior branch of the two-anna zamindars of Ponabalia to take to government service was Manoranjan Raychaudhuri, who became a postmaster. From about the end of the nineteenth century, the income from the zamindari was no longer sufficient to maintain the numerous family of the Ponabalia Raychaudhuris.

of the two-anna zamindars of Ponabalia), were bound in the long run to weaken their control of raiyats. The existence of a long chain of zamindars, taluqdars, osat taluqdars, haoladars, osat haoladars, nim haoladars, karshadars (ordinary cultivators), and bargadars (sharecroppers) was also likely to tilt the balance of power in favour of those occupying the lower positions against those in higher ones.[63] The great zamindars in Bakarganj were in any case perpetual absentees who could

[63]The zamindars, of course, tried to solve the problems created by subinfeudation by acquiring fresh subinfeudatory rights themselves, elongating the chains of subinfeudation in the process. Where 'estates' were scattered, acquisition of a new lease in the intruding lands tended to consolidate properties. This method of acquiring tenures under existing zamindars and first or second grade tenure-holders in order to bring intruding lands under control was employed on an extensive scale by the Teota Babus, the Murapara Babus, the Ghoshes of Shikharipara, and in the petty interlaced estates of Bikrampur (see *Final Report on Dacca*, p. 63). Within their own zamindaris many co-sharing zamindars made a practice of acquiring any under-tenures which had been brought to public sale by decrees. The Ponabalia Raychaudhuris did this on an extensive scale in order to enhance their control of the zamindari and to strengthen their own position against their powerful co-sharing opponents, the Nawabs of Dacca. It was, in fact, contests between co-sharing zamindars about purchasing or otherwise taking possession of under-tenures in their joint estates, which, in Beveridge's experience, led to so much fighting among them in and out of courts. Writing in 1876 Beveridge observed: 'One use frequently made of the large number of under-tenures is to enable a man to retain his hold on a property after one or more of his rights has been sold. . . .Suppose, for instance, that a zamindar's right and title in his zamindari are sold for arrears of revenue, or in satisfaction of a decree, it might be imagined that this would terminate his connection with his estate; but as a general rule, this would be far from the case. The *mazul*—i.e., quondam zamindar—does not surrender his hold on the land so readily. If he cannot in any way impeach the sale by showing that he did not get notice of it, that the estate was sold below its value, that the decree was fraudulent , etc., or that the property did not belong to him, but was his wife's or his brother-in-law's, he proceeds to another battle-field, and claims to hold a nij taluq—i.e., a taluq belonging to the zamindar, or a howala, or other under-tenure . . . . The last fight of all made by a dispossessed proprietor is generally that for the khanabari or paternal homestead, and is literally a fight *pro ara et foco*. The most serious riots in the district have their origin in disputes between the auction purchaser and the old proprietor, and the *casus belli* is then generally a dispute about an under-tenure. Beveridge, op. cit., p. 199-200.

never play the role of powerful resident landlords: the holders of the three largest properties in the district—the Nawabs of Dacca, the Tagores of Calcutta and the Ghoshals of Bhukailas (near Calcutta)—had never even set foot in the district.[64] The vast estates of the Nawabs of Dacca were so scattered and so complex that the cost of direct management would have been prohibitive. So the Nawabs of Dacca, instead of collecting directly from cultivators, created under-tenures as a means of simplifying the difficulties of management and control.[65] The lesser zamindars who lived in Bakarganj, such as the Ponabalia Raychaudhuris, were generally too poor to have absolute power over their tenants. They lived a long way off from portions of their scattered estates, and owing to the difficulties of communication in a deltaic area, seldom visited the outlying mahals. Most family members of the Ponabalia Raychaudhuris hardly ever stirred out of the village of Ponabalia, except to go to the district headquarters of Barisal or the metropolis of Calcutta. In the cold season, when the aman (winter rice) harvest had been gathered and the raiyats had cash in hand, energetic zamindars and taluqdars toured through the accessible mahals, collecting dues and presents. 'But for nine months in the year', observed Beveridge,[66] 'the under-tenantry are left to themselves and the land stewards. Even the latter are not always present, for as they are generally Hindus, they do not like to live in the midst of a Mahomedan population. They go to their homes at the time of the durga puja, and do not return for two or three months. As, therefore, the zamindars cannot, or do not, live on their estates, they are forced, in Burke's phrase, to govern with

[64]Beveridge, op. cit., p. 192.

[65]*Final Report on Dacca*, p. 63. This method of collecting through tenure-holders was employed in many complex estates to reduce cost. Creation of under-tenures was not as absurd as it sometimes looked on paper. In most cases a proprietor, whether he be zamindar, taluqdar, or haoladar, created an under-tenure when he could not with advantage to himself collect directly. An absentee or weak proprietor might not be able to collect his dues effectively from troublesome tenants. In such a case he would invariably seek out a locally powerful man, perhaps one of his troublesome tenants, and give him an under-tenure to collect on the proprietor's behalf.

[66]Beveridge, op. cit., p. 193.

a loose rein, and to allow the under-tenantry to create or acquire transferable rights.'[67]

While the various grades of registered 'landlords' divided the jama among themselves, equally numerous grades of 'tenants' controlled the land, cultivating themselves with the help of hired labour or letting out to sharecroppers on the half produce system. These powerful and large tenants were usually Muslims of peasant stock who called themselves 'Sheikhs' (as distinct from Saiyads who were sharif or noble Muslims of supposedly foreign origin). In Bakarganj these tenants held transferable and hereditary tenures like haolas, osat haolas, and nim haolas for the lands which they cultivated, so that their raiyati right was additionally protected and screened by a tenurial right. It was the acquirement of tenures by cultivators which made the chains of subinfeudation in Bakarganj noticeably longer than in any other district of Bengal. During J.C. Jack's survey and settlement of Bakarganj from 1900 to 1908, 64 per cent of the land was held and cultivated by ordinary occupancy tenants, and 27 per cent of the land was in the possession of prosperous cultivators who held tenures for the lands which they cultivated.[68] These bigger Muslim cultivators, in Bakarganj as well as in Dacca, enjoyed vast acres which they could not possibly cultivate by themselves; the practice was to distribute the excess land to under-tenants and sharecroppers. Ascoli calculated during his survey and settlement of Dacca (1910-1917) that 10 per cent of the land was cultivated by sharecroppers, most of whom had no status at all and were frequently ejected from their holdings. Their employers claimed that the sharecroppers were servants or hired labourers and that the whole crop belonged to themselves except the portion given to the bargadars as wages of labour.[69] These sharecroppers were also, like the majority of

[67]Not all zamindars, of course, were mild, happy-go-lucky landlords. There was the other type, frequently encountered in Dacca, who were landlords and money lenders at the same time. Many zamindars, headed by the Murapara Babus, lent to their raiyats at 37½ per cent interest, and gradually acquired the raiyati holdings, reducing the tenants to sharecroppers. *Final Report on Dacca*, pp. 75-77.

[68]*Final Report on Bakarganj*, p. 58.

[69]*Final Report on Dacca*, pp. 75-77.

their immediate landlords, Muslims of peasant stock and considered themselves to be liable to ejection. Resistance from Muslim sharecroppers to ejection or rent enhancement was a possibility only in those cases where the immediate landlords happened to be high caste Hindus and there were ambitious Muslims in the neighbourhood who were competing with such Hindus for local leadership. In general, the hold of the cultivating haoladars over their under-tenants and sharecroppers was absolute, and, while they regularly increased the rents of the actual cultivators holding under them, it was extremely difficult for superior non-cultivating proprietors to obtain increases of tribute from these powerful and entrenched haoladars. In consequence there was a very substantial margin between what the cultivating haoladars obtained from their under-cultivators and what the superior proprietors obtained from the haoladars. The haoladars were not averse to paying, from time to time, increases of tribute to their taluqdars or zamindars, but they were absolutely set against any attempt to limit their demand from under-tenants and sharecroppers. In the 1870s the haoladars in Bakarganj strenuously opposed an attempt on the part of the government to record the tenants (prajas) under them and fix a prajawari jamabandi (rent-roll of under-tenants). So fierce was their opposition that the government had to desist from the project.

It was this class of cultivating Muslim haoladars who obtained possession and control of the new land in the south which was reclaimed from the forest after the Permanent Settlement. The haolas, osat haolas, nim haolas, and osat nim hoalas possessed by these large cultivators arose mostly in the process of the extension of cultivation. In Bakarganj, cultivation of the jungle was not accomplished by squatters, as was frequently the case in Bankura where roving tribes of Santhals reclaimed forests and moved on, when pushed out by Bengali landlords who seized the newly cultivated lands. Nor was reclamation of the forest achieved with the capital and enterprise of zamindars or other superior proprietors, who refused to move out from the more settled areas north of the Sunderbans. It was the cultivating haoladars and nim haoladers, usually hardy and enterprising Muslim agriculturists possessing men and money, who brought the Sunderbans and the chars of Dakshin Shahbazpur under cultivation.[70] An enterprising agriculturist who took a large grant of forest on a haoladari lease usually clubbed together with neighbours, friends, or relatives to clear the forest, but as the cultivation advanced and the lands became marked off in aliquot portions he was obliged, since he could not cultivate more than a certain amount of land, to let out portions in nim haolas to his partners or his dependants employed in the enterprise. In the course of time nim haolas became so generally prevalent that they constituted fully one-quarter of the under-tenures recorded by J.C. Jack in Bakarganj.[71]

Besides the favourable tenure possessed by Bakarganj cultivators, there was another very effective weapon in their armoury against oppressive zamindars and taluqdars. This was the practice of zimma by which a cultivator transferred his allegiance from his proper overlord to a third party, called zimmadar (caretaker), who undertook to pay the revenue on behalf of the cultivator. A zimmadar was usually a powerful zamindar or taluqdar in the neighbourhood to whom the cultivator transferred his tenure and received it back as an under-tenure. Zimma was especially prevalent in joint estates owned by quarrelling co-sharers; the tenants found it advantageous to place themselves under the protection of one of the co-sharers to escape from the oppressions committed by the others. Ambitious and powerful zamindars also used it as a means of extending their influence in neighbouring estates on which they had designs. But, in general, the effect was to put some restraint on the actions of oppressive proprietors who knew that the raiyats, if driven to extremity, would seek the protection of a zimmadar. 'In other districts', remarked

[70]Beveridge, op. cit., p. 195.

[71]A large number of nims and osats seem to have originated after the Great Wave of 1882, which drowned the great body of karshadars (ordinary tenants) in Bakarganj. Haoladars had to make strenuous exertions in order to keep lands under cultivation and in their great competition for labour they attracted cultivators by the offer of nims and osats. *Final Report on Bakarganj*, pp. 47-48.

Beveridge, 'ryots run away when too much trampled upon; in Bakarganj they go to a zimmadar'.[72]

The substantial Muslim cultivators constituting the primary landholding class in Bakarganj had, moreover, a reputation for violent resistance which compelled the absentee Hindu zamindars to be wary in their dealings with them. Taking advantage of quarrels between co-sharing zamindars, these Muslim peasant-proprietors often promoted their own subordinate interests by violent aggressions. The widespread riots in Bakarganj in 1854, arising from a dispute between Hindu co-sharers in the zamindari of Saiyadpur, illustrated the way in which violent bands of Muslim villagers could virtually replace the authority of the zamindars with their own rule, enforced from embattled strongholds, over the population of an area.[73] The ready disposition to

[72]Beveridge, op. cit., pp. 206-207. It was not always, of course, that the practice of zimma succeeded in breaking the hold of a powerful overlord. The Mahalanavises of Basinda, large taluqdars in pargana Selimabad, took a lease of village Kal Megha in the Sunderban estate of Gyanpara for reclaiming the forest. They financed the reclamation of the forest by giving advances to cultivators, who were attracted by the promise of permanent leases, but when a good deal of land had been cleared a dispute arose between the Mahalanavises and the cultivators, upon which the Mahalanavises refused to grant permanent leases. The cultivators, in retaliation, placed themselves under the zimma of Sidam Mia, a Muslim taluqdar in the neighbourhood who was instigating them against the Mahalanavises. The Mahalanavises fearing that they would be deprived of the fruits of their endeavours and expenditure, hired clubmen to keep Sidam Mia out of the village. This led to several affrays, for Sidam Mia was the superior proprietor of the estate of Gyanpara and contended that the under-right claimed by the Mahalanavises was false and that the area cleared by them was part of his private lands. The dispute continued for several months till Sidam Mia died and eventually his family submitted to the larger purse of the Mahalanavises. His share in Gyanpara was put up for sale in execution of a decree and was bought by the Mahalanavises, so that they came to possess both the superior and subordinate rights in the estate. Beveridge, op. cit., pp. 202-205.

[73]Pargana Saiyadpur belonged in portions of 10 annas and 6 annas to Lala Mitrajit Singh, a descendant of the original zamindar at the time of the Permanent Settlement, and Briju Ratan Das, a new co-sharer by purchase. There were several lucrative taluqs in the pargana and the object of the two rival co-sharers was to get exclusive possession of as many valuable properties as possible. Summary suits were pressed against the taluqdars, and their tenures purchased for a song. In some cases the taluqdars fought the

resort to violence in order to protect or promote their land rights was especially evident among Muslim agriculturists of the Faraizi sect, who were noticeably 'more vigorous and less tractable than ordinary Mahomedans'.[74]

---

purchasers, in other cases a purchase by one of the zamindars led to disputes with his co-sharer. Resolving to put down opposition, from whatever quarter it might come, by violent measures, Lala Mitrajit Singh approached the two most notorious characters in the district, Gagan Mir and Mohan Mir, and obtained the aid of these two Muslim brothers by promising them the certain taluqs. Soon afterwards Mitrajit Singh, breaking his compact with two brothers, refused to complete the transfer of a taluq, and the two brothers became his worst enemies. Numerous criminal cases were brought by these parties, against each other. But the long purse of Mitrajit Singh soon exhausted the small means of the Mias in this expensive and profitless warfare, and, leaving the zamindar to the court, they turned to plundering the zamindar's kachari (office and treasury) and robbing and oppressing all who were in his party. By regular plunder and warfare, the Mias were able to collect, without any money of their own, a force with which Mitrajit Singh's hired bands were not strong enough to cope. The rival co-sharer, Briju Ratan Das, hoping to bring about the utter ruin of Mitrajit Singh, joined hands with the Mias, who thereby felt so strong that they defied not only the 10-anna zamindar but also the police. A fortified house was built, from which the rabble of that part of the country issued to plunder the inhabitants. The police were powerless to put down this armed band of Muslim villagers and the district was in a state bordering on insurrection. Frightened by the state of affairs, the two zamindars compromised their differences. Thereupon the Mias no longer confined their depredations against the adherents of the 10-anna zamindar, but robbed and plundered everyone without discrimination. The Magistrate of Bakarganj had to take the field in person, and at length Gagan Mir was captured and Mohan Mir surrendered. The brothers were sentenced to fourteen years and the combination of rioting villagers came to an end. Beveridge, op. cit., pp. 239-244.

[74]Beveridge, op. cit., pp. 254-255. The Faraizis were not Wahabis, with whom they were often identified, though there was undoubtedly a resemblance between their creeds. Both represented an attempt to return to the doctrines of Muhammad and to purge the superstitions and idolatrous practices which had been gathered round the earlier creed by lapse of time and by contact with infidels, especially Hindus. In other words, they were primitive church movements. In their political tendencies, however, the two sects were quite different. The Faraizis did not challenge the British and their revolutionary views did not extend beyond disputing the zamindars' illegal claims for excess collections. Muin-ud-Din Ahmad Khan, *History of the Fara'idi Movement in Bengal* (*1818-1906*), (Karachi 1965), pp. 114-115.

The areas in East Bengal where the Faraizi movement attained its greatest strength were Faridpur, Bakarganj, and Dacca. The founder of the sect, Haji Shariatulla, was a small land-holder born of a petty taluqdar family in the village of Shamail in Madaripur subdivision of Bakarganj district (later transferred to Faridpur district). His movement, initiated in 1818 after his return from a pilgrimage to Mecca, was anti-zamindar from the beginning, since he was opposed to the payment of idolatrous taxes imposed by Hindu zamindars over their Muslim raiyats. The Hindu zamindars were alarmed at the spread of the new creed and when Shariatulla attacked and looted a whole village in 1831 in order to impose his creed they were instrumental in having him deported from Nayabari, in Dacca district, where he had settled. Violent fighting and large-scale affrays between Faraizi peasants and Hindu zamindars, however, did not break out until the assumption of headship of Shariatulla's son and successor, Dudu Mian, who organized a large band of clubmen. He struck terror in the hearts of the Hindu zamindars of Faridpur in 1842 by leading at night an expedition of 800 Faraizi peasants against the powerful Ghoshes of Faridpur. During this night raid the zamindar Madan Ghosh was carried off and drowned in the river Padma.[75] Dudu Mian's son and successor, Naya Mian, was able to further consolidate the power of the Faraizi sect in Madaripur by successfully backing the claim of an excluded Hindu co-sharer in the big zamindari of Palong, the zamindars of which were notorious oppressors of Faraizi raiyats. 'In this area', testified a subdivisional officer of Madaripur in his Bengali autobiography, 'Naya Mian established a state of his own within the British regime. In every village, he appointed a superintendent and a footman through whom he kept the Faraizis in control. No dispute of the village could be submitted to the civil or criminal courts without the permission

[75]Ibid., pp. 1-47. Dudu Mian allegedly misused the great power and financial resources placed in his hands for religious purposes by purchasing an estate for himself. He also acquired no less than 18 wives during his colourful career, one of whom was a Brahman girl forcibly carried off during a raid.

of the superintendent.'[76] The Muslim peasants in the different Faraizi settlements were all brought under the authority of the head of the sect through a regular chain of command of gaon khalifas (village agents), superintendent khalifas (in charge of ten or more villages forming a gird), and uparasta khalifas (advisers of the head of the sect) who constituted the siyasi or political branch of the Faraizi sect as distinct from its dini or religious branch.[77]

Though the initial impulse for the Faraizi movement came from the Islamic revivalist movements which spread through the subcontinent after the decline of Muslim power in North India due to the British occupation, the acquirement of a mass peasant following by the Faraizi movement in the lower deltaic formation of East Bengal, so far away from the centres of Islamic revivalism (such as Delhi and Patna), can only be explained in terms of specific changes in the social and economic conditions of the delta. Muin-ud-Din Ahmad Khan, the historian of the Faraizi movement, has pointed out that the movement spread along the banks of the deltaic rivers down which the Muslim missionaries floated by boats in order to preach the cult to Muslim peasants. But while the route of the missionaries might have influenced the geographical location of the Faraizi movement, it must be emphasized that it was precisely along the banks of the rivers running south, where chars were constantly springing up and from which forests could be reached most easily, that the frontiers of cultivation were being extended by enterprising Muslim cultivators. The work was arduous and dangerous and demanded unity and discipline among the bands of Muslim cultivators engaged in the task, so the sectarian organization of the Faraizi movement fulfilled a genuine local need. The attempt of Hindu zamindars and taluqdars, recognized by the Permanent Settlement as 'landlords' of lands where there had never been any cultivation, to enhance rates on new lands as soon as they were brought fully under cultivation, naturally created resentment among the prosperous and enterprising leaders of the Muslim bands along the rivers who regarded the land as theirs by right. The ideology of

[76]Navin Chandra Sen, *Amar Jivana*, Vol. III (Calcutta 1317 B.S.), p. 149.

[77]Muin-ud-Din Ahmad Khan, op. cit., pp. 105-111,

the Faraizi movement was tailormade to the needs of Muslim agricultural entrepreneurs who were determined to retain the fruits of their enterprise, by violent action if necessary. Between the Hindu gentry, declared landlords at the Permanent Settlement, and the land-reclaiming Muslims, defined as tenants by the same settlement, competition for local power became increasingly sharper over time.

On the whole, the local Hindu gentry, who had been a more influential element in Dacca-Jalalpur than in any other district before 1793, remained predominant for a long time after the Permanent Settlement, and their position strengthened vis-a-vis the large zamindars. Yet the fact that these Hindu gentry never participated in agricultural operations, unlike their Rarhi counterparts in Burdwan or Bishnupur, prevented them from converting their title to the land into actual possession of it, and there was, therefore, no massive intrusion by these gentry into the structure of land-holding and village politics. The growth of a prosperous Muslim agricultural class which succeeded in appropriating the increased rents resulting from extension of cultivation gradually weakened the position of the Hindu gentry at this level, although they benefited at another level from the destruction of the bigger magnates after 1793. The emergence of two distinct social groups—the smaller Hindu gentry and the larger Muslim agriculturists—as the leading elements in the structure of politics in the localities led, in time, to an explosive situation in these localities which powerfully fed communalism in the province as a whole.

PART III

CONCLUSION

10

Continuity and Change in Bengali Agrarian Society

The studies of a few selected areas of Bengal, ranging from the huge zamindaris of Bishnupur, Burdwan and Dinajpur to the innumerable petty taluqs of Dacca and Midnapur, have shown that each area had its own peculiar structure of hierarchically organized land rights, which was shaken up more profoundly at the top than at the bottom by the Permanent Settlement. To deal in a methodical way with the impact of the transfer of rights under the Permanent Settlement, each local structure has been examined from the top downwards and the enquiry has shown that changes in the top did not necessarily percolate to the bottom. For want of adequate local data the area studies have provided only a brief clue as to what happened at the village base of each structure, and it is necessary, in view of the importance of the village in the organization of society, to pursue this clue in the light of whatever evidence is available.[1] It is now proposed, in the first place, to summarize the findings about the changes wrought in the upper layers of the local revenue-collecting structures by the Permanent Settlement; and secondly, to direct enquiries downwards to the actual happenings at the level of the land-holding structure within the villages.

[1]The available evidence is more or less confined to Rangpur and Dinajpur, where Buchanan-Hamilton carried out the only survey of this period.

The introduction of this work stated two counter-factual propositions, often recorded as statements of belief by administrators and scholars who have written on the subject, which provide an analytical framework within which to organize our enquiries into changes in the upper and lower levels of the hierarchy of land rights in various localities. Both propositions claim that the Permanent Settlement created new classes of landlords in Bengal. The first emphasizes the legal innovations of the Permanent Settlement—the creation of absolute property in land by law and its passing from an ancient aristocracy of zamindars to an urban commercial class of landlords under the ruthless operations of the market for land established by the sale regulations of 1793. The second emphasizes the growth of the market value of land due to commercialization of crops and its passing to a rich village landholding class of jotedars from self-sufficient peasants who became share-croppers and landless labourers on their own lands.

In a despatch to the Court of Directors, the Governor General-in-Council observed in 1830, 'In the provinces of Bengal, Bihar and Orissa a large portion of the zemindaries formerly held or managed by natives, has, you are aware, been transferred, by public or private sale, to persons having no hereditary connexion with the tracts of which they have so acquired the property or management. Of the purchasers many are the inhabitants of Calcutta, who or whose families acquired wealth, either by commercial speculations, conducted in close communication with Europeans, or in the service of the Government under European superiors.'[2] Echoing a similar thought

[2]Report of the Select Committee on the Affairs of the East India Company, Vol. 1, General Appendix, No. 47, letter from Governor General-in-Council to Court of Directors, 1 January 1830, *Parliamentary Papers*, sess. 1831-32, Vol. VIII. In his evidence to the Select Committee James Mill also remarked in 1831: 'To a very great degree the original possessors in Bengal have, from their own improvidence and other causes lost their estates. Few of the old zamindars now exist. The men who hold the property are not resident; they are capitalists who reside in the towns, and manage by their agents'. Ibid., James Mill's statement 9 August 1831 Question 3344, Minutes of Evidence taken before the Select Committee on the Affairs of the East India Company, *Parliamentary Papers*, sess. 1831, Vol. V.

B.M. Bhatia remarks in a recent essay: 'Cornwallis through his Permanent Settlement conferred proprietary rights on the zamindars . . . . The merchant class purchased the zamindaris ousting the old zamindars who in any case were mere revenue farmers and not proprietors. By 1882, at least two-thirds of the agricultural land in Bengal had passed into the hands of Banias in Calcutta.'[3]

The underlying assumption that agricultural land as such (i.e. physical possession of it) passed from an ancient aristocracy to a merchant class under the Permanent Settlement has hitherto led to an undue preoccupation with the transfer of zamindaris after 1793 in discussions of change in agrarian society. Because of this emphasis on the transfer of zamindaris, the question has been dealt with at some length in the area studies; and it has been shown that what usually changed hands were titles to revenue, collection, not lands. By itself the change of proprietorship in zamindaris and taluqs, the substance of which lay not in ownership of land but in dominion over villages (in their aspect as mauzas), could not bring about a massive redistribution of agricultural lands.[4] The transfer of titles after 1793 was merely an acceleration of a process which had been going on at a fairly rapid pace from 1700. The acquirement of zamindari rights by native Bengalis employed in the service of the government, upon which the Governor General-in Council commented in a letter to the Court of Directors, was a time-honoured practice among Brahman, Kayastha, and Vaidya officials of the Mughal governors. Because of the fluidity in the composition of the zamindar class, it was misleading to conceive the Bengal zamindars as an ancient aristocracy. With a few exceptions, the big zamindaris within which the parganas in Bengal were agglomerated were built up in the fifty years before Plassey; the zamindari of the deputy

[3]B.M. Bhatia, 'The Elite Approach to study of Modern Indian History' in B.R. Nanda and V.C. Joshi (eds.), *Studies in Modern Indian History* (New Delhi 1972), p. 49.

[4]Dr. Bhatia himself partly admits this when he says: 'These merchants, however, had no interest in farming. They employed very often the earlier proprietors as putnidars for collection on (sic) revenue'. Ibid., p. 49.

governor of Dacca, Maharaja Rajvallabh, was younger even than Plassey. To put it in a nutshell, the Permanent Settlement brought about a great circulation in titles, but not of lands; and circulation of titles had been going on before at such a rate that the zamindars whom the British recognized as landlords were mostly a mushroom class of adventurers raised to their position of pre-eminence in the first half of the eighteenth century by the reduction of older proprietors. Many of the reduced older proprietors no doubt survived as small taluqdars.[5] And it was this smaller class of taluqdars and zamindars who succeeded in buying up the greatest number of the titles brought into circulation by the sale of the zamindaris. The detailed area studies confirm the recent finding, put forward by Islam as an all-Bengal proposition, that the principal group among auction purchasers were the existing zamindars, and not the Calcutta merchants.

But zamindars, of course, were of all kinds, ranging from the ancient Rajput dynasty of the kingdom of Bishnupur to the petty taluqdar and service families of Dacca who had acquired a few scattered mauzas in different parganas by fraudulently altering the revenue accounts entrusted to them by the government or the bigger zamindars. To treat the term zamindar as an abstract category would be to conceal changes which took place within complex local systems of revenue-collecting rights which, for the sake of administrative convenience, the Mughal government treated as zamindaris by appointing or confirming at the head of each local system a local magnate designated zamindar or chaudhuri. The government of the East India Company, through a newly organized district administration of permanently resident collectors and magistrates, pressed much more firmly on the local tribute-collecting political systems than did the Nizamat. The breakdown of the political power of the large zamindaris and the need to meet a rigid British revenue demand led to the growth of a system of smaller properties, vertically (i.e., subinfeudation), or laterally (i.e., subdivision) divided, which vastly increased the number of small proprietors. These

[5]For instance, the Bikrampur taluqdars who survived the onslaught of Maharaja Rajvallabh, who merely imposed a zamindari jurisdiction over the existing taluqs in Bikrampur. See ch. 9, case study of Dacca.

changes in the structure of titles consolidated the position of the high caste local gentry who had filled the middle ranks of the local tribute-collecting hierarchies headed by Rajas and zamindars. But the changes brought about by the circulation of titles did not bring about a redistribution of land, for land was held much lower down the hierarchy of land rights and it was not until one reached the village, or mauza at the bottom of the hierarchy that people actually concerned with the land were to be encountered.

The area study of Burdwan showed that after the Permanent Settlement the high caste local gentry grasped the profitable levels of tribute-collection (through their newly acquired patnis), leaving the Raja—a powerfal prince of whom they had formerly stood in awe as their sovereign—a mere annuitant. However, it was at the lower rungs of the ladder that the battle had to be fought for local land control, and here the dominant village elites—in many cases agricultural Sadgops who had been the principal power in the region before the rise of the Burdwan Raj—succeeded in preventing themselves from being displaced. In Bishnupur, on the other hand, the view from above revealed a much more fundamental revolution in the local political system, for here the ancient Bishnupur Raj and its farmers (relations and dependents of the Raja) were more or less completely replaced by outsiders—the Burdwan Raj and its patnidars from Burdwan, Hugli, Nadia, etc. The hereditary enemy of the Bishnupur Raj, Maharaja Tejchand of Burdwan, was a territorial magnate whose enormous power and resources enabled him to effect this complete displacement of the Bishnupur family from their dominant position: it was certainly not an operation to be successfully accomplished by rich men from Calcutta, who gave up their purchased titles after violent resistance from relations of the Bishnupur Raja. But the view from above, if it did not penetrate far enough, would have been misleading in this case for the new landlords from outside Bishnupur did not make much headway in their attempt to resume the extensive lands endowed by the Bishnupur Rajas for the military and religious establishments of their kingdom. Widespread disturbances amongst the militia greeted an attempt at resumption in 1808, and in the end the Raja of Burdwan and his patinidars succeeded in resuming only a small part of the lands held by the local Brahman gentry, the officers of the frontier guardsmen, and the influential village headmen. Although there was a complete revolution of landed interests at the top, there was hardly any transfer of land at the village level.

In Dacca and Midnapur the local gentry were already in possession of innumerable taluqs, which were recognized at the Permanent Settlement and freed from the overlordship of the bigger pargana zamindars through whom the Mughal government had dealt with the taluqdar class. In these districts, where an exceptionally large number of existing properties were confirmed by law at the Permanent Settlement, a great number of the mahals sold for arrears of revenue seemed to circulate within the same small taluqdar class. But, on the whole, this class gained at the expense of their social heads—the bigger local rajas who had formerly been ruling over them from forts (dismantled by the British after 1760).[6] Not only did the smaller taluqdars gain freedom from the rapacious supervision exercised over them by zamindars appointed or confirmed by the Mughal government but they also succeeded in buying up many of the mahals of the Rajas offered for sale, since often enough they were officials of the bigger zamindars and advantageously placed to exploit their position in zamindari administration. In Dacca the local gentry who acquired the proprietary rights confirmed by the Permanent Settlement were high caste gentry who had never taken part in agriculture, and were, therefore, easily disposed to create sub-tenures. And since there was plenty of reclaimable forest southwards they gave out permanent leases for reclamation to the prosperous Muslim cultivators who constituted the land holding class in the villages under their taluqs. In this way, a very complicated chain of subinfeudated tenures arose in Dacca which virtually shut off the gentry, already precluded by caste from agriculture, from the land. It was the

[6]For instance, the Rajas of Chandradvip, the heads of the Kayastha samajs in their areas, and the Rajas of Mainachoura, the heads of the Kaivarta samajs within their zamindari. The forts of both houses were in ruins by 1800.

prosperous Muslim and Namasudra cultivating classes who obtained possession of the vast new lands reclaimed from forest in Dacca, Faridpur, and Bakarganj. When the high caste gentry tried to press their demands for a share in this increased rent from land, the Muslim and Namasudra village land-holding elites violently resisted the pressure; the Faraizi and Namasudra movements against high caste zamindars and taluqdars were symptoms of the gradually weakening position of the high caste Hindu gentry vis-a-vis an enterprising, prosperous, and violent peasant landlord class. While the emergence of a complex land tenure system through subdivision and subinfeudation reflected the kaleidoscopic changes in the upper levels of the revenue-collecting structure in Dacca, Faridpur and Bakarganj, lower down the scale peasant landlords not only continued to hold their lands at favourable rates but extended their hold to new lands in the forest. In Midnapur, where the Kaivarta taluqdar class were of agricultural stock, there was no subinfeudation of this sort and the tenurial structure remained relatively simple. Since the cultivating population was also Kaivarta, and the taluqdar gentry were part of a larger Kaivarta jotedar class, there was no communal conflict as in Dacca. But wherever there were estates possessed by non-Kaivarta or outside zamindars in this thickly-settled Kaivarta country (such as the Brahman Rajas of Mahisadal, the government estates in Contai, the Seals of Calcutta and the Rajas of Burdwan), violent combinations among Kaivarta tenants enabled the prosperous section among them to appropriate a large part of the increased rent of the land.

It is not implied, of course, that nowhere did 'new' outside landlords succeed in establishing a solid and profitable foothold in the localities. In Rangpur, as we have seen, the Tagores of Calcutta and the Nandys of Kasimbazar obtained and successfully managed the extremely valuable zamindaris of Patiladaha and Baharband. But, in general, outsiders were powerfully discouraged by the manipulation of the sale mechanism by local 'rings' — such as the faction operating from the civil jail in Midnapur, and the combination between officers of the Raj, the collectorate and the courts in Dinajpur. In other words, the market for titles created by the Permanent Settlement was not a free market operating under conditions of perfect competition, at which anyone with capital could obtain possession of a profitable property by bidding without knowledge. Only men with inside information could make valuable purchases under such a peculiar structure of the market for titles, so that in Dinajpur and Midnapur the agents of the zamindars who ran the rings picked up the most valuable bits from the break-up of the big zamindaris.[7] There were of course men of capital in Calcutta who purchased zamindaris, taluqs, and patnis all over Bengal. Where such transfers of property were effective, as in parganas Baharband and Patiladaha, the purchase by Calcutta merchants did not reflect actual transfer of lands at the village level, which continued to be held by big jotedars holding secure leases which could not be set aside at will.

It must not be supposed that it was the invariable practice of all men of capital in Calcutta to invest their money in zamindari properties in the interior. The wills and inventories of men of substance in Calcutta and other towns between 1763 and 1850, preserved in the old record room of the High Court of Calcutta, show that the main form in which these men invested their capital was urban house and ground property and not revenue-

[7]Comparable developments took place in areas which have not come under our scrutiny. In the Jessore Raj, the Raja purchased a few sold-up mauzas of his pargana, Sahos, in the names of Banamali and Ramnarasingha Basu, Biswanath Basu, Ramkumar Mitra, and others who were then (1797) in his service. The following year he granted a mortgage of pargana Sahos including the fictitiously sold mauzas to Banamali and Ramnarasingha Basu for a loan of Rs 7,500. The holders of the mortgage allowed the pargana to fall into arrears before the expiry of the mortgage and purchased it in the name of Biswanath Basu. In the general dismemberment of the Jessore Raj, these officers of the zamindar colluded with the young Raja's guardian to have their dependent patni talqus (consisting of 22 mauzas) within the zamindari recorded as independent properties by unconditional sale. The patnidars were Banamali Basu, Biswanath Basu, and Ramtanu Basu, elder brother of Ramnarasingha Basu. Proceedings of the Bengal Sudder Board of Revenue, Wards Branch, August 1830, No. 7, Collector of Jessore to E.R. Barwell, Commissioner of Revenue for Jessore, dt. 20 May 1829.

bearing or rent-free landed estates[8] (see Table 10.1). Ramdulal Dey, one of the principal commercial magnates in Calcutta, possessed, according to an inventory,[9] a large amount of money lent on interest, ready money to the extent of Rs 33 lakhs, more than a dozen houses all over Calcutta, four suburban gardens, considerable urban ground in Calcutta and Benaras, and two godowns in New Chinabazar in Calcutta. In addition to this vast urban property and lent-out money and cash, he had only a small piece of rent-free brahmottar land of 10 bighas in 24 Parganas, a more substantial lakhiraj or rent-free property of 1,088 bighas in Burdwan, and a small taluq in pargana Dorodumnan in Midnapur.[10] Urban house and ground property

[8]Of the men whose wills and inventories (1763-1850) are preserved in the High Court, 50 per cent left urban property in the form of ground and buildings. Next in order of importance were: ornaments and household effects—45%, revenue-bearing landed estates--21%, mercantile concerns shops and godowns—21%, banking houses and money lent on interest—21%, rent-free lands—17%. High Court, Old Record Room, Wills and Inventories, see description in Bibliography.

[9]Ibid., Ramdulal Dey CW 10402.

[10]There were of course a number of new rich families, both in Calcutta and elsewhere, who invested a more considerable portion of their wealth in landed properties. See, for instance, the list of taluqs, zamindaris, etc., bought by Gokul Ghoshal, a banian of Calcutta, in BRP, 20 April 1798, Nos. 5-14, and the list of taluqs bought by Maharaja Nabakrishna Deb, Clive's diwan, in BRP, 2 February 1798, No. 57. Once these families became established zamindars and gave up their entrepreneurial activities, they indulged in repeated buying and selling of landed properties, which became the main field of investment of their profits from land. It is, however, clear from the zamindari papers of these new families that this circulation of titles took place largely among their own set, in settlement of claims against one another. For instance, one of the Tagore branches in Calcutta, being indebted to mahajans and unable to pay the revenue, sold a taluq in pargana Balia near the Sunderbans in 24 Parganas (at that time included in Chakla Hugli) to Nabrakrishna Deb in 1792. Bengali deed of sale, from Ramratna Tagore and others to Nabrakrishna Deb and others, 2 Agrahayan 1198 B.S., Raja Digambar Mitra Estate Papers, Box No.3, Satkhira documents. Gopimohan Deb, who inherited the taluq from Nabrakrishna, created in 1824 a patni under the taluq in favour of Ramnarayan Raychaudhuri (Ekrarnama for patni taluq from Ramnarayan Raychaudhuri to Gopimohan Deb, 1231, B.S., Ibid.) who in turn mortgaged and then sold the patni to Kasinath Raychaudhuri in 1834. Bengali letter from Kasinath

TABLE 10.1

WILL AND INVENTORIES OF RESIDENTS OF CALCUTTA AND OTHER TOWNS IN THE HIGH COURT OF CALCUTTA 1763-1860: (BREAKDOWN OF THE NUMBER OF PEOPLE UNDER DIFFERENT HEADINGS OF INVESTMENT).

Item of Property	*Number of Proprietors*
Ready money	48
Urban property-ground and buildings	45
Ancestral residence and dwelling houses	43
Gardens, garden houses and tanks	22
Bazaars	1
Household effects, ornaments, jewels, etc.	40
Revenue-paying estates — taluqs, zamindaris, etc.	19
Rent-free lands — devottar, brahmottar, etc.	15
Lands (undefined)	10
Jotes and agricultural lands	2
Movable and immovable property (undefined)	10
Company's 'papers' securities, etc.	11
Mercantile concerns, shops, godowns, etc.	19
Banking houses and money lent on interest	19
Indigo factories	1
Investment in European business houses	2
Boats and carriages	2
Total number of owners leaving property	89

Source: Calcutta High Court, Old Record Room, Wills and Inveutroies.

Raychaudhuri to Gopimohan Deb, 23 Bhadra 1240 B.S. Ibid. But the patni changed hands repeatedly after this and finally in 1844 Gopimohan's successor Radhakanta Deb, the superior taluqdar, sold it for realization of arrears of dues from his under-tenure holder to a new patnidar, Ramkrishna Ghosh, under the Patni Regulation of 1819. Bengali letter from Radhakanta Deb to Ramkrishna Ghosh, 5 Asharh 1251 B.S. Ibid. In 1857, however, Radhakanta Deb sold his own taluq, under which the patni existed, to the rising Raychaudhuris of Satkhira (Article of Agreement on 4 May 1857 between Radhakanta Deb and the Raychaudhuris of Satkhira, Ibid.), so that under the Patni Regulation of 1819 Ramkrishna Ghosh's patni ceased to exist. It was the tremendous rise in the value of the taluq, which was situated near the Sunderbans and contained much reclaimable waste, that led to so much speculative buying and selling. For though Nabrakrishna Deb purchased it from the Tagores in 1792 for only Rs 25,000 his grandson Radhakanta Deb sold it in 1857 to the was a much safer field of investment for bankers, merchants, and money lenders in Calcutta than was landed property in the mufassal. The market for urban property was not vitiated by fraud and there was no problem of taking possession of such property; whereas in the case of landed properties brought to sale for arrears of revenue, the bidder had to gain inside information about profitable 'lots' and had subsequently to negotiate with the existing under-tenure holders and the former proprietors for taking possession of the purchased lots.

New purchasers, when they did succeed in obtaining possession of zamindaris and talqus in spite of being outsiders, usually managed to ritualize their position within two generations. The families of the entrepreneurs who rose in the service of Europeans quickly adopted the life-style of the older magnates.[11] The zamindari

Raychaudhuris of Satkhira for Rs one lakh which was four times the original price. Similar evidence of buying and selling of landed properties among a set of rising new zamindars is available from the zamindari papers of the Palchaudhuris of Maheshganj in Nadia and the Sarkars of Surul in Birbhum. Deed of grant of patni by Zamindar Annadaprasad Banerjee of Telinipara to Prankrishna and Nabakrishna Palchaudhuri, Zamindari Papers of the Palchaudhuris of Maheshganj; share of Ila Palchaudhuri. In Birbhum the new zamindars of Surul, Raipur, and Supur rose in commercial association with John Cheap, the Company's commercial Resident. Later some co-sharers among the Surul zamindars became indebted to the Sinhas of Raipur (family of Lord S.P. Sinha) and the Rays of Supur and their share was bought by the zamindars of Raipur and Supur in a sale for a decree in satisfaction of debt. Zamindari papers of Surul, Ekrarnama from Ramchandra Sarkar, etc. to Gurucharan Sarkar, 15 Agrahayan 1246; also Birbhum district records, Surul Estate Bundle Tauzi No. 26, darkhast of Gurucharan Sarkar.

[11]Warren Hasting's favourite, Gangagovinda Singh, spent Rs 20 lakhs on his mother's funeral ceremony, attended by Rajas and zamindars from all over Bengal and presided over by the venerable Brahman Raja of Nadia, Sibchandra. Here is a description of the shrine at the ancestral residence of Gangagovinda's family, the Paikpara zamindars of Calcutta, in Kandi (Murshidabad): 'Of all shrines, the shrine at Kandi is maintained with the greatest liberality. The god here seems to live in the style of the great Mughal. His masnad and pillows are of the best velvet and damask richly embroidered. Before him are placed gold and silver salvers, cups, tumblers, pan-dans, and jugs of various size and pattern. He is fed every morning with fifty kinds of curry and ten kinds of pudding. His breakfast over,

papers of the Surul zamindars of Birbhum reveal the characteristic manner in which 'new men' would eventually ritualize their position in local society. Srinibas Sarkar, the ancestor of the Surul zamindars, came from an agricultural Sadgop family in Nilpur in Burdwan where the family had some agricultural lands.[12] He settled in Surul and acquired wealth as a gomasta by supplying indigo, sugar, and cloth to John Cheap, the Commercial Resident of Birbhum immortalized by Hunter in his Annals of Rural Bengal.[13] He purchased a zamindari in 1797 in the name of Ramnarayan Sarkar from the Raja of Birbhum, Muhammad Zaman Khan, whose zamindari was breaking up.[14] By the next generation the Surul family had become resident traditional zamindars in Surul, whose ritual position was indicated by two Bishnupur-style temples to Jorasib (Shiva) and Narayan (Vishnu) erected in 1831,[15] and a palatial mansion in mixed European and Bengali style which dominated the village.[16] The great social authority which they acquired in the village was seen in their arbitration in all local disputes ranging from land disputes between tenants[17] to the seduction of a householder's wife[18] and unauthorized fishing by 'a man of great consideration' in the village bathing tank which was rendered muddy by the

---

gold hookahs are brought to him to smoke the most aromatic tobacco. He then retires for his noonday siesta. In the afternoon he lunches and at nights sups upon the choicest and richest viands with new names in the vocabulary of Hindu confectionery. The daily expenses at the shrine are said to be Rs 500, inclusive of alms and charity to the poor. Bholanath Chandra, *Travels of a Hindu*, pp. 65-67, quoted in W.W. Hunter, *A Statistical Account of Bengal*, Vol. IX, pp. 80-81.

[12]Account by the joint manager of the Surul co-sharers given to the author in 1970.

[13]W.W. Hunter, *Annals of Rural Bengal.*

[14]Birbhum District Records, Surul Estate Bundle Tauzi, No. 26, deed of sale by Muhammad Zaman Khan to Ramnarayan Sarkar, dated 1204 B.S.

[15]Inscription on the Jorasib and Narayan temples in Surul.

[16]Visited by the author in 1970.

[17]Bengali letter from Chattopadhyaya to (undecipherable), 3 Asharh 1294 B.S. A dispute between two tenants, Laksminarayan Sadhu and Uday Deyali, in which the zamindar paiks gave possession to one of the parties. Surul Zamindari Papers.

[18]Bengali letter (torn) to Mohini Mohan Sarkar, 1293 B.S. Ibid.

sport.[19] They maintained a school in the village,[20] lent money to their tenants,[21] and kept a close watch, through their agents, on all thefts and violence within the zamindari.[22] Their domination of Surul was so complete that even when the neighbouring zamindars of Supur and Raipur acquired a share in the zamindari in satisfaction of a decree for debt, their influence and authority remained unimpaired around Surul. By acquiring proprietary rights over every important means of the village economy, such as homestead lands, tanks and trees,[23] and by giving loans at high interest to the villagers, the Surul family built up a ring-fence around Surul (in pargana Barbakshahi) within which they had control of every aspect of its social, economic, and political life. But in the villages beyond their residence, their authority and influence was by no means unchallenged, especially as quarrels between co-sharing branches of the Sarkars enabled the Rays of Supur and the Sinhas of Raipur to obtain a foothold in the zamindari.[42] In the distant villages, the Surul zamindars often encountered serious oppositions from combinations of substantial tenants, especially from Muslim tenants (possibly of Pathan origin) who were disposed

---

[19]Bengali petition of residents of Daksinpara, the public of Surul to Mohini Mohan Sarkar, 12 Jyaishtha 1294 B.S. Ibid.

[20]Letter from Ramesh Chandra Mukherjee, 5 October 1885, asking for extra payment in addition to regular subscription for Bandgara School, Ibid.

[21]Bengali ikrar from Gaur Garain in Asananda Sarkar for a loan of Rs 15, dt. 11 Asvin 1228 B.S. (1822). Many other similar ikrars exist in the Surul Zamindari Papers.

[22]Bengali letter from Magaram Devasharman, 20 Phalgun 1227 B.S. and Kabulati letter from Dhananjay Konar, 19 Bhadra 1240 B.S. Ibid.

[23]Deed of sale of homestead and brahmottar by Kalisankar Chatterjee to the zamindar, 1229 B.S.; deed of sale of tank and trees by Chinibash Mandal to the zamindar, 1222, B.S.; deed of sale of homestead land by Nafar Chandra Sarkar to Guru Charan Sarkar, 6 Jyaishtha 1226 B.S.; Ibid.

[24]Bengali letter from Ramchandra Sarkar et al. to Gurucharan Sarkar 15 Argrahayan, 1246, B.S. Ibid. For later quarrels leading to the appointment of a joint manager, see Bengali letter from Kedarnath Sarkar to Bireshwar Sarkar, 8 April 1891, Ibid.

to violence.[25] Srinibas Sarkar, the tough architect of the family fortunes, himself had to appeal for the help of the district judge and magistrate of Birbhum when the tenants in his taluqs in the distant pargana of Manoharshahi opposed his attempt to carry out a measurement of lands under Regulation 7 of 1799.[26] Later on there were piteous appeals to the collector of Birbhum by the Surul zamindars for an order to the tenants to pay revenue.[27] A violent Pathan named Muhammad Akmal forcibly took possession of 71 bighas of land by ejecting 13 tenants of Srinibas Sarkar from his purchased taluq 'lot' Marga in pargana Manoharshahi and cultivated these lands within the latter's taluq with the help of his own men from 1807 to 1811 without paying any dues. It was only after a long prosecution in court that Srinibas Sarkar succeeded in persuading Muhammad Akmal to give up the forcibly occupied lands.[28]

What the clever manipulation of Regulation 7 of 1799 by Srinibas Sarkar and the procedure of the courts demonstrated was that by exploiting the apparatus of a modern bureaucratic state the 'landlords' recognized by the state could apply very considerable pressure on the existing dominant groups in the villages. Under such continuous pressure, the considerable economic differences between the various peasant households of the villages might also be liquidated, for increases in rates of assessment would wipe out the margins enjoyed by the better-off sections. If the new landlords ritualized their position and acquired local influence by residence, there might well be a change not only in the structure of titles, but in the distribution of lands, at least within a certain radius around their residence. The purchase of talqus by the Sarkars in the area around Surul, where there was an enormous concentration of the village

[25]Correspondence for 1292, B.S. referring to attempts of Paran Sheikh Badal Sheikh and other troublesome tenants trying to instigate combinations for withholding dues, Ibid.

[26]Bengali letter from Srinibas Sarkar to the Judge of Birbhum, [2 Asvin, 1214 B.S. Ibid.

[27]Birbhum District Records, Surul Estate Bundle Tauzi No. 26, entry for 1838.

[28]Bengali letter from Muhammad Akmal to Srinibas Sarkar, 23 Phulgun, 1218 B.S., Surul Zamindari Papers.

economy in their hands, caused a fundamental alteration of the social structure. And it was brought about by their acquirement of all resources (including the most secure and inviolable of properties—bastu or homestead lands). The zamindari title was not the only or even the most important of rights, but by long residence the Sarkars of Surul turned this title into physical possession of land to the exclusion of all other rights in the village, a feat which the powerful but absentee Nandys of Kasimbazar and Tagores of Calcutta could not achieve in Baharband and Patiladaha. Nevertheless, it is noteworthy that the Sarkars could establish this ring-fence only around village Surul (mauza Nij Krishnagar) in their taluq Krishnagar under pargana Barbakshahi. In the more distant pargana Manoharshahi, where also Srinibas Sarkar acquired three 'lots' by purchase, the authority of the Sarkars was openly flouted by troublesome tenants who would not submit to a measurement of their lands under Regulation 7 of 1799 and by violent Pathans of the type of Muhammad Akmal who forcibly occupied lands and paid no dues for a quinquiennium at a stretch.

It should, moreover, be borne in mind that before the establishment of the imposing economic empire by the Sarkars in Surul at the time of the Permanent Settlement, there were other little economic empires in Birbhum, though admittedly less impressive in extent and grandeur, run by precisely the kind of men, such as Muhammad Akmal,[29] who proved so troublesome to the new zamindars. While for the villager in Surul the world must have changed around him during the buildup of power by Srinibas Sarkar under new administrative rules and economic connections, from the over all view of rural society and rural economy, the change was less striking. Through land-holding and credit-giving—the same methods employed by Srinibas Sarkar though on a scale possibly unprecedented in the neighbourhood—other men had dominated villages, but they did not enjoy the undisputed and unrivalled mastery within their

[29]Muhammad Akmal was the master of 9 Muslim peasants whom he settled on the seized lands in the lot of Marga taluq, Ibid.

localities acquired by the Surul zamindars.[30]

There is a widely accepted argument that such concentration of economic resources within the villages did not exist before the Permanent Settlement and was brought about only afterwards by the commercialization of agricultural production. This is the second counter-factual proposition referred to before and which, because of its importance, will bear repetition. According to this proposition, the traditional village community was constituted, on the basis of equality and fraternity, by a single class of self-sufficient peasants producing for their households and not for the market. But the gearing of agricultural production to the demands of the market after 1793 initiated a process of concentration of land-holding, on the one hand, and loss of land and pauperization on the other. Production of commercial crops required advances; and the possibility of profit from land as a means of producing commercial crops provided an economic incentive to creditors to appropriate the lands of their debtors. There emerged a new landlord class of peasant jotedars giving credit and monopolizing land, and as a corollary large sections of the peasant fraternity of the former village republics became sharecroppers and agricultural labourers. Village society was remodelled into a three-tier class structure of landed jotedars, self-sufficient peasants, and landless tillers.

If true, this was indeed a fundamental transformation of rural society. But as it happens, there is a considerable body of contemporary evidence, referred to before, which shows that the change was by no means so drastic after the Permanent Settlement, since the land-holding pattern in the villages was already very unequal before it. Speaking of the difficulties of the collector's position in Rajshahi district in the heart of central Bengal, Peter Speke wrote to the Board of Revenue in 1787:

[30]While the Surul family combined the social authority, prestige and large resources of zamindars with the economic influence of jotedars, these men had only the economic hold of jotedars to back their power within the village and their margin of economic superiority was not so great as to set them above challenge from other villagers in circumstances of roughly comparable prosperity.

> There is a class of tenants of some substance, given pattas at Khos Kass or residing at pleasure mokarrari, who are not husbandmen, but who take large tracts of land and who both from their responsibility and from their being obliged to hire labourers, are allowed easier terms and to pay in one sum. If zamindars did not break engagements with this valuable class of tenants it would be one certain means of bringing much waste land into cultivation.[31]

Three years later, J.H. Harrington, who carried out a survey of pargana Swaruppur in Rangpur district in order to detect fraud in the revenue assessment, mentioned in his survey report on Swaruppur dated 20 March 1790 that in this pargana there was a body of considerable raiyats to whom the common peasants paid rent over and above the tribute claimed by the zamindar. The principal raiyats took leases for large tracts of land from the zamindar and cultivated these lands through poor cultivators who paid two-thirds of the produce to the jotedars.[32] This represented a large margin of profit per bigha to the jotedars when the revenue claimed by the zamindar was deducted from it. The average rate assessed by the zamindar for cultivated land in this pargana was 10 annas and 12 gandas. Since the value of the produce per bigha was estimated by Harrington to be Rs 2-6, the jotedars, who obtained Rs 1-9 per bigha out of this (i.e., two-thirds of Rs 2-6), made a profit of 150 per cent more than the rate paid by them to the zamindar. This practice of a division of produce between the rich farmer and poor peasant to whom the former had let the lands leased from the zamindar—in other words the supposedly new economic relation-

[31]BRP, 13 April 1787, Collector of Rajshahi to BR, dt. 1 March 1787. But as we have seen in our area study of neighbouring Dinajpur, if big tenants were dissatisfied with the zamindar they simply left the land with their dependents, so that the zamindar was the ultimate loser for breaking faith.

[32] Evidently the present practice of a division of the crop in many parts of West Bengal, by which the tiller of the soil (krishan) gets one-third of the produce and the landlord (jotedar) takes two-thirds, had prevailed before the Permanent Settlement, at any rate in Swaruppur. Home Miscellaneous, Vol. 385, Seroopore.

ship between the jotedar—rich farmer and bargadar—landless peasant—was also commented upon with disapproval as early as 1794 by H.T. Colebrook in his *Remarks on the Husbandry and Commerce of Bengal* :

> This class of middle men is numerous. Some are authorised by the nature of their tenure, where the rent and limits of the farm are fixed and ascertained; others have an express permission inserted in their lease;[33] most have no justification for this practice,[34] which has grown up by abuse, and which is highly detrimental. The under-tenants, depressed by an excessive rent in kind, and by usurious returns for the cattle, seed, and subsistence, advanced to them, can never extricate themselves from debt. In so abject a state, they cannot labour with spirit, while they earn a scanty subsistence without hope of bettering their situation. Wherever the system of an intermediate tenantry subsists, the peasantry is indigent, the husbandry ill-managed.[35]

Being chronically short of capital, the sharecroppers borrowed from their masters not only seed and food, but also money for cattle and implements at a usurious rate of interest varying from 25 to 50 per cent. Referring to their perpetual indebtedness and semi-slavery enforced by the system of advances under sharecropping arrangements, Colebrook commented: 'We cannot then wonder at the scenes of distress which this class of cultivators exhibits, nor that they are often compelled, by accumulating debts, to emigrate from province to province.'[36]

The only available statistics giving a rough measure of this type of concentration of the village economy at this early period pertain to Dinajpur and Rangpur, where Buchanan-Hamilton carried out his survey in 1808. The area study of Dinajpur revealed that, according to figures given by Buchanan-Hamilton,

---

[33]That is, to let out their lands to under-tenants.

[34]The practice of sharing the crop with a bargadar.

[35]H.T. Colebrook, *Remarks on the Husbandry and Internal Commerce of Bengal* (London reprint 1806), p. 64.

[36]Ibid., p. 103.

6 per cent among the agricultural classes controlled 36.5 per cent of the raiyati lands within the district. At the other end of the scale, 52 per cent of the cultivators had no land and worked for the richer agriculturists as sharecroppers and attached or casual labourers. This enormous difference in land-holding naturally enabled some of the peasant households to lend out sums at high interest but on extremely bad security,[37] while other households in the village were forced to take loans on terms which nothing but accident could ever enable them to repay. 'The consequence', wrote Buchanan-Hamilton in his report on Dinajpur, 'is, that the rich man, in place of a capital which can be realized, acquires a number of necessitous dependents, to whose wants he must administer, in order to procure a share of their labour in place of interest, and these dependents are reduced to perhaps one of the worst kinds of slavery, that of insolvent debtors.'[38] There was thus a very close connection between the land-holding pattern and the credit mechanism, as has already been pointed out in our account of the village economy in Part 1. Those who borrowed grain or money would fill the ranks of sharecroppers and hired or tied labourers; those who lent would be able to have their lands cultivated by their debtors at the lowest wages. The description which Buchanan-Hamilton gave of the mode of concentration within the village economy deserves to be quoted in full, even though we have referred to it before, because of its keen insight and lucidity:

> About one farmer in 16 may rent from 30 to 100 acres. These seldom labour with their own hands, but keep as many ploughs as they have dependent relations, or hire two or three additional men. The remainder of their lands they give to people who cultivate it for a share. These men in general have large capitals, and advance money or grain both to those who cultivate for a share, and to their other necessitous

[37]The rate of interest on loans was found by Buchanan to be much higher than the ordinary gains of commerce or agriculture, so that rich peasants were willing to take considerable risks in lending grain or money to poor fellow villagers. Only residents within the village could take such risks, not urban money-lenders.

[38]Francis Buchanan, *Geographical Description of Dinajpur*, p. 241.

> neighbours, to enable them to live, while the cultivation is going forward. It may indeed be said that their stock carries on at least one-half of the whole cultivation of the country. Most of the adhiars and small farmers are more indebted to them than the whole value of their stock, and for six months in the year would starve, did not the wealthy farmers advance them grain to eat. It is they who even furnish the seed; so that, whenever one of them is discontented, he gives up his farm, and retires with all his dependents to some other estate, where there are waste lands, which his stock enables him to clear. The village which he left is then for some years unoccupied, until the landlord can find a fugitive of the same kind, and in general must use a good deal of solicitation before he can induce the farmer with his dependents to settle. On this account, the landlords do not like this class of men; but it is evident that they are absolutely necessary, unless the landlords themselves would advance money to their necessitous tenantry .... It is true, that these large farmers exact enormous profits for whatever they advance to their necessitous dependents, but still they are of infinite use to these people, who without their assistance would be instantly reduced to the state of common labourers, and often, to beggary.[39]

Buchanan-Hamilton evidently looked upon the jotedar class with a much kindlier eye than did Colebrook, who held sharecropping to be responsible for slovenly cultivation and the existence of an intermediary tenantry to be the cause of general poverty in their neighbourhood. In strong contrast to this view, Buchanan-Hamilton opposed the imposition of a land ceiling of 50 bighas, said to have been introduced by collector Hatch in Dinajpur at the time of the Parmanent Settlement in order to do away with sharecropping and to eliminate property inequalities.[40]

[39]Ibid., pp. 235-236.

[40]'With whatever view it was framed, or alleged (sic) to be framed, I have no doubt in stating, that the observance of such a regulation would be highly injurious both to agriculture and to the labourer. These people, who cultivate for a share of the produce, are in a better state than common

He noted with approval that in Rangpur, where no such 'useless and pernicious' regulation existed, the flourishing state of pargana Baharband was due to the existence of large jotedars who 'either employ those, who cultivate for a share, in which case they furnish stock, or they let the land at rackrent to under-tenants, who are thus compelled to be more industrious'.[41] The research of modern agricultural economists would suggest that Colebrook might have been more correct in his appreciation than was Buchanan-Hamilton. Buchanan-Hamilton himself recorded evidence in his account of Rangpur tending to show that it was the system of advances from village landlords to sharecroppers which was responsible for pauperization, migration, and slavery in rural society. In parts of Rangpur, the sharecroppers received not only food and seed, but also cattle, from their employers; and their suffering increased in direct proportion to their indebtedness. Deprived of any means, they were entirely dependent on their employers, who often took the whole produce (instead of the customary half share) for having advanced the cattle in addition to the seed.[42] Krishans or agricultural labourers, who unlike sharecroppers were hired for money and supplied with ploughs, mortgaged their labour for a year in Dinajpur on account of money paid in advance. But in fact the accumulation of interest compelled them to prolong their service beyond the stipulated year as

---

labourers, and must fall to that level, unless they are employed as at present, for they have no stock sufficient to enable them to cultivate without assistance. Besides the reducing farms to 50 bigas would compel every rich man to give up agriculture, and to remove his stock to some other employment, which of all other circumstances would be that most destructive. Like other useless or pernicious regulations, however, this is constantly evaded and leases for 50 bigas each are granted to five or six persons of the same family; it being understood that the whole belongs to the principal person.' Ibid., p. 234.

[41]Buchanan-Hamilton Manuscripts, Mss. Eur. D. 75, Account of Ronggopur, Vol. II, p. 96.

[42]Ibid., pp. 110-11. This category of sharecroppers, who were worse off than the ordinary adhiars (half crop shares, adhi=half), presumably included the peasants, found by Harrington in Swaruppur, who paid two-thirds of the crop to their masters.

virtually tied labourers.[43] In the eastern parts of Rangpur, the terms of an advance on wages were even more disastrous for poor villagers: 'The servant, on receiving the money in advance, engages to repay it in a certain time, and during that period he and his family work for the person who lends, and this labour is considered merely as adequate to their support, and to the interest of the money. If the money is not paid at the stipulated period, the whole family become slaves, and may be sold jointly or separately, in whatever manner the master pleases.'[44]

There were thus many kinds of landless villagers in Bengal in the early years of British revenue administration. The argument of increasing concentration of landholding and steady augmentation of landless labour logically assumes a point in the past when land was equally distributed among the village households. This point has been placed by a Bengali sociologist, in accordance with the widely accepted assumptions of Marx and Maine, in the period immediately before the Permanent Settlement.[45] But at this point there were already in existence several types of peasants working for superior peasant landlords: rackrented under-tenants (chukanidars or prajas), half-crop sharers (adhiars), sharecroppers paying two-thirds of the produce (and in some circumstances, the whole crop), casual field labourers, agricultural labourers hired for the year, bonded labourers, and slaves and household servants (golams). The size of this landless group in rural society is an important problem in considering the argument about an increasing concentration

[43]According to a common instance given by Buchanan-Hamilton, a young krishan, in order to defray the expenses of his marriage, bound himself to a master for two years and took the whole of his wages as an advance, which was immediately exhausted in the ceremony. For the next two years the newly married bride had to provide for herself by whatever means that were available, but if she fell ill or became pregnant, the krishan had to mortgage his labour for a fresh advance at an enormous interest, 'and of course the family always continued in debt, and the extremity of wretchedness'. Buchanan, *Geographic Description of Dinajpur*, p. 245.

[44]Buchanan-Hamilton Manuscript, Mss. Eur. D. 75, Account of Ranggo pur, Vol. II, p. 113.

[45]Ramkrishna Mukherjee, *The Dynamics of a Rural Society.*

of land-holding and the emergence of village landlords and village labourers under British rule. Hamilton-Buchanan's estimate of the proportion of landless cultivators among the agricultural population, based on rough calculations made by his native assistants during the pargana-by-pargana survey and therefore liable to a large margin of error, was for Dinajpur 52.1 per cent and for Rangpur 50.0 per cent. The next estimate of the proportion of landless villagers was made in 1872-73 by the Special Deputy Collector of Rangpur who concluded that cultivators with no lands and bullocks accounted for 35 per cent of the Rangpur agriculturists. This was, however, too restrictive a definition of landless villagers, for there were many cultivators with a pair of bullocks (sometimes owned jointly by more than one poor household) who did not have sufficient lands of their own and employed their cattle and plough on the fields of rich neighbours on a half-crop system. The proportion ascertained by the sample survey of the Bengal Land Revenue Commission of 1938-40 was 37.3 per cent for Dinajpur and 32 per cent for Rangpur. But this sample survey excluded many sharecroppers and labourers with a few bighas of land of their own. The Census of East Pakistan in 1961 showed the proportion of sharecroppers, agricultural labourers, and poor owner-cultivators working part-time on other people's lands by hiring themselves out for labour, sharing the crop, or renting the lands (as prajas) to be 46.6 per cent for Dinajpur and 38.2 per cent for Rangpur. Buchanan's rule of the thumb survey possibly overestimated the proportion of landless villagers, and no firm conclusion can be based on such shaky statistics. These statistics, such as they are, do not provide any support for the theory of a great concentration of land-holding and swelling of landless labour under British rule (see Table 10.2.)

The area study of Rangpur and Dinajpur leads to the conclusion that if at the top a new commercial landlord class did not entirely take over the landed estates of an ancient aristocracy neither did a new peasant landlord class at the bottom appropriate on a massive scale the agricultural lands of a self-sufficient peasantry. No doubt there were developments in this direction on a limited scale with the growth of population

TABLE 10.2

LANDLESS AGRICULTURAL CLASSES IN DINAJPUR AND RANGPUR (PERCENTAGE TO AGRICULTURE POPULATION)

	1808	1872	1938	1961
Dinajpur				
Sharecroppers	34.0	N.A.	13.8	9.2
Agricultural labourers	18.1	N.A.	23.5	16.0
Cultivators owning part, renting part, working for hire	N.A.	N.A.	N.A.	31.4
Total landless	52.1	N.A.	37.8	46.6
Rangpur				
Sharecroppers	39.4	N.A.	19.1	6.0
Agricultural labourers	11.6	N.A.	12.9	14.8
Cultivators owning part. renting part, working for hire	N.A.	N.A.	N.A.	17.4
Cultivators with no land or bullocks	N.A.	35.0	N.A.	N.A.
Total landless	51.0	35.0	32.0	38.2

Note: The figures are not strictly comparable as the definition of landless classes as well as the boundary of the districts differed on each occasion.

Sources: Buchanan, *Geographical Description of Dinajpur*, pp. 236, 244; Buchanan-Hamilton Manuscripts, Mss. Eur. G. 12, Account of Ranggopur, Vol. II, Table No. 36; Gopal Chandra Das, *Report on the Statistics of Rungpore for the Year 1872-73* (Calcutta 1874), p. 85; *Government of Bengal Report of the Bengal Lanu Revenue Commission*, Vol. 11, Table No. VIII (d), (Alipore 1940); *Census of Pakistan 1961*, Vol. II, p. 5-16.

pressure on land,[46] but if we are to believe Buchanan-Hamilton's evidence, the process had already gone quite far

[46]Referring to the privileged Brahman and Rajput raiyats and wealthy raiyats of some other ranks an officer wrote from Dharampur in 1827: 'These self-privileged land-holders, who are the principal or Jheit Ryots of every Talook or Village, and most of the Brahminical Caste, become in this manner the petty tyrants of their village and take up the best lands about them. They are ever greedy to extend their possessions beyond

before the economic changes under colonial rule began to take widespread effect. A class of village landlords, whose property was measured in the amount of bighas and not in the number of mauzas (like that of zamindars), had already come into existence. Harrington's survey of Swaruppur in1790 showed that transfers of raiyati lands were frequent before the Permanent Settlement, so much so that it was difficult for him to find out the amount of land held by each raiyat;[47] and the Midnapur collectorate records are full of manuscript deeds of sales of agricultural lands in the first half of the eighteenth century.[48] A market for agricultural lands existed because most raiyati plots produced commercial crops in addition to grain for subsistence. Buchanan noticed in the western parts of Rangpur that there was scarcely any cultivator who lived by the cultivation of grain alone. Almost every raiyat paid a considerable portion of his rent by marketing tobacco, betel nut or sugarcane.[49] It is not unlikely that in the course of the nineteenth century further commercialization of agriculture provided greater incentives to the jotedar to appropriate more village lands, but even before this, whenever an opportunity had presented itself, such as the famine of 1770, he had taken over the lands of other villagers.[50] In economic terms, the class of large farmers found by Buchanan-Hamilton in Dinajpur in 1808

---

their individual capability of cultivation; but the most fruitful lands being occupied by them, and having by various means absorbed the jotes of the low and poor class, they are at no loss to keep them in cultivation. They derive indeed great profit by reletting them to poor cultivators, from whom they exact the highest rates in money or take a moiety of the produce; which last is the most usual practice, in order that their claim to the Jote or Jumma registered in their possession in the Zemindarry Books, should not be invalidated by the fact or appearance of another actually occupying the land.' BRP, 16 October 1827, No. 37, enclosure from Mr G.A. Blake.

[47]Home Miscellaneous, Vol. 385, Seroopore.

[48]Midnapur District Records Room, Permanent Settlement Records including Resumed Estate Kabubiyats. See, for instance, serial Nos. 2 and 36.

[49]Buchanan-Hamilton Manuscripts, Account of Ronggopore, Vol. II, Book IV, Agriculture of Ronggopore.

[50]See pp. 62-63.

was the same as the jotedar class observed in the district in the 1930s by the next surveyor, F.O. Bell. Bell was equally struck by the inequality in the social life and the standard of living of different rustic families. In almost every village he found large families of substantial cultivators who exercised leadership over the village and constituted the principal source of rural credit. These families, holding more than 30 acres of land, were the financiers of the countryside and marketed much of the exported surplus of the district. Comparing the conditions in Dinajpur in his own time with those prevailing at the time of Buchanan-Hamilton's survey—a comparison which revealed to him little change in the technique of agriculture and the class structure of agrarian society—Bell observed: 'This well-to-do jotedar class is no new feature of the district, and no creation of the Permanent Settlement.'[51]

The appropriate question, therefore, is not whether the Permanent Settlement created a new class of village landlords, but how this existing class was affected by the recognition of the zamindars above them as 'landlords' by Cornwallis. The area studies, especially those of Baharband, Patiladaha, Ponabalia, and Surul show that, depending on particular local circumstances there could be four possible lines of developments. First, the existing land-holding village elites might be completely displaced by the new purchasers of the zamindari title, who by long residence would convert the legal title into physical occupation of agricultural lands belonging to the former village elites. Second, powerful absentee zamindars might succeed—by the introduction of periodical survey and regular bureaucratic management—in so far increasing and equalizing assessment rates that the surplus of the village elites (bound to be small compared to that of the urban rich considering the total size of the village economy) would be wiped out reducing them to the economic level of ordinary raiyats while they perhaps retained their political influence as village heads. Third, the new zamindars might succeed in raising assessment rates over inferior raiyats by reaching an understanding with the village land-holders that would enable the latter to retain their margin. And fourth,

[51]*Final Report on Dinajpur*, pp. 16-17, 45.

absenteeism, quarrels between co-sharers, scattered distribution of subdivided and subinfeudated properties might so far weaken the local position of the 'landlords' recognized in 1793 that the resident village landlords of peasant stock, especially if they were energetic, violent, and well-skilled in the art of formenting combinations of raiyats, would raise their margin by appropriating the increases in the economic rent of land arising from rising prices, new cash crops, and clearance of forest. Of these alternatives, the particular course of development in a locality would depend very much on whether there was much reclaimable waste, or possibility of commercial agriculture in the neighbourhood, of whether a relatively inexpansible social surplus had to be shared out among different groups of landlords.

The village of Surul, where the new zamindar family of the commercial agent Srinibas Sarkar settled permanently, witnessed the first of these possible lines of development. The proliferating branches of the family secured the proprietary right to the bastu (household) lands in the village, secured possession of its tanks, trees, and rent-free lands (mainly Brahmottar), and acquired its best agricultural lands on which they employed krishans on the two-third system of crop-sharing (i.e., two-thirds for the landlord and one-third for the labourer).[52] When Srinibas Sarkar purchased the zamindari, the area around Surul was already well cultivated and the agricultural production of the locality was highly commercialized due to large exports of indigo, sugar, and fine cloth through the factory of Sonamukhi which had its headquarters at Surul. There was apparently no great scope for extension of cultivation. The subsequent dismantlement of the factory and the decline of valuable exports must have led to contraction of the economy and stimulated intensive cultivation of rice—the only recourse for an area of growing population and limited acreage. These were the circumstances in which the branches of the Surul family turned away more

[52]When the author visited Surul in 1970, the dominant mode of production was sharecropping under the Surul landlords who got two-thirds of the crop as rent. This was the traditional mode of cultivation in Surul and other villages around Santiniketan, but there is no indication in the Surul Zamindari Papers as to when first the branches of the Surul family engaged in this type of cultivation.

and more from the export business in cloth, indigo, and sugar with shippers in Calcutta and put increasing emphasis on moneylending and physical occupation of the land.[53] However, it was not throughout the whole zamindari, scattered over many parts of Birbhum district due to the haphazard purchase of 'lots' and patnis offered for sale, that the family succeeded in converting its purchased title to actual possession of the land. In view of the purchase of shares in the zamindari by outsiders like the Sinhas of Rajpur and the Rays of Supur, the quarrels between rival branches of the Surul family,[54] the management of distant taluqs through dishonest gomastas (from whom elaborate undertakings[55] had to be taken), the grant of ijaras of distant villages to revenue farmers (after obliging them to supply respectable men as securities),[56] and the creation of patnis in favour of under-tenure holders in scattered lots ruled out conversion of purchased titles into actual possession even if it had been physically possible to occupy distant lands under a village-based technology of agriculture. In villages where zamindari families came to reside permanently, it was not unusual for the new resident landlords to create ring-fences around their places of habitation. But such ring-fences could not include more than a few villages, beyond which the older village elites naturally

[53]The early records of the zamindari are very much concerned with the shipping of cloth, indigo, and sugar from Calcutta (for instance, undated Bengali letter to Sibnath Sinha and Bengali letter to Sibnath Sinha dt. 16 Sravan 1228), but as late as 1870 there are stray references to export of indigo to the firm of Colving Coloving in Calcutta by the Surul zamindars (for instance, English letters from Colving Coloving to Babu Ram Burmo Sircar, dt. 20 December 1869 and 2 February 1870). Nevertheless the growing preoccupation with the details of zamindari management, rent collec. tion and moneylending is unmistakable, although moneylending seems to have been one of the earliest activities of the family.

[54]See printed letter issued by Ashutosh Sarkar warning the mandals, paiks and prajas of Lot Krishnagar not to pay rent to Ramanath Sarkar, dt. 1299 B.S.

[55]Kabulati letter of Dhananjay Konar, 19 Bhadra, 1240 B.S. Sural Zamindari Papers.

[56]Malzaminati letter from Anantaram Devasharma to Prankrishna Sarkar guaranteeing to pay dues in case of default by farmer of mauza Seranti in pargana Barbakshahi. 18 Asharh 1228 B.S., Ibid.

continued to enjoy power. Moreover, it should be borne in mind that since the same technology of agriculture and relations of production continued to prevail in the ring-fences created by resident zamindars (i.e., the collection of produce from share-croppers and tied labourers in the framework of small-scale agriculture rather than large-scale capitalist farming through wage labourers and improved techniques), there was no social revolution in the villages brought into their physical possession. They replaced the older dominant groups in the villages, but there was no change in the economic basis of the structure of domination.

The majority of the zamindars and taluqdars who acquired the title of landlord under the Permanent Settlement were not of agricultural stock, as were the Sadgop zamindars of Surul. Their object was not to take physical possession of land,[57] but to appropriate as much as possible of the surplus produced by the village through enhancement and equalization of assessment rates. Where the pressure of the jama assessed by the new landlords was exceptionally heavy, an egalitarian village structure might emerge although the higher village castes would continue to exercise leadership politically as the representatives of the village before the all-powerful outside landlord. Lalbehari Dey's famous novel of the life of the peasant hero, Govinda Samanta, in the village of Kanchanpur in Burdwan, where a powerful patnidar of the Raja of Burdwan residing near the village ruled with an iron hand and broke the ringleaders of a peasant combination (based on a true story),[58] portrayed exactly this kind of situation in the late nineteenth century, when there was no wasteland left in Burdwan and pressure of population had led to a five-fold increase of rates of assessment on raiyati holdings since the Permanent Settlement.[59] There is no evidence to show, however, that the elimination of the economic margin of the village elites was a general development all over Bengal immediately after the

[57]Being mostly Brahmans and Kayasthas, they had as a rule no interest in cultivation.

[58]Lalbehari Dey, *Bengal Peasant Life*. The village of Kanchanpur has been identified and surveyed by Bengali sociologists.

[59]See case study of Burdwan.

Permanent Settlement, when there was considerable scope for extension of cultivation in all parganas except the old settlements surrounded by intensively cultivated rice-producing plains.[60] The new enterprising zamindars of Calcutta with a business-like bent of mind entertained notions of measuring lands and fixing equal rates according to the capacity of the soil.[61] But in practice it

[60]A judicial report on Nadia in 1816, seems to indicate that in parts of this well-cultivated district, existing dominant village groups were economically crushed by new auction purchasers: 'Almost the whole of this District has been disposed of, either by public or private sale; the landholders are now no more, and the new purchasers are, for the most part, opulent native merchants at the Presidency, who have bought the lands as a mere speculation, and will part with them again after they have thoroughly fleeced them. These men are, of course, non residents (a circumstance of itself unfavourable to landed property) and they consequently have been farmed, and rack-rented, and old respectable Raiyats, hopeless and oppressed, have either fled from the fields of their forefathers or sought redress in the Courts of Justice'. Home Miscellaneous, Vol. 775, Judicial Nuddea, 1816.

[61]The famous Bengali entrepreneur and zamindar, Dwarakanath Tagore, issued the following instructions to J.C. Mitter when he appointed the latter as the manager of his estate of Shahzadpur: former actual jamas of different mauzas and jotes to be ascertained; assessment to be revised with justice and equity without overlooking the zamindar's interests and without oppressing the raiyats; villages to be measured and rates to be fixed according to quality of the land and local conditions; waste lands to be brought under cultivation by settling raiyats there; rates to be increased on reclaimed lands if possible later; lands to be parcelled among raiyats settled on the estate rather than outsiders, enquiries to be held to prevent encroachment; and in order to repossess the lands now held illegally by principal raiyats, information to be gathered as to the nature of their tenures before filing law suits. Manuscript Tagore Family Letter Books, Dwarakanath Tagore's Correspondence, 1835-1842, Vol. 1, Part 1, No. 6, English letter from Dwarakanath Tagore to J.C. Mitter, dt. 14 January 1836. In the second generation Dwarakanath's son, Debendranath Tagore, did not lose this profit-oriented attitude to zamindari as an investment from which adequate returns had to be secured by proper management. In a characteristic Bengali letter he wrote to Nagendranath Tagore: 'This time I am visiting the zamindari in order to make such arrangements that there will be no losses in future and to introduce such rules as to yield larger profits this year'. Tagore Family Letter Books, Babu Nagendranath Tagore's Correspondence, Vol. II, No. 278, Debendranath Sharma to Nagendra, dt. Shahzadpur, Pabna, 20 July 1852. Under proper management the zamindari did yield splendid profits to the Tagore family and the huge

was not easy to carry out such projects. In Baharband, as we have seen, Lokenath Nandy's survey and measurement for equalization of rates and elimination of privileges was defeated by a combination of large jotedars;[62] and in Patiladaha the dependence of the Tagores on the big Muslim jotedars for the extension of cultivation necessarily led to consolidation of the latter's privileges.

However, both in Baharband and Patiladaha the new zamindars were able to obtain increases of tribute—by an understanding with the big jotedars—far in excess of the amount justified by the extension of cultivation. This, the third of the possible lines of development, was by far the commonest in the settled parts of the country. After the passing of Regulation 7

debts incurred by Dwarakanath Tagore after the failure of Carr, Tagore & Company, amounting to Rs 306, 178, were paid off by Debendranath Tagore from these profits. Manuscript Documents of the Tagore Family, Debt of Late Babu Dwarakanath Tagore; Babu Nagendranath Tagore's correspondence, Vol. II, No. 235, N.N. Tagore to Nagendra, no date. Zamindari was a perfectly rational and very intelligent insurance against business losses.

[62]Such combinations of raiyats took place from time to time in the first half of the nineteenth century, but not so frequently as in the late eighteenth century up to the passing of Regulation 7 of 1799. In Chakla Bhusna under the zamindari of Rajshahi, where the jotedars were so 'notorious for their turbulent, fraudulent conduct' that the zamindar and the officers of the government found it difficult and often impossible to make them pay a just revenue, there was apparently an improvement in the situation in 1799 after the passing of Regulation 7. BRC, 29 August 1799, No. 5, enclosure from Board of Revenue, dt. 2 July 1799, by J.H. Harrington. Nevertheless, agrarian disturbances and peasant combinations continued to cause periodical alarm among the zamindars and in 1854 the British Indian Association complained to the government that a serious cause of agrarian disorder arose from the combination of raiyats made under solemn mutually-exchanged pledges, known as ekajoti (combination) and dharmaghat (strike or refusal to pay), to oppose the planter or zamindar in the exercise of his rights. British Indian Association Publications (manuscript bound volumes), Petition of the British Indian Association on the bill for the more effectual suppression of affrays concerning the possession of property. For an instance of such a combination by influential raiyats in a Dinajpur village, see Birbhum Old English Correspondence, Receipt Register from January 1821-December 1825, extract from a letter from the acting collector of Dinajpur, dt. 13 April 1821.

of 1799 and Regulation 5 in 1812, by which the government definitely declared its backing of the zamindars, there was a switch in the policy of the village oligarchs from resistance to collaboration in regard to the superior lords of the territory. In 1828, commenting upon the fast pace at which rates of assessment were rising, the indigo planters of Jessore observed in reply to a query from the government that whenever zamindaris belonging to old proprietors were sold at auction to new purchasers, the latter had to face jotedars possessing old leases who were in a strong position to resist any attempt to dispossess them or to enhance the rates assessed on their privileged holdings. In such zamindaris, where the amount collected by the traditional zamindars was usually quite low according to prevailing standards, the auction purchasers invariably sought to enhance the rates to the highest standard in existence. The indigo planters noted in their communication that the new landlords seldom failed to achieve their ends as they secured the co-operation of the larger jotedars by confirming their old leases.[63] There was, thus, an informal alliance between the superior landlords and the village leaders that facilitated the great increase of assessment after 1799 in the settled parts of the country where the extension of cultivation was by no means sufficient to account for the enhancements obtained.[64] When there was no understanding between the superior landlord and his jotedars, the former, if he was weak and unskilful, stood no chance whatever against a few energetic village landlords 'backed by the spears, bamboos, and clubs of the cultivating tenants.'[65] If on the other hand, the zamindar happened to be rich and strong, the issue of the conflict remained wide open.

But in parts of Bengal, such as Dacca and Bakarganj, there were numerous petty taluqdars with interlaced and subinfeudated estates, who were neither rich, nor strong; and by coincidence, there was in this area a great belt of forest available for clearance and the natural human element available for clearing it was a tough and violent type of Muslim villager possessing both men and money.

---

[63]BRP, 7 March 1828, No. 27.

[64]BRP, 7 March 1828, No. 47, Mr. Halhed's minute.

[65]*Bengal Village Biographies*, (Calcutta 1858), p. 21.

This leads to the fourth possible line of development, which occurred over large parts of Dacca and Bakarganj, especially in small zamindaris like that of the Ponabalia Raychaudhuris. The fact that in this area zamindaris and taluqs, when they underwent partition, were invariably divided into anna-shares in the rupee (i.e., unseparated shares in the whole) and not in separate territorial blocks of mauzas showed that the numerous grades of tenures and sub-tenures which had sprung up in the niabat of Dacca long before the Permanent Settlement (reflecting the dense habitations of the high caste Hindu gentry, such as the Bikrampuri babus) were circulating titles to revenue-collection without any direct connection with the land. The seven-anna Haveli Selimabad zamindari of the Ponabalia Raychaudhuris was at first subdivided into one and six annas; then the six annas into four annas (Srikrishna branch) and two annas (Manohar branch); and finally the two annas into bara hisya (elder branch = one anna) and chhota hisya (junior branch = one anna). Even before the Permanent Settlement, chains of taluqs, haolas, and osat haolas had intervened in Haveli Selimabad between the zamindars and the cultivators, and many of the richer cultivators were already in possession of very favourable tenures for clearing forest which could not be set aside, so that acquirement of the tenures by purchase was the only course left open to the zamindars to impose control over villages. This was the course on which the two-anna zamindars of Haveli Selimabad set out after the Permanent Settlement, but their policy of purchasing under-tenures was largely frustrated by the acquirement of the four-anna share by the hostile Nawabs of Dacca and by constant bickering between the bara hisya and the chhota hisya of the Ponabalia Raychaudhuris. It was only with a limited number of actual cultivators that the Ponabalia Raychaudhuris succeeded in establishing direct relationship, although the Permanent Settlement declared them to be landlords. The rising economic rent of the zamindari, a splendid rice surplus area with plenty of waste for extension of cultivation, was intercepted by prosperous agricultural Muslims possessing virtually impregnable haolas, osat haolas, and nim haolas. Growing economic pressure, arising from a long and costly litigation with the Nawabs of Dacca and from the interception of profits by under-tenure holders, compelled the petty Vaidya landlords of Ponabalia to turn to service and professions in the late nineteenth century. The violent Faraizi movement among the class of enterprising Muslim agriculturalists engaged in reclaiming chars and forests in Dacca, Faridpur, and Bakarganj shut out many petty Hindu landlords of similar circumstances from obtaining a share in the rising rent of this steadily expanding and highly prosperous alluvial tract. The Muslim village landlords, organized by Dadu Mian into the united and disciplined Faraizi sect,[66] appropriated the benefits of an expanding agricultural economy.

The broad picture of the village land-holding class, then, was that although they were economically levelled down in certain pockets of high population pressure at certain points in time, they generally managed, in settled areas, to retain an economic margin by shifting the increased burden of assessment to poor villagers, and in border areas with plenty of waste they succeeded in improving their economic position by taking possession of new lands on favourable terms. Depicting rural society on the basis of an actual survey of two villages (probably in Jessore) in the middle of the nineteenth century, the unnamed author of an essay entitled *Bengal Village Biographies* advised persons interested in rural society

> to look out, first, for the Zemindar or Talookdar paying revenue to Government, who collects from one village, from half a dozen or from the whole Pergunnah; next, for the substantial small proprietors, who, in appearance middleman, *own* a quarter, one-eighth, or one-half of the village,

[66]Such unity and discipline was necessarily imposed on colonizing agriculturists who needed to pool their labour power and resources for reclaiming a marshy, river-intersected, forest country. It was the prospect of prosperity, and not the burden of poverty imposed by the Permanent Settlement, that led to the emergence of the Faraizi sect among Muslim agriculturists.

> we care not by what title they are designated;[67] next, for any cultivating ryots with clear proprietary rights if there be such, who practically will not differ much, except in status, from the aforesaid small proprietors; and finally, for the class of men who squat, take leases, temporary or permanent and do the main business of cultivation, with rights hardly defined, but quite capable of definition all over the country.

The author of the *Bengal Village Biographies* recognized that the impact of the Permanent Settlement on villages varied according to local circumstances, but still, taking one thing with another, he concluded that

> the rural population are not by any means so utterly crushed and annihilated as is supposed. What with the general lightness of the land tax, the surprising fertility of the country, the expansion of commerce, the divisions of estates, the creations of small tenures, the temporary alienations, the farms, the puttunis, the power of combination which, however, is so often misdirected, the immense number of paid situations which our administration as well as the whole Zemindary system creates and maintains—what with all this, we say, the village, one step above a ploughman or day labourer, has several chances. All are not yet reduced to one dead level of equality[68].

[67]"These small proprietors in the neighbourhood of the place we are writing from, and in several other districts, are termed gantidars. But we care little about a local term, which conveys no distinct impression to the mind, and which may mean the same thing as half a dozen very different terms in use in other parts of the country. What we do care about is the significant fact, that in such men we find those who appear to us to be the real proprietors of the soil. Their rate of rent is fixed and cannot be enhanced, except under some very peculiar circumstances; they plant and dig, prune and cut down, and build up, transfer, sell, mortgage, alienate and establish ryots on their lands, exactly as they please. The miles of date gardens which meet the eye in every direction over thousands of plains, are mainly their creation; they collect from half a dozen mere ryots on the one hand, or cultivate, by hired labour, a small home farm on the other; they have all those attributes which, to minds not wilfully blind to facts, nor wedded to theories, nor beyond the power of conviction, are descriptive of virtual, tangible, *de facto* ownership of land. *Bengal Village Biographies* (Calcutta 1858), p. 20.

[68]Ibid., p. 22 ff.

11

EPILOGUE

Bengali Rural History from the Permanent Settlement to the Abolition of Zamindari

The Permanent Settlement of 1793, long regarded as the propelling force behind a revolution in Bengali rural society, would appear to have effected a less fundamental change in the agrarian base of society than is usually supposed. There were striking changes in the higher orders of society in the towns and rural centres which drew tribute from the villages in the interior, passing on a part of this surplus to the metropolis of Calcutta. From a total view of the structure of society, the most significant among these changes in the long run was the consolidation of the smaller local high caste gentry, who became an independent propertied class with a more secure base for striking out in new directions. Rammohan Ray, the embodiment of the new age, was a typical representative of the dependent grihastha class living under the authority of big Rajas who seized the opportunity afforded by the breakup of the Rajs under the Permanent Settlement to convert their inchoate rights in the local rent-sharing systems into legally recognized titles to collection of jama. The rearranged local tenurial systems which emerged after the Permanent Settlement effected a broader distribution of tribute from the land among a large number of literate gentry.[1] The small but secure shares in the tribute from the

[1]A number of rich Calcutta families, who had made money in commercial association with Europeans or in the services of the Company's government,

villages which they obtained under this redistribution provided an incentive to the mobile elements among them who had a long tradition of service under the Mughal state (such as the Bikrampuri babus) to fill up the new urban professions and salaried positions created under British rule. These petty landlord families, with sons employed in service or engaged in practising law, came in time to form the politically conscious section of the nation in the countryside. It was the destruction of the territorial magnates by the Permanent Settlement (in their aspect as rulers of principalities) that opened the way to these new developments. Towns like Burdwan, Bishnupur, Krishnagar, Jessore, and Dinajpur were formerly overshadowed by the presence of magnates exercising administrative authority over the surrounding countryside. Now these towns came under the influence of smaller literate gentry capable of political dialogue with the local representatives of the supreme government and closely concerned with their policies. They proved keenly receptive to the new movements of social reform and cultural modernization emanating from Calcutta;[2] and during the Swadeshi movement they provided the political constituency of the Indian National Congress in rural Bengal.[3]

While these changes were taking place in the higher orders of society in Bengal, the framework of social relations inside which the villages in the interior carried on agriculture showed a strong tendency towards crystallization and solidification. A traditional mode of production controlled by a creditor class of village

bought large estates and came to constitute a new class of landed rich. Rammohan Ray's orthodox opponent, Radha Kanta Deb, belonged to this class. But the penetration of the new rich class of Calcutta in local land control systems was not as massive as has hitherto been imagined. The new anded families of Calcutta like the Debs and the Tagores, and surviving lolder magnates like the Rajas of Burdwan, came to form a rich zamindar group above the smaller gentry and constituted the uppermost stratum of Bengali society in the nineteenth century.

[2]See for instance the Bengali autobiography by Krishna Kumar Mitra, *Krishna Kumar Mitrer Atma-Charitra* (Calcutta 1937). The author came from a small taluqdar family of Mymensingh and became a member of the Brahmo samaj and a leader of the Bengal Moderates.

[3]*Final Report on Dacca*, p. 45.

landlords persisted on the basis of a backward technology of agriculture. Large-scale capitalist farming through increased capital inputs and improved techniques, as envisaged by the framers of the Permanent Settlement, did not develop in Bengal. Instead there was an accentuation of certain traditional features of the production relations in the villages—the small size of plots, labour-intensive farming through sharecroppers and bonded labourers, and the master-serf type of relationship between jotedar and bargadar. The existing mode of production—small farms, sharecropping, and technological backwardness arising from the unprofitability of modern inputs—prevented the conduct of cultivation through large estates (in the economic sense of the term) managed by capitalist landlords. Agriculture continued to be necessarily village-based, carried on within the framework of small holdings cultivated by peasants who borrowed capital from village landlords of the traditional jotedar type. Zamindars could not, even if they were willing, profitably get personal possession of all the lands of their so-called 'estates' (which were hotch-potch collections of rent-sharing rights over scattered mauzas and parganas), although resident zamindars usually did manage to create ring-fences around their own villages within which they controlled all economic activities. While it was possible for them, by converting themselves into landlords of the jotedar type, to dominate the villages around them, but it was economically unprofitable, in the prevailing state of agricultural technology, to extend this domination further. For no legal innovation, in the absence of the type of economic change which led to the transition from the manor to the estate in England, could suddenly alter the social basis of production and lead to the emergence of estates.

It must not be supposed that the new men who became zamindars by auction purchase invariably turned themselves into idle annuitants subscribing to social values which prevented them from becoming better landlords. Evidence of their extensive involvement in enterprises like the manufacture and export of cloth, silk, sugar and indigo is available from existing zamindari papers. Far from frittering away capital in non-productive activities and converting themselves into idle annuitants living off rent, many of the new zamindars invested the greater part of the profits from their landed properties in the cultivation and processing of valuable export products.[4] The factor which prevented these enterprising zamindars from playing the part of model landlords assigned to them by Cornwallis was the difficulty of acquiring physical control of land at the local level. As Justice Phear observed in an annual address to the Bengal Social Science Association, unless the zamindar was exceptionally situated, middlemen, permanent tenures, and rights of occupancy effectually barred him from direct action relative to the possession of, and dealings with, the land itself. 'How different is this from the perfect freedom of the English landlord, and how impossible it is to reason in the one case by analogy with the other. In truth, the property in the soil, which the Bengal zamindar enjoys, is not that of the landowner in England; and it was from want of perceiving the distinction that the authors of the Permanent Settlement formed expectations which could never be realised.'[5] Would conferment of landlord status on the jotedar class by a direct settlement with them have led to the result desired by Cornwallis? It has been recently argued, by Dr. A. Bhaduri, on the basis of a survey of 26 villages in

[4]Expressing his anxiety about the financing of household expenses in Calcutta, Debendranath Tagore writes in a letter to Girindranath Tagore while on tour through the zamindari: 'Indigo is being cultivated on 6,700 bighas of land. Unless accident intervenes, 400 maunds of indigo is likely to be produced. If money is not available at the right time, losses result. The money now being sent from the zamindari is tied up in financing indigo production and in addition a loan will have to be taken from Madan Babu. To send money from here at this time will hamper the indigo business. But I am worried as to how expenses in Calcutta will be met. If you can manage the household expenditure there with the money from the ijara of Janipur, Shalimpur and Kumarkhali, it will be excellent. Sale of indigo brings in the whole money at a time and that is more profitable. Advise me after considering this matter.' Babu Girindranath Tagore's Correspondence, Part II, 1845-1854, No. 64, undated letter from Debendranath Sharma. Some time afterwards, sanctioning Rs 1,000 for erecting a silk factory and exporting silk to Calcutta, Debendranath wrote again to Girindranath that the silk business would have to be financed by the profits of zamindari. Ibid., No. 67, undated letter from Debendranath Sharma.

[5]'Annual Address' by J.B. Phear, delivered before the Bengal Social Science Association on 7 January 1869, *Transactions of the Bengal Social Science Association*, Vol. III, 1869.

Birbhum district in 1970, that the specific character of the economic and political domination of the villages by the jotedar class inhibited improvement in productivity. The jotedar, in his combined role as landlord and moneylender, realized more from his bonded sharecroppers than he could expect from a marginal increase in productivity which, while increasing his share of the crop (that is to say, rent), might set his sharecroppers free of debt, ending his profit from interest and his political control of the village.[6] There is, however, no reason why the jotedar would not have invested in improvement of agriculture if the profitability of new inputs had risen sufficiently (due to changed economic circumstances like greater availability of irrigation water) to outweigh any possible loss of interest or political control (which, moreover, might not follow necessarily). But the zamindari papers of the Surul family, who stood effectively (in economic terms) in the position of jotedar with regard to the Surul area, strongly suggest that throughout the nineteenth century sharing the crop and lending money was more profitable to the village landlords than direct capital-intensive farming with new inputs.[7]

---

[6]A. Bhaduri, 'A Study in Agricultural Backwardness under Semi-Feudalism' *Economic Journal*, March 1937.

[7]The explanation for this set of conditions is beyond the scope of this study. An answer may be sought both in supply-oriented hypotheses—for instance irrigation facilities—and in propositions emphasizing the demand aspect—such as the size of the local market and the opportunities for export. Presumably it was a question of both the rate of capital formation in agriculture and the rate of growth of the domestic—especially rural—market for agricultural produce. For major changes leading to acceleration of the rates of capital formation and market expansion, the researcher will turn expectantly to the impact of new cash crops. It may be noted in this connection that indigo—the only new cash crop to occupy a sufficiently large part of the cultivated area after the Permanent Settlement as to constitute a 'leading sector' in agriculture—did not stimulate the peasant economy in a large way. Its production was dominated by European planters who kept, down the prices offered to the peasants by a usurious system of advances largely because the income elasticity of demand for indigo in the world market was not sufficient to enable the planters to offer attractive prices to the peasants. The typical complaint of the raiyats against indigo planters was that the latter forced them, often using violence, to perform greater labour and that after this extra labour they received no part of the profits.

In the absence of any breakthrough in technology, the new demands made upon agriculture by a growing population, a modernized administration, and a developing urban civilization compressed rural society in the long-settled and closely cultivated parts of the country into a narrow mould of domination by the existing village elites, who managed to preserve their rule by an agreement with the superior agencies of tribute collection to raise greater tribute from their villages.[*] It was the tightening of the structure of government that forced the village oligarchies to submit to these harder terms—terms which effected a redistribution of the social surplus and laid the foundations of the new urban social order of the Bengali gentry and literati and the imperial economic and political order of the British Raj. The new domination imposed over the village by outside agencies, such as the estates, the government, and the indigo factories came to rest squarely on the old domination by the land-holding and money-lending families within the village. The composition of this dominant class within the village might change considerably over time, but the specific character of the domination seemed to persist. Through the years of changeless change, some village households rose into the jotedar class, while others fell from it to the level of subsistence farmers. But while there was considerable mobility within this class structure, especially between the classes of rich jotedars and ordinary raiyats (cases of upward mobility among agricultural labourers, mainly composed of tribals and untouchables, were rare), the structure itself sufficiently retained its distinctive identity to be described in exactly similar terms by Buchanan in 1808, Westmacott in 1876, and Bell in 1940 for the district of Dinajpur.

Thus the new sharing-out of the social surplus under the administrative or reorganization of the Permanent Settlement provided the basis of a social structure that was substantially reformed at the top but only marginally modified at the bottom. Formerly this social structure had consisted of the Mughal nobility, the regional Rajas, and the dependent local gentry at the top, and the village heads, the ordinary raiyats, and the

See a petition to the Church Missionary Society by some Christian raiyats in Church Missionary Papers, CI/1/019/14.

landless villagers at the bottom. The body of raiyats, including the village heads, were the physical possessors of agricultural holdings and as such they obtained, in the first instance, the economic rent of the land, from which they paid a share as jama (tribute for rulers), which was shared out between the Nizamat, the Rajs, and the subordinate local grihasthas collecting the tribute from the localities. Some of the raiyats, variously known in different regions as mandals, jotedars, gantidars, and haola dars, enjoyed such large holdings that the margin of the economic rent which they retained after paying the jama was sufficient to enable them to lend money and grain and to employ sharecroppers and labourers. But the greater body of raiyats who had small holdings had to work their own farms since the share in economic rent which was left to them after payment of the jama gave them only a small margin of superiority to sharecroppers and agricultural labourers who worked for others. This was the prevailing system of distribution of the rent from land which was modified through administrative action on a massive scale from 1786 to 1812, leading to the emergence of a social structure consisting of a European merchant-administrative class, rich absentee landed magnates, smaller propertied gentry in towns and rural centres, village-controlling jotedars, ordinary raiyats, and landless villagers. The government raised enormously and fixed permanently its own tribute, and also contracted out its right to increase jama on a perpetual basis to a vastly increased number of proprietors—both rich urban magnates and smaller local gentry—who carved out the Rajs among themselves. The new powers given by the government to the proprietors for collecting the increased tribute, such as laws, courts and police, enabled the perpetual contractors of revenue in time to increase their own share in the rent from land by reducing the total size of the social surplus left to the villages. By the middle of the nineteenth century, the poor raiyats in the densely inhabited parts of the country probably enjoyed a smaller portion of the economic rent in spite of the increase in its total size and from this portion they had to pay interest calculated on a possibly increasing size of debt incurred on account of greater commercial production of crops. The number (and also perhaps the proportion) of villagers living at subsistence level—whether as raiyats with a few bighas or as full-time workers for others—increased in the mid-nineteenth century with the growth of population pressure on land. But the incidence of the increased burden on the villages was highly differential: the village landlords managed to retain a much larger margin of the economic rent of land than the common raiyats by an adroit combination of collaboration with, and resistance to, the superior collectors of tribute. In the second half of the nineteenth century changed political circumstances led to a gradual improvement in their position vis-a-vis the outside landlords.[8] The share in the rent from land retained by the village in general, and by dominant village groups in particular, increased relative to the diminishing share of the social surplus collected by outside landlords from the 1880s onwards. But the increased margin of economic rent received by the body of raiyats from 1880 to 1920 was probably offset by the increase in the number of people sharing it. Moreover, the great spurt in population growth after 1920 brought about a crisis in agriculture which engulfed even the village landlords during the depression of the thirties.

The currents in village life which arose from these tensions over the sharing-out of rent—especially between village landlords and superior landlords—did not feed the new movements towards cultural 'renaissance' and 'national' awakening among the higher orders of Bengali society in the towns and rural centres. The ideologies which were promoted in the villages by such tensions—the Faraizi movement (conscious practice of orthodox Islam among energetic and prosperous Muslim agriculturists engaged in reclaiming new lands and determined to resist enhancement of rates on them by Hindu zamindars and taluqdars), the Namasudra agitation (Sanskritization and education under Christian missionary patronage among prosperous 'Chandals' who keenly resented their low ritual status vis-a-vis the high caste local gentry), the obscure peasant cults and caste movements—were alien to the rent-receiving Bengali gentry and useless to the gentry-based Bengal Congress. The

[8]It should be noted that in case of resident zamindars practising cultivation in their own village, such as the Surul zamindars, the distinction between outside and village landlords did not apply.

loss of cohesion and buildup of tension in the localities began, in time, to feed into broader and more abstract communal divisions in an emerging structure of provincial politics and ultimately saw political embodiment in the partition of Bengal. Yet it must be noted that the way in which local tensions linked up with movements in provincial politics differed from region to region in accordance with local circumstances, which lent a complex and asymmetrical pattern to the patchwork of nationlist and separatist politics in the arena of the province. In East Bengal the Bengal Congress rested squarely on privileged but hard-pressed social elements like the high caste Bikrampur taluqdars who pushed the Swadeshi movement in the interior to the extent that made it such an impressive success in Dacca, Faridpur, and Bakarganj. Despair at their diminishing income from the land in a prosperous alluvial tract drove them to the Congress platform, and then in turn to revolutionary terrorism, Hindu communalism, and international (rather than local) communism. But it was in these very districts, where the prosperous Muslim and Namasudra jotedars entered into increasingly fierce competition for power in their own localities with the numerous high caste local gentry, that the movements for 'Muslim' power at the centre and reservation of seats for the 'depressed classes' under the banner of the Krishak Praja Party attained the greatest momentum. By contrast, in the Muslim majority areas of North Bengal like Rangpur and Dinajpur, the communal disharmony and rioting which progressively disfigured village social life in East Bengal from 1926 onwards remained significantly absent. For here the locally dominant class of Muslim jotedars did not face tough competition for local power from a high caste Hindu gentry allied with the Congress. But if communalism did not spread like a virus in Rangpur and Dinajpur, nor did the national movement make much headway in these districts, for the rural Hindu gentry who pushed the national movement and provoked Muslim separatism in Dacca, Faridpur, and Bakarganj, were very thin on the ground in North Bengal. It was only in West Bengal, in parts of Midnapur, Hugli, and Bankura, that the Congress campaign of Civil Disobedience was fed by peasant participation under the leadership of jotedars of respectable agricultural castes, such as the

Mahishyas (Kaivartas), who felt no local antagonism against high caste gentry (who were virtually absent in parts of Midnapur, and were themselves agriculturists in Bankura and Hugli) but nursed local grievances against the government.[9]

It would appear, in retrospect, that the framers of the Permanent Settlement constructed an artificial category, named 'landlord' which did not accord well with the complex realities on the ground; those who were included by administrative fiat in this new category hardly deserved the description, but there were others, included by fiat in the complementary category of 'tenant', who might have laid a more serious claim to it. By creating this permanent tension between legal fiction and economic reality in each locality, the Permanent Settlement pushed local conflicts into the broader territorial sphere of government activity. There immediately ensued a struggle between the *de jure* and the *de facto* landlords in each locality over the sharing out of rent, in which both parties followed with keen attention each measure of general and particular policy emanating from the district and provincial headquarters. In this struggle the government was at first allied with the zamindars in its own interest, since the punctual payment of an enhanced (even if fixed) revenue—which was the prime consideration of the government at that time—would have been impossible for the newly constituted landlords without superior powers against troublesome village cliques. But this attitude on the part of the government began to change when the payment of the revenue became easier and the zamindar began to appropriate the increasing tribute to which the government—due to the hasty action of Cornwallis in 1793—could no longer lay claim. By destroying the principalities and erecting its own district administration, the government had acquired the means of intervention in the localities. As the British Indian Association observed in a memorial to the government, in the struggle for local power between contending parties—zamindar, planter, village clique—the collector held the key to the alternate success

[9]John Gallagher, 'Congress in Decline: Bengal, 1930-39', forthcoming article in *Modern Asian Studies*.

or defeat of each party.[10] Government had at first assumed that it could not manage the country without the zamindars. Now it became increasingly evident that it could manage the country much better by direct bargains with the influential village cliques. The balance turned more and more against the zamindars as the government embarked on a course of tenancy legislation which, while conceding nothing to sharecroppers and agricultural labourers, bolstered the position of the jotedars. Having realized how much better it could have done without the 'landlord', government was now backing its other category—'tenant'. But, as usual, its policy was enveloped in fiction: it was not backing the body of peasants against the village landlords, but was only favouring the village landlords against the superior landlords. The process was finally brought to a neat conclusion through the abolition of zamindari in the 1950s by the broader-based and more powerful governments which emerged in the two Bengals on the basis of jotedar support in elections under universal adult franchise.

[10]British Indian Association Publications, Third Annual Report 1854, section on the Affray Bill.

Bibliography

[The primary sources consulted for this thesis are in English, Bengali and Persian and the main repositories of these sources are the India Office Library and Records, the British Museum, the Church Missionary Society and the Baptist Missionary Society in London; the Centre of South Asian Studies and the University Library in Cambridge; the West Bengal State Archives, the Calcutta High Court, the British Indian Association, the West Bengal Secretariat Library, the National Library, and the Sahitya Parishad in Calcutta; the District Record Rooms of Midnapur, Bankura. Burdwan, Birbhum and Nadia in West Bengal; the Bengali Manuscript Department of the Visvabharati University, Santiniketan; and various private collections in old zamindari houses in Jhamapukur (Calcutta), Rabindra Sadan (Santiniketan), Surul (Birbhum), Supur (Birbhum), Krishnagar (Nadia), Bishnupur (Bankura), Maheshganj (Nadia) etc.]

Government Records

West Bengal State Archives

[The following section is extracted from the printed handbook of the State Archives entitled 'Catalogue of English Records Preserved in the Historical Record Room of the Government of Bengal 1758-1858'. The main series of proceedings consulted for this thesis, the Proceedings of the Board of Revenue, is in a much better state of preservation in the West Bengal State Archives than in the India Office Library and Records, and the proceedings under each date are numbered throughout the series, whereas proceedings numbers are lacking for the India Office Records and Library series before 1794 The Archives have also several volumes of very useful printed (but not published for general information) 'Alphabetical Index to the Proceedings of the Board of Revenue 1786-1858' which gives admirable abstracts of all minutes and letters but which is not available in the India Office Library and Records or elsewhere.]

English Records

Judicial (Civil) 1793-1815.
Judicial (Criminal) 1793-1815.
Judicial, Civil - Lower Provinces 1816-1834.
Judicial, Criminal - Lower Provinces 1816-1834.
Board of Revenue at Fort William 1786-1822.
Board of Revenue - Lower Provinces 1822-1828.
Board of Revenue - Sadar 1829-1850.
Board of Revenue - Lower Provinces 1851-1858.
Printed Index to the Proceedings of the Board of Revenue 1786-1858.
Sadar Board of Revenue - Settlement—1837-1843. (Copies of Memoranda on Certain Settlements in Bauleah, Cuttack, Chittagong and Murshidabad Divisions by F.J. Halliday 1837-1838, 1 volume).

Miscellaneous Records—Revenue Department.

(*a*) Proceedings and Reports 1774-1858. Proceedings of the Commissioners appointed by a letter dated 12th March 1788 to make enquiries and investigations relating to the State of Rungpore, Kuch Bihar and Rubrampore 30 April —10 November 1788, 1 vol.

(*b*) Accounts and Registers relating to lands and land revenue 1758-1842.

(*i*) Account of Izaradars and Ihtimandars of the 24 Parganas showing the annual rent for the year 1758, 1 vol.

(*ii*) Settlement accounts and kistbandi of several districts of Bengal and Bihar 17 [ ]-1789, 2 vols.

(*iii*) Five years' settlement accounts of Bengal and Bihar 1772-1777, 1 vol.

(*iv*) Accounts of Bazi Zamin or alienated lands of Vishnupur, 54 vols.

Bazi Zamin of Mahisadal and its dependencies, 1 vol.
Bazi Zamin of Birbhum, 1 vol.

(*v*) Hustabud or revenue accounts of Birbhum, Vishnupur, Bhagalpur, Chittagong, Calcutta, Dacca, Fatesingh, Hijli, Hoogly and Hatinda districts 1772-1776.
Jahangirpur, Jessore, Khas Taluks, Lashkarpur, Mahmudshahi, Mysadul, Midnapur and Nadia districts 1772-1776.
Purnia, 24 Parganas, Panchete, Rajshahi, Rokanpur, Rangpur, Rajmahal, Saidpur and Sujamutha districts 1772-1776.

(*vi*) General Registers of malguzari mahals showing the names of parganas, mahals and malguzars, amount of jama, management, partitions, decrees and details of encumbrances, 24 vols.

(*vii*) General Registers of Lakhiraj mahals for several parganas of Hijli and Midnapur, 2 vols.

Miscellaneous Records—Board of Revenue.

(*a*) Office Records.

(*i*) Salary receipt book or register showing the names and salary of the establishment of the office of the Board 1793-1836, 4 vols.

(*ii*) Establishment register or statements showing the establishment of the office of the Board and of subordinate offices and collectorates in several districts with an abstract 1803-1804.

(*iii*) Notes and minutes by the Secretary and the members of the Board, drafts of letters from the Secretary to Commissioners and other authorities, copies of letters to and from various officers, 1822, 1830-1836, 4 vols.

(*iv*) Receipt books or registers of letters received by the Board from several authorities, arranged alphabetically under certain heads 1823-1858.

(*v*) Notebook of particular cases, i.e., Board's office notebook or memo book containing references to important cases on various subjects, with an index 1831-1850.

(*vi*) 'Lay Books' or registers of letters laid before the officers of the Board together with references to the consultations 1836-1843.

(*vii*) Board Books or registers with an index, containing abstracts of letters placed before the Sadar Board of Revenue with their notes of discussion thereon 1836-1859.

(*b*) Registers, etc., relating to lands and land revenue.

(*i*) Revenue account or account settlement i.e. register containing settlement, kistbandi, general jama wasil baki accounts etc. of the following districts, Murshidabad, Birbhum, Ramgarh, Jessore, Dacca 1786-1787, 1 vol.
Bengal and Behar 1786-1789, 1 vol.
Rajshahi 1789-1790, Jessore 1789-1790, Rajmahal 1789-1790, Belleah 1800-1804.

(*ii*) Comparative statement of the adjustment of decennial settlement assessment and the jama for the year 1196 Fasli of Zilla Midnapur.

(*iii*) Survey of parganas in Midnapur of register containing accounts of the survey of 12 parganas in Midnapur with genealogy and succession of the zamindar, 1788.

(*iv*) Decennial Settlement accounts submitted by Collectors relating to

Saran and Champaran
Mymensingh
Nadia 1791-1799.
Dacca-Jalalpur (undecipherable).

(*v*) Quinquennial Register for Rangpur for 1202 B.S.

(*vi*) Account Sale or statement of lands sold for arrears of revenue in the following districts. There are the original statements submitted by the Collectors and bound into volumes:

Nadia 1793-1811
Jessore 1793-1813
Mymensingh 1793-1813
Dacca 1793-1817

Dinajpur 1793-1817
Tipperah 1793-1807
Murshidabad 1794-1813
Midnapur 1794-1816
Burdwan 1794-1817
Chittagong 1794-1817
Rajshahi 1794-1817
Rungpur 1795-1815
Birbhum 1795-1807
24 Parganas 1801-1807, and other districts in Bihar and Orissa.

Vernacular Records

1. Bengali Records:
   (*a*) Copies and abstracts of Hooghly Collectorate papers (missing).
   (*b*) Papers relating to the Mahisadal Zamindari, 1 bundle.
   (*c*) Moazinal Dahsala (standard of fixing the assessment of jama for the decennial settlement), 11 bundles.
2. Persian Records 1624-1828.
3. Mixed Persian and Bengali Records 1764-1827 (largely missing). Boards bundle no. 262, Kabuliyats in Persian and Bengali.
4. English, Persian and Bengali Registers relating to Baze Zamin daftar 1764-1827.
5. Big bundles of various departments.

India Office Library and Records

Proceedings of the Governor-General-in-Council.
1. Bengal Criminal and Civil Judicial Consultations 1793-1794.
2. Bengal Criminal Judicial Consultations 1795-1842.
3. Bengal Civil Judicial Consultations 1795-1841.
4. Bengal Revenue Consultations 1793-1858.

Proceedings of the Board of Revenue of Bengal.
1. Board of Revenue, Bengal, Proceedings 1786-1822.
2. Board of Revenue, Lower Provinces of Bengal 1822-1829.
3. Sadar Board of Revenue Proceedings 1829-1855.

Court Proceedings

1. Inventories of deceased persons' estates sworn to in the Mayor's Court, Calcutta 1758-1776. Proceedings and Copies of Wills 1727-1774.
2. Inventories of deceased persons' estates sworn to in the Supreme Court of Calcutta 1775-1779. Copies of Wills 1774-1779.
3. Sadar Dewani Adalat Proceedings 1773-1801.

Manuscript Reports

Bengal Commercial Reports 1795-1815.

Home Miscellaneous Series

Vol.	*Particulars*
47	Burdwan—Lands upon which salt is made—extract of letter from John Johnstone to the Governor-General-in-Council, 22 August 1762. Midnapore-zamindari of Myna Choura—John Johnstone to Committee of new lands at Fort William, 8 June 1760.
205	Vansittart's Nuddea Deputation, 1783.
206	Amini Commission Report, 25 March 1778.
385	Seroopore. Decennial Settlements Reports from Collectors to Board of Revenue on Burdwan, 20 May 1788; Calcutta 8 April 1788; Chittagong, 19 January and 31 May 1788; Tippera 12 April 1788; Dacca, 17 January 1788; Dinajpur 15 January 1788; Jessore 25 June 1788; Murshidabad, 24 February 1788; Mymensingh, 13 February 1788; Nadia, 15 February 1788; 24 Parganas, 17 May 1788; Purnia, 7 March 1788; Rajashahi, 23 May 1788; Rangpur, 16 December 1788; and Sylhet, 24 November 1789.
434	Estimate of the fertility of Bengal, Bihar and Orissa.
530	Rights conferred on zamindars by the Bengal Regulations—(i.e. the Permanent Settlement—Cumming's Observations. Rights of Zamindar and Ryots, Notes prepared by Cumming.
692	Police in the Territories under the Supreme Government, March 1811.

775 Reports of Judicial Officers 1814-18—Judicial Nuddea 1816—Report on the District of Burdwan.

1815 Rennell Letters.

Burdwan Collectorate Records Room

Old English correspondence 1786-1820

Estate Bundles or Tauzi Records. Originally 6900 bundles, 400 removed to Bankura and Hugli.

[Tauzi No. 2, registered in the name of the Burdwan Raj, shows Burdwan Raj Estate No. 2 sub-leased by patni to the Mukherjees of Uttarpara. Most estate bundles of this collectorate belong to the Burdwan Raj, but they reveal these estates to be sub-leased to various subinfeudatory patnidars and darpatnidars.]

Register of Lakhiraj Lands, lists rent-free lands.

Chakran Settlement Records, relate to service lands.

Daul and Kistbandi, Decennial Settlement Papers.

Ward's Records, papers of Ward's estates administered by the collector of Burdwan.

Chalans or accounts and receipts.

Putni Sale Records.

Quinquennial Register, list of all proprietors paying land revenue revised every five years.

Quinquennial Papers.

Taidad or rent-free estates.

Bankura Collectorate Records Room

Old English correspondence 1800-1847.

[Bankura was originally a magistracy, not a collectorate, and the revenue jurisdiction of the Bishnupur part of the magistracy belonged to Burdwan. The Old English correspondence of this district is therefore different in nature from that of other districts and is full of long and informative reports, not concerned so much with the details of the revenue business as with land disputes, rural control and local political organization.]

Tauzi Records.

[Tauzi No. 1 is the original Bishnupur estate bundle and contains very old Persian documents. Tauzi No. 72 appertains to a resumed Lakhiraj estate of which the Bishnupur family retained possession. The big tauzis all belong to the Burdwan Raj and indicate sub-leasing to patnidars and darpatnidars. The Tauzis are full of 'taluqdari decree cases', i.e., suits filed by the Burdwan Raj for the sale of patni or darpatni taluqs for revenue arrears under the Patni Regulation, and 'lakhiraj' (revenue-free) claims against the taluqdars by local tenants. The absentee taluqdar class in Bankura was apparently subject to a dual pressure from above and below and, not surprisingly, the composition of the class was constantly changing.]

Quinquennial Register of 1795. Records of Quinquennial Register 1802.

[No further quinquiennial registers were made in this district, and the same failure to bring the register up to date every five years with the purpose of keeping track of changes in landed property occurred in all districts of Bengal. The Quinquennial Register of 1795 has the following heads: name of pargana, name of zamindar or taluqdar, name of ijaradar (revenue-farmer) and darbasti jama which included mufassal charges of collection (saranjami) and proprietor's allowance (malikana).]

Birbhum Collectorate Room

Old English correspondence 1786-1837.

Tauzi Records.

[The Tauzis in Birbhum are full of Persian and Bengali documents.]

Midnapur Collectorate Record Room

Old English correspondence

[Temporarily removed to the Census Office in Calutta.]

Tamluk Salt Letters.

[According to the reports of the Historical Records Survey Commission, the Midnapur collectorate had many other series of correspondence which are now missing.]

Rent Free Registers or Taidads.

Decennial Settlement Papers, Persian documents.

Permanent Settlement Records, bandobast kabuliyats (settlement acceptance deeds) mostly in Persian, some in Bengali.

Register of Patwaris.

High Court of Calcutta

Appelate Side. Sadar Diwani Adalat Records.

[These records are kept in bundles, but there is no order in their preservation, nor any guide to location of particular case records.]

Original Side. Supreme Court and Mayor's Court Records.

[These are in a somewhat better order due to consolidation of cases into bundles with titles by P.J. Marshall.]

Old Record Room. Wills and Inventories.

[Each will or inventory is numbered. The people who left wills were mostly inhabitants of Calcutta, though there were a few who belonged to neighbouring districts. Some of the wills numbered in the catalogue are missing. There are some old wills belonging to the 1760s and 1770s, but until the beginning of the nineteenth century the number of wills is rather insufficient to base firm conclusions upon.]

Records of Association and Societies

British Indian Association, Calcutta

Publications of the British Indian Association 1854-1860.

[Manuscript bound volumes containing printed correspondence, papers, and annual reports of the Association, which represented the big zamindar lobby in Calcutta.]

Baptist Missionary Society, London

Correspondence of Carey, Ward, Thomas, Marshman, etc. (manuscript letters), 1799-1824.

Annual Reports of the Committee of the Baptist Missionary Society (printed).

Church Missionary Society, London

Files of correspondence, reports, vernacular documents. etc. 1830-1860.

[This is a rich collection of reports, journals, narratives of tours and diaries submitted by individual missionaries, as well as their correspondence. The files contain Bengali documents, such as a malzaminati (revenue security) letter to Maharaja

Tejchand (CI 1/022/9/1) dated 26 Agrahayan 1237 B.S. and a muchleka (undertaking) of paiks in Burdwan to the ijaradar of the zamindar which throw light on social and economic conditions and revenue matters.]

Private Collections and Manuscripts

India Office Library and Records

Mss. Eur. D. 231. Regulations for the Criminal Courts in Bengal.

Mss. Eur. D. 281. Historical Review of the External Commerce of Calcutta from 1750 until 1830.

Buchanan-Hamilton Mss. Account of Ranggopur, Mss. Eur. D. 75.

Francis Mss. E. 13C, Mss. Eur. E. 28.

Richard Temple Collection Mss. Eur. F. 86.

Centre of South Asian Studies, Cambridge University

G.M.G. Bell Papers

Rabindra Sadan, Santiniketan

Tagore Family Letters Books

Vol. I, Part 1: Babu Dwarakanath Tagore's Correspondence 1835-1842, 1844-1845.

Vol. I, Part 2: Babu Girindranath Tagore's Correspondence 1845-1854 (letters from Debendranath Tagore).

Vol. II: Babu Nagendranath Tagore's Correspondence 1853-1858 (letters from Debendranath Tagore)

Vol. V: Babu Girindranath Tagore's Correspondence (no dates, numbered letters).

[Illuminating letters regarding family business and finances, management of zamindari, indigo, and silk factories.]

Zamindari Papers

Rabindra Sadan, Santiniketan

Documents of the Tagore family.

[Contains the Last Will and Testament of Dwarakanath Tagore, Debt of Late Babu Dwarakanath Tagore, document on storage of paddy in Pandua for lending to tenants at 25% interest per annum. etc.]

Loan Registers.

[Loan Register for 1306 B.S. lists debtors, their professions and the amount of debt and interest repayable. It was the established practice for the Tagore family to advance money to their tenants at roughly 3 per cent a month. The professions of the debtors are all mentioned as agriculture and the amount of their debt varies from Rs 5 to Rs 50. The number of borrowers for 1306 B.S. (1899) was 293 and for 1307 B.S. (1900), 133. Some of the debtors were from the village headman or jotedar class called mandals, pramaniks, sardars, and mirdhas and the large size of their loans sometimes as much as Rs 50, seems to indicate that they sub-lent their loans to poorer tenants at higher interest.]

Bengali Manuscript (Puthi) Department of Visvabharati University, Santiniketan

Surul Zamindari Papers

[The Puthi Department has acquired a large selection of papers from the Surul collection which is being catalogued. But the bulk of the papers are still in the records room of the Surul Rajbari in Village Surul, Birbhum, lying in utter confusion. The letters are in old Bengali, apart from a few Persian and English letters and documents. The earliest documents in the collection date back to 1743, consisting of Bengali accounts. A letter dated 12 Agrahayan (1759) reports the loss of a sanad for rent-free lands due to Maratha incursions. The Surul zamindari itself seems to have been found in 1797 but the family acquired older papers relating to the mahals and lands included in their zamindari.]

Majumdar family of Supur, Birbhum

Supur Zamindari Papers

[Seven bundles were examined by the author in Bolpur, since due to disturbances in 1970 she could not go to Supur village itself. These bundles date mostly from 1855 and are concerned mainly with rent suits, but there are a few statements of lands to be sold dated 1800 and 1807.]

Family of the Palchaudhuris of Maheshganj, Nadia

Papers of Ila Palchaudhuri's share

Papers of Jaydurga Debi branch

[These papers are rotting in the cattle-shed of the old house in Maheshganj. The author located some Bengali letters of 1839-1848 from the pile of papers.]

Nadia Rajbari, Krishnagar, Nadia

Nadia Raj Papers

[Most of the papers are purported to have been destroyed. A few documents are still in the possession of the present Maharaja in his Calcutta mansion.]

House of Raja Digambar Mitra, Jhamapukur, Calcutta

Jhamapukur Estate papers (Estate of Raja Digambar Mitra)

[This estate was acquired in the 1850s but the collection contains older papers of the respective estates of the family. Box No. 3, Satkhira, contains papers of estate inherited from the Satkhira family, which includes pre-1793 letters. Box No. 4, Halta and Sonakhali, includes mostly documents of 1850s.]

Personal possession of the Author (a member of the Ponabalia Raychaudhuri family).

Ponabalia Zamindari Papers

[Contains letters, deeds, documents of judicial cases and manuscript books giving accounts of tenures on which the Ponabalia Raychaudhuris, two-anna zamindars of Haveli Selimabad, fought prolonged judicial battles with the Nawabs of Dacca, the four-anna zamindars of Haveli Selimabad. The bulk of the collection is in the old Bakarganj dialect of Bengali, but many important judicial documents are in English.]

Newspapers and Periodicals

Samachar Chandrika 1830-1831 (Bengali periodical).

Transactions of the Bengal Social Science Association 1869-1872.

Government Publications

Unspecified Government or Department of Government.

A Statistical Account of Bengal, 20 vols. W.W. Hunter (London 1875-1877).

Board of Revenue, Bengal.

Selections from the Correspondence on the Resettlement of the Majnamuta and Jellamuta Estates in the District of Midnapur (Calcutta 1881).

Government of Bengal.

Agricultural Report on Dacca District, A.C. Sen (Calcutta 1885).

Bengal District Gazetteers: Burdwan, J.C.K. Paterson (Calcutta 1910).

Midnapur, L.S.S. O'Malley (Calcutta 1911).

Bengal District Records (edited by W.K. Firminger)

Dinajpur, 2 vols. 1786-1788

Midnapur, 3 vols. 1763-1774

Rangpur, 2 vols. 1770-1782.

Final Report on the Survey and Settlement Operations in the District of Bakarganj 1900-1908, J.C. Jack.

Bankura 1917-1924, F.W. Robertson

Burdwan 1927-1934, K.A.L. Hill and Phanindra Kumar Banerjee

Dacca 1910-1917, F.D. Ascoli

Dinajpur 1934-1940, F.O. Bell

Faridpur 1904-1914, J.C. Jack

Midnapur 1910-1918, A.K. Jameson

Mymensingh 1908-1919, F.A. Sachse.

Rangpur 1931-1938, Arthur Coulton Hartley

The Letter Copy Books of the Resident at the Durbar at Murshidabad, edited by Walter K. Firminger (Calcutta 1919).

Memoranda of Midnapur, by H.V. Bayley (Calcutta 1902).

Proceedings of the Controlling Council of Revenue at Murshidabad, 1770-1772, 11 vols. edited by Walter K. Firminger (Calcutta 1919).

Report of the Bengal Land Revenue Commission 1938-40, 6 vols. (Alipore 1940-1941).

A Report on the District of Jessore. Its Antiquities, its History and its Commerce, J. Westland (Calcutta 1874).

A Report on the District of Rungpore, 2. vols, E.G. Galzier. vol. 2 :

Further Notes on Rungpore Records (Calcutta 1873-1876).

Report of the Rent Law Commission, Vol. 1 (Calcutta 1880)

Report on the Statistics of Rungpore for the Year 1872-73, Gopal Chunder Dass (Calcutta 1874).

Government of Eastern Bengal and Assam

Eastern Bengal and Assam District Gazetteers.

Dacca, B.C. Allen (Allahabad 1912)

Dinajpur, F.W. Strong (Allahabad 1912)

Rangpur J.A. Vas (Allahabad 1911)

Government of West Bengal

West Bengal District Records, New Series.

Burdwan. Letters Received 1788-1802, Asok Mitra ed. (Calcutta 1955).

Burdwan. Letters Issued 1788-1800, Ranajit Guha and Asok Mitra eds. (Calcutta 1956).

Birbhum 1786-1797 1855, Asok Mitra ed. (Calcutta 1954).

Midnapore. Letters Received 1786-1803, J.C. Sengupta and Sanat Kumar Bose ed. (Calcutta 1958).

Murshidabad. Letters Received 1789-1803, Sanat Kumar Bose and A Mitra eds. (Calcutta 1958)

Government of Pakistan

Census of Pakistan 1961, Vol. 2, *East Pakistan, Population 1961.*

Parliamentary Papers

Fifth Report of the Select Committee on the Affairs of the East India Company, sess. 1812, Vol. VII.

Report from the Select Committee on the Present State of the Affairs in the East India Company, sess. 1831, Vols. V & VI.

Report from the Select Committee on the Affairs of the East India Company, sess. *1831-32, Vols.* IX-XIV.

English Translations of Persian Works

Abul Fazl-i-Allami — *Ain-i-Akbari*, Vol. II, translated by H.S. Jarrett, Calcutta 19 .

Ziauddin Barani — *Tarikh-i-Firozshahi* translated by H.M. Elliot, *The History oj India as Toldby Its own Historians*, Vol. III (London 1871).

Francis Gladwin — *A Narrative of Transactions in Bengal* (being a translation of Salimulla's *Tarikh-i-Bangla*).

Ghulam Husain Salim — *Riyazu-s-Salatin*, translated by Maulavi Abdus Salam (Calcutta 1902).

Printed Articles in Journals

Bhaduri, A. — 'A Study in Agricultural Backwardness under Semi-Feudalism', *Economic Journal*, March 1973.

Chaudhuri, S.B. — "Pattani (Patwi) Tenures", *Calcutta Review*, Vol. 62, 1876.

Cohn, Bernard E. — 'The Initial British Impact on India', *Journal of Asian Studies*, August 1960.

Gallagher, John — 'Congress in Decline: Bengal, 1930-39', forthcoming article in *Modern Asian Studies*.

Phear, J.P. — 'One some Features of Litigation in Bengal', *Transactions of the Bengal Social Science Associations*, Vol. VI, 1872.

Ray Chaudhuri, Tapan — 'The Agrarian System of Mughal India', *Enquiry*, Spring 1965.

Sanyal, Hitesranjan — 'Continuities of Social Mobility in Traditional and Modern Society in India: Two Case Studies of Caste Mobility in Bengal, *Journal of Asian Studies*, February 1971.

——— — 'Territorial Aristocracy of Bengal', No. 1, 'The Burdwan Raj' *Calcutta Review*, Vol. LIV.

——— — 'The Zamindar and the Ryot', *Calcutta Review*, Vol. VI, Part II, 1846.

Theses

Chakravarty, Santosh — The History of the Relations of the Rajas of Burdwan and the East India Company, 1760-1832, University of Burdwan.

Chaudhuri, Benoy B. — Agrarian Relationships in Bengal after the Permanent Settlement 1873-1819, Calcutta.

——— — Agrarian Economy and Agrarian Relationship between 1859-1885, Oxford.

Islam, M.S. — Permanent Settlement and the Landed Interest in Bangal 1793-1819, SOAS 1972.

Mahmood, A.B.M. — The Land Revenue History of the Rajshahi Zamindari (1765-1793), SOAS 1966.

Printed Books — English

Adam, William — *Reports on the State of Education in Bengal (1835-1838)*, Anath Nath Basu, (ed.) (Calcutta 1941).

Ahmad, Salauddin — *Social Ideas and Social Change in Bengal 1818-1835* (Leiden 1965).

Baden-Powell, B.H. — *The Land Systems of British India*, 3 vols. (Oxford 1892).

——— — *The Origin and Growth of Village Communities in India* (London 1899).

The Indian Village Community (London 1896).

Beveridge, H. — *The District of Bakarganj, Its History and Statistics* (London 1876).

Bhattacharya, Jogendra Nath — *Hindu Castes and Sects* (Reprint, Calcutta 1968).

Beech, Robert & Mary Jane, eds., — *Bengal: Change and Continuity* (East Lansing 1971)

Bose, Nirmal Kumar — *Modern Bengal*, (Calcutta 1959).

Buchanan Francis (Hamilton) — *A Geographical, Statistical and Histori-*

cal Description of the District, or Zilla, of Dinajpur, in the Province or Soubah, of Bengal (Baptist Mission Press, 1883).

Bradley-Bart, F.B. *The Romance of an Eastern Capital* (London 1906).

Broomfield, J.H. *Elite Conflict in a Plural Society: Twentieth Century Bengal* (Berkeley, California 1968).

Chandra, Bholanath *Travels of a Hindu* ( ).

Chatterjee, Anjali *Bengal in the Reign of Aurangzeb 1658-1707* (Calcutta 1967).

Chowdhury, Benoy *Growth of Commercial Agriculture in Bengal, 1757-1900* (Calcutta 1964).

Colebrook, H.T. *Remarks on the Husbandry or Internal Commerce of Bengal* (Calcutta 1804).

Datta, Kalikinkar *Alivardi and His Times* (Calcutta 1939).

Day, Lal Behari *Bengal Peasant Life*, ed. Mahadebprasad Saha, (Calcutta 1969).

Desai, A.R. *Social Background of Indian Nationalism* (Bombay 1966).

Dutt, R. Palme *India Today* (Bombay 1949).

Elliot H.M. *The History of India as Told by Its Own Historians*, Vol. III (London 1871).

Firminger, W.K. *Historical Introduction to the Bengal Portion of the Fifth Report* (Reprint, Calcutta 1962).

Frykenberg, Robert Eric *Guntur District 1748-1848: A History of Local Influence and Central Authority in South India* (Oxford 1965).

———, ed. *Land Control and Social Structure in Indian History* (Madison 1969).

Ghose, Lokenath *The Modern History of the Indian Chiefs, Rajas, Zamindars* (Calcutta 1881).

Ghoshal, H.R. *Economic Transition in the Bengal Presidency 1793-1833* (Patna 1950).

Gopal, Sarvepalli *The Permanent Settlement and Its Effect on Bengal* (London 1949).

Guha, Ranajit *A Rule of Property for Bengal* (Paris 1963).

Habib, Irfan — *The Agrarian System of Mughal India (1556-1707)* (London 1963).

Harrington, F.H. — *Analysis of the Bengal Laws and Regulations*, 3 vols. (Calcutta 1805-1817).

Hunter, William Wilson — *Annals of Rural Bengal* (Reprint, Calcutta 1965).

——— — *Bengal M.S. Records*, 4 vols. (London 1894).

Jack, J.C. — *The Economic Life of a Bengal District: A Study* (Oxford 1916).

Karim, Abdul — *Murshid Quli Khan and His Times* Dacca 1963).

Khan, Abdul Majed — *The Transition in Bengal, 1756-1775: A Study of Saiyid Muhammed Reza Khan* (Cambridge 1969).

Khan, Muin-ud-Din Ahmad — *History of the Fara'idi Movement in Bengal (1818-1906)* (Karachi 1965).

Khan, Raja Mahendralal — *The History of the Midnapur Raj* (Calcutta 1889).

Kling, Blair B. — *The Blue Mutiny. The Indigo Disturbances in Bengal 1859-1862* (Philadelphia 1966).

Kopf, David — *British Orientalism and the Bengal Renaissance, 1773-1836* (Berkeley & Los Angeles 1969).

Kumar, Dharma — *Land and Caste in South India : Agricultural Labour in The Madras Presidency during the Nineteenth Century* (Cambridge 1965)

Kumar, Ravinder — *Western India in the Nineteenth Century: A Study in the Social History of Maharashtra* (London 1968).

Low, D.A. ed., — *Soundings in Modern South Asian History* (London 1968)

Maine, Sir H.S. — *Village Communities in East and West* (London 1876).

Mann, Harold H. *The Social Framework of Agriculture, India, Middle East, England* (Bombay 1976).

——— *Medieval India: A Miscellany.* Vol. 1 (Aligarh 1969)

Martin, Montgomery ed. *The History, Antiquities, Topography and Statistics of Eastern India* (London 1838).

Misra, B.B. *The Central Administration of the East India Company 1773-1834* (Manchester 1959).

——— *The Indian Middle Classes* (London 1961).

——— *The Judicial Administration of the East India Company in Bengal 1765-1782* (Delhi 1961).

Moreland, W.H. *The Agrarian System of Moslem India* (Cambridge 1929).

——— *From Akbar to Aurangzeb: A Study in Indian Economic History* (London 1923).

——— *India at the Death of Akbar* (London 1920).

Morris, Morris D., Toru Matsui, Bipan Chandra, & T. Raychaudhuri *Indian Economic History in the Nineteenth Century: A Symposium* (Delhi 1969).

Mukherjee, Ramkrishna *The Dynamics of a Rural Society* (Berlin 1957).

Nag, Kalidas and Debajyati Burman eds. *The English Works of Raja Rammohun Roy* (Calcutta 1945-51).

Nanda, B.R. and V.C. Joshi eds. *Studies in Modern Indian History* (New Delhi 1972).

Neale, Walter C. Economic Change in Rural India; *Land Tenure and Reform in Uttar Pradesh, 1800-1955* (London 1962).

Patel, Surendra J. *Agricultural Labourers in India and Pakistan* (Bombay 1952).

Philips, C.H. *The East India Company 1784-1834* (London 1949).

Raychaudhuri Tapenkumar *Bengal under Akbar and Jahangir* (Calcutta 1953).

Risley, Herbert Hope *The Tribes and Castes of Bengal*, 2 vols. (Calcutta 1891).

Roy, Atul Chandra *History of Bengal : Mughal Period 1726-1765* A.D. (Calcutta 1968).

Rouse, C.W.B. *Dissertation Concerning the Landed Property af Bengal* (London 1791).

Saran, P. *The Provincial Government of the Mughals* (Allahabad 1941).

Siddiqi, Asiya *Agrarian Change in a Northern Indian State, Uttar Pradesh 1819-1833* (Oxford 1973).

Singh, Iqbal *Rammohun Roy : A Biographical Enquiry into the Making of Modern India* (Bombay 1958).

Sinha, J.C. *The Economic Annals of Bengal* (London 1927).

Sinha, Narendra Krishna *The Economic History of Bengal from Plassey to the Permanent Settlement*, 2 vols. (Calcutta 1956-1962).

——— ed. *Fort William—India House Correspondence* (Public Series) Vol. 5, 1767-1769 (Delhi 1949).

Sinha, Nirmal (ed.) *Freedom Movement in Bengal, 1818-1904 : Who's Who* (Calcutta 1968).

Sinha, Pradip *Nineteenth Century Bengal, Aspects of Social History* (Calcutta 1965).

Stewart, Charles *History of Bengal* (London 1812).

Thorner, Daniel and Alice *Land and Labour in India* (London 1962).

Tripathi, Amales *Trade and Finance in the Bengal Presidency 1793-1833* (Calcutta 1956).

Varghese, T.C. *Agrarian Change and Economic Consequences : Land Tenures in Kerala 1850-1960* (Calcutta 1970).

Verelst, H. *A View of the Rise, Progress and Present State of the English Government in Bengal* (London 1771).

Whitcombe, Elizabeth *Agrarian Conditions in Northern India* (Berkeley, California 1972).

Wilson, H.H. *Glossary of Judicial and Revenue Terms* (London 1855).

(Unnamed author) *Bengal Village Biographies* (Calcutta 1868).

(Unnamed author) *Zemindary Settlement of Bengal*, 2 vols. (Calcutta 1879).

Printed Books — Bengali

Banerjee, Bhabani-charan *Kalikata Kamalalay* (Calcutta, 1343 B.S.).

Chakravarti, Harish Chandra *Bhranti Vijaya*, Part I, Brahman Kanda (Andul, Hourah, 1319 B.S.).

Gupta, Ambika Chanan *Hugli*, (Calcutta 1321 B.S.).

Mitra, Krishna Kumar *Krishna Kumar Mitrer Atma-Charitra* (Calcutta 1937).

Pradhan, Bhagabati Chanan *Aryaprabha* (Tamluk 1318 B.S.).

Ray, Basanta Kumar *Mahishya Bibriti* (Babur Bazar, Dacca, 1322 B.S.).

Sarkar, Prakash Chandra *Mahishya Prakash* (Calcutta 1912).

Sen, Navin Chandro *Amar Jivana*, Vol. 3 (Calcutta 1317 B.S.).

Sen, Rohini Kumar *Bakla* (Bakarganjer Pratna—tattva o Adhunik Itihas) published by Sudhangshu Kumar Sen (Kirtipasa, Barisal, 1915).

APPENDICES

NOTE ON APPENDICES ON SALES OF REVENUE-COLLECTING RIGHTS

The following Appendices are based on manuscript figures of sales of zamindaris and taluqs contained in the following records series in the West Bengal State Archives:

Miscellaneous Records, Board of Revenue, Registers, etc., relating to Lands and Land Revenue, Account Sale or Statement of Lands Sold for Arrears of Revenue.

This series is based on original statements supplied by the Collectors of different districts. It does not include all the sales that took place, as will be evident in comparison with the annual statement of sales for revenue arrears in the Bengal Revenue Consultations series, on which Dr. Islam has based his study. But while the Miscellaneous Records series of the Board of Revenue is less complete than the statististical tables prepared for the Revenue Consultations of the Governor-General-in-Council, the series does give particulars about the residence and professions of purchasers which are not to be found in the annual statement.

APPENDIX II

MIDNAPUR—SALES OF REVENUE-COLLECTING RIGHTS IN DIFFERENT PARGANAS IN TERMS OF JAMMA (IN RS) 1794-1816

TOTAL JAMMA OF THE DISTRICT—RS. 1,063,709

Parganas in which sales took place	*Assessment on each pargana Rs*	*Purchased by residents within pargana*	*% of assessment*	*Purchased by residents outside the pargana but in district*	*Purchased by residents outside district*	*Residence unknown*	*Total*	*% of assessment*
Agrachour	13,103	249	1.90	5,952	152	294	6,201	47.33
Ammercy	32,305	515	1.59	5,637	258	516	6,598	20.42
(Taluk) Battie Takie	11,885			1,932			2,706	22.77
(Bhelorachour	4,869	847	17.40	2,114			2,961	60.81
Bhooiamoota	22,563			1,687			1,687	7.48
Budgerpore	5,015			312		2,152	2,464	49.13
Burrichour	7,972			167		134	301	3.78
Chucksmailpore	4,796				129	584	713	14.87
Coorulchour	16,268	3,042	18.70	903			3 945	24.25
Cossijoora & Shawpore	263,403	44,409	16.86	60,825	56,606	88,810	250,650	[95.16
Cuckrajeet	1,762			5,258		516	5,774	327.70
Dautoonchour	9,775			2,433	75	64	2,572	26.31
(Tuppa) Dharinda	4,073	862	21.16	3,569	2,065		6,496	159.49
Duttomoota	7,075	174	2.46			306	480	6.78
Gugnapore	8,165			7,532	1,185	424	9,141	111.95

Gunissur	8,203	151	1.84				151	1.84
(Havillee) Jellasore	8,796	294	3.34	5	2,078	110	2,487	28.27
(Tanna) Jehanpur	5,660			66			66	1.17
Julcapore	4,551			875		881	1,756	38.58
Khundar	93,222	7,682	8.24	817	549	1,303	10,351	11.10
Khurrugpore	18,298			780			780	4.26
Khutnagur	22,318	90	0.40	525	239	652	1,506	6.75
Lapoochour	9,896	1,748	17.66	4,487	2,412	2,882	11,529	116.50
Midnapore	113,728	3,062	2.69	2,424	10,771		16,257	14.29
Mutcudpore	1,304			307			307	23.54
Mynachoura	73,154	52,795	72.17	38,957	17,360	26,305	135,417	185.11
Narringachour	2,295	206	8.98				206	8.98
Ooterbeyhar	11,157	240	2.15	592	69	307	1,208	10.83
Pertabban	10,558			1,788		1,211	2,999	28.41
Raje Gurr	4,493	395	8.79	412		228	1,035	23.04
Sheepore	25,556	672	2.63	193	372		1,237	4.84
Subbung	91,864	17,662	19.23	23,635	5,710	15,400	62,407	67.93
Turcooachour	17,263	13	0.08				13	0.08
Mutcudabad	1,490			507			507	34.03
Keessaree	3,158			177			187	5:92
Burrajeet				1,300			1,300	
Denkiabazar				726			4,332	
Others		3,606		1,975	2,677	388	5,040	
Total		138,714		178,879	102,707	143,467	563,767	

APPENDIX III

MIDNAPUR

YEAR BY YEAR SALES OF REVENUE-COLLECTING RIGHTS IN TERMS OF JAMMA (in Rs) 1794-1816

Year	*Purchased by residents within pargana*	*% of total assessment*	*Purchased by residents outside the pargana but in district*	*Purchased by residents outside district*	*Residence unknown*	*Total*	*% of total assessment*
1794					25,192	25,192	2.37
1795	79	0.01	3,442	9,842	57,381	70,744	6.65
1796	1,280	0.12	13,835	5,086	46,284	66,485	6.25
1797	3,833	0.36	11,494	315	10,564	26,206	2.46
1798	46,265	4.35	21,062	14,018	3,263	84,608	7.95
1799	21,153	1.99	15,442	16,396		52,991	4.98
1800	3,016	0.28	3,969	938		7,923	0.74
1801	29,276	2.75	23,394	48,432		101,102	9.50
1802	5,592	0.53	15,227	1,188	294	22,301	2.10
1803	1,961	0.18	6,628	1,117		9,706	0.91
1804	13,418	1.26	22,430		192	36,040	3.39
1805	5,044	0.47	789	128	112	6,073	0.57
1806	229	0.02	3,753			3,982	0.37
1807	931	0.09	4,090	348		5,369	0.50
1808	1,121	0.11	1,773		185	3,079	0.29

1809	890	0.08	299			1,189	0.11
1810	1,524	0.14	1,863			3,387	0.32
1811	31	—	1,636			1,667	0.16
1812	138	0.01	723			861	0.08
1813	125	0.01	1,786	114		2,025	0.19
1814	1,198	0.11	20,440	4,785		26,423	2.48
1815	820	0.08	4,804			5,624	0.53
1816	790	0.07				790	0.07
TOTAL	138,714		178,879	102,707	143,467	563,767	
% of Assessment	13.04		16.82	9.65	13.49	53.00	
Annual Average	6,031		7,777	4,466	6,238	24,512	
% of Average	0.57		0.73	0.42	0.58	2.30	

APPENDIX IV

DACCA—SALES OF REVENUE-COLLECTING RIGHTS IN TERMS OF JAMMA (IN Rs.) 1797-1802

Total Jama of District Rs. 1,285,800

Year	*Dependent Rights*	*Independent Rights*	*Unknown*	*Total*	*% of Total*
1797	308	3,792	58	4,158	0.47
% of Assessment	0.02	0.29	0.01	0.32	
1798	372	66,588	358	67,318	7.59
% of Assessment	0.03	5.18	0.03	5.24	
1799	2,767	260,739	42	263,548	29.71
% of Assessment	0.22	20.28	—	20.50	
1800	16,105	4,526	285	20,916	2.36
% of Assessment	1.25	0.35	0.02	1.62	
1801	342,702	106,640	1,740	451,082	50.85
% of Assessment	26.65	8.29	0.14	35.08	
1802	53,279	24,272	2,477	80,028	9.02
% of Assessment	4.15	1.89	0.19	6.23	
TOTAL	415,533	466,557	4,960	887,050	100.00
% of Assessment	32.32	36.28	0.39	68.99	
Place of Residence of Purchasers					
Dacca	339,725	219,017	4,620	563,362	63.51
% of Assessment	26.42	17.03	0.36	43.81	
Burdwan	579	16,474		17,053	1.92
% of Assessment	0.05	1.28		1.33	
Murshidabad		1,080		1,080	0.12
% of Assessment		0.08		0.08	
Nadia	2,402	15,278		17,680	1.99
% of Assessment	0.19	1.19		1.38	

Calcutta	612	9,073		9,685	1.09
% of Assessment	0.05	0.70		0.75	
Rajshahi		2,280		2,280	0.26
% of Assessment		0.18		0.18	
Government	67,611	199,826	315	267,752	30.19
% of Assessment	5.26	15.54	0.03	20.83	
Jessore	464	346		810	0.09
% of Assessment	0.03	0.03		0.06	
Unknown	4,140	3,183	25	7,348	0.83
% of Assessment	0.32	0.25	—	0.57	
TOTAL	415,533	466,557	4,960	887,050	100.00
% of Assessment	32.32	36.28	0.39	68.99	

Glossary

Abkari — Excise

Abwab — Irregular cess over and above the revenue to be paid

Adhiar — Half crop-sharer

Aima — Land grants, free of rent or subject to small rents for the first few years and assessable subsequently at fixed or progressive rents

Amil — Revenue collector of the Diwani department incharge of a sarkar or district

Amin — Measurer, surveyor or revenue officer in pargana who distributed the revenue demand in detail on the raiyats

Amla — Officer

Arcot rupee — Depreciated rupee

Asal jamma — Original revenue fixed by Todar Mal

Babuan land — Private land

Baje gaon paikasht — Other village non-resident raiyat

Bandar — Riverine trade centre

Banian — Native merchant or officer connected with European officers of the East India Company

Bara Bhuiya — Twelve lords of the land

Bara hisya — Senior Branch

Bargadar — Sharecropper

Barkandaz — Matchlock men, footmen under direct order of Sadr Kachari

Baruas — Village heads in Midnapur

Bastu — Homestead

Batta — Exchange of depreciated rupee, change
Batwara — Division
Bazars — Urban Marts
Baze mahal — Land on quit rent
Baze zamin — Revenue free land
Benami — Fictitious
Bepari — Merchant, grain trader
Bigha — Measure of land which varied from region to region, standard bigha = $\frac{1}{3}$ acre
Bish — Unit of land
Brahmottar — Rent free lands granted to the Brahmans (alienable to non-Brahmans)
Britti — Land for maintenance of zamindar, Brahman, etc.
Busnia — Village headman

Chakla — Large division of country
Chapee — Concealed
Char — New alluvial formation on river beds
Chasi — Cultivator
Chaudhrai — Jurisdictions of chaudhuri
Chaudhuri — Hereditary local official for collecting the revenue, theoretically distinct from the zamindar but often identical in practice
Chengra — Small farmer and part-time labourer
Chhota hisya — Junior Branch
Chitta — Demand for the monthly instalment of revenue
Chowki — Watch post
Chow patni — Fourth degree of patni lease
Chuar — Savage
Chukanidar — Under-tenant of a jotedar

Dafadar — Head of a party of police or soldiers
Daradarpatni — Permanent lease at fixed dues under darpatni
Darchukanidars — Under-teanant of chukanidar
Darijaras — Sub-farms
Daroga — Police officer of a thana

Darpatni	— Permanent lease at fixed dues under patni
Dastur	— Customary percentage of zamindar
Dastur-ul-amal	— Administrative regulation
Daul bandobast	— Settlement register of the zamindar
Devottar	— Rent free land for the maintenance of idols and temples
Dewania	— Tout, adviser and leaders of villagers
Dewry Mahals	— Corruption of diwara, island formed on river bed. Dewry Mahals of Burdwan Raj consisted of lands gained by recession of river
Dihis	— Collection of villages
Dini	— Religious branch of the Faraizi sect
Diwan	— Manager, regent
Diwani	— Revenue department
Diwani sanad	— Title deed granted to zamindars by the diwani department
Ekajoti	— Combination
Ekji navis	— Assessment specialist
Etmamdar	— Charge holding farmer, temporary officers appointed to collect revenue from village and parganas
Farman	— Mandate, order, patent
Faujdar	— Military officer of the district
Faujdari thana	— Police jurisdiction
Ferari	— Deserted
Gamochcha	— Towel
Ganjs	— Commercial centres
Ganti	— Agricultural land of village revenue farmer
Gaon khalifas	— Village agents of Faraizi sect
Garh sardar	— Commander of the fort
Ghatwal	— Guardsman of the frontier passes
Gola	— Store for keeping gain
Golam	— Slave
Gomasta	— Agent, village officer of zamindar
Gram saranjami	— Charges of revenue collection from villages
Grihastha	— Literally householder, respectable non-cultivating gentleman

Guzastha jamma — Increasing jamma

Haola — Tenure under taluq
Haptam — 7th Regulation of 1799
Hast-o-bud — Investigation and survey, detailed inquiry
Hat — Weekly fair, rural markets
Hazira — Actual sources of revenue
Hisya — Share
Huda — Lot or division of zamindari
Huzuri — Head, directly under superior authority
Huzuri jotedar — Jotedar in Kuch Bihar, paying revenue directly to the treasury
Huzuri taluqdar — Taluqdar paying revenue directly to the government

Ijaradar — Farmers
Ikrar — Deed
Ikrarnama — Deed

Jagirs — Assignment of revenue made by the State to its officers in lieu of salaries
Jal — Wet
Jalpai land — Salt manufacturing land
Jamma — Assessment
Jamabandy — Revenue roll
Jamadar — Leader of the footmen, leader of detached police parties on assignments
Jama hasil — Assessment and collection
Jama navis — Assessment scrutineer
Jangal bari — Forest Clearance
Jangal bari taluq — Taluq created from forest clearance
Jheit raiyat — Principal raiyat
Joar — Revenue unit, unit within zamindari
Jote — Direct raiyati lease under zamindar, etc., large agricultural holding
Jotedar — Rich farmer, raiyat holding land direct from zamindar

Kabulati — Undertaking
Kachari — Office

Kalà	— Black loam
Karkun	— Clerk, writer, registrar, inferior revenue officer
Karmachari	— Zamindar's village officer, collectors of village revenue
Khamar	— Waste land in personal possession of the zamindar cultivated by contract and not by settled tenants
Karshadar	— Ordinary cultivator
Khanabari.	— Rent free homestead land
Kharija taluq	— Formerly dependent taluq separated from zamindari
Khas	— Direct
Khazanchi	— Treasurer
Khidmat	— Service
Khudkast raiyat	— Non-resident raiyat
Khut	— Hereditary revenue officer
Killa	— Fort
Kist	— Instalment of revenue
Kotwal	— Chief police officer from town, officers of militia
Krishan	— Agricultural labourer
Kulin	— High-ranking
Lakhiraj	— Rent-free land
Madhya Svatta	— Middling right
Madhya Svatta asthayi	— Temporary middling right
Mahajan	— Money-lender
Mahal	— Division of Pargana
Mahal Kachari	— Revenue office of a Mahal or division of pargana
Maharaja	— Great King, title conferred on zamindars
Maharaj Bahadur	— Title conferred on zamindars
Mahattran	— Rent-free holding belonging to the mandals
Mal	— Land revenue
Malangi	— Salt worker

Malguzari land	— Revenue paying land
Malikana	— 10% allowance on collection made to the proprietor (or often ex-proprietor) by the person who happened to engage for the revenue in recognition of the former's lost rights
Malzaminati	— Securityship of revenue
Mandal	— Village headman
Mansabdar	— High Officers
Mauza	— Revenue unit corresponding to village
Mazkuri	— Dependent
Mazul	— Former, removed
Mindaran	— Land grants to barbers, washermen, milkman, blacksmiths and other service groups
Mirdhas	— Head of spearmen, messenger of a Zamindar
Mokarari	— Permanent
Mokarari jotedar	— Jotedar paying fixed revenue
Muchleka	— Written undertaking
Mudivamsa	— Grocer's line
Mufassal	— Interior
Mufassal kachari	— Local office
Muhrir	— Accountant, writer
Mukhya	— Village head
Muktar	— Legal agent
Munsif	— Judicial officer
Muqaddam	— Village headman, village zamindar
Mutsuddi	— Writer, revenue officer, accountant
Muzafat	— Agglomerated pargana or taluqs
Nagdian troops	— Troops paid in cash
Naib	— Regent, manager
Naib diwan	— Deputy finance minister
Naib nazim	— Regent of nazim or governor
Naib qazi	— Deputy qazi or judicial officer
Nankar	— Proprietary allowance of zamindar, private lands of zamindar
Nawab	— Independent ruler of the suba after the break-up of the Mughal Empire
Nawara	— Fleet

Nazar — Fee, present
Nazim — Governor
Nazir — Military officer, inspector, court officer
Niabat — Deputy governorship
Nij — Own
Nij gaon paikasht — Own village non-resident raiyat
Nij haola — Own haola of zamindar or taluqdar
Nij jotes — Home farms
Nij taluq — Own taluq of zamindar
Nilamdar — Auction purchaser
Nim haola — Under-tenure below haoladar
Nirikh — Prevailing rates of rent in the parganas
Nizamat — The military governorship of the province
Nizmat adalat — Criminal court
Paiks — Village militia, footmen, infantry
Paikan — Land of paiks or village footmen
Paikan establishment — Local police establishment at the village level
Paikasht raiyat — Non-resident raiyat
Panchaki jama — Ouit rent
Panjam — 5th Regulation of 1812
Paramanik — Village head
Pargana — Unit of revenue assessment comprising many villages
Pargana Saranjami — Charges of revenue collection from parganas
Patni — Permanent leases at fixed dues under zamindari or taluq
Patwari — Village accountant
Parwana — Warrant
Patta — Lease
Peada — Sadr footmen
Peshkar — Subordinate officer in a department employed for keeping accounts
Peshkash — Fixed tribute in cash
Plateka — Rated revenue of lands deserted but still kept on survey
Poddar — Money changer

Praja	— Subject or under-tenant of a jotedar
Prajawari jamabandi	— Rent roll of under-tenants
Pulbandi	— Embankment
Punyaha	— Annual revenue collecting ceremony
Qanungo	— Record keeper
Qanungo daftar	— Office of land registrar
Qazi	— Judge, judicial officer
Qutqina	— Revenue farm of a village held by an influential local man under a superior farmer of revenue
Qutqinadar	— Village farmer, under-farmer in the mufassal
Raiyat	— Literally a subject, cultivating (sometimes non-cultivating) holder of land paying revenue to zamindars, etc., tenant
Raiyati	— Land of a raiyat
Raiyatwari	— Settlement with raiyats
Raj	— Kingdom, subordinate principality, large zamindari.
Raja	— King, big zamindar
Rajbari	— Palace
Raje-ul-mulk	— Law of the land
Rani	— Queen, big female zamindar, wife of big zamindar
Rasum	— Allowance for zamindar or qanungo
Rattan	— Cane
Royroyan	— Corruption of Rai Raiyan, high revenue officer of state
Sabek ijaradar	— Original, permanent revenue farmer
Sadr amin	— Chief measurer
Sadr chaudhuri	— Chief hereditary revenue collecting officer of district
Sadr diwani adalat	— Provincial civil court
Sadr ijara	— Revenue farms held directly from the zamindar, etc.

Sadr jama	— Assessment payable to government from zamindari headquarters after deducting mufassal charges
Sadr kachari	— Head office
Sadr mustajir	— Head revenue farmer
Sadr nizamat adalat	— Provincial criminal court
Sadr officer	— Zamindari officer at headquarters
Sadr qanungo	— Chief record keeper of the district
Salami	— Present to a superior, gratuity or receiving a lease
Samaj	— Local society
Samajpati	— Social leader
Sampanna chasi	— Rich peasant
Saraf	— Banker and money changer
Sanad	— Official title-deed
Sarasari jotedar	— Jotedar in Kuch Bihar paying revenue to the revenue farmers
Sarbarakar	— Manager, steward, trustee
Sardar	— Leader, vassal, general
Sarkar	— Manager
Sarkar	— District
Sayer	— Customs duties
Sebait	— Care taking worshipper
Senapati	— Militia, commanding officer
Senapati mahals	— Lands for the support of militia
Serais	— Inn
Sezawal	— Attaching or supervising officer employed by the government
Sherista vakil	— Departmental official
Sheristadar	— Departmental officer, presiding officer
Shiqdar	— Revenue-collecting and peace-keeping officer in pargana; farm servant
Sikka rupee	— Standard rupee
Siyasi	— Political branch of the Faraizi sect
Suba	— Province
Subadar	— Governor to Suba or province
Sudra	— Fourth caste, farm servants employed for agricultural operations
Swadeshi	— Nationalist movement of 1905 1908

Tahsildar — Revenue collecting officer
Tahud — Temporary revenue engagement
Taluq — Proprietary revenue collecting right from portion of a pargana
Taluqdar — Small landholder within a pargana
Taraf — Collection of mauzas and villages, division of a pargana
Tappa — Detached portion of a pargana
Taqavi loans — Official loans to agriculturists
Tauzi — Estate bundle in collectorate, a revenue payable amount
Thakur — God
Thakurani — Goddess
Thakurbari — Temple
Thakurseba land — Temple land
Thana — Police jurisdiction
Thanadar — Police officer of a thana
Thanadari establishment — Police establishment at country level
Tuxeembandy — Revenue settlement
Uparastha khalifa — Advisers of the head of the Faraizi sect
Vakil — Agent
Vilayati chaudhuri — Chaudhuri appointed to parganas in Orissa
Wadadar — Farmer of the pargana
Zamindari — Hereditary revenue collecting jurisdiction
Zilla — Unit of collection within district
Zimma — Charge, collecting circle from small taluqs within zamindari, intervening tenure between zamindari and raiyat, transfer of allegiance by raiyat
Zimmadar — Caretaker, collector of revenue from small taluqs, intervener between zamindar and raiyat
Zurkharid taluq — Dependent taluq, the holder of which is at liberty to sell it by bill of sale without the sanction of the zamindar.

Index

Note—The letter 'n' in the pagination statement refers to the footnotes on the respective pages.

Index to the Introduction